Crossing Platforms
A Macintosh/Windows Phrasebook

Crossing Platforms

A Macintosh/Windows Phrasebook

Adam Engst and David Pogue

O'REILLY®

Beijing · Cambridge · Farnham · Köln · Paris · Sebastopol · Taipei · Tokyo

Crossing Platforms: A Macintosh/Windows Phrasebook
by Adam Engst and David Pogue

Published by O'Reilly & Associates, Inc., 101 Morris Street, Sebastopol, CA 95472.

Editor: Mark Stone

Production Editor: Clairemarie Fisher O'Leary

Printing History:

November 1999:   First Edition.

ISBN: 1-56592-539-4

Table of Contents

Introduction

The Macintosh and Windows are the most popular computer platforms on Earth. But the relationship between them, and between the people who use them, has never been smooth. For years, Macintosh fans felt robbed by Microsoft, who, they felt, stole the best features of the Macintosh when designing Windows. And Windows users, for their part, often resented what they perceived as the excessive enthusiasm Macintosh fans felt for their underdog platform.

Today, much of the anger has subsided. Microsoft, it turns out, is enthusiastic in its support of the Mac OS, happy to support its sole competitor (if only to show the U.S. Justice Department that Microsoft is no monopoly). The Macintosh, moreover, benefits greatly by Microsoft's Macintosh software division, whose Office suite and Internet tools rank among the most popular Macintosh applications. Meanwhile, Apple has helped itself to some of the best ideas from Windows in the latest versions of the Mac OS, bringing the two systems even closer together.

Bilingual Education

As a result, we now live in an era of unprecedented shifts from one operating system to another. During Apple's financial slump of 1995 to 1997, thousands of Macintosh fans reluctantly started using Windows out of a fear that their favorite computer maker might not be around to support the Macintosh for long. Then, during Apple's subsequent recovery, thousands of frustrated Windows users embraced the simplicity and style of Apple's smash-hit iMac computer. It's increasingly common for someone to use a Macintosh at home, but Windows at work; Windows in Accounting, but a Macintosh in the art department; Macs for the kids, Windows for their parents. And among computing professionals—network administrators, consultants, and web page designers—familiarity with both platforms is becoming ever more important.

With all the emotion clearing like smoke, one fact becomes clear: whether at Apple or Microsoft, the designers of an operating system must solve the same set of challenges. They need to offer you, the user, a means of interacting with your files and folders, access to preference settings to tailor the operating system to your purposes, a system of printing and going online, and so on. Sometimes Apple and Microsoft solved these puzzles in similar fashions, other times they took drastically different approaches, but the problems themselves are the same. Once you study both platforms, the parallels become crystal clear: a Macintosh alias is essentially identical to a Windows shortcut; the Mac's Trash can matches the Windows Recycle Bin; the Mac's Network Browser and the Windows Network Neighborhood both access other computers on your network; and so on.

But knowing one set of terminology isn't much help in figuring out the other. Who would guess that a shortcut and an alias have the same function? And more important, when you're plopped in front of the platform you don't know, how can you figure out the important differences between aliases and shortcuts?

This book is the answer. It's designed like a foreign-language translation dictionary. For instance, if you're a Macintosh user trying to use a Windows machine and you want to create an alias, you look up *alias* to find out it's a *shortcut* in Windows. Like a French-English/English-French phrasebook, this one is split in half; one set of alphabetical entries is written for the person who's switching to Windows, and the other set is written for people going to Macintosh.

How to Use This Book

Crossing Platforms assumes that you already know your native computer; it makes no attempt to start from such basics as pointing, clicking, or how RAM and hard disks work. Its mission is to make you operational on the less familiar platform as efficiently as possible, to help minimize your groping for important controls in an unfamiliar vehicle.

The key to using this book is simple: Turn to the appropriate half of the book—"For Mac Users Learning Windows" or "For Windows Users Learning the Mac." Then look up the term you already know.

If you're a Macintosh user, then, use this half of the book. Look up such Macintosh-specific terms as *alias, Disk First Aid,* and *Option key,* or generic computing terms like *file sharing, moving files,* and *printing files.* Either way, you'll find out exactly what the equivalent component is in Windows, and you can read about how it differs from the one you already know. Words in **boldface** are cross-references—other related terms in this same half of the book that you can look up.

As you become increasingly familiar with Windows, you'll likely recognize more and more familiar landmarks. Eventually, you'll grasp the stylistic differences of the world's two most famous system software companies, and maybe you'll even anticipate where Microsoft stashed things. At that point, you won't need this book as often, and you'll have attained a most impressive status—as a truly bilingual computer user. When that time comes, you won't even bat an eye when taking what was once an inconceivable leap: crossing platforms.

Operating System Versions

Both Apple and Microsoft update their operating systems constantly. This book covers the most widely used, recent versions of each: Windows 95 and 98, and Mac OS 8 through 8.6. The book doesn't explicitly cover Windows 2000, but almost all of this book's Windows discussions should apply equally well to the newer Windows.

The Ten Most Important Windows Differences

This entire book is dedicated to documenting the differences between the Mac OS and Windows. But if today is your first day in front of a Windows PC, here are the ten differences most likely to trip you up.

1. **Turning the machine on and off.** There's no keyboard on/off button on the PC, as there is on every Macintosh. Instead, your PC probably has a power button on the front panel; push it to turn on the computer. To shut down, choose Shut Down from the Start menu at the lower-left corner of the Windows screen.

2. **Mouse buttons and contextual menus.** The Windows mouse has two buttons instead of one. Use the left button for everyday clicking. Use the right mouse button where you would Control-click something on the Macintosh—that is, to bring up contextual pop-up menus.

3. Menu bars. In Windows, a separate menu bar appears at the top of every single window. There's no single menu bar at the top of the screen, as on the Macintosh.

4. Keyboard shortcuts. Many keyboard shortcuts are the same in Windows as on the Macintosh—but you should substitute the Ctrl key for the Command key, and the Alt key for the Option key.

5. Window controls. To close a Windows window, click the tiny square (containing the X) in the upper-right corner. To move it, drag the title bar as usual. And to resize it, drag the lower-right corner, exactly as you would on the Macintosh. Dragging the edges of a window makes the window bigger or smaller instead of moving it, as it would on the Macintosh. The other two small squares in the upper-right corner of every Windows window are the *minimize* button (makes the window disappear, having collapsed down to a single tile on the Taskbar) and the *maximize* button (expands the window to fill the screen, regardless of what's in the window).

6. The Taskbar. The strip of buttons at the bottom of the screen is called the *Taskbar*. It contains an icon "tile" for every window of every running program. Click one of these tiles to bring that window to the front. When a window is minimized, click its corresponding Taskbar tile to make the window reappear.

7. Application windows. Quitting a Windows program doesn't necessarily close all of its windows; in some programs, the window may remain on the screen even after you've used the Exit command (which is the Windows equivalent of Quit). Don't be alarmed; just close the window and go on with your life. Conversely, closing the final window in some Windows programs quits the program.

8. The Start menu. The Start menu, whose icon appears at the bottom-left corner of the screen, resembles the Apple menu in many ways. You should know about a few important differences, however: first, *every* program on your PC is listed in the Programs submenu, which is a convenient launching mechanism. Second, although you can add your own items to the Start menu, doing so isn't quite as straightforward as adding something to your Mac's Apple menu. See Apple Menu in this half of the book for step-by-step instructions.

9. Disks. When you insert a disk—a floppy, CD-ROM, or Zip, for example—into a Windows PC, no icon appears on the Desktop. To see what's on the disk, you must open the My Computer icon; the resulting window contains icons representing each disk. Double-click those icons to open the corresponding disk windows. To eject a disk, don't attempt to drag its icon to the Recycle Bin (the Windows version of Trash)! Instead, use your PC's front-panel pushbuttons to eject floppies, CDs, and so on.

10. Avoiding passwords. Many Windows machines are set to prompt you for a username and password on startup. If you're the only person using the PC, you don't need to suffer this behavior, especially since it provides essentially no security. See Password Security Control Panel for details on how to eliminate the login dialog box.

11. Bonus Difference: Troubleshooting. Wherever you find a Windows machine, you also find a toll-free technical-support number—or a paid consultant on the premises. Troubleshooting is not generally something you can do yourself. For example, few Windows machines come with a startup CD, and performing a clean system install is almost unheard-of. The troubleshooting tools included with your PC are generally good, but most people require professional assistance in using them. See Troubleshooting in this half of the book for some starting points.

About This Program

In Windows: About This Program

To find out what version of a Macintosh program you're using, you choose the About command, always the first item in the Apple menu. But to ferret out the same information in Windows, you need to look instead for an About menu item in the Help menu for the application you're using. It's usually the last item in the Help menu, and it produces a dialog box filled with version numbers, serial number, and other info, exactly as in Macintosh "About" boxes.

To learn more about Windows itself, choose Help → About Windows 9X in any Desktop window (such as a folder or Explorer window). The resulting dialog box tells you the version you're running, to whom it's licensed, the physical memory available, and the system resources usage level (see Figure A-1).

ADB (Apple Desktop Bus)

In Windows: Keyboard Port, Mouse Port, USB

Older Macintosh models rely on a technology (a jack and cable-connector style) called ADB (Apple Desktop Bus) to connect keyboards, mice, trackballs, and joysticks, along with a few other types of devices. On the PC, though, there's no technology equivalent to ADB and no single standard port for input devices (although someday USB may become such a standard). So, if you're adding a keyboard or a mouse to your PC, make sure to check the ports before purchasing.

Some PC keyboards have a large 5-pin round (DIN) connector, but others connect to a smaller 6-pin, round, mini-DIN port (also known as a PS/2 connector). The 6-pin connector appears commonly on laptops, where space is limited.

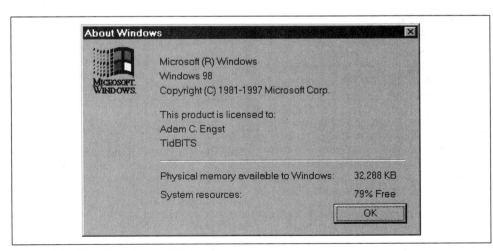

Figure A-1. About Windows 98 dialog box

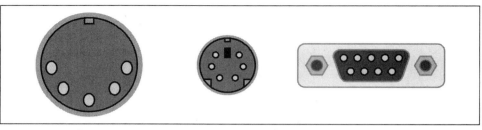

Figure A-2. Different ports for connecting PC keyboards and mice

PC mice, too, come in two basic varieties: the serial mouse (which connects to a 9-pin DB-9 connector) and the bus, or PS/2, mouse, which connects to the 6-pin mini DIN port. See Figure A-2 for diagrams of the three different ports. Depending on your PC, your back panel might be labeled with icons for the different ports.

Windows offers no standard means of daisy-chaining multiple keyboards and mice, as you can on the Macintosh, although Windows 98 does let you use multiple mice at the same time. This configuration is handy if your laptop has a trackball, for instance, and you'd like to hook up a serial mouse as well. In fact, many laptops let you attach a second keyboard or mouse so you can avoid using the cramped built-in keyboard and pointing device.

Adobe Acrobat
In Windows: Adobe Acrobat

Adobe Acrobat is a cross-platform program (versions exist for the Macintosh, Windows, and Unix) that lets you see documents on-screen as they were meant to be seen on paper, complete with graphics, typography, and original layout. You can also print these documents without loss of quality, even if you lack the documents' original fonts.

Some companies choose to distribute online in Acrobat format—more accurately called PDF or Portable Document Format—because of this guarantee of display quality. Other uses of Acrobat include sending proofs of documents to people who may lack both the necessary program and the necessary fonts to view the original file, and distributing forms such as the IRS tax forms, which must be printed out accurately.

Adobe put a lot of effort into making Acrobat files totally cross-platform. If you create an Acrobat file using Acrobat Distiller on the Macintosh, you can send that file to a Windows user who can read and print it using the free Acrobat Reader—and vice versa.

You can find much more information about Adobe Acrobat on Adobe's web site at *http://www.adobe.com/*.

Alias
In Windows: Shortcut

A Macintosh alias is an icon that represents some other file, folder, or disk and takes up very little disk space, yet opens the original icon when double-clicked. In effect, it lets a file, folder, or disk icon be in more than one place at once. A common usage: put the alias for a commonly used item in your Apple menu or on your Desktop. In Windows, the equivalent icon duplicates are called shortcuts.

Creating shortcuts. To create a shortcut, right-click a file, folder, or disk; from the pop-up menu that appears, choose Create Shortcut. Windows creates the shortcut next to the original, calling it "Shortcut to Applications" (or whatever the name of the original was, as shown in Figure A-3). Shortcut icons match the originals, with the addition of an arrow branded on the icon (exactly as in Mac OS 8.5 and later). Once you've created a shortcut, you can rename it, move it, or copy it anywhere you like; double-clicking it opens the original file.

As an alternative method of creating a shortcut, open the window where you'd like the finished shortcut to reside. Then choose File → New → Shortcut. The Create Shortcut

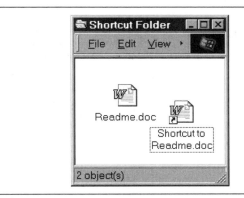

Figure A-3. An original file and its shortcut

wizard walks you through the steps of creating a shortcut: choosing the original, naming the shortcut, and sometimes choosing an icon.

Note

When you're asked to select an icon for the shortcut, the Browse dialog box defaults to showing you only programs. You must choose Files of type → All Files to see other types of files from which you can steal icons.

Windows also offers several shortcuts to creating shortcuts:

- Right-click any blank spot on the Desktop or in a Desktop window; from the resulting pop-up menu, you can choose New → Shortcut to place a new shortcut on the Desktop.

- If you right-click and drag an icon, Windows asks if you want to move the original to the new location, copy the original to the new location, or create a shortcut in the new location.

- If you press Ctrl-Shift when dragging, Windows displays the same pop-up menu, but defaults to making a shortcut of the original in the new location (your cursor changes to indicate that it will create a shortcut).

You'll find that Windows is distinctly different from the Macintosh in one regard: if you try to drag a program's icon to a different window, Windows makes a shortcut in the new location instead, unbidden. To move or copy the actual program you must right-click and drag, or Shift-drag, its icon.

Special shortcut features. Windows shortcuts offer more control than Macintosh aliases. To access these additional features, right-click the shortcut icon and choose Properties from the resulting pop-up menu. In the Properties dialog box, click the Shortcut tab for information about the shortcut, such as target type and target location. The Target field contains the full pathname to the original.

The "Start in" field specifies the folder that contains the original item. (It may also identify a folder that contains files related to the original item, such as a folder containing documents to open at launch.)

More useful is the "Shortcut key" field, which lets you define a keystroke that launches, or switches to, the program referenced by the shortcut. (In other words, Windows has a built-in function that does what, say, QuicKeys does on the Macintosh—launches your favorite programs and documents from the keyboard. See **Macros** for more information on macro programs in Windows.) To specify such a shortcut key, click in the field and press any key except Escape, Enter, Tab, Spacebar, Print Screen, or Backspace; your finished keystroke is Ctrl-Alt-[whatever key you chose].

Note

Windows lets you duplicate shortcut keys for different shortcuts; the most recent one defined should overrule any duplicates. If a previously assigned shortcut keystroke is giving you trouble, however, right-click the offending shortcut, and choose Properties → Shortcut → Shortcut Key → Delete.

Finally, the Run pop-up menu lets you specify which kind of window will open when you launch a program from its shortcut: a normal window, a window that's minimized to an icon on the Taskbar, or a window that's maximized to take up the full screen. This option is especially useful for shortcuts in the StartUp folder that run at startup; you may want certain background applications, such as speech-recognition engines or screen capture utilities, to launch automatically at startup but to minimize themselves to get their windows out of your way.

Finding the original item. The Properties → Shortcuts dialog box offers two useful buttons. To find the original item, click Find Target; Windows opens the folder containing the original icon. (This mechanism is exactly the same as the Show Original command applied to a Macintosh alias.) To change the shortcut's icon, click Change Icon and choose an icon from those listed in the Change Icon dialog box.

Note

Even in Windows 98 shortcuts aren't as smart as aliases. Beware of creating shortcuts for items on other networked computers or on removable disks, for example—Windows still isn't smart enough to prompt you to insert the appropriate removable disk or make the specific network volume accessible when you double-click such a shortcut.

If you change the name of the original file, a Windows shortcut still works. But in Windows 95, if you move the original file to a different folder, your shortcut "breaks," so that it no longer launches the proper file

when double-clicked. In fact, it may open a random file in the original's home folder! There's no workaround other than to upgrade—in Windows 98, shortcuts can locate their originals even after they've been moved.

Appearance Control Panel
In Windows: Display Control Panel, Sounds Control Panel

In Mac OS 8.0 and 8.1, the Appearance control panel let you adjust a few subtle cosmetic interface options: highlight color, menu font, and the like. In Mac OS 8.5 and later, though, the Appearance control panel is a full-fledged application that governs a broad array of "look and feel" settings—what pattern or picture you'd like as your Desktop backdrop, what fonts you prefer for your windows and menus, what sound effects should accompany your Finder activity, and so on.

In Windows, you'll find these features and more, but they're scattered among several different control panels. Here, tab by tab of the Mac OS 8.5 Appearance control panel, is where to find them.

Themes and Appearance tabs. The Macintosh Appearance control panel's Themes tab lets you name and save a single "theme" that incorporates dozens of settings in the Appearance control panel; the Appearance tab lets you choose color schemes for icons, windows, selected text, and so on.

In Windows, the closest corresponding feature is called Schemes; you access it from Control Panel → Display → Appearance (see Figure A-4). The Item menu lets you choose every conceivable interface component (icon, menu, message box, and so on, right down to the inactive window border)—at which point the dialog box's Size, Color, and other pop-up menus let you modify that element. You can save your creations and, when you create a truly ugly one (an easy task), delete them.

A scheme, however, stores only window color schemes and font choices on your PC—not the full array of sounds and Desktop patterns stored by Macintosh theme.

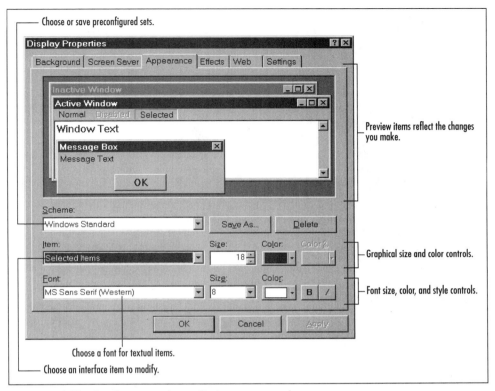

Choose or save preconfigured sets.

Preview items reflect the changes you make.

Graphical size and color controls.

Font size, color, and style controls.

Choose a font for textual items.

Choose an interface item to modify.

Figure A-4. The Display control panel's Appearance tab

Fonts tab. The Mac's "Smooth all fonts on screen" setting in Appearance → Fonts is equivalent to the "Smooth edges of screen fonts" checkbox in Control Panel → Display → Effects in Windows. To change the actual font choices for Windows windows, menus, and so on, visit Control Panel → Display → Appearance, as described previously.

Desktop. Follow these steps to apply a picture to the background of your Desktop in Windows (see Figure A-5):

1. Open Control Panel → Display → Background.

2. Select a picture in the Wallpaper list to preview it.

3. Choose Center, Tile, or Stretch from the Display menu (experiment to see the differences).

4. Click Apply to preview the new background at full size. If you don't like the way it looks, repeat the previous steps.

5. Click Close when you're happy with the background you've chosen.

Windows comes with a few graphics files, most of which are designed to be tiled, but you can add your own in several ways:

• You can use any bitmap file (*.bmp*); click Browse and find it on your hard disk in the Open File dialog box.

• If you see a graphic you like on the Web and you're using Internet Explorer, you can right-click the graphic and choose Set as Wallpaper. Doing so creates a picture named "Internet Explorer Wallpaper" in the list; note that setting another graphic as wallpaper replaces (and deletes) whatever you were using before.

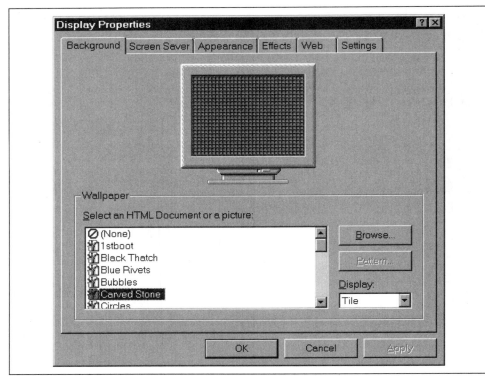

Figure A-5. Display control panel's Background tab

- You can also right-click a graphic in a web page and choose Save Picture As, then save it as a bitmap file. Once it's saved on your hard disk, you can use it as a background as you would any other bitmap file.

Although most of the pictures in the Wallpaper list look like a Mac's standard built-in patterns, they're actually individual graphics files. To use a pattern rather than a picture, follow these:

1. Open Control Panel → Display → Background.
2. Select None at the top of the list.
3. Click Pattern.
4. Choose a pattern and click OK to set it as the pattern for your Desktop.

You can edit the pixels that make up the pattern, or create new ones, by clicking Edit Pattern. Give the pattern a new name in the

> **Note**
>
> In Windows 98, you can't change the pattern's color in the Pattern Editor. The pattern is simply a black overlay over the colored Desktop. (You change the Desktop color in the Display control panel's Appearance tab.)

Sound. Mac OS 8.5 marked the official debut of sound effects in the Mac OS—subtle sounds that can accompany such system actions as dragging icons and opening and closing windows. (Apple actually showed this feature back in the early 1990s with the Sonic Finder, a version of the Finder that was never officially released. Several third parties also provided it in early versions of the Mac OS.) Windows provides control over these system action sounds in the Sounds control panel (Control Panel → Sounds).

Although you can assign sounds to individual actions or events in Windows (see Figure A-6), you're more likely to choose a sound scheme, which is a collection of related sounds. If any given sound bugs you, though, you can just turn it off (much to the relief of those driven nearly insane by the Utopia scheme's shutdown laughter).

Options. The Mac's Smart Scrolling option in Appearance → Options (which creates a double-headed scroll-bar arrow at one end of each scroll bar, instead of the usual one-arrow-at-each-end arrangement) has no equivalent in Windows.

Nor does Windows offer an equivalent to the Mac's "Double-click title bar to collapse windows" option (in Appearance → Options). But double-clicking a window's title bar in Windows always does some-

thing anyway—it maximizes the window, making it fill the entire screen.

Apple Guide
In Windows: Help

Apple Guide is the online help technology that walks you through various tasks, such as adjusting the sound volume or setting up a printer. To use it, you click through successive tutorial screens, with animated red circles pointing out items on the screen that you're supposed to click or adjust.

In Windows, the online Help system frequently takes the form of step-by-step, successive tutorial screens, just like Apple Guide, but without nearly as much interaction or animated red highlighting. For more information about different online help options in Windows, see **Help**.

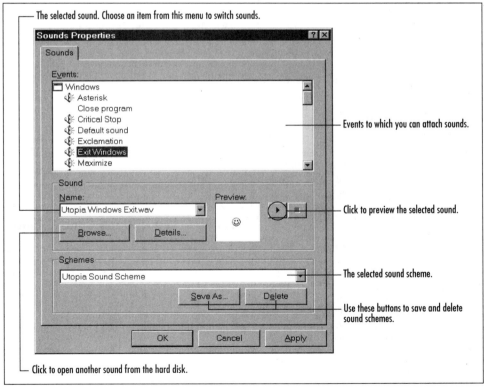

Figure A-6. Sounds control panel

Apple Menu
In Windows: Start Menu, Favorites Menu

The Mac OS's Apple menu is user-configurable; by moving files and folders in and out of the System Folder → Apple Menu Items folder, you can control what's listed in the Apple menu. Such important elements as the Chooser, the Control Panels item, and Recent Applications, Recent Documents, and Recent Servers items—along with your favorite documents, disks, folders, and programs—also call the Apple menu home.

In Windows, the Apple menu's equivalent is the Start menu, although the two aren't identical. As on the Macintosh, you can add items to this menu—but in Windows, you can't remove most of the default menu items. Windows 98 also offers a Favorites menu (a submenu in the Start menu), exactly as in Mac OS 8.5 and later; it's closer in spirit to the Mac's Apple menu, since you can easily add folders to your system-wide list of favorites and access them from Start → Favorites.

User-specified items. Just as you put aliases in the Apple Menu Items folder on the Macintosh, so you can put shortcuts into the Start Menu folder in Windows. Such items are listed above the Programs item in the Start menu. Here's how to add items to the Start menu:

- Right-click the Start menu. Choose Open (to open the Start Menu folder) or Explore (to view it in an Explorer window). Then right-drag a file or folder into the Start Menu folder, and choose Create Shortcut Here from the pop-up menu.
- Right-click a blank area of the Taskbar, choose Properties, and click the Start Menu Programs tab in the resulting dialog box. Clicking the Add button runs a wizard that walks you through finding a file to add and placing it appropriately. If you click Remove, a dialog box lets you remove items from the Start menu. Click Advanced to view an Explorer window that shows the Start Menu folder's contents; from there, you can drag shortcuts in or out to add or remove them from the Start menu.

- In Windows 98, drag an icon onto the Start menu, pause briefly without releasing the mouse button, and then drag the item anywhere you want within the menu. You can even put things into your Programs or Favorites folders this way.

Adding folder shortcuts to the Windows 98 Start → Favorites menu is even easier. Whenever you're viewing a folder window, choose Favorites → Add to Favorites. If you are used to the Mac OS 8.5-style Favorites menu, you may be confused that the Favorites command lists both shortcuts to web pages as well as to favorite folder windows.

Other items. Most of the remaining Apple-menu elements familiar to Macintosh users—the Chooser, Control Panels, and the Recent Items listings—have equivalents in Windows. See their individual listings.

One aspect of the Windows Start menu frequently throws Macintosh users making the switch: unlike the Apple menu, you can't open any Start-menu folder directly in the Start menu. You must slide the cursor sideways onto the submenu and make a selection there.

For example, on the Macintosh, you can choose Favorites, Recent Documents, or Control Panels from the Apple menu and release the mouse—the corresponding window appears. On Windows, however, you're not allowed to choose those commands in the Start menu. You must choose one of the items in their submenus.

Apple Menu Options Control Panel
In Windows: No direct equivalent

The Apple Menu Options control panel adds two useful features to the Macintosh. First, it lets your Apple menu sprout four levels of submenus, thus letting you select, from this menu, files that are deeply nested in folders within folders. Second, Apple Menu Options adds three commands to your Apple menu: Recent Applications, Recent Documents, and Recent Servers. These commands (and their matching System Folder subfolders) list the most recently used applications, documents, and servers that you've opened.

Windows offers the same submenu-listing feature, but gives you no control over the number or type of menus. It can, however, offer easy access to your most frequently used items, as follows:

- Start → Documents works almost exactly like Apple → Recent Documents, tracking your most recently used documents.

- Start → Programs lists all Windows programs—not just those most recently opened—on your hard disk. Since Macintosh users may find Windows navigation difficult at first, the Programs menu can prove helpful—it's easier to launch programs from the Programs menu than to find them in your folder hierarchy.

Apple System Profiler

In Windows: System Information, Windows Report Tool

On the Macintosh, you generally don't need to know the technical details of your sys-

tem. When you do, though, you can fall back on Apple System Profiler, which provides detailed information about your Mac's hardware and software configuration. In Windows, the System Information program does roughly the same thing.

If you have Windows 95, you're out of luck; there's no such program or built-in method of creating a system profile. In Windows 98, however, you can find System Information at Start → Programs → Accessories → System Tools → System Information. The program provides a two-pane interface, with all the hardware and software components of your system listed on the left, and details about the selected component on the right (see Figure A-7).

If you're a Macintosh user using a Windows machine for the first time, the system information may not mean much to you. But the system information can prove extremely useful to a support technician you manage to get on the phone.

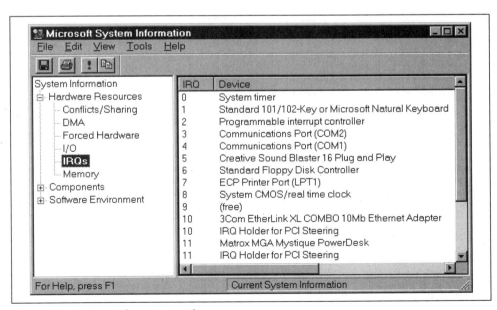

Figure A-7. System Information utility

If you're asked to submit a report detailing your system's hardware and software configuration, use the Windows Report Tool (accessible from Tools → Windows Report Tool in the System Information program) to create a report. In it, describe your problem, what you thought should happen, and any steps necessary to reproduce your problem. Along with that information, Windows Report Tool takes a snapshot of the settings on your computer and bundles it all up for sending.

AppleCD Audio Player
In Windows: CD Player

If you're used to wasting the vast computing power of your Macintosh by playing audio CDs on your CD-ROM drive, you'll appreciate the fact that you can do the same thing under Windows (assuming of course, that your PC has a sound card installed). When you pop an audio CD into your PC's CD drive, the Windows equivalent of the Mac's AppleCD Audio Player launches itself—something called CD Player—and starts playing the CD. (You can also launch CD Player manually in Windows 98 from Start → Programs → Accessories → Entertainment → CD Player, or in Windows 95, from Start → Programs → Accessories → Multimedia → CD Player.)

To prevent CD Player from launching automatically, press Shift when you insert the CD. Or, if you never want a CD to start automatically, right-click My Computer and choose Properties. Switch to the Device Manager tab, open the CD-ROM branch, and double-click your CD-ROM drive to open its Properties window. Switch to the Settings tab and turn off "Auto insert notification."

CD Player, like its Macintosh equivalent, offers all the controls of a CD player: random, continuous and intro modes, pause, stop, play, eject, next and previous track, skip forward and back buttons, and so on (see Figure A-8). The View → Volume Control command summons a separate Volume Control application, absolutely teeming with individual sound-tweaking controls.

CD Player lets you switch among three display modes: Track Time Elapsed, Track Time Remaining, and Disk Time Remaining. CD Player can also show the artist's name, the title of the CD, and the name of the current track number—if it knows this information. Unfortunately, you must teach it—by choosing Disc → Edit Play List. In the resulting dialog box, you can type in disc, artist, and track information, and also specify which tracks you'd like to hear. CD Player stores the play list information in a file called *cdplayer.ini*, which is limited to 64K; if you have a huge CD collection, you're out of luck.

As an alternative, check out the extensive list of CD-playing software that works with the CDDB CD Database on the Internet. It's at *http://www.cddb.com/downloads/*.

AppleScript
In Windows: Batch Language, Windows Scripting Host

Long ago, DOS users jeered that the Mac OS had no equivalent to the DOS batch language. That was true, although the DOS batch language was nothing to write home about (it lacks many programming constructs necessary to write more than the simplest programs). When Apple added scripting capabilities to the Mac OS, they took the form of the full-featured AppleScript, which provides far more access to the internal workings of Macintosh applications than batch files ever did for DOS programs.

In other words, if you're used to the power of AppleScript, you may be sorely disappointed in what you can do with batch files in Windows. Luckily, Windows 98's Windows Scripting Host lets you write and run scripts in a variety of powerful scripting languages, including Microsoft's VBScript and JScript, plus JavaScript, Perl, PerlScript, Python, and TCL. Windows 95 and NT 4.0 users can download Windows Scripting Host from *http://msdn.microsoft.com/scripting/default.htm?/scripting/windowshost/*.

Batch language. Batch files are ASCII text files that contain commands that you could execute at the DOS prompt, as well as rudimentary programming constructs like looping and conditionals. These files can't use the name of any internal DOS programs,

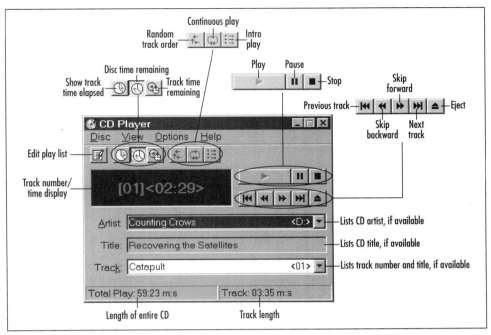

Figure A-8. CD Player's basic interface

and their names must end in *.bat*. Each command must be on a line by itself; each command executes sequentially.

These limitations might seem onerous, but you can perform some useful tasks in batch files. Possibilities include making sure a network connection has been established before running an Internet program, or creating a specific set of folders and files before starting a new project.

If you're interested in pursuing the Windows batch language, check out O'Reilly & Associate's *Windows 95 in a Nutshell.*

Windows Scripting Host. Macintosh users will probably feel more at home with Windows Scripting Host, which lets you execute scripts written in a variety of scripting languages. Unfortunately, though not surprisingly, AppleScript isn't among those languages. But if you have experience with scripting in Unix, you can use any one of several Unix scripting languages.

The huge advantage of Windows Scripting Host over the DOS batch language is that some of these scripting languages, such as

the freely downloadable PerlScript (see *http://www.activestate.com/pw32/*), let you access the internals of Windows programs, much as AppleScript does for Macintosh applications.

Scripts written in any of these languages are still ASCII text files, although they have specific extensions that enable Windows to identify them as scripts and run them through the Windows Scripting Host. For instance, VBScript scripts have *.vbs* extensions, whereas JScript scripts use the *.js* extension.

For more on this kind of Windows scripting, *Learning Perl on Win32 Systems* might prove helpful, since it's specific to PCs.

AppleShare
In Windows: Microsoft Networks, File Sharing, Client for Microsoft Networks

Macs have always had built-in Ethernet or LocalTalk ports for networking. The software protocol for sharing files over a network is AppleShare—but that term may refer to any of three things:

- The overall technology for sharing files on the Macintosh over AppleTalk or TCP/IP networks.

- The server software used to serve files over a network to Macs.

- The client software used to access AppleShare servers over a network.

AppleShare file sharing technology. The Windows counterpart to the AppleShare technology is Microsoft Networks, which lets you share files among networked Windows machines. Microsoft Networks can use any of the network protocols installed on your PC, including TCP/IP, IPX, NetBEUI, and so on. Remember, protocols are the languages used to communicate over a given network. Microsoft Networks uses your selected protocol to provide file and printer sharing services.

(To share files between Macs and PCs, see **Transferring Files to Windows**.)

AppleShare server. Apple sells a server called AppleShare; the latest version, called AppleShare IP, adds Internet server capabilities (Web, FTP, DHCP, and electronic mail) to its standard file and print serving capabilities. In the Windows world, you'd probably rely instead on Windows 98's big brother, Windows NT, for similar server duties. Windows NT is an industrial-strength operating system designed for use on servers, although it comes with an equally beefy learning curve.

If you don't need such power, the built-in file and print sharing in Windows may be sufficient, since it's roughly on the same level as personal file sharing in the Mac OS. You set up file and print sharing in the Network control panel in Windows. For more information, see **File Sharing** and **Printer Sharing**.

AppleShare client. On the Macintosh, to access AppleShare servers and other Macs running file sharing, you click the Apple-Share icon in the Chooser. In Windows, you can access available servers from the Network Neighborhood icon on the Windows Desktop.

Adding a Windows PC to an AppleShare network. If you're in the uncommon position of trying to make a Windows PC hook up to a primarily Macintosh-populated network, several excellent commercial software products await. The best-known, and among the most stable, is PC MACLAN (*http://www.miramarsys.com/*). Once installed on the Windows PC—not a difficult proposition, thanks to the excellent phone support—it lets you access the network's Macintosh printers and hard disks through the standard Network Neighborhood interface.

As a bonus, PC MACLAN can also make the Windows machine available to the Macs on the network—using the same Chooser or Network Browser software the Macintosh users would ordinarily use to access other networked Macs. There's even a version (PC MACLAN Remote) that lets you dial into a Macintosh network from a Windows laptop (or other remote Windows machine).

AppleTalk
In Windows: NetBEUI

You can think of network protocols as languages that computers use to speak to one another. AppleTalk is the standard Macintosh network protocol, although Macs can use other protocols, such as the Internet's TCP/IP. In the Windows world, the standard network protocol is NetBEUI (pronounced "net-booie").

AppleTalk Control Panel
In Windows: Network Control Panel

AppleTalk is the Macintosh control panel that lets you specify what kind of network the Macintosh is using: Ethernet, infrared, LocalTalk, and so on.

In Windows, you use the Network control panel for such configurations. Unfortunately, the Windows Network control panel can be intimidating to the Macintosh user; if you're a first-timer, see **Networking** before reading ahead.

To configure a PC to see other machines on a network, just as you'd set the AppleTalk control panel to use the Ethernet port on a

A–C

Macintosh, here's what you'd do. See Figure A-9 for additional information.

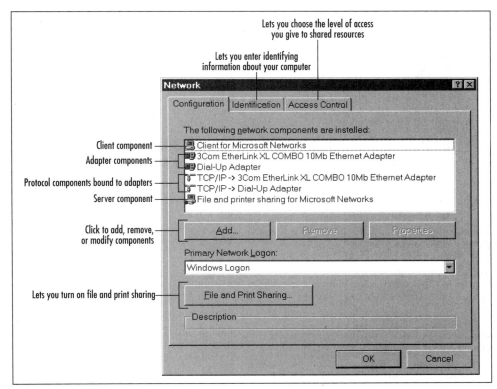

Figure A-9. Network control panel's parts and pieces

1. In the Network control panel's list of network components, make sure you have an adapter for the hardware device that connects you to the network (probably a network card). If not, add one by clicking Add → Adapter and picking the appropriate item from the lists. If you're using a modem, use the Dial-Up Adapter. Adapter icons look like little PCI cards.

2. See if the appropriate protocol is included in the list of installed components in the Network control panel. (It should be the same as the other computers with which you want to communicate, generally NetBEUI or TCP/IP.) Protocol icons look like network wires. If your desired protocol is not present, add it by clicking Add → Protocol and

picking the appropriate protocol from the lists. This step causes Windows to create network components for that protocol for each adapter. If your desired protocol is present, but it doesn't seem to be bound to your adapter (the protocol components in the Network control panel list the adapter to which they're bound), try adding the protocol again.

3. Depending on the protocol you've chosen, you may have to configure the protocol component. That's primarily true for TCP/IP, which you're likely to use if you also want to access the Internet. Select the protocol and click Properties, or double-click the protocol to display a Properties dialog box. TCP/IP requires the most configuration. See

TCP/IP Control Panel for detailed configuration instructions.

4. If you want to connect to other servers on your network, make sure to add and configure the Client for Microsoft Networks component as well. Adding a client is just like adding an adapter or protocol; in this case, click Add → Client → Microsoft → Client for Microsoft Networks. To configure Client for Microsoft Networks, double-click it to display its Properties dialog box.

5. Click OK in the Network control panel, after which Windows installs any necessary files from the Windows CD-ROM and asks you to reboot. (Now you'll pine for the AppleTalk control panel on the Macintosh, which never requires you to restart the Macintosh.)

After configuring the Network control panel to use the appropriate adapter, protocol, and service, test your connection by opening the Network Neighborhood icon on your Desktop (assuming there are other servers you can access). If you see their icons, you're all set. If not, return to the Network control panel and double-check your settings for the adapter, protocol, and client. It's worth checking the advanced settings for your network adapter's component—the occasional PC Card Ethernet adapter requires you to specify the type of Ethernet cabling in the Advanced tab.

Application Menu
In Windows: Taskbar

To switch between running applications on the Macintosh, you can choose an application's name from the application menu in the upper-right corner of the menu bar. (In Mac OS 8.5 and later, you can instead press Command-Tab to cycle through your active applications, exactly as in Windows.)

In Windows, there's no application menu; instead, you switch between open programs by clicking their icons on the Taskbar, the strip at the bottom of the screen. You can, however, move the Taskbar to other edges of the screen by dragging it to a new location.

In fact, the Taskbar offers many more functions than the Mac's application menu (especially in Windows 98), including toolbar management and window management. There are innumerable combinations of items you can place on your Taskbar, in your choice of sizes and positions; take some time to experiment.

Window switching. The Taskbar doesn't just list all your active applications, as on the Macintosh—in fact, it contains icons for every window in every application with independent windows (some applications, like Microsoft Word, create a single parent window and keep all the document windows inside the parent window). If you have two web browser windows open, two buttons appear on the Taskbar (see Figure A-10). The more open windows, the more icons on the Taskbar, to the point where they become too small to fit.

To switch to a different window, click its icon on the Taskbar. If you click the button belonging to the frontmost window, Windows 98 minimizes that window, turning it into an icon on the Taskbar.

To drag something (some selected text, for example) from one application to another when both windows aren't visible simultaneously, you can use the Taskbar as an intermediary. Drag the selection over the destination's icon on the Taskbar; wait until Windows displays the corresponding window; then release the mouse. The selection appears in the destination window (if the software accepts such a drag-and-drop).

Toolbars in Windows 98. Windows 98 lets you add several different toolbars to your Taskbar, which you may consider either handy or overly cluttered. Most toolbars let you place unopened items—shortcuts to folders, documents, applications, or web pages—on your Taskbar, which otherwise lists only open windows (see Table A-1).

To add a toolbar, right-click the Taskbar and choose from the Toolbars submenu. To remove a toolbar from your Taskbar, either choose it from the Toolbars submenu again (a checkmark appears next to its name), or right-click it and choose Close. You can

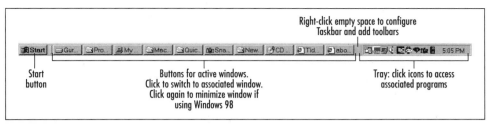

Figure A-10. A loaded-down Taskbar

move and resize toolbars by dragging their left edges.

Toolbars are a special type of window. You can add items to a toolbar by dragging icons onto it—Windows makes a shortcut to the item (or offers to). You can also drag Desktop icons onto toolbar icons as another way to move files or folders, or to open documents with specific applications. (This technique may sound familiar to Macintosh users if you've ever dragged document icons onto application icons, or onto the Mac OS 8.5 Application Switcher palette.)

In fact, because toolbars are special types of windows, you can even drag them off the Taskbar onto the Desktop, where they become free-floating windows. Or drag a toolbar to an edge of the screen; Windows "docks" (fastens) it to that edge, just as in Microsoft Office programs on the Macintosh. As with the Taskbar, right-clicking a toolbar provides a menu from which you can set the toolbar to be always on top and, if it's docked, to hide itself.

The Address toolbar is the most unusual of the toolbars: it duplicates the function of the Run command from in the Start menu. Type the name of a folder, program, or web page in the Address toolbar and press Enter to open that folder, program, or web page. If you misspell one word, though, Windows

assumes you're looking for a web page; you must then wait as it opens an Internet Explorer window that doesn't find anything. Misspell in a multiple-word string, and Windows searches Yahoo's web catalog for those words.

You can make your own toolbars, too. Right-click the Taskbar; choose Toolbars → New Toolbar. In the resulting dialog box, choose a folder or type a web address. (Making a toolbar to a web page is strange, since you end up with that web page displayed in your Taskbar. You can drag that toolbar off the Taskbar to the Desktop, where it becomes its own window, but why not just open a window in Internet Explorer?)

Window management. One problem Macintosh users encounter in Windows is that they can't hide all the windows that belong to an application at once, as they can on the Macintosh. As a result, you may find it difficult to work on the Desktop among all the windows cluttering it up. Pressing the WIN key-M (in Windows 95) or clicking the Show Desktop button on the Quick Launch toolbar (in Windows 98, as shown in Figure A-11) is like choosing Hide All from the Macintosh application menu while in the Finder—it hides all other programs'

Table A-1. Toolbars Available on the Windows 98 Taskbar

Toolbar	Functions
Address	Opens a window displaying a folder's contents, a program, or a web page when you type a folder name, program name, or URL in the Address field.
Links	Shows the contents of your Links toolbar from Internet Explorer.
Desktop	Shows any icons that are sitting out on your Desktop.

Table A-1. Toolbars Available on the Windows 98 Taskbar (continued)

Toolbar	Functions
Quick Launch	Displays small buttons that, when clicked, run Internet Explorer, run Outlook Express, view channels, or minimize/restore all the windows on your Desktop.
Custom Toolbar	Shows the contents of a folder or a web page that you select.

open windows. Click the Show Desktop button (Windows 98) again to simulate the Mac's Show All command.

One more note on window management (in Windows 95 or 98): When you right-click an empty portion of the Taskbar, the contextual menu provides commands to cascade the windows currently open on the Desktop, tile them horizontally or vertically, or minimize/restore them all. Although some individual Macintosh applications offer this feature, it's not built into the Mac OS.

Taskbar display. The Taskbar is generally always visible, although you can set it to appear only when you move your cursor to the corresponding edge of the screen. In addition, applications generally don't cover the Taskbar, although you can change that behavior, too. To change these options, right-click the Taskbar → Properties. If you want the Taskbar to appear only when you move your cursor to the Taskbar's edge of the screen, turn on "Auto hide." To permit application windows to overlap the Taskbar, turn off "Always on top." (But in general, there's little reason to do so unless you're working on a tiny screen.)

If the Taskbar isn't large enough for everything you want it to display, you can enlarge it by dragging an edge. It can grow as large as half the size of the Desktop, though increasing it more than a line or two is seldom necessary.

To make your Windows 98 Taskbar occupy two lines, devoting one to the Address toolbar, increase the size of the Taskbar first, then display the Address toolbar.

As you open more windows, the number of buttons on the Taskbar increases and the size of each icon shrinks (to a minimum of 16 by 16 pixels each). Icons without names aren't particularly useful at that size, but if you move your cursor over the icon, a ToolTip pops up, identifying the full name. In the worst situation, you may have too many icons to fit on the Taskbar, even at the smallest size. In that case, an arrow appears on end of the row of icons; click it to see those that are hidden from view.

You can choose which edge of the screen holds the Taskbar; click an empty area of the taskbar and drag to another edge of the screen. Macintosh users may prefer to see the Taskbar at the top of the screen, but that positioning may obscure the title bar of some Windows applications. If so, press Alt-Spacebar, then M, and then use the arrow keys to move the offending window. (Or press Alt-Spacebar, then X to maximize the window.)

Clock. The Taskbar's Properties dialog box also lets you hide the clock at the end of the Taskbar. Moving the cursor over the clock displays a ToolTip with the current date; right-clicking the clock brings up the Taskbar's contextual menu with a command that lets you set the time and date. For more information, see **Date & Time Control Panel**.

Tray. The area at the right edge of the Taskbar, next to the clock, is called the Tray. The icons of startup applications often appear in the Tray; they take up less space than full Taskbar icons that way (and, presumably, you don't need to switch into these applications often). They too often have ToolTips in case you don't understand the icons. A number of other icons in the Tray display system status indicators or provide direct access to settings like volume or bit depth, much like the Mac's Control Strip.

Applications
In Windows: Programs

For a list of applications that are similar to the Macintosh applications you're used to, see **Cross-Platform Applications**.

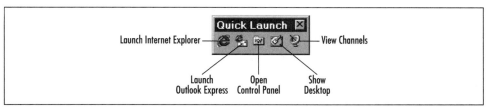

Figure A-11. Quick Launch toolbar.

Assistant
In Windows: Wizard

Some tasks on the Macintosh require a number of steps in various control panels or applications. To help new users complete these tasks, Apple created assistants—programs that walk you through the task, step by step, one configuration screen after another. (In Mac OS 8 and later, for example, you may remember having used the Mac OS Setup Assistant or the Internet Setup Assistant.)

In Windows, these assistants are called wizards, and they're far more prevalent than on the Macintosh. You'll find yourself using them all the time with little alternative. Unless you're familiar with what the wizard is doing for you, you probably won't be able to circumvent it. And in most cases, it's not worth the effort.

ATM (Adobe Type Manager)
In Windows: ATM (Adobe Type Manager)

Adobe Type Manager, commonly known as ATM, is a font utility designed to display clear, sharp characters of any size on screen and on non-PostScript printers. ATM works with Type 1 PostScript fonts; TrueType fonts, which exist for both Windows and the Macintosh, don't require ATM to perform the same feat. (Without ATM, PostScript fonts often look jagged on the screen and on inkjet printouts.)

ATM is available for both Windows and the Macintosh, but you're more likely to see it on the Macintosh, since a limited version of ATM is installed with the Macintosh version of Adobe Acrobat's free Acrobat Reader. A commercial product with additional type-manipulation capabilities, ATM Deluxe, is available for both Windows and the Macintosh. See *http://www.adobe.com/* for more information.

Auto Power On/Off Control Panel
In Windows: None

Auto Power On/Off works with only a small number of Macs, including the Quadra 840AV and the Power Macintosh 7100 and 8100. It serves the same purpose as the more recent Energy Saver control panel, letting you specify when the Macintosh turns on and off automatically. For information on similar features in Windows, see **Energy Saver Control Panel**.

AutoRemounter
In Windows: Client for Microsoft Networks Logon Options

When PowerBooks go to sleep, they lose network connections. This control panel automatically remounts servers when you wake the PowerBook. In 1998, Apple incorporated this feature into the Energy Saver control panel. In Windows, you can find the corresponding option in Control Panel → Network → Client for Microsoft Networks → Properties → "Logon and restore network connections."

B

Balloon Help

In Windows: ToolTips, Context Sensitive Help in Dialog Boxes

On the Macintosh, if you're trying to find out more about an item on the screen, you turn on balloon help by choosing Help → Show Balloons from the ubiquitous Help menu. Windows offers two features that are comparable to the Mac's balloon help: Tool-Tips, for explaining toolbar icons, and context-sensitive help in dialog boxes. For more information about getting help in Windows, see **Help**.

BinHex

In Windows: BinHex

BinHex is a bit of an anomaly on the Macintosh—it's both a binary packaging format that lumps the two Macintosh file forks together and a transfer encoding format that converts the resultant 8-bit file into 7-bit ASCII text for transmission via email or downloading from FTP or web sites.

BinHex is neither used nor necessary in the Windows world, where files have only a single fork. Some, but not all Windows email programs can decode BinHex files received from Macintosh users. If you find yourself with a binhexed file on a Windows machine, several utilities can decode it; the best will be Aladdin Expander from Aladdin Systems. You can download Aladdin Expander—and learn more about related products from Aladdin—from *http://www. aladdinsys.com/*.

For more information, see **Transferring Files to Windows**.

Boot Disk

In Windows: Boot Disk

Although both the Macintosh and Windows support multiple disks, not all of these disks can boot a Windows PC. Any disk can boot a Macintosh if the disk contains valid System and Finder files and is selected in the Startup Disk control panel. The situation isn't as simple when you're using Windows PC.

PCs generally boot from the first floppy drive (the A: drive) or the first hard disk (the C: drive). Most newer PCs also have a bootable CD-ROM drive. The order in which your PC checks for bootable disks is determined by the BIOS (like the Mac's ROM), and can be changed in your BIOS setup menu.

A disk is bootable if it contains the necessary files. At a minimum, these must include *autoexec.bat*, *command.com*, *config.sys*, *drvspace.bin*, *io.sys*, and *msdos.sys*.

To create a startup floppy disk that can boot your PC, follow these steps:

1. Open Control Panel → Add/Remove Programs → Startup Disk → Create Disk.

2. Insert a floppy disk when prompted—note that all files already on the disk at that point will be erased. Windows may ask for your Windows CD-ROM.

PC boot sequences prevent you from using a Zip disk or an external hard disk to boot the machine in case of problems with your main hard disk. Nor do Windows PCs generally come with a system-software startup CD, as Macs do. As a result, make sure you have a floppy disk that can boot your PC—and don't lose your Windows CD. You may need both disks, since you may need the combination to recover from hard disk corruption.

> **Note**
>
> Third-party software like Norton Utilities or System Commander offer a means of creating boot disks and recovery disks.

Button

In Windows: Button

Along with menus, buttons are one of the most common elements of a graphical user interface. Buttons are generally rectangles in Windows and rounded rectangles on the Macintosh. On both platforms, the button name fits inside the rectangle. To activate a button, press it by moving the cursor over the button and clicking. But you undoubtedly already knew all that.

What you may not know is that you can click many buttons in both systems from the keyboard, without using the mouse at all. Most dialog boxes have at least OK and Cancel buttons.

Like the Macintosh, Windows lets you click default buttons (which are outlined) by pressing Enter or Spacebar. Similarly, you can "click" Cancel buttons in dialog boxes from the keyboard—just press the Esc key, exactly as on the Macintosh.

Except in Microsoft and some former Claris programs, where many dialog box elements have keyboard equivalents, the OK and Cancel buttons are usually the only ones you can trigger from the keyboard on a Macintosh. But in Windows, you can "click" virtually any button, checkbox, pop-up menu, or radio button in a dialog box from the keyboard. One button, generally the most likely one you'll use, is always highlighted (with a thin line inside the button outline) when the dialog box appears, but you can also change which button is selected by pressing the Tab key repeatedly (see Figure B-1). Pressing Shift-Tab reverses the order of selection.

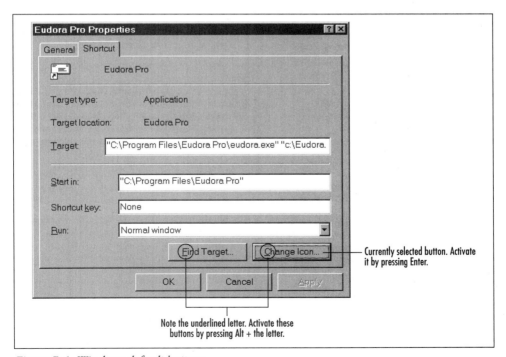

Currently selected button. Activate it by pressing Enter.

Note the underlined letter. Activate these buttons by pressing Alt + the letter.

Figure B-1. Windows default buttons

C

Calculator

In Windows: Calculator

Windows has a desk accessory Calculator, just as the Macintosh does. You open it by choosing Start → Programs → Accessories → Calculator. Actually, the Windows version is significantly more powerful than the Mac's—using the View menu, you can switch between standard four-function mode and full, HP-style, scientific mode.

CD Drives

In Windows: CD Drives

CD drives for accessing CD-ROMs and audio CDs are standard equipment on Macs and PCs today, with the notable exception of laptop computers that lack room for a CD drive. For the most part, using CDs on Windows is similar to using them on a Macintosh, with a few caveats.

Inserting and removing CDs. Inserting CDs in both Macintosh and PC CD drives works the same—press the eject button on the drive, insert the CD, and press the button

again to close the tray. Don't be alarmed when your CD icon doesn't show up on the Windows Desktop—it never will. Instead, you must open the My Computer window to see the CD icon.

When a CD is loaded, the My Computer window displays the name of the CD (see Figure C-1); when empty, it displays only the CD drive's drive letter. Once they've been inserted, you use CDs just like any other disk in Windows (except that you can't write data to a CD, of course).

Removing CDs is different, however. On the Macintosh, you're probably used to ejecting CDs by dragging their icons to the Trash or choosing Special → Eject. The Mac OS doesn't let you eject a CD by pressing the CD drive's eject button.

In Windows, however, pressing the eject button on the CD drive does eject the CD. If you have windows open, displaying files on the CD, Windows automatically closes them if you manually eject the CD. Avoid pressing the eject button when the Busy light on the CD drive's front panel is illuminated,

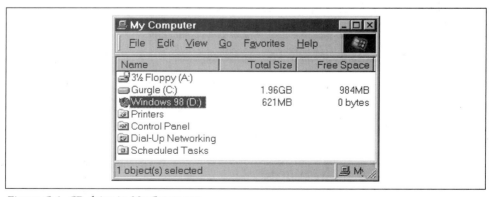

Figure C-1. CD drive in My Computer

which means that a Windows program is trying to access data from the disc.

If you'd rather not worry about whether or not the CD is ready to be ejected, right-click the CD icon in My Computer and choose Eject from the contextual menu.

AutoPlay on CD insertion. Some CDs for both the Macintosh and Windows come pre-programmed to launch a program—often an installer—automatically when you insert the CD. Although you've probably rarely seen this feature in action on the Macintosh, Windows CDs often launch a shell program or installer when inserted. You can turn off this auto-launch behavior using the TweakUI control panel's Paranoia tab (see **ResEdit** for more information about TweakUI), but if you do so, you may have trouble figuring out which program you're supposed to launch when you insert the CD.

Settings. You can modify two aspects of CD use in Windows: the letter Windows uses to refer to the CD drive and the amount of memory it uses when caching data from the CD (a speed-enhancement scheme).

You can choose a drive letter for the CD drive in Control Panel → System → Device Manager → CD-ROM → your CD drive → Properties → Settings.

As for caching, make sure that the settings in Control Panel → System → Performance → File System → CD-ROM match the speed of your CD-ROM drive (probably 4X or faster on recent models). Unless your PC has less than 12 MB of RAM, set the supplemental cache size to the largest setting, 1238K, using the slider.

Chooser
In Windows: Printers, Network Neighborhood

The Chooser, of course, is the original Mac OS method for selecting a printer or logging onto another hard disk on the network. (In recent versions of the OS, the Desktop printers and Network Browser software supplement the Chooser.)

There's no Chooser in Windows, but there are close analogues to the Mac's more recent printer and server-choosing software.

Printers. In Windows, printers are Desktop objects in My Computer → Printers. You can open the Printers folder directly from My Computer, by choosing Start → Settings → Printers, or from within the Control Panel folder. See **Desktop Printers** for details.

Servers. You mount remote servers in Windows via the Network Neighborhood icon on your Desktop. (If you don't have a Network Neighborhood icon, add a Client for Microsoft Networks using Control Panel → Network → Add → Client → Microsoft → Client for Microsoft Networks.)

For details, see **Network Browser**.

Clean Install
In Windows: Clean Install

Like the Mac OS installer program, the Windows installer is designed to replace only those components of the operating system that need updating, as a convenience to you. Unfortunately, that means that if a system file is corrupted, it stays corrupted. The only way to guarantee a virginal, all-new System Folder (on the Macintosh) or Windows folder (on Windows) is to perform a clean install. A clean install on Windows, as on the Macintosh, produces a machine that seems more responsive and less trouble-prone. You'll find five pages of dense, single-spaced instructions on how to perform a clean install of Windows at *http://www.zdnet.com/zdtv/callforhelp/projects/jump/0,3652,2217113,00.html.* Another approach is provided at h*ttp://www.winmag.com/library/1998/0701/cov0076.htm#clean.*

Windows is a sprawling, deeply entrenched operating system. You can't simply replace the Windows folder, which contains the guts of the operating system, as you can replace the System Folder on the Macintosh. If you replace your Windows folder, you must also reinstall all your fonts, drivers, and so on—and all your applications.

In Windows, the clean install is a technique of last resort; it's not a casual, foolproof troubleshooting step, as it is on the Macintosh. If you're getting inexplicable crashes or other intractable problems, first try a standard Windows install-in-place. Attempt a clean install only if you have all of your original master disks for applications, drivers, and so on—and a lot of time. Tweaking and further troubleshooting is almost always required after a clean install.

Clipboard
In Windows: Clipboard

Windows and the Macintosh offer similar clipboard features. In essence, you can cut or copy information from one program to an invisible clipboard storage area, and then switch to another application to paste that information.

In Windows, however, you can also copy and paste a file icon—a quick way of moving a file from one window into another.

In Windows, there's no Show Clipboard command, as there is on the Macintosh; however, the Clipboard Viewer performs the same function. In Windows 98, it's accessible at Start → Programs → Accessories → System Tools → Clipboard Viewer. In Windows 95, you may have to install it from Control Panel → Add/Remove Programs → Windows Setup → Accessories → Clipboard Viewer, after which it appears in Start → Programs → Accessories → Clipboard Viewer.

Clipping Files
In Windows: Scraps

In many Macintosh programs, you can drag selected text or graphics out of the original window and onto the Desktop. There an icon appears—a clipping file—containing the selected material. You can double-click this icon to view the material, or drag the icon back into an application window to "paste" it there.

Windows 95 has no equivalent feature, but in Windows 98, you can drag text or graphics out of some applications to create "scrap" files on the Desktop. These work almost exactly like Macintosh clipping files,

except that you can double-click a scrap file to open it in the application from which it was created. Unfortunately, relatively few Windows applications support scraps (Microsoft applications do, as you might expect).

To create a scrap file, select some text or a graphic and drag it to the Desktop. To use a scrap file in another document, drag the clipping file's icon from the Desktop to the desired point in an open document.

Clock
In Windows: Clock

The Mac's clock appears on the right side of the menu bar; in Windows, it shows up in the Tray, on the right side of the Taskbar.

On a basic level, the clocks are similar, telling the current time and date. (Hold the Windows cursor over the time display to see a ToolTip with the date.) Unfortunately, the Windows clock isn't nearly as configurable as the Macintosh clock is; you can't modify the way it looks or set periodic chimes, as you can on the Macintosh.

For more information about time in Windows, see **Date & Time Control Panel**.

Closing Windows
In Windows: Closing Windows

To close a Windows window click the close button in the upper-right corner of the window (see Figure C-2). Alternatively, choose System menu → Close (or press Alt-F4). To close a window and all windows you opened to get to it, Shift-click a window's close button.

You can also close minimized windows in Windows by right-clicking an icon in the Windows Taskbar and then choosing Close.

When you quit a Macintosh application, all open windows in that application close automatically. But in Windows, the connection between quitting an application and closing a window is quite different. Some programs (such as Internet Explorer and Outlook Express) treat each window as a separate task; closing one doesn't affect any

Close button

Figure C-2. Close button

others. Other applications (like Microsoft Word) treat document windows just as the Macintosh does—quit the program, and all document windows close automatically. See **Windows** for more details.

Double-clicking the system menu icon (the tiny icon just above the first menu in each Windows window, in the same place as the Mac's close box), also closes the window. If you, a Macintosh user, instinctively dive for the upper-left corner of a Windows window to close it, get into the habit of closing windows by double-clicking this system menu icon.

For information about closing windows by hiding them, see **Hiding Applications** and **Collapsing Windows**.

Collapsing Windows
In Windows: Minimizing Windows

When you want to shrink a window you're not using on the Macintosh, you can either

hide the application or click the collapse button. In Windows, you have only one option—click the minimize button (see Figure C-3) to reduce the window to an icon on the Taskbar. Alternatively, right-click the window's icon on the Taskbar and choose Minimize or choose System menu → Minimize. To restore a minimized window, click its icon on the Taskbar.

Command Key
In Windows: Ctrl Key

Although most Macintosh keyboards have a Control key, the primary modifier key has always been the Command key.

In Windows, though, the Ctrl key remains the principal modifier key. Fortunately, Microsoft copied many of Apple's keyboard shortcuts, so if you remember to swap the Ctrl key for the Command key, you already know many common Ctrl key keyboard shortcuts. For a list, see Table C-1.

Minimize button

Figure C-3. Minimize button

Table C-1. Keyboard Shortcuts Using the Control Key

Keyboard Shortcut	Function
Ctrl-A	Select All
Ctrl-Alt-x	User-defined keyboard shortcut for opening Windows shortcuts. See **Alias**.
Ctrl-Alt-Del	Quit a frozen program. See **Force Quit**.
Ctrl-arrow keys	Scroll without moving the selection.
Ctrl-C	Copy to clipboard. Works with file icons as well as high-lighted material in document windows.
Ctrl-click items	Select an item without deselecting currently selected items, as Shift-click does in the Finder.
Ctrl-drag an icon in the Explorer	Copy a file. Works like Option-drag on the Macintosh.

A-C

Table C-1. Keyboard Shortcuts Using the Control Key (continued)

Keyboard Shortcut	Function
Ctrl-End	Moves to the end of a document.
Ctrl-Esc	Same as clicking the Start menu.
Ctrl-F4	Closes document windows within application windows (such as in Microsoft Word).
Ctrl-Home	Moves to the start of a document.
Ctrl-Shift-drag an icon in the Explorer	Displays the contextual menu that you'd see if you right-dragged the icon.
Ctrl-Tab	Press repeatedly to cycle through open windows.
Ctrl-Shift-Tab	Same as Ctrl-Tab, but in reverse.
Ctrl-V	Paste from clipboard.
Ctrl-X	Cut to clipboard.
Ctrl-Z	Undo. Also works on file operations.

Connect To
In Windows: Taskbar's Address Toolbar

Mac OS 8.5 and later comes with a tiny utility called Connect To (Apple menu → Connect To). Open it, type a URL, and press Return; Connect To sends the Internet address you typed to the appropriate Internet application.

To simulate this effect in Windows 98, follow these steps:

1. Right-click the Taskbar.
2. Choose Toolbars → Address.
3. If you want the Address toolbar to float on your Desktop instead of being part of the Taskbar, drag it off the Taskbar (see Figure C-4).

To use the Address toolbar, just enter a URL and then press Enter, or choose one from the drop-down menu (see Figure C-4).

For more information about toolbars, see **Application Menu.**

Contextual Menus
In Windows: Contextual Menus

Because contextual menus are relatively new to the Mac OS, and because they duplicate the commands in normal menus, many Macintosh users aren't in the habit of using them. When you use Windows, though, many functions are accessible only through contextual menus, which tends to frustrate and confuse Macintosh users. If you can't find some essential command in Windows, remember that many additional commands and options are hidden within contextual menus.

Using contextual menus. To make contextual menus appear in Windows, click an item—an icon, the Desktop, a toolbar, and so on—using the right mouse button. (Some laptops may not have a two-button mouse, but a "right mouse button" will be available in some form.) Alternatively, select the item in question with a single click of the left mouse button, and then press the Application key. This key is usually to the right of the Spacebar and has an image of a menu

Figure C-4. Address toolbar

on it. (On the other hand, if you actually know a Windows user who uses the Application key, you're one in a million.)

Modifying contextual menus. On the Macintosh, you can add items to contextual menus by dropping appropriate files—contextual menu plug-ins—into the System Folder → Contextual Menu Items folder. You can add new contextual menu commands to Windows, too, but not manually—in general, the utility you're trying to install comes with an installer that does the job.

Control Key

In Windows: Control (Ctrl) Key, Right-Clicking

In the Mac OS, you use the Control key primarily for displaying contextual menus. The Ctrl key in Windows is more akin to the Mac's Command key; to display contextual menus in Windows, right-click the item on the screen—a button, toolbar, or icon, for example—as described in the previous entry.

Control Panels

In Windows: Control Panel

You configure most aspects of the Mac OS in pseudo-applications—control panels—in the Control Panels folder. The Windows Control Panel is almost identical.

Accessing the Windows Control Panel. You can access Windows control panels in different ways:

- Open My Computer → Control Panel.

- Choose Start → Settings → Control Panel.

- Windows 98: Add a toolbar to your Taskbar (see **Application Menu** for instructions), drag the Control Panel folder icon to the toolbar, and then click the Control Panel icon.

- Individual control panels may have alternate methods of access. For instance, you can access the System control panel by right-clicking My Computer and choosing Properties.

- Access individual control panels directly through a hierarchical menu, just as you would on the Macintosh. Follow these steps to create a hierarchical Control Panel menu in your Start menu, for example:

  a. Right-click the Start menu, and then choose Open to open the Start Menu folder.

  b. Choose File → New → Folder. Windows creates a new folder.

  c. Rename the folder as follows: *Control Panel.{21EC2020-3AEA-1069-A2DD-08002B30309D}*.

You'll see your new menu command, called Control Panel, in the Start menu, with a submenu listing the contents of the folder. It may take a few seconds to draw the first time you use it each session, but it should be faster for the rest of the session.

The following are some facts about the Windows Control Panel:

- Unlike Macintosh control panels, Windows control panels are not normal files that you can move in and out of the Control Panel folder. To remove a control panel, you must uninstall it from Control Panel → Add/Remove Programs.

- Each Macintosh control panels lets you configure something, whereas some Windows control panels are simply shortcuts to folders (such as Fonts and Printers), or wizards (like Add New Hardware).

- Some Windows control panels interact in potentially confusing ways. For instance, you can set default dialing properties in the Modem control panel, but an identical Properties dialog box accessible from a Dial-Up Networking connection overrides the defaults. Similarly, you don't configure TCP/IP settings for your Dial-Up Adapter in the Network control panel, but instead in each Dial-Up Networking connection.

- You can choose the Control Panels command in the Mac's Apple menu to open the Control Panels folder. But you can't choose the Settings command in the Windows Start menu—you must proceed to choose an item from its sub-menu.

Control Strip
In Windows: Tray

The Control Strip, a fixture of the Macin-tosh interface, provides direct access to set-tings in numerous control panels. You can also extend it with modules installed in the Control Strip Modules folder.

The closest equivalent in Windows is the Tray, the area on the right side of the Task-bar that holds icons for special programs. Some of those icons sprout pop-up menus providing direct access to Control Panel set-tings, exactly as on the Macintosh Control Strip.

It's difficult to identify some of these tiny Tray icons, but if you hold the cursor over one, a ToolTip appears to identify it. Try clicking or right-clicking these Tray icons to see what they do, exactly as you might on the Control Strip.

Controlling the Tray icons. Removing or rearranging the tiles on the Macintosh Con-trol Strip is easy. Doing so is slightly harder

on the Windows Tray—see Table C-2 for a list of Tray items and where you turn them on and off.

Copy
In Windows: Copy

The Windows Copy command (Ctrl-C) works exactly the same as it does on the Macintosh—it transfers highlighted text or graphics onto the invisible clipboard, ready for pasting into another document or another part of the same document.

In Windows, however, you can also use Cut, Copy, and Paste to move and copy *files* from one folder window to another. Although this technique may seem clumsy, it can be helpful when it's difficult to get the source and destination folder windows visi-ble at the same time.

To copy files and folders using the Copy command, follow these steps:

1. Select one or more icons in a window.

2. Choose Edit → Copy (Ctrl-C).

3. Click on the window you want to switch to.

4. Choose Edit → Paste (Ctrl-V).

Table C-2. Tray Items

Item	Control Location
Clock	Taskbar → Properties → Taskbar Options → Show clock
Display resolutions	Control Panel → Display → Settings → Show settings icon
Dial-Up Connection	Dial-Up Networking → Connections → Settings → Show an icon on Taskbar after connected
FilterKeys	Control Panel → Accessibility Options → Keyboard → FilterKeys → Settings → Show FilterKeys status
Language	Control Panel → Keyboard → Language
MouseKeys	Control Panel → Accessibility Options → Mouse → MouseKeys → Settings → Show MouseKeys status
PC Card (PCMCIA)	Control Panel → PC Card (PCMCIA) → Show control
Power Status	(In Windows 98): Control Panel → Power Management → Advanced – Show power meter (In Windows 95): Control Panel → Power → Show battery meter
StickyKeys	Control Panel → Accessibility Options → Keyboard → StickyKeys → Settings → Show StickyKeys status
Volume	Control Panel → Multimedia → Audio → Show volume control

Using Copy on filenames. On the Macintosh, you can highlight group of icons, and then choose Edit → Copy to copy the highlighted files' names to the Clipboard, ready to paste into, say, an email or a word processor. You can't use this technique in Windows.

You can use the Copy command while renaming an icon, but only after you've actually typed a change to a file's name. If you use Copy when the "renaming rectangle" has appeared but you haven't yet made any changes, Windows copies the entire file instead of the highlighted part of the file's name.

Copying Files
In Windows: Copying Files

Copying files on the Macintosh is a simple proposition—just drag them from one disk to another. That technique works in Windows, too, but Windows offers a few additional methods. When you're copying a file in Windows, the mouse cursor generally acquires a small plus character badge (see Figure C-5).

- To copy files between disks, drag icons from a window on one disk to a window on another disk.

- To copy files to another window on the same disk, Ctrl-drag the icons to the new location. (This technique is akin to Option-dragging on the Macintosh.) If

you don't hold down the Ctrl key, the files will be moved instead.

- Select one or more icons, and then choose Edit → Copy (Ctrl-C). Alternatively, right-click one of the selected items and choose Copy. Then switch to another window and choose Edit → Paste.

- Right-drag any file or folder from one window to another on any disk, and then choose Copy Here from the contextual menu. If you create a copy of a file in the same folder as the original in this manner, Windows creates a duplicate of the file, prefixing the name with "Copy of."

Windows obeys certain rules when copying files:

- If you drag an application icon, Windows makes a shortcut in the destination instead of a copy. If you're sure that you actually want to move the application itself—which may sometimes mean that it won't work, since Windows applications are often folder-dependent—press Shift as you drag.

- You can change a move into a copy by pressing Ctrl while dragging.

- You can cancel a copy in progress by right-clicking or by pressing Escape. You can't move a file into or out of the My Computer window. Anything you drag out of this window becomes a shortcut.

Figure C-5. Plus badge on cursor when copying

Figure C-6. Curved-arrow badge on cursor when making a shortcut

• Copying files in two-pane Explorer windows works just like moving them in the normal folder windows; just drag files or folders from the left pane to a folder in the right pane.

Note

You can tell if you'll be successful in dragging an application by its cursor shape. If the cursor has a curved arrow badge, Windows plans to make a shortcut (see Figure C-6). For more information about shortcuts, see Alias.

Creator Codes
In Windows: File Type Mappings

Behind the scenes, every Macintosh file has two four-letter codes associated with it: the creator code and the type code. The creator code identifies the application that created the file (such as Photoshop), and the type code specifies the file type (JPEG, GIF, PICT, etc.). Together, these codes define what file icons look like and which program is launched when you double-click a file in the Finder.

In Windows, the situation is completely different. Files all have three-letter extensions that specify the type of file, so a Microsoft Word document's name ends with the letters *.doc*; an Excel document, *.xls*; and so on. You may not be able to see these extensions, though you can reveal them by deselecting View → Folder Options → View → "Hide MS-DOS file extensions for file types that are registered."

Although type and creator codes are separate on the Macintosh, in Windows, every type of file can have only one application associated with it. So, if you double-click a file whose name ends in *.txt*, Windows will always try to open the file in NotePad. On the Macintosh, a text file could open in SimpleText, BBEdit, Word, or Nisus Writer, depending on the creator code.

Windows applications sometimes "steal" files from one another. For instance, Internet Explorer and Netscape Navigator will each try to take over the *.htm* extension,

since whichever one has it will open all HTML files by default.

You can reset these associations manually if necessary using the following steps:

1. Open View → Folder Options → File Types.

2. Select the desired file type from the list (type a letter to jump to entries starting with that letter), and then click Edit.

3. In the Edit File Type dialog box, select "open" in the Actions list, then click Edit.

4. In the Editing action dialog box, click the Browse button and select a new application to associate with the Open action.

Cross-Platform Applications
In Windows: Cross-Platform Applications

In the past, the hardest part of switching between Windows and the Macintosh was that you had to use completely different applications. Today, the most popular programs are available in nearly identical Windows and Macintosh versions. Plus, it's likely that the two versions share the same file format, which is important when moving back and forth between the two platforms. Here are some of the most popular:

Database

• AppleWorks (Apple Computer):
  http://www.apple.com/appleworks/
• FileMaker Pro (FileMaker):
  http://www.filemaker.com/

Graphics and illustration

• Adobe Illustrator (Adobe Systems):
  http://www.adobe.com/prodindex/illustrator/main.html
• Adobe PhotoDeluxe (Adobe Systems):
  http://www.adobe.com/prodindex/photodeluxe/main.html
• Adobe Photoshop (Adobe Systems):
  http://www.adobe.com/prodindex/photoshop/main.html
• Adobe Streamline (Adobe Systems):
  http://www.adobe.com/prodindex/streamline/main.html

- AppleWorks (Apple Computer):
  http://www.apple.com/appleworks/
- Bryce (MetaCreations):
  http://www.metacreations.com/
- Canvas (Deneba):
  http://www.deneba.com/
- CorelDRAW (Corel):
  *http://www.corel.com/products/
  graphicsandpublishing/draw8/index.htm*
- DeBabelizer (Equilibrium):
  http://www.equilibrium.com/
- FreeHand (Macromedia):
  *http://www.macromedia.com/software/
  freehand/*
- Kai's Photo SOAP (MetaCreations):
  http://www.metacreations.com/
- Kai's Power Tools (MetaCreations):
  http://www.metacreations.com/
- Painter (MetaCreations):
  http://www.metacreations.com/
- Ray Dream Studio (MetaCreations):
  *http://www.metacreations.com/
  products/rds/studio.html*

Internet

- America Online (America Online):
  http://www.aol.com/
- Eudora (Qualcomm):
  http://www.eudora.com/
- Microsoft Internet Explorer (Microsoft):
  http://www.microsoft.com/
- Microsoft Outlook Express (Microsoft):
  http://www.microsoft.com/
- Netscape Communicator (Netscape Communications):
  http://www.netscape.com/

Multimedia

- Adobe After Effects (Adobe Systems):
  *http://www.adobe.com/prodindex/
  aftereffects/main.html*
- Adobe Premiere (Adobe Systems):
  *http://www.adobe.com/prodindex/
  premiere/main.html*
- Macromedia Director (Macromedia):
  *http://www.macromedia.com/software/
  director/*

Page layout and publishing tools

- Adobe Acrobat (Adobe Systems):
  *http://www.adobe.com/prodindex/
  acrobat/main.html*
- Adobe FrameMaker (Adobe Systems):
  *http://www.adobe.com/prodindex/
  framemaker/main.html*
- Adobe InDesign (Adobe Systems):
  *http://www.adobe.com/prodindex/
  indesign/main.html*
- Adobe PageMaker (Adobe Systems):
  *http://www.adobe.com/prodindex/
  pagemaker/main.html*
- QuarkXPress (Quark):
  http://www.quark.com/

Personal finance

- Quicken (Intuit):
  http://www.intuit.com/
- Kiplinger TaxCut (Block Financial):
  http://www.taxcut.com/

Spreadsheet

- AppleWorks (Apple Computer):
  http://www.apple.com/appleworks/
- Microsoft Excel (Microsoft):
  http://www.microsoft.com/office/

Web graphics and authoring

- Adobe GoLive (Adobe Systems):
  *http://www.adobe.com/prodindex/
  golive/main.html*
- Adobe ImageReady (Adobe Systems):
  *http://www.adobe.com/prodindex/
  imageready/main.html*
- Adobe ImageReady (Adobe Systems):
  *http://www.adobe.com/prodindex/
  imageready/main.html*
- Adobe PageMill (Adobe Systems):
  *http://www.adobe.com/prodindex/
  pagemill/main.html*
- Home Page (FileMaker):
  http://www.filemaker.com/
- Macromedia Dreamweaver (Macromedia):
  *http://www.macromedia.com/software/
  dreamweaver/*

- Macromedia Flash (Macromedia): *http://www.macromedia.com/software/ flash/*

- Macromedia Fireworks (Macromedia): *http://www.macromedia.com/software/ fireworks/*

- Macromedia Generator (Macromedia): *http://www.macromedia.com/software/ generator/*

- Macromedia ShockWave (Macromedia): *http://www.macromedia.com/ shockwave/*

- NetObjects Fusion (NetObjects): *http://www.netobjects.com/*

Utilities

- Aladdin DropStuff (Aladdin Systems): *http://www.aladdinsys.com/dropstuff/*

- Aladdin Expander (Aladdin Systems): *http://www.aladdinsys.com/expander/*

- Norton AntiVirus (Symantec): *http://www.symantec.com/*

- Norton Utilities (Symantec): *http://www.symantec.com/*

Word processing and presentation

- AppleWorks (Apple Computer): *http://www.apple.com/appleworks/*

- Corel WordPerfect (Corel): *http://www.corel.com/products/ wordperfect/index.htm*

- Microsoft PowerPoint (Microsoft): *http://www.microsoft.com/office/*

- Microsoft Word (Microsoft): *http://www.microsoft.com/office/*

Cut

In Windows: Cut

The Windows Cut command (Ctrl-X) works exactly as it does on the Macintosh—it removes highlighted text or graphics from an application window, placing it onto the invisible clipboard ready for pasting into a different place.

In Windows, moreover, you can use the Cut command to move files in conjunction with Paste—a handy technique when you're having trouble getting the source and destination folder windows open on the screen at the same time.

To move files and folders using the Cut command, follow these steps:

1. Select one or more icons in a window.
2. Choose Edit → Cut (Ctrl-X). The selected icons become transparent.
3. Click on the windows you want to switch to.
4. Choose Edit → Paste (Ctrl-V).

For notes on using Cut to edit filenames, see **Copy**, which works similarly.

D

Date & Time Control Panel

In Windows: Date/Time Control Panel

In the Mac's Date & Time control panel, you can set the Macintosh clock's date, time, and time zone, switch between different date and time formats, and modify a wide variety of options for the menu bar clock.

The Windows Date/Time control panel, accessible in Control Panel → Date/Time, is less full-featured. You can set the date and time by following these steps.

1. Choose the month from the Month menu.

2. Enter a year in the Year field.

3. Click the appropriate date in the calendar display.

4. Enter the appropriate time in the Time field, below the analog clock display (see Figure D-1).

The analog clock display is purely ornamental, as is the map display in the Time Zone tab, where you can choose a time zone from the list. (In other words, you can't click to set the time or location.)

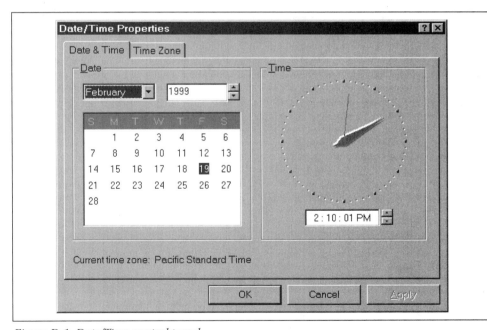

Figure D-1. Date/Time control panel

To change the time or date display formats, use the Windows Regional Settings control panel (Control Panel → Regional Settings), which has tabs for both time and date (see Figure D-2).

Del Key

In Windows: Delete Key

The forward delete, or Del, key, which is grouped with the navigation keys (Page Up, Home, and so on) on Macintosh keyboards, deletes text to the right of the insertion point. (In graphics programs, it simply functions as a duplicate Delete key.) Maybe that's why Apple eliminated the forward-delete key altogether from the keyboard that accompanies its current computers.

In Windows, though, the forward delete key (called simply Delete, to avoid confusion with the Backspace key) has a few additional functions:

- Select a file and press Delete to send that file to the Recycle Bin (like pressing Command-Delete in Mac OS 8 and later).

- Press Shift-Delete to delete the file instantly from your hard disk. Be careful using Shift-Delete, since you don't have a second chance to recover the file, as you do when you put a file in the Recycle Bin.

- The well-known Ctrl-Alt-Delete combination (originally used to restart DOS-based PCs) now brings up the Close Program dialog box, from which you can quit misbehaving programs.

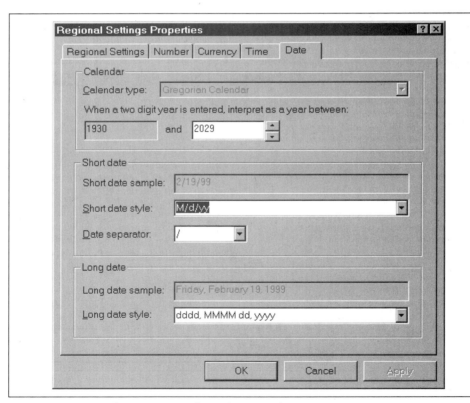

Figure D-2. Regional Settings control panel's Date tab

Delete Key

In Windows: Backspace Key

Many Macintosh users still think of this key as the Backspace key, although on the standard Macintosh keyboards it's labeled "Delete." In Windows, though, it's labeled "Backspace," so we'll make the same distinction.

In addition to its usual function—deleting the highlighted item, or deleting text to the left of the insertion point—the Backspace key has another function in Windows. Whenever you're in a window that lists files, such as a standard folder window, Windows Explorer, or an Open or Save dialog box, pressing Backspace moves you up one level in the disk hierarchy. (Power users recognize this concept as the Command-up arrow shortcut on the Macintosh.)

Deleting Files

In Windows: Deleting Files

You can delete files and folders in Windows the same way you're used to on the Macintosh—by dragging them to the Recycle Bin. However, Windows offers additional ways to delete files; see **Trash** for a full list.

Desktop

In Windows: Desktop, My Computer

For the most part, the Macintosh and Windows Desktops are quite similar. Like the Windows Desktop, the Macintosh Desktop is, behind the scenes, actually a folder that contains files and other folders that appear on the backdrop, the Desktop, when you first turn on the computer. And anything you'd do on the Macintosh Desktop is likely to work on the Windows Desktop: renaming files, opening folders, dragging icons, and so on. You can drag document icons on top of application icons to open files. You can right-click objects on the Windows Desktop to summon a contextual menu, much like the one that appears when you Control-click the Macintosh Desktop.

On the other hand, the two Desktops are also different in subtle ways.

- When you insert a disk or CD of any kind, you're used to seeing its icon appear on your Macintosh Desktop. In Windows, no icon appears; you must open the My Computer icon on your Desktop to access your disk drives. See **Disk Space** for more information.

- The Macintosh Desktop can hold files and folders from any disk, since each disk has its own invisible Desktop Folder. In contrast, the invisible Desktop folder in Windows lives only on the C: disk, so the Windows Desktop can hold only files and folders from the C: disk.

- In Mac OS 8 and later, Desktop Printer icons appear on the Desktop; in Windows, Printer icons are stored in a special folder at My Computer → Printers. (Of course, you can create a shortcut to a Printer icon and store the shortcut on your Windows Desktop.)

- In Mac OS 8.5 and later, the Network Browser appears in the Apple menu. The Windows equivalent, the Network Neighborhood, sits on the Desktop.

Removing icons from the Desktop. It's easy to remove most icons from the Macintosh Desktop, but it can be more difficult to remove items from the Windows Desktop. In fact, you may find doing so impossible without the aid of the TweakUI control panel, an optional utility on the Windows 98 CD-ROM. (If you use Windows 95, you can download TweakUI from *http://www. microsoft.com/windows95/downloads/ default.asp.*)

To remove "stuck" items from your Desktop, rename them, or create files from them so you can move them. (Note that you can't necessarily apply all of these actions to each item; right-click each one, as shown in Figure D-3, to see which actions are allowed.)

1. Install TweakUI by installing the Windows 98 Resource Kit Tools Sampler on the Windows 98 CD-ROM at *Windows 98\tools\restkit\setup.exe.*

2. Open Control Panel → TweakUI → Desktop.

D–G

Figure D-3. Modifying Desktop settings with TweakUI

3. Click the box next to each icon's name to remove or add a checkmark. Checked items appear on the Desktop.

4. Double-click the names of items to edit them.

5. If you'd like to move a Desktop icon to a new location on your hard disk, select its name, click Create As File, and then save the resulting file to the new location.

If you're a fan of the Mac's Button view, in which only a single click opens an icon, you can simulate that arrangement in Windows with a little work.

The Windows Desktop versus Finder Desktop. The most significant difference between the Windows and Macintosh Desktops, however, is that the Macintosh Desktop "belongs" to the Finder, along with all other Finder windows. So, when you switch into the Finder (by clicking any visible Desktop area, for example), all Finder windows appear over whatever other application windows you have open.

The fact that Finder windows appear over other windows when you click the Desktop exemplifies the different way the Macintosh and Windows handle tasks. In Windows, every *window* is a separate task that appears separately on the Taskbar. On the Macintosh, though, every *application* is a separate task that appears in the Application menu. Windows belonging to those applications are not separate tasks, and thus appear or disappear all at once.

As a Macintosh user, you may find it difficult to work in Desktop windows that contain files and folders, because windows from other applications can get in the way more easily then they would on the Macintosh. If your Desktop is too cluttered, special tricks await.

In Windows 98, enable the Quick Launch toolbar on your Taskbar, and then click the

Making Windows Look Like a Macintosh

If you're feeling lost at sea the first time you use Windows, remember that its alien feeling stems primarily from its different look; beneath the surface, most of the elements are the same as on the Macintosh. With a few choice adjustments and shareware morsels, you can give Windows a facelift to make it look exactly like the Macintosh Desktop. Here are some starting points:

The amazing freeware program WinMac makes Windows look exactly like a Macintosh—complete with Desktop icons, a fixed-at-the-top Finder menu bar, the Charcoal font for menus, and more. The program even adds Macintosh menu commands to your "Finder," such as Empty Trash, Eject Disk, Edit Menu items, and an Application menu. WinMac is free from *http://www.niklas.com/w.html*.

As a less radical alternative, download the Mac95 Plus! theme for use with your Windows Appearance control panel. It replaces the graphics used for your hourglass cursor, arrow cursor, My Computer icon, hard disk, and floppy icons, along with sounds, Desktop backgrounds, fonts, color settings, and startup/shutdown sounds. It's available from *http://www.geocities.com/SiliconValley/Way/2736*. The same web site offers other utilities that turn your Start menu into a multicolored apple, change your dialog boxes to resemble those on the Macintosh, make your control panel icons look like the Mac's, and so on. WinShade, another shareware morsel available at this web site, lets you roll up windows into their title bars, exactly as the Macintosh does, and Mac95 Integrated Video and Sound for DOS (Mac95ivs) even gives you the Mac OS startup screen. (Mac95 requires the Themes program from the Microsoft Plus add-on package.)

You can also make Windows look more Macintosh-like by moving the Start menu into Apple-menu position—at the top of the screen. To do so, click any empty area of the gray Taskbar and drag straight up to the top of the screen. Unfortunately, doing so may cover up your programs' menu bars—a problem easily solved with the $15 shareware program Shove-it, available from *http://www.phord.com/*.

You'll be able to find your files more easily if you put them where you'd expect to find them on the Macintosh. Open the My Computer window; drag the icons for the various disk drives (hard disk, floppy, CD-ROM, and so on) to the right side of your screen, where these disks would appear on a Macintosh. Unlike a Macintosh, the resulting shortcuts will always appear there, even when no disk is inserted, but at least you'll know where to look.

Finally, there's the matter of your Desktop background. Fortunately, moving your favorite Macintosh Desktop patterns to Windows is easy enough. On the Macintosh, open the Appearance or Desktop Pictures control panel; choose Edit → Copy, and paste the pattern into, for example, Photoshop. Save the file as a BMP (bitmap) file, which is the standard Windows Desktop pattern format, and add the suffix .bmp to its name. Copy the file over to the PC (see Transferring Files to Windows). On the Windows machine, open the C: drive, open the Windows folder, and drag the BMP file into the window. Finally, use the Display control panel (click Background) to choose your new Desktop pattern.

Show Desktop button to minimize all open windows In Windows 95, press the WIN key with the letter M. In both cases, you jump directly to the Windows Desktop, and all windows from other applications are hidden. (Click their taskbar buttons to bring them forward again.)

Changing the Desktop picture or pattern. For information about changing the Windows Desktop's background, see **Appearance Control Panel**.

Desktop Patterns Control Panel
In Windows: Display Control Panel's Background Tab

In Mac OS 7.5 and 7.6, you switch Desktop patterns using the Desktop Patterns control panel. The same feature is accessible in Windows from the Background tab of the Display control panel. For more information, see **Appearance Control Panel.**

Desktop Pictures Control Panel
In Windows: Display Control Panel's Background Tab

In Mac OS 8.0 and 8.1, you switch Desktop patterns and pictures using the Desktop Pictures control panel. The same feature is accessible in Windows from the Background tab of the Display control panel. For more information, see **Appearance Control Panel.**

Desktop Printers
In Windows: Printers Folder

With Mac OS 8, Apple introduced Desktop Printers, icons on your Desktop that represent printers. You can drag documents onto these icons to be printed, making it easy to specify which printer you want to use for each printout. You can also open Desktop icons to review the print queue—to see which document is printing or to determine why a document may not have printed, for example.

In Windows, the same task is handled by the Printer icons located in My Computer → Printers. (You can also access these Printers by choosing Control Panel → Printers and Start → Settings → Printers.)

An Add Printer wizard walks you through the process of setting up a new printer, after which that printer shows up in the Printers folder. You can use printer icons much like Macintosh Desktop printers—drag documents to a Printer icon to print, open a Printer icon to view and control your print

queue, and so on (see Figure D-4). For more information, see **Printing Files.**

If you need to modify a printer's settings, right-click it and choose Properties (or choose Printer → Properties when you have the queue open). The options vary by printer, of course, but you can change things like paper size, paper source, font rendering, and so on.

One printer is always your default printer, which means only that it's the default printer when you print a document from within an application. You can always choose a different printer in the Windows Print dialog box, just as on the Macintosh.

DialAssist Control Panel
In Windows: My Locations

You use the Mac's DialAssist control panel to modify how other control panels, such as the Remote Access control panel in Advanced mode, dial phone numbers. The same capability is available in Windows in the Telephony control panel. You'll find this either in Control Panel → Telephony → My Locations (Windows 98) or in Control Panel → Modems → Dialing Properties → My Locations (Windows 95). For more information, see **Location Manager Control Panel.**

Dialog Boxes
In Windows: Dialog Boxes

On the Macintosh, you're used to seeing dialog boxes in a wide variety of situations: changing settings, opening documents, printing, and so on. Windows uses dialog boxes for similar tasks, but there are differences that you may find either confusing or helpful.

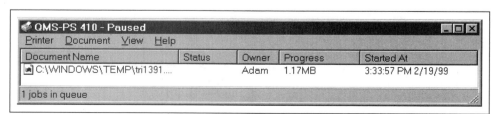

Figure D-4. Print queue

Modality. The Macintosh has two types of dialog box. First, there's the *application modal* type, which lets you work in other applications before closing the dialog box; this kind of box generally has a title bar, which you can drag to move the window. *System modal* dialog boxes, on the other hand, must be closed before you can return to work. (The Print and Save dialog boxes take this form.) These usually lack a title bar and can't be moved; if you click anywhere outside of such a window, the Macintosh rewards you with only a beep.

Most Windows dialog boxes, on the other hand, are application modal. Windows has only a few system modal dialog boxes, such as the Shut Down dialog box, which prevent you from doing anything else until you've closed the dialog box.

Help in dialog boxes. Although relatively few Macintosh users rely on Balloon Help in dialog boxes, you can always choose Help → Show Balloons on the Macintosh. In Windows, you access the same kind of context-sensitive help by clicking the question-mark button in the corner of most dialog boxes, and then pointing to the various elements of the dialog box, as shown in Figure D-5.

Alternatively, you can right-click an item in a dialog box to display a What's This? button; click the button to display the pop-up help window. For more information, see **Help.**

Tabbed dialog boxes. In Windows dialog boxes, tabs separate different panels, exactly as in Microsoft programs for the Macintosh. Tabbed dialog boxes work well except when there are multiple rows of tabs. When you click a tab, the rows swap positions, which can be disorienting.

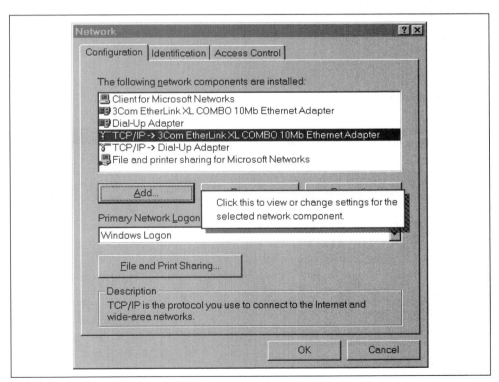

Figure D-5. Pop-up Help window in a dialog box

Dialog box buttons and keyboard shortcuts. Most Macintosh dialog boxes have OK and Cancel buttons; if you're a keyboard fan, you can press the Return or Esc keys, respectively, instead of clicking them. Windows dialog boxes also have OK and Cancel buttons, and once again the Enter and Esc keys trigger them. However, Windows settings dialog boxes commonly provide an Apply button that saves the changes you've made without closing the dialog box, as clicking OK would do.

In Windows, you can control far more parts of dialog boxes from the keyboard. For example, you can trigger every button, checkbox, pop-up menu, and other element using keyboard equivalents, indicated on the screen by underlined letters (see **Button** for details). You can also press Tab repeatedly to select different controls within the dialog box. When you've managed to highlight the button or control you want, you can press Enter or Spacebar to "click" it.

Disk Cache
In Windows: Vcache

The Mac's Memory control panel lets you change the *disk cache* settings. The disk cache is a standard computer feature in which frequently used data from the hard disk is temporarily stored in RAM in the event it's needed again. Since RAM is so much faster than hard disks, the cached data is available almost immediately the next time it's requested.

Windows offers a disk cache, too. However, most of the time you don't have to change the Windows disk cache settings, since Windows manages them automatically. For more on memory management, see **Memory Control Panel**.

Disk First Aid
In Windows: ScanDisk

Disk First Aid is the standard Mac OS hard disk-repair program. On Windows, the corresponding program is called ScanDisk. As with Disk First Aid in Mac OS 8.5 and later, ScanDisk runs automatically after a system crash in the hopes of nipping fresh hard-disk problems in the bud. You can also run ScanDisk manually from Start → Programs → Accessories → System Tools → ScanDisk. Its interface is simple, primarily offering you the choice of standard or thorough tests (see Figure D-6).

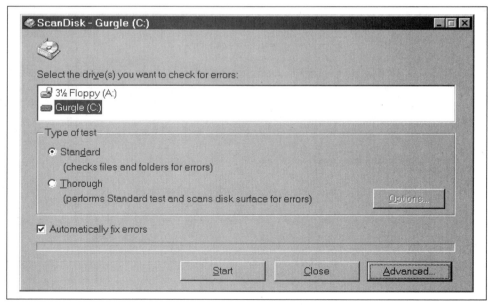

Figure D-6. ScanDisk interface

A standard test works like Disk First Aid: it checks files and directory structures for damage. The thorough test also scans the surface of the disk for bad blocks, which takes much longer and need not be run frequently, perhaps once a month at the most. (Most modern hard disks have bad blocks mapped out when they're formatted; it's relatively unlikely for them to develop more.) ScanDisk can automatically fix problems or ask you for each one—automatic fixing is generally best.

As with Disk First Aid, it's a good idea to run a ScanDisk standard test once every week or so. The easiest way to do that is using Windows' Scheduled Tasks, available in the My Computer window. For more information about scheduling tasks, see **Macros**.

Disk Space
In Windows: Hard Disk Properties

To find out how much space is available on a disk in Windows, open the My Computer icon, right-click the disk icon (such as the C: hard disk); from the pop-up menu, choose Properties. The resulting dialog box shows you how much disk space is available, complete with a useful pie chart.

Disks. For the Macintosh user moving to Windows for the first time, few surprises are as disorienting as the issue of disks and disk icons. When you insert a CD, floppy disk, or Zip disk, for example, no icon appears on the Windows Desktop. Even the hard disk doesn't have an icon on the Desktop.

Fortunately, Windows isn't without disk icons altogether—it just keeps them in a different place. Double-click the My Computer icon in the upper-left corner of the screen to reveal the full array of disk icons.

Think of these as disk-drive icons, not disk icons, because they're permanent installations in the My Computer window, even when no disks are actually in the drives. The CD-ROM icon may change visually when a CD is actually in the PC. But when you insert another kind of disk, there's only one way to find out whether or not it's properly inserted and working: try double-clicking the corresponding icon in the My

Computer window. If the disk window now opens, everything is fine—otherwise, you get an error message.

If you miss the directness of being able to access your disk icons on the Desktop, you're not condemned to having to open the My Computer window every time you want to view your disk icons. Make shortcuts for these icons and place them at the right edge of the screen, exactly as on the Macintosh. (See **Alias** for more on Windows shortcuts.) Although these icons appear permanently there, whether or not disks are actually in the drives they represent, at least this step brings you one step closer to the familiar Macintosh environment.

Ejecting disks. Don't attempt to eject a disk by dragging its icon to the Recycle Bin, thinking that it will work like dragging a disk to the Trash on the Macintosh—you'll wind up erasing the files!

Instead, right-click the disk's icon and choose Eject Disk from the pop-up menu. Alternatively, alarming as it may feel at first, you can eject a disk manually by pressing the eject button on the front panel of your PC—there's one each for the Zip drive, floppy drive, CD-ROM drive, and so on. The disk pops out on its own.

Note

Never manually eject a Windows disk by pressing its eject button while the little activity light is flashing. That indicator tells you that the PC is still recording to or reading information from the disk. Wait until the light goes out before pushing the eject button.

Erasing disks. To erase a Windows disk, such as a floppy or Zip, bring its icon into view by double-clicking the My Computer icon on your Desktop. Right-click the disk icon; from the pop-up menu, choose Format. A dialog box appears, offering such options as Quick Erase (deletes the files but doesn't check the disk surface for problems) or Full (takes longer, but locates bad spots on the disk and marks them as off-limits). See **Erase Disk** for details.

Renaming disks. You can't rename a Windows disk as you do other files. Instead, right-click a disk's icon and choose Properties from the pop-up menu. Change the disk's name in the Label field, keeping in mind that no disk name can be longer than 11 letters.

Drive Setup
In Windows: Formatting Disks

The software you need to reformat a PC hard disk is built into Windows; it's not a standalone application. For information on reformatting disks in Windows, see **Hard Disks**.

Drivers
In Windows: Drivers

A driver is a small program that lets a computer, either a Macintosh or a PC, communicate with some piece of hardware, be it a printer, modem, or scanner. Drivers are a much bigger deal in the PC world than in the Macintosh world, for two reasons:

- Since there are many more manufacturers of hardware for PCs than for Macs, the possibilities for problems and conflicts are much greater.

- Apple often writes generalized drivers that work for an entire class of hardware devices, which relieves manufacturers from having to create their own drivers. For instance, most laser printers use Apple's LaserWriter driver, and many USB devices can use Apple's generic USB driver. Many drivers, such as those for the mouse, keyboard, monitor, hard drive, speakers, and so on, are invisible and built into the Macintosh ROM.

Interestingly, one of the most important reasons for the success of Windows 95 is the huge amount of effort Microsoft put into creating and testing drivers for hardware peripherals. Other PC-based operating systems (including Windows NT, ironically) lack similarly good driver support, which

proved to be a significant advantage for Windows 95.

Even so, drivers can be a major source of headaches on the PC because there are so many of them. Conflicts are relatively common and difficult to troubleshoot. Video card drivers are among the worst, since they can conflict with seemingly unrelated features of the computer. (Even problems as seemingly unrelated as an inability to read Internet newsgroups have occasionally been traced to outdated video-card drivers.)

Windows includes a huge database of drivers, but it's only as current as the day Windows was released. (Windows 98's updated driver collection alone is a good reason to upgrade.) All peripherals should come with the necessary drivers on disk, of course, and you should be able to download updates from most manufacturers' web sites. It's worth creating bookmarks to the web sites for products you own, so you can quickly check for driver updates when you're trying to troubleshoot.

Microsoft's Windows 98 Update Device Driver wizard can check for new drivers from the Microsoft Windows Update web site.

To check for an updated driver, follow these steps:

1. Open Start → Settings → Control Panel → System → Device Manager.

2. Click the name of the peripheral device whose driver you'd like to update.

3. Click Properties → Driver → Update Driver. (If the Properties dialog box lacks a Driver tab, you can't update the driver.)

4. The Update Device Driver wizard asks if you want to search for a driver, then gives you an opportunity to specify where it should look: floppy drives, the CD-ROM drive, Microsoft Windows Update, or another location.

5. If the Update Device Driver wizard finds a new driver, it offers to install the driver for you.

E

Edit Menu
In Windows: Edit Menu

The Edit menu in the Finder's menu bar is mirrored within the Edit menu of every folder window in Windows. Most of the menu items—Cut, Copy, Paste, and so on—have the same names and keyboard shortcuts as on the Macintosh, except that you use the Ctrl key instead of the Mac's Command key.

The commands in the Windows Edit menu work exactly as they do on the Macintosh—you can cut, copy, or paste highlighted material in your applications. At the Desktop, however, Windows offers a unique feature—you can use Cut, Copy, and Paste on Desktop icons themselves, thus moving or copying actual files to other windows. Although this method of moving and copying files may seem unfamiliar, give it a try. You may find it easier than dragging files around in Windows.

For information on the main commands in the Edit menu, Cut, Copy, Paste, and Undo, see their respective entries. Among the other Edit menu items are:

Clear. Windows has no equivalent to the Mac's Clear command, but Macintosh users never use it anyway (it's easier to press the Delete key).

Select All. The Windows Select All command (Ctrl-A) works almost identically to the Macintosh Select All command (Command-A), selecting everything (all icons, all text, all graphics, or whatever) in the current window. However, the Mac's Select All command can also select all the text of a file while you're editing it, which isn't possible in Windows.

Show Clipboard. Windows has no direct equivalent to the Mac's Show Clipboard command, which displays whatever textual or graphical information you've most recently cut or copied to the clipboard—an occasionally handy option. However, the Clipboard Viewer performs the same function. In Windows 98, it's accessible at Start → Programs → Accessories → System Tools → Clipboard Viewer. In Windows 95, you may have to install it from Control Panel → Add/Remove Programs → Windows Setup → Accessories → Clipboard Viewer, after which it appears in Start → Programs → Accessories → Clipboard Viewer.

Preferences. Most Macintosh programs, including the Finder, offer a Preferences command in the Edit menu. In Windows, the same command is usually called Options, and—especially in Microsoft programs—it's frequently found in a menu called Tools.

At the Desktop level, Windows lacks anything comparable to the Finder Preferences dialog box (Edit → Preferences). That makes sense, since most of the options in that dialog box—spring-loaded folders, control over grid spacing, and labels—don't exist in Windows.

Ejecting Disks
In Windows: Ejecting Disks

On the Macintosh, you eject a disk using a menu command (or by dragging a disk icon to the Trash). On a PC, however, most people push the manual eject button on the front panel of every floppy, Zip, CD, and other drive.

Don't eject the disk while the PC is accessing it—that is, when the small light on the front panel of the disk drive is illuminated.

It's best to close the window to the floppy disk before ejecting it, too; otherwise, the PC may access the drive, looking for the disk and possibly damaging it.

Since PCs don't eject floppy disks automatically when you shut down or restart, you're likely to find your PC trying to start up from the floppy disk the next time you turn it on. Obviously, unless the floppy disk has the necessary system files to boot, the PC won't get far—a confusing error message on a black screen is all you get. When this situation happens to you, eject the disk and press any key to force the PC to boot from the hard disk.

Although most PC users are in the habit of ejecting disks by pressing the manual eject button on the front panel of the computer, that's not the only way to do the job on some PCs and with some types of disk drives. You can also eject some disks by opening the My Computer icon under Desktop, right-clicking the corresponding disk-drive icon, and choosing Eject from the resulting contextual menu.

Email Attachments
In Windows: Email Attachments

One of the best ways to transfer files from a Macintosh to a PC running Windows is by attaching the files to an email message. Unfortunately, although this technique can work well, it's fraught with pitfalls. For more information on how to transfer files successfully, see the email section of **Transferring Files to Windows**.

Emulators
In Windows: Emulators

This book assumes that you have access to a physical PC or a physical Macintosh. However, several third-party programs let you run Windows—and Windows software—on the Macintosh; there are even programs that let you run Macintosh programs, in a limited way, on a PC.

Running Windows on the Macintosh. For the most part, the only successful emulators run PC software (DOS, Windows, and even

other operating systems) on the Macintosh. Note, however, that running Windows software through an emulation program is much slower than using the same software on a real PC.

Virtual PC (Connectix)

Virtual PC has an excellent reputation. One advantage of Virtual PC over Soft-Windows (described next) is that it emulates an entire PC, not just Windows. Thus, you can use Virtual PC to run PC-compatible operating systems other than Windows, such as Windows NT or even OS/2. You can learn more about Virtual PC at the web site *http:// www.connectix.com/html/connectix_ virtualpc.html.*

SoftWindows (Insignia Solutions)

SoftWindows (and its predecessor, SoftPC) have been around for many years. Its price and feature list are very similar to Virtual PC's; one pleasant feature is TurboStart, which memorizes the state of your emulated Windows environment when you quit the program (Virtual PC has a similar feature). The next time you resume SoftWindows, it starts up in a fraction of the time an actual PC would take to start up. You can find more information on SoftWindows and other Insignia products at *http://www.insignia.com/.*

Whether emulation software makes sense for you depends on your proposed uses. Emulation works well if you need to run Windows programs only occasionally; you're more likely to encounter flakiness if you use the system heavily.

If you want to run Windows software on a Macintosh, but don't want to put up with the slow speeds of emulation software, many Macintosh fans look into an Orange Micro OrangePC. This PCI card includes a Pentium processor and the other circuitry found in a real PC, and can therefore run software at about the same speeds. You save considerable desk space and (if you have a fancy monitor, keyboard, and ergonomic setup) equipment cost.

On the other hand, compare prices—it may actually be less expensive to buy a PC. Furthermore, you may occasionally experience glitches when trying to move data back and forth between the two operating systems.

You can find more information about Orange Micro's products at *http://www.orangemicro.com/*.

Running Macintosh software on a PC. Running Macintosh software on a PC is a much more difficult proposition, and attempts to write such programs have had decidedly mixed results. Such programs can't run many Macintosh programs because their creators can't legally copy necessary code from the Macintosh ROM chips. The most successful Macintosh emulator, called Executor, comes from a company called ARDI. You can find more information about Executor (and the compatibility list of software it can run) at *http://www.ardi.com/*.

Energy Saver Control Panel

In Windows: Power Management Control Panel

The Mac OS's Energy Saver control panel lets you set when your Mac's components to go to sleep after a period of inactivity. In Windows, the Power Management control panel provides similar functions, including the capability to put the PC into standby mode, turn off the monitor, and turn off hard disks (see Figure E-1).

Although the Power Management control panel lets you create groups of settings, called "schemes," display a power meter in the Tray, and require a password when coming out of standby, it lacks the Mac's controls for going to sleep and waking up at specified times.

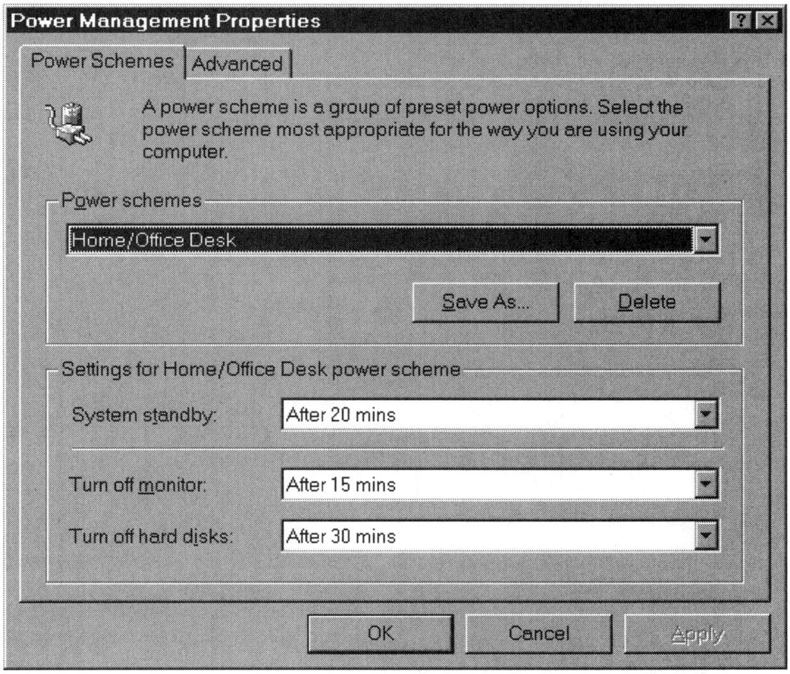

Figure E-1. Power Management control panel

Not all PCs support power management features—they must support APM (Advanced Power Management), which must be turned on in the BIOS (which is like the Mac's ROM). Consult your PC's manual for details on its support for APM.

Erase Disk
In Windows: Formatting Disks, Hard Disks

Erasing a Macintosh disk is as simple as selecting the disk and choosing Special → Erase Disk. In Windows, the process is nearly as simple:

1. Double-click the My Computer icon.

2. Right-click the floppy icon, and choose Format from the pop-up menu.

3. In the Format dialog box (see Figure E-2), choose the capacity of the disk, the format type, and other options.

4. If you want to name the floppy disk, enter a name into the Label field, since you can't rename a disk directly within Windows.

5. Click Start.

A Quick format merely erases the disk's directory, whereas a Full format also scans the entire disk surface for bad sectors. The "Copy system files only" option creates a disk that can boot your PC (instead of creating an empty floppy). For additional information, see **Hard Disks**.

Esc Key
In Windows: Esc Key

On the Macintosh, the Esc (generally known as Escape) key has little purpose beyond its ability to cancel a dialog box. In Windows, however, Esc has more functions, as you can see in Table E-1.

Ethernet
In Windows: Ethernet

Ethernet is a networking protocol that's supported equally well by the Macintosh and Windows, so it's an excellent method of connecting a Macintosh and a PC to transfer files or share other network resources. For more information on configuring a PC running Windows to connect to an Ethernet

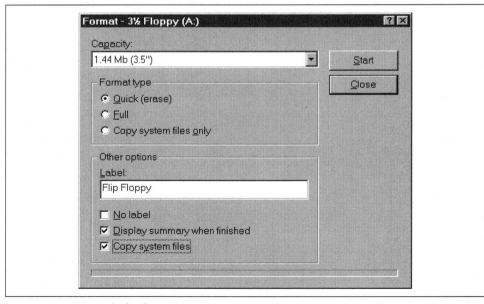

Figure E-2. Format dialog box

Table E-1. Windows Shortcuts Using the Escape Key

Keyboard Shortcut	Function
Esc	Closes a dialog box or menu without performing any operations, exactly as on the Macintosh. Esc also cancels a Cut/Copy operation in progress, as Command-period does on the Macintosh.
Alt-Esc	Sends the current window behind all the other open windows.
Ctrl-Esc	Displays the Start menu.

network, see **Networking**; for more about moving files back and forth, see **Transferring Files to Windows**.

Eudora
In Windows: Eudora

Qualcomm's Eudora is one of the oldest and most popular Internet email programs on the Macintosh, having first appeared in 1988. It's also popular in Windows, and the two versions are extremely similar, often down to the keyboard shortcuts. If you're used to Eudora Light or Eudora Pro on the Macintosh, you should try it in Windows, since it's easy to switch.

The other advantage of using Eudora in both Windows and the Macintosh is that you'll experience the fewest problems when sending attachments back and forth.

For more information, or to download a free copy of Eudora Light, visit *http://www.eudora.com/*. Also check out *Eudora 4.2 for Windows & Macintosh: Visual QuickStart Guide*, described at *http://www.tidbits.com/eudora/*.

Extensions
In Windows: Drivers

On the Macintosh, extensions are the files in the System Folder → Extensions folder. Some extensions are drivers, and make it possible for the Macintosh to use unusual pieces of hardware. Other extensions patch the Mac OS and modify its standard behavior, making possible such features as Internet connections, faxing, and screen savers.

Windows has drivers, too, but it doesn't have extensions. However, programmers can't patch Windows as they can the Mac OS. Instead, Windows relies on background applications, often with little or no interface, to fulfill the same purpose as Macintosh extensions. (You may see the icons of such self-launching background apps in your Taskbar system tray.) These applications "listen" to system events and perform various actions based on what they hear. The advantage of this technique is that it doesn't allow as much leeway in modifying the operating system in potentially dangerous ways.

Extensions Folder
In Windows: StartUp Folder

Since Windows uses applications for the kinds of things that are handled by Macintosh extensions, Windows has no equivalent to the Mac's Extensions folder. The closest equivalent is the StartUp folder, which you can view by right-clicking the Start button and choosing Open. Then open Start Menu → Programs → StartUp.

There are other ways to control Windows startup applications, too, as described in the following entry.

Extensions Manager Control Panel
In Windows: Manual manipulation of files, Third-Party Utilities

Because Windows uses applications rather than Macintosh-style extensions, Microsoft never saw the need to provide a utility for turning startup applications on and off. As a result, if you want to create different sets of applications to launch at startup, you must create a "StartUp (Disabled)" folder and

D–G

move items between it and the real StartUp folder. Here's how to do this:

1. Right-click the Start button, and choose Open.

2. Open Start Menu → Programs → StartUp.

3. Choose New → Folder and name it StartUp (Disabled).

4. Drag the StartUp (Disabled) folder to a different location, such as the Desktop.

5. Make a shortcut to the StartUp folder in the same location by right-dragging it to the new location, and then choosing Create Shortcut.

6. Drag shortcuts from the StartUp folder into the StartUp (Disabled) folder to disable them.

7. Drag shortcuts back from the StartUp (Disabled) folder into the StartUp folder to enable them again.

If you're a Macintosh user, this process should sound familiar—moving files between the Extensions and Extensions (Disabled) folders is exactly how Extensions Manager (and rival Conflict Catcher) works. Luckily, numerous third-party freeware and shareware utilities can manage the startup process; search for "startup" in an online software library like ZDNet's Software Library at *http://www.zdnet.com/swlib/* for a selection. Be careful when using these utilities, since any program that can modify the Registry can cause problems if something goes wrong.

Extensions Off
In Windows: Safe Mode

In times of troubleshooting, you wouldn't get far without some means of starting a computer from Ground Zero, its native, virginal, factory-fresh state, free from any software you've added to its operating system. On the Macintosh, of course, you start up your Macintosh with the Shift key pressed to boot with all extensions turned off. (Doing so in Windows just prevents applications in the StartUp Folder from launching.)

In Windows, restoring the OS to its bare minimum components is called booting in Safe Mode. To do so, choose Start → Shut Down → Restart. In Windows 95, press the F5 key when you see the words "Starting Windows 95." In Windows 98, press Shift as the computer starts up again. It's normal for Windows to take much longer to start up in Safe Mode. Eventually, you'll be prompted to acknowledge that Windows is running in Safe Mode; click OK.

When the startup process is finished, you'll see the words SAFE MODE in each corner of the screen. Your Desktop may look very different, lacking its customary background and monitor settings. Software that loads automatically (screen savers, virus protection utilities, and so on) is now turned off. So are all of your device drivers except the keyboard, mouse, and basic monitor software; your CD-ROM, network, and Internet "extensions" are turned off, exactly as they would be on the Macintosh.

The troubleshooting work is halfway done: you can now begin the business of adjusting your control panel settings, or installing updated driver software, in hopes of solving whatever problem you were having (see **Troubleshooting**).

To exit Safe Mode, choose Start → Shut Down → Restart and let the computer start up again normally.

F

Favorites Menu
In Windows: Favorites Menu

In Mac OS 8.5, Apple introduced the Favorites command in the Apple menu—in conjunction with the File → Add to Favorites command, the Favorites submenu offers a convenient means of tagging frequently used files, folders, and disks for easy access.

Windows 98 provides a Favorites menu (in the Start menu), too. This command stores bookmarks to both frequently visited web pages and designated folders.

Note

It's easy to get confused by the Windows 98 Favorites menu—there's no logical reason it should hold both web page bookmarks and folder shortcuts. Consider making extremely clear distinctions between your web page favorites and your folder favorites, perhaps by organizing them in different folders or starting their names with different characters so they're sorted together.

To add a web page or a folder to your Favorites menu, choose Favorites → Add to Favorites from Internet Explorer, an Explorer window, or any window on the Desktop. Once you've added a number of favorites, you may wish to arrange them in folders. Choose Favorites → Organize Favorites to open the Organize Favorites dialog box (see Figure F-1).

In the Organize Favorites dialog box, you can create folders, move items into and out of folders, rename them, or delete them. Buttons facilitate these tasks, but you can also move items by dragging them into folders, rename them by selecting them and

then clicking in the name, and delete them by dragging them to the Recycle Bin. As usual, right-clicking an item displays a contextual menu that offers all these options and more.

Faxing
In Windows: Faxing

If you have used Macintosh fax modems, and the accompanying software, with mixed success, it may come as some relief that faxing software is built-in to Windows 95, though not Windows 98. Exactly as on the Macintosh, you can send faxes directly from the programs you create them in, such as Microsoft Word. (To do so, choose File → Send To → Fax Recipient.)

For complete instructions on receiving faxes, double-click the InBox on your Windows Desktop. (If you don't see it, insert your Windows CD and reinstall Microsoft Exchange.) Once Microsoft Exchange launches, choose Help → Microsoft Fax.

In Windows 98, you must install Windows Message and the Microsoft Fax program from your Windows 98 CD-ROM. Open *Windows 98/tools/oldwin95/message/us* to find the installers for Windows Message and Microsoft Fax, along with an informational document about these now obsolete programs.

File Assistant
In Windows: Briefcase

For some time, the Mac OS included a utility called File Assistant (or PowerBook File Assistant). File Assistant was a file-synchronization utility, and it was replaced in Mac OS 8.1 with the **File Synchronization Control Panel**.

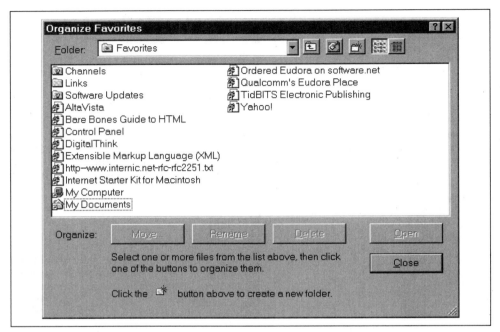

Figure F-1. Organize Favorites dialog box

File Exchange Control Panel
In Windows: File Types

Like its predecessor, the PC Exchange control panel, the modern Mac's File Exchange control panel lets the Macintosh read PC-formatted floppy disks. It also offers file translation features that let you open files in applications other than those that created them.

By default, a Windows PC cannot read Macintosh-formatted disks, although several third-party utilities provide this feature. See **Transferring Files to Windows** for details.

The file translation and extension mapping capabilities of the File Exchange control panel mimic the way Windows relies on filename extensions to connect documents to the applications that can open them. Windows handles mapping filename extensions automatically, but you can modify those settings in Views → Folder Options → File Types. For more information, see **File Types**.

File Menu
In Windows: File Menu

The File menu in the Mac's menu bar is similar to the File menu in every Windows folder window. Windows, however, displays different commands in the File menu depending on what is selected. For instance, if no document is selected, Windows doesn't show the Print command.

New Folder. The Windows File menu has a direct equivalent to the Mac's File → New Folder command, though it's hidden in File → New → Folder. The File → New menu lets you create things other than folders, including shortcuts and documents of various types. Some application installers, furthermore, add new document types to this menu. Finally, if a document icon is selected, the File → New command creates a duplicate of the selected document.

Open. The Macintosh and Windows Open commands are essentially identical, although Windows also offers a File → Quick View command that can be useful for looking at a file's contents without having to launch the parent application.

Move To Trash. The Mac's Move To Trash command corresponds to the Windows File → Delete command, which puts the selected icons in the Recycle Bin.

Close Window. Close Window on the Macintosh is exactly the same as File → Close in Windows, closing the current window when chosen. Although it's not shown in the menu itself, Ctrl-W also closes the window.

Get Info. To find the kind of information (file size, modification date, etc.) that you're used to seeing in the Get Info window, select an icon in Windows and then choose File → Properties (Alt-Enter). (Alternatively, right-click any icon and choose Properties from the pop-up menu.) For more information, see **Get Info Command**.

Label. Windows has no equivalent to the Mac OS's labels, so there's no equivalent to the Label command.

Duplicate. Although Windows has no Duplicate command, you can duplicate files in several different ways:

- Press Ctrl and drag a file within the same window.

- Select a file, choose Copy (Ctrl-C), then choose Paste (Ctrl-V).

- Highlight an icon, and then choose File → New to create a duplicate of the file in the appropriate application.

Make Alias. The Mac's Make Alias command corresponds to the File → Create Shortcut command in Windows. For more information, see **Alias**.

Add To Favorites. Windows doesn't have an equivalent to the Add To Favorites command in Mac OS 8.5 and later. Instead, you add favorites to the Windows Favorites menu from Favorites → Add to Favorites. See **Favorites Menu**.

Put Away. Windows has no equivalent to the Mac's Put Away command, which restores items moved to the Desktop or Trash to their original location.

Find. The Windows Find command is in Start → Find, rather than in the File menu. For more information, see **Find**.

Show Original. To find the original icon from which an alias (shortcut) was made in Windows, select the shortcut icon, and then click File → Properties → Shortcut → Find Target. Windows opens the folder containing the target file, though it doesn't select the file, as does the Macintosh.

Page Setup. Although some Windows applications (including Microsoft Word) have Page Setup commands in their File menus, there's no equivalent in Windows Desktop windows.

Print Desktop. Windows has no equivalent to the Mac's Print Desktop command. If you really want to print a picture of the Windows Desktop, use the Print Screen command (see **Screen Capture**).

File Sharing
In Windows: File Sharing

One of the great strengths of the Macintosh is its built-in personal file-sharing feature, which first appeared in System 7 in 1991. To Windows 95 and Windows 98, though, Microsoft added file and print sharing as well. File sharing lets you access files on remote computers over the network, much as though the shared folders were disks attached to your computer. For information about setting up networking in general, see **Networking**.

Configuring file and print sharing. To turn on file and print sharing in Windows, follow these steps:

1. Open Control Panel → Network → Identification. Fill in a name, workgroup, and description for your computer.

2. In Control Panel → Network → Configuration's list of network components, make sure the same protocol is used on both the machine sharing the files and the machine you want to be able to access the files. TCP/IP or NetBEUI work fine.

3. In Control Panel → Network → Configuration's list of network components, make sure you see the "File and printer sharing for Microsoft Networks" service-component. If that component isn't in your list, add it by clicking Add → Service → Microsoft → "File and printer sharing for Microsoft Networks." Service icons look like little computers.

4. Also in the Network control panel, click the "File and Print Sharing" button, and check "I want to be able to give others access to my files" (see Figure F-2). For

information about sharing printers, see **Printer Sharing**.

5. Right-click the folder or disk you want to share, and choose Sharing from the contextual menu.

6. In the Sharing dialog box, enter a name for the shared item, a comment that others can see if they use View → Details in Network Neighborhood, the appropriate access, and passwords (see Figure F-3).

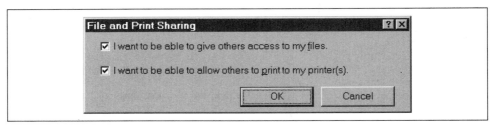

Figure F-2. File and Print Sharing dialog box

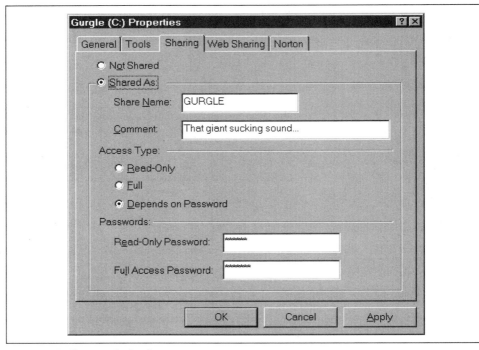

Figure F-3. Sharing dialog box

7. When you close the Sharing dialog box, Windows asks you to confirm your passwords.

> **Note**
>
> Consider strictly limiting access to your hard disk if security is an issue—that is, if a large number of other people are connected to the same network or if you have a permanent Internet connection via a cable modem or DSL connection. See **Users & Groups Control Panel** for details.

Accessing files via file sharing. To connect to and access files on a machine running file sharing, follow these steps. For more information, see **Network Browser**.

1. Repeat steps 2 and 3 of "Configuring file and print sharing."

2. Double-click the Network Neighborhood icon on your Desktop. Consider switching to Details view by choosing View → Details; you'll see more information about the shared computers.

3. Double-click the icon for the computer whose files you want to access. Double-click the shared folder you want to access and enter the appropriate password. You can choose to have Windows remember the password, though doing so could be a security risk.

4. Once your password is accepted, Windows opens a window showing all the files in the shared folder. Depending on the access privileges you've been given, you may only have read access; otherwise, you have full access to read, write, and delete files.

Simplifying access. There are two ways you can simplify access to shared folders once you've connected for the first time.

- Make a shortcut to the folder. Place it on your Desktop or in some other easily accessed location.

- Right-click the shared folder and choose Map Network Drive. Then pick an unused drive letter and indicate whether or not you want to reconnect to the drive on logon (see Figure F-4). Once you've done this, the shared folder shows up in your My Computer window as a drive.

Monitoring shared folders. To monitor just who has connected to your shared folders, use the Net Watcher utility (Start → Programs → Accessories → System Tools → Net Watcher). In Net Watcher, you can disconnect users and also see precisely what resources are shared on your system.

File Sharing Monitor Control Panel
In Windows: Net Watcher

In Windows, you can see who is using your shared resources—and disconnect them if desired—using the Net Watcher utility. To open it, choose Start → Programs → Accessories → System Tools → Net Watcher. For more information, see **File Sharing**.

File Synchronization Control Panel
In Windows: Briefcase

Working with multiple computers—such as a laptop and your desktop PC—raises the thorny issue of tracking different versions of the same file on different computers. The obvious solution is to copy files to the laptop before a trip, and back to the desktop

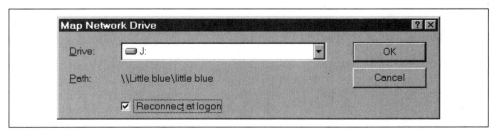

Figure F-4. Map Network Drive dialog box

on your return. Unfortunately, if you're not careful, you could end up with modifications in both copies of a file.

You can automate the file-copying process on the Macintosh by using the File Synchronization control panel (or the File Assistant utility, in an older version of the Mac OS). Microsoft solved the same problem by coopting a metaphor from the office world—the briefcase. You might use a real-world briefcase to carry papers home from work, and the next day bring them back in the briefcase. The electronic Briefcase in Windows serves much the same purpose, although it has quite a few more features than your standard alligator-covered box.

Windows may have created a default Briefcase for you, called My Briefcase and located on the Desktop. If not, you can install a new one by first installing the Briefcase components from Control Panel → Add/Remove Programs → Windows Setup → Accessories. Then right-click the Desktop, or an empty space in a window, and choose New → Briefcase from the New submenu. (Alternatively, choose File → New → Briefcase in a window.)

Windows copies any files you drag into a Briefcase (which looks like a normal folder window when open), along with a "sync link," which links the Briefcase's copy of a file to the original on the hard disk. The Briefcase tracks the original, and notes when you need to update the Briefcase to account for changes. To update the Briefcase, right-click the Briefcase and choose Update All, or with the Briefcase window open, choose Briefcase → Update All.

Once you have files in a Briefcase, you're ready to take it home. In the simplest situation, you move it to a removable disk, such as a Zip or floppy disk; the Briefcase disappears from your hard disk. Note that you must move and not copy the Briefcase! Creating copies can cause untold confusion. You can also move the Briefcase to another computer over a network.

Moving the Briefcase over a network avoids one limitation of using a floppy—although Windows asks for multiple floppies if the Briefcase is too large for one disk, all the files copied to floppies other than the first

disk lose their sync links. So, if you're using a floppy disk, keep your Briefcases small and use multiple Briefcases if necessary.

After you've moved the Briefcase to another location, you can work on the files in it. It's safest to work on the files without removing them from the Briefcase; if you're using a floppy or Zip disk, leave the Briefcase on it. (The rationale: if you copy the files out of the Briefcase to your home hard disk, the files gain another sync link. Now you have three copies of the files on your various machines and disks, which is just asking for trouble.)

When you're working on files in the Briefcase on a removable disk, or on another computer, they behave as though they're in a normal folder. However, when you return to your main machine, either with the laptop or with the floppy/Zip disk, be sure to move the Briefcase back to the original hard disk. Right-drag the Briefcase icon to the desired location and, from the pop-up menu that appears, choose Move Here. Next, open the Briefcase window by double-clicking it, and make sure it's in Details view. Check to see if any of the files have "Needs updating" in the Status column, and if so, choose Briefcase → Update All (see Figure F-5).

Try the Briefcase with a few unimportant files in a relaxed situation before you entrust it to an important report you have to present to upper management. Make sure you're comfortable with the way the Briefcase works before you rely on it, since making a mistake (like forgetting to update it before leaving work) could cause problems.

File Translation
In Windows: File Translation

The most frustrating aspect of working with Macs and Windows-based PCs is file translation. It's hard enough to move files back and forth physically (see **Transferring Files to Windows**), but trying to find the appropriate translator for them can be truly annoying. You have three options when trying to share Macintosh files with programs on Windows: use cross-platform applica-

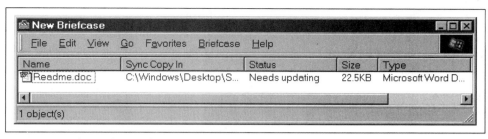

Figure F-5. Files in the Briefcase that need updating

tions, rely on universal file formats, or use file-translation software.

Cross-platform applications. The easiest way to share files between Windows and Macintosh programs is to use programs that have almost identical versions on both platforms. Most Microsoft, Adobe, and Macromedia applications fall into this category, as do many other popular programs. See **Cross-Platform Applications** for a list.

Note that you must generally use parallel versions of cross-platform applications for file formats to be similar. For instance, you might have trouble opening a Windows Word 97 document in Word 4 on the Macintosh.

Also, even when cross-platform applications don't share the same file format, they generally come with translators that let you read and write the appropriate formats. Sometimes, as with older versions of Microsoft Word, you may have to visit the company's web site to find the appropriate translators.

Universal file formats. Some file formats are sufficiently universal that most applications in the same category (graphics, word processing, etc.) can read them. For instance, any word processor can read a text file, and almost any word processor can read RTF (Rich Text Format) files. Similarly, any graphics program should be able to open a GIF or a JPEG file. For more details, see **GIF**, **JPEG**, and similar entries.

You can use these universal file formats to move data between programs that otherwise cannot read each other's files. But keep in mind that universal file formats don't offer as many features as proprietary

file formats. In other words, if you save a file from Word 97 as RTF, and then try to open the resulting document in WriteNow on the Macintosh, you may lose some formatting in the process.

Note

When moving a file to Windows, remember to add the necessary three-letter suffix to its name, a requirement on Windows. Otherwise, the Windows-using recipient won't be able to double-click your file to open it. See **File Types** for a list of typical Windows extensions.

File translators. If you need to convert files from one format to another, you need a file translation utility.

The best utilities for translating between PC and Macintosh file formats come from DataViz. This company's MacLinkPlus can convert most Windows word processing and spreadsheet files to Macintosh equivalents, and Conversions Plus converts most Macintosh files in their Windows equivalents. (MacLinkPlus was included with the Mac OS until Mac OS 8.5.)

Both programs offer a large list of translators, plus tips on dealing with common formats for which DataViz doesn't have translators. No file translation product can be perfect, but DataViz's products are among the best. For more information, visit *http://www.dataviz.com/.*

A number of older Macintosh programs supported an Apple technology called XTND, which could translate many popular file formats. XTND is moribund today, but you

D–G

may still run into it on occasion, and it's worth trying if you don't have MacLinkPlus.

File Types

In Windows: File Types

When it comes to figuring out which application to launch when you double-click a document, the Macintosh and Windows work quite differently. Windows has no equivalent to the Mac's invisible file type and creator codes, and instead relies on three-letter filename suffixes (such as *.doc* and *.txt*). You set up these suffixes in the File Types dialog box, accessible from View → Folder Options → File Types (see Figure F-6).

The entries in the File Types dialog box map an extension, such as *.doc*, to an application, such as Microsoft Word. Every time you double-click a file whose name ends with *.doc*, Windows knows to open Word. That sounds similar to the way the Mac's behind-the-scenes, four-letter type and creator codes work, but in fact it's significantly more limiting. On the Macintosh, you can name a file anything you want—it still opens in the correct application, thanks to its creator code. The creator code also means that you can have one text file that opens in SimpleText and another one that opens in Microsoft Word.

You can modify the file extension mappings in the File Type dialog box, but for the most part there's no reason to do so. That's because when you install a program, its installer registers any new file extensions with Windows. The problem with this method, and the reason you might occasionally want to reset a file type, is that Windows programs occasionally try to take over common extensions. For instance, since both Microsoft Internet Explorer and Netscape Communicator are web browsers, they'll both try to take over the *.htm* and *.html* filename extensions. Depending on which one you installed most recently, you may need to go into the File Types dialog box and reset the *.htm* and *.html* extensions properly.

Filenames

In Windows: Filenames

For years, the names of your files on a Windows PC were limited to the so-called "eight-dot-three" format: eight characters, a period, and then a three-letter suffix.

If you believe the brochures, Windows 95 radically increased the maximum length of filenames to 260 characters. Unfortunately, behind the scenes, the eight-dot-three system lurks as a parallel filename universe. Every Windows 95/98/2000 document still requires a three-letter suffix, even though it's often hidden; moreover, you'll encounter thousands of files that retain the eight-dot-three convention in order to remain compatible with Windows 3.1 or even DOS.

Filename extensions. Windows filenames must end in three- (or four-) letter extensions, separated from the name with a period. Without the filename extension, Windows has no way of identifying the file's type and wouldn't be able to open it in the right application. Most of the time, Windows appends the proper extension for you. (That's not true, however, if you're sent a file from a Macintosh by email, network, or disk—even if it's a file from a cross-platform program, such as Microsoft Word, you must still add the suffix before you attempt to double-click it.)

Reserved characters. Although you can use most characters in Windows filenames, several are off-limits (compared to one on the Macintosh—the colon). Characters you cannot use, mostly because they still have specific uses in DOS, include the following:

$ % < > | * . \ / " ~ : ? = ;

Case sensitivity. Both Windows and the Mac OS are case insensitive—you cannot create files called FILENAME and FileName in the same window. That said, both preserve case in filenames, so you can use mixed case whenever you want without fear of losing the capitalization.

Changing a file's name. To rename a Windows icon, click once to select it, and then click the filename. (Another way: right-click its icon; from the pop-up menu, choose

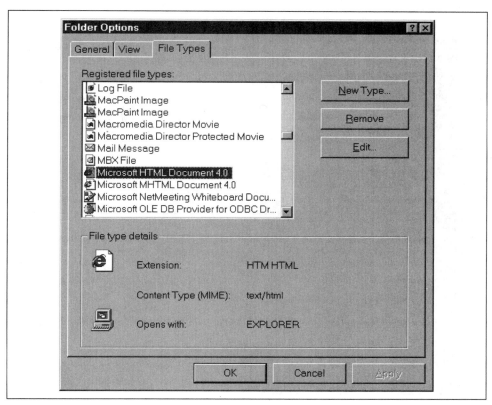

Figure F-6. File Types dialog box

Rename, or type M.) Either way, a special editing rectangle appears; type the new name or edit the existing name. Press Enter (or click elsewhere) to confirm the new name.

Editing filenames. You can edit filenames using all the basic tools you'd expect in a text-editing environment, including arrow keys; the Backspace and Delete keys; and Cut, Copy, and Paste.

Find

In Windows: Find

In Windows, you find files and folders on your hard disk exactly the way you do on the Macintosh—using a Find program.

Searching by filename. The Windows Find Files or Folders utility offers most of the same features as the Macintosh Sherlock or Find File utility. You can search specific disks or folders for files or folders by name, contents, modification date, creation date, last access date, file type, and size. Here's how you search for filenames containing the word "player," for example. Figure F-7 shows how the Find dialog box should look.

1. Choose Start → Find → Files or Folders to open the Find dialog box.

2. Enter "player" in the Named field.

3. From the Look In menu, choose My Computer to search all mounted disks and make sure "Include subfolders" is checked.

4. Click Find Now.

Find Files or Folders then shows the results of the search in the lower half of the win-

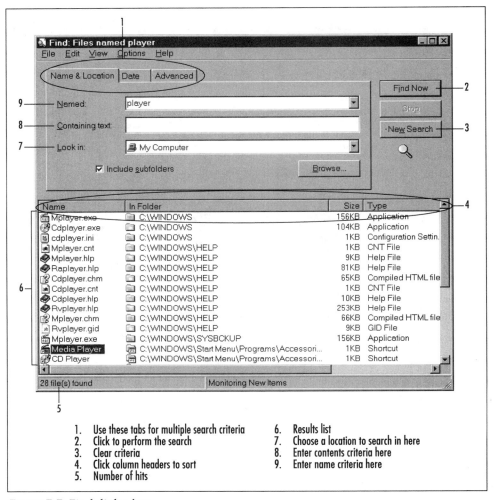

1. Use these tabs for multiple search criteria
2. Click to perform the search
3. Clear criteria
4. Click column headers to sort
5. Number of hits

6. Results list
7. Choose a location to search in here
8. Enter contents criteria here
9. Enter name criteria here

Figure F-7. Find dialog box

dow. The Results window works much like other Windows Desktop windows, so you can sort it by name, folder, size, type, or modification date by clicking the appropriate column headers. Double-clicking an icon opens it, and you can right-click icons to perform any standard actions on them.

Identifying a file location. At first, you may be puzzled that Windows doesn't show you where your found files are, as the Macintosh does. Actually, it does, but in a less intuitive format. Instead of showing you a graphic folder hierarchy, as the Macintosh

does, Windows shows you—to the right of each found file's name—a string of text like this:

```
C:\\Windows\Start Menu\Programs\
Accessories\Multimedia
```

(The default column arrangement generally isn't wide enough to show you this complete pathname. If that's the case, drag the tiny vertical column header divider between the In Folder and Size columns to the right, widening the In Folder column.)

This notation indicates the location of the file you found. C: means that the file is on the main hard disk, on which there's a folder called Windows, inside of which is a folder called Start Menu, and so on.

It may occur to you that this arrangement makes it impossible to jump to the window containing the file you've found, as you can on the Macintosh by double-clicking one of the tiny folders in the location hierarchy display. You'd be right—after using the Windows Find command, you can only open or drag one of the results, not view it in its home folder.

Searching by date or file type. To create more sophisticated searches, you can enter date ranges or search for specific file types. To search by date, click the Date Modified tab in the Find window; to search by file type, click the Advanced tab.

Be careful using these tabs, however. If you switch back to the Name & Location tab during the same Find session, the criteria you establish on these alternate tabs remain in place. You may discover that the Find Files & Folders program can't find files that you're certain exist—unaware that your searches are being restricted by hidden information on these other tabs.

Find by Content. As in Mac OS 8.5 and later, Windows can actually search for text within your files—words you've typed into word processing files, for example. But whereas Sherlock's Find by Content feature is sophisticated, with relevance ranking and full indexed searching, Windows content-searching is slow and not very intelligent. Still, to search for words inside files, choose Start → Find → Files or Folder and click the Advanced tab. Now type your search phrase into the "Containing text" field and click Find Now.

Search Internet. You can search multiple web sites straight from Sherlock on the Macintosh, but in Windows, choosing Start → Find → On the Internet merely opens a web browser window to your specified search site. Windows can also search the Internet for information about people, accessible from Start → Find → People. The People search connects to a specified directory web

site and looks for contact information about the person you've entered. Bear in mind that these sites often have incorrect or out-dated information—check out what a search for Bill Clinton turns up in Figure F-8.

Find network servers. Windows can also locate individual servers on a large network—a feature lacking on the Macintosh. Choose Start → Find → Computer and enter the name of the computer to find servers that match your search term. The feature is primarily useful if your PC is connected to a very large network—otherwise, it's easier to open the Network Neighborhood and find the server by reading the server names.

Finder
In Windows: Explorer

Technically, the Finder is the program that creates and maintains the Macintosh Desktop and the other visible aspects of the Macintosh interface. The equivalent program in Windows is the Explorer, which provides all the behind-the-scenes work in displaying the Windows interface.

But the Explorer—not to be confused with Internet Explorer, the web browser—has another mode used more frequently by Windows users then by Macintosh users. If you right-click a folder or disk and choose Explore from the contextual menu, a two-paned hierarchical window opens. Folders appear in the left pane, whereas files and folders show up in the right pane (see Figure F-9).

Functionally, the Explorer works like a Finder list view: clicking the + signs lets you see folders within folders, exactly as you might click the disclosure triangles next to folder names on the Macintosh. Macintosh users will probably find the Explorer interface more foreign than the standard Windows interface, but it can occasionally be useful, since arranging windows on the Windows Desktop can be clumsy.

Everything you can do in a normal Desktop window works in two-paned Explorer windows as well—you can change views, open files, rename files and folders, and so on.

D–G

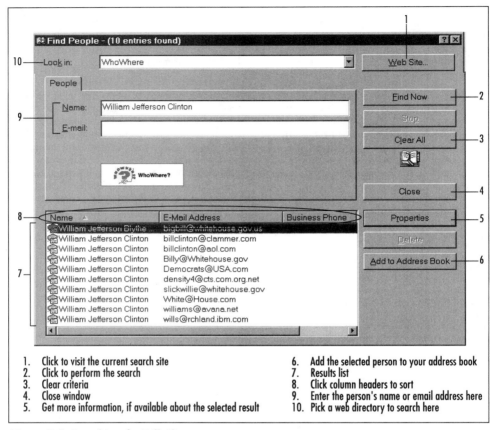

Figure F-8. Searching for Bill Clinton

1. Click to visit the current search site
2. Click to perform the search
3. Clear criteria
4. Close window
5. Get more information, if available about the selected result
6. Add the selected person to your address book
7. Results list
8. Click column headers to sort
9. Enter the person's name or email address here
10. Pick a web directory to search here

Figure F-8. Searching for Bill Clinton

A few things are different. To display the files in a folder in the right pane, click the folder in the left pane. To see the folders nested within a folder in the left pane, either double-click the folder or click the + sign next to the folder name (which then turns to a minus sign). You can move and copy files using the same methods that work in normal Desktop windows.

Fkeys
In Windows: Function Keys

See Function Keys (Fkeys).

Floppy Disks
In Windows: Floppy Disks

Although floppy disks are becoming less important in both Windows and the Macintosh, they remain popular for transferring small files. Unfortunately, Windows and the Macintosh format floppy disks differently, so they cannot read each other's disks without special software. On the Macintosh side, that software is File Exchange, a control panel that comes with the Mac OS. In Windows, various utility programs let you read Macintosh floppy disks; see **Transferring Files to Windows** for details.

Inserting floppy disks. When you insert a floppy disk on Windows, no icon appears on the Desktop. Instead, you must double-

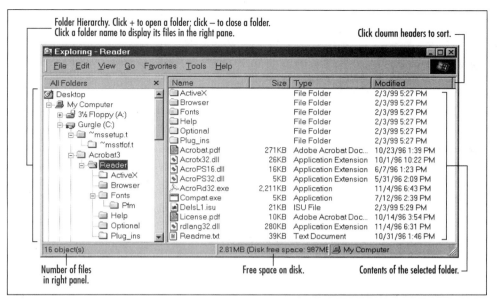

Figure F-9. *Two-paned Explorer window*

click the My Computer icon on the Desktop to view the floppy-drive icon (called 3½ Floppy (A)). Double-click it to open the floppy disk window, if one is inserted. (If you double-click the floppy icon window before the disk is inserted, you'll just get a cryptic error message.)

Formatting disks. When you insert a blank disk into a Windows machine, no message appears automatically asking you to format the disk, as on the Macintosh. Instead, Windows won't offer to format the disk until you actually try to open the floppy disk window. Of course, you can also format disks in Windows manually—see **Erase Disk** for details.

Booting from a floppy disk. Windows can create an emergency startup floppy disk for you—use it to start up the machine when troubleshooting; you won't be offered the full Windows interface, but at least you'll have basic DOS access your files. It's a good idea to have such a disk on hand for emergencies; see **Boot Disk** for instructions.

Ejecting a floppy disk. You'll quickly discover that you can't eject a floppy disk from

a Windows PC by dragging its icon to the trash, as you can on the Macintosh. Instead, most Windows users eject a disk by pushing the physical button on the front panel of the floppy drive, taking care never to do so when the floppy-drive light is illuminated.

Alternatively, on some PCs you may be able to right-click the 3½ Floppy (A) icon (in the My Computer window) and choose Eject from the contextual pop-up menu.

Folders
In Windows: Folders

At their heart, folders are almost exactly the same in Windows and on the Macintosh—they're containers for holding files and other folders. You can move and copy folders just as you would files, but the two operating systems work slightly differently.

Some folders have special functions in Windows, as shown in Table F-1. Avoid manipulating these folders or their contents unless you know what you're doing.

Fonts

In Windows: Fonts

One of the most attractive aspects of working with graphical interfaces like Windows and the Mac OS is that they let you create documents using different fonts. Before

graphical interfaces, fonts were specific to programs, rather than being accessible to any program.

Types of fonts. Exactly as on Windows, fonts on the Macintosh come in two varieties: TrueType and PostScript. Functionally,

Table F-1. Special Folders in Windows

Folder	Contents	Location
Briefcase	Documents for synchronizing with other machines. See **File Synchronization Control Panel**.	*Desktop*
Command	DOS programs.	*C:\Windows*
Control Panel	Control panels. Not really a folder, Control Panel is populated with .cpl files located in *C:\Windows\System*. See **Control Panels**.	*My Computer*
Desktop	Items that appear on the Desktop.	*C:\Windows*
Dial-Up Networking	Software for connecting to the Internet.	*My Computer*
Favorites	Shortcuts to items on your computer or on the Internet for populating the Favorites menu.	*C:\Windows*
Fonts	Contains fonts.	*Control Panel*
My Computer	Contains your disks, plus special folders for Printers, Control Panel, Dial-Up Networking, and Scheduled Tasks. See **Desktop**.	*Desktop*
My Documents	Default location for saving documents.	*Desktop*
Network Neighborhood	Access to remote servers on the network. See **Network Browser**.	*Desktop*
Online Services	Signup files for various online services.	*Desktop*
Printers	Printer icons. See **Printing Files**.	*My Computer, Control Panel*
Programs	Shortcuts to all your programs.	*C:\Windows\ Start Menu*
Recycle Bin	Items that have been dragged to the Recycle Bin. See **Trash**.	*Desktop*
Scheduled Tasks	Tasks to execute on a regular basis. See **Macros**.	*My Computer*
Start Menu	Items that appear in the Start menu. See **Apple Menu**.	*C:\Windows*
StartUp	Items that launch automatically at startup. See **Startup Items Folder**.	*C:\Windows\ Start Menu\ Programs*
System	Various system files.	*C:\Windows*
Windows	Equivalent to the Mac's System Folder.	*C:*

the two font technologies are similar, although they use different underlying mathematical algorithms. TrueType fonts are predominant on both Macintosh and Windows because they offer many advantages: for example, they appear smooth and attrac-

tive at any size, both on screen and when printed; furthermore, on the Macintosh, each TrueType font requires only a single font file in your System Folder, making font management simpler.

PostScript fonts, on the other hand, are more frequently used in professional publishing and graphics, despite numerous drawbacks—each font requires several components to manage in your System Folder (separate files for the screen display and print out, for example), and these fonts can look jagged on the screen unless you've also installed Adobe Type Manager (ATM). Nonetheless, a wider variety of high-quality fonts are available in PostScript format, and most professional publishing equipment works better with PostScript than with True-Type fonts.

Technically, there's a third kind of font format—bitmapped fonts. This very old font format prints jaggedly on any printer and look jagged on the screen at some sizes. TrueType and PostScript fonts are far superior because they eliminate these limitations.

Font suitcases. Windows has no direct equivalent of the Mac's font suitcases, which can combine screen fonts and TrueType fonts in a single suitcase. In Windows, if you look in the Fonts folder, you see a separate font file for each font variant—Arial, Arial Black, Arial Bold, Arial Bold Italic, and so on. To hide the different variants, choose View → Hide Variations. (Hide Variations just hides the different files—it doesn't combine them into font suitcases.) A single screen-font file in Windows can contain all the different point sizes, so you don't see a separate file for each size.

Installing and removing fonts. To install fonts in Windows, you can copy fonts into the Fonts folder, place shortcuts to the fonts in the Fonts folder, or follow these steps:

1. Open Control Panel → Fonts.

2. Choose File → Install New Font to display the Add Fonts dialog box.

3. Select a drive from the Drives menu, and then select a folder from the Folders list. Windows searches the selected folder and displays available fonts.

4. Select the fonts you want to install, and then click OK. If you want to copy the font files to the Fonts folder, select the "Copy fonts to Fonts folder" checkbox. If that checkbox is unselected, Win-

dows instead places shortcuts to the selected fonts in the Fonts folder.

To remove fonts from the Fonts folder, drag them out of the Fonts folder, or right-click them and choose Delete.

Viewing fonts. To see what a font looks like, double-click it. The sample font display in Windows provides a lot more information than you're used to with the Macintosh (see Figure F-11).

Windows offers another feature in the Fonts folder that doesn't exist on the Macintosh. If you choose View → List Fonts By Similarity, a menu appears at the top of the Fonts folder. When you choose a font from that menu, Windows organizes the fonts by their similarity to the one you've chosen. This feature can be useful if you're not familiar with all the specific fonts.

Choosing fonts. You use fonts in Windows exactly as you do on the Macintosh—simply choose a font from your application's Fonts menu. You can also specify which fonts you'd like used in the Windows interface itself—just open Control Panel → Display → Appearance; for details, see **Appearance Control Panel**.

Why the difference between Windows and the Macintosh? If you've ever viewed the same web page or Word document on both Windows and the Macintosh, you may have wondered why the two platforms seem to render the same fonts at different sizes. For instance, a web page that looks good in Windows has tiny text on the Macintosh, and a document that looks fine on the Macintosh has huge text in Windows.

The problem is related to the fact that the Mac OS assumes a screen resolution of 72 dpi, whereas Windows assumes a screen resolution of 96 dpi. For a detailed explanation of the problem, see Geoff Duncan's article in *TidBITS* at *http://db.tidbits.com/getbits.acgi?tbart=05284*.

Unfortunately, there is no easy way around the problem, although workarounds exist if you only run into the problem occasionally:

• If you use Internet Explorer as your web browser on the Macintosh, you can click the Larger or Smaller icons on

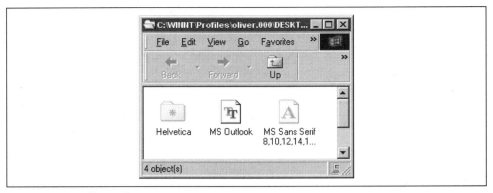

Figure F-10. Different font icons

the toolbar to adjust the overall type size—an instant quick fix for web pages with tiny type on the Macintosh.

- If you're using Microsoft Word, you can scale the document up for the Macintosh or down for Windows using the Zoom menu on the main toolbar. Or, if you must work in a stylesheet-heavy document for a long time, you can redefine the main styles to use a larger or more readable font. For instance, when opening a Windows document in Times 10-point type—a nearly unreadable style on the Macintosh—consider redefining the Normal style to the Mac's New York or Palatino 12-point font.

Force Quit
In Windows: End Task

If a Macintosh application is frozen, you can often force it to quit by press Command-Option-Esc and then clicking the Force Quit button. In Windows, if you need to discipline a badly behaved program by quitting it forcibly, press Ctrl-Alt-Delete, click the name of the misbehaving program, and then click the End Task button. The hard part of all this, of course, is figuring out which program to quit, since the names of the programs in the Close Program dialog box are often the short DOS-style names, which you may not recognize.

If you press Ctrl-Alt-Delete again while in the Close Program dialog box, you restart the PC, much like pressing Control-Command-Power on the Macintosh. It's safer for your PC to use the Shut Down button in the Close Program dialog box instead.

Forks
In Windows: None

Behind the scenes, Macintosh files can have two distinct parts, or forks: the resource fork and the data fork. For instance, the code-defining menus, windows, and dialog boxes are generally stored in an application's resource fork; the contents of the document are often stored in the data fork. A few exceptions have appeared over the years. For instance, documents generated by the word processor Nisus Writer are straight text files, but they store their formatting in the resource fork. Thus, any text editor can read a Nisus Writer document, losing only the formatting.

The problem with dual-forked files is that most other operating systems, including Windows, don't support multiple forks in files. Windows programs generally understand only the data fork of documents. When you try to send a Macintosh document to a Windows machine, therefore, assume that only the data fork will transfer.

When transferring files to Windows, therefore, there are three techniques:

- Combine both the resource and the data forks into a single file. This is how

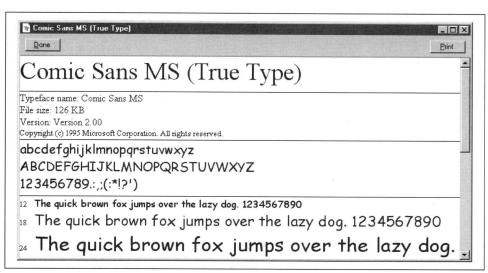

Figure F-11. Font sample

the *MacBinary* and *BinHex* file formats work behind the scenes.

Unfortunately, Windows itself doesn't understand the MacBinary file format, so your recipients will need a Windows utility like Aladdin Expander (see *http://www.aladdinsys.com/* for more information) to open such files, which may have a *.bin* extension, for use in Windows. These utilities decode the MacBinary file, throwing out the resource fork and retaining the data fork for use in a Windows program.

You might also consider using MacBinary when transferring a file from one Macintosh to another via a Windows machine (or a computer running some other operating system, like Unix). Without MacBinary, the file would be rendered unopenable during that intermediate step.

BinHex, another file compression scheme, combines the two forks of a Macintosh file, exactly as MacBinary does—but it also encodes the resulting compressed file as a stream of plain text, which must then be decoded before being used. Few Windows programs can decode BinHex; Eudora and

Aladdin Expander are the exception. See **BinHex** for more information.

- Split the resource and data forks into separate files. The *AppleDouble* email attachment format, in conjunction with MIME, uses this approach. It works well for sending email attachments to people using Windows machines because MIME creates two separate parts for the attachment, one containing the resource fork and the other containing the data fork. Then, on the Windows side, the email client discards the resource fork and reads only the data fork. For more information, see **Transferring Files to Windows**. This splitting also takes place when you copy a Macintosh file with two forks to a PC-formatted disk, and then view the files in Windows. A hidden folder called *Resource.frk* contains all the resource forks of the Macintosh files, leaving the data forks accessible to Windows programs.

- Transfer only the data fork. The *uuencode* and *Base64* attachment encoding formats in email use this technique. Since no other platform can read a Macintosh resource fork, these schemes don't even bother to transmit it. On the other hand, if you send a Macintosh file with a resource fork using one of those formats to another Macintosh, that file will be unopenable. For more information, see **Transferring Files to Windows**.

Formatting Disks

In Windows: Formatting Disks, Hard Disks

See **Erase Disk** and **Hard Disks**.

Function Keys (Fkeys)

In Windows: Function Keys

As a Macintosh user, you probably use the function keys at the top row of the keyboard (F1, F2, and so on) only rarely. But in Windows, these function keys are frequently useful. See Table F-2 for a list of the standard function keys and their uses.

Table F-2. Uses of the Function Keys

Function Key	Use
F1	Opens Windows Help.
F2	Selects the name of the selected item for renaming.
F3	Opens Start → Find.
F4	Opens the drop-down folder hierarchy in Save dialog boxes.
Alt-F4	Closes the active window (or, in cases like Microsoft Word, closes the program). If no windows are active (click the Desktop), displays the Shut Down dialog box.
Ctrl-F4	Closes a document window in an application that has multiple windows inside the application window.
F5	Refreshes the current window to make sure it reflects the current contents.
F6	Moves the "focus" between different panes in the Explorer.
F10	Selects the first menu on the menu bar; press Enter to open the menu, or Tab to select a different menu.
Shift-F10	Displays the contextual menu for the selected item—identical to right-clicking.
F11	In Windows 98 only, toggles the current window between normal and full-screen mode.

G

General Controls Control Panel
In Windows: None

The General Controls control panel contains a hodge-podge of unrelated settings. Windows has no equivalent catch-all control panel. In fact, many features made possible by the Mac's General Controls panel, such as the options to hide the Desktop when in an application, protect the System Folder or Applications folder, govern insertion point and menu blinking, and change the location for saved documents, have no equivalents in Windows.

Automatic hard disk checking. Only one General Controls option has a Windows counterpart: the "Warn me if computer was shut down improperly" checkbox. When turned on, this option automatically uses Disk First Aid to check your startup hard disk for problems after a crash.

By default, Windows 95/98 does the same thing with its disk maintenance program, ScanDisk. Turning this behavior on and off, however, is a much more complicated endeavor that's possible only in Windows 98 and later. Here are the steps:

1. Open the C: window, and choose View → Folder Options → View → Show all files.

2. Right-click *Msdos.sys*, choose Properties, and turn off the Read-only checkbox. Close the Properties dialog box.

3. Double-click *Msdos.sys* and open it in Notepad.

4. Make the second-to-last line in the file read AutoScan=1 (to turn on the automatic scanning after a crash) or AutoScan=0 (to turn off this feature).

5. Save the file, quit Notepad, and reset the Read-only attribute in the *Msdos.sys* Properties dialog box.

Get Info Command
In Windows: Properties Command

In the Mac OS, you choose File → Get Info to open a Get Info window for a selected icon. The information in the Get Info window varies by icon type, but you can count on seeing information about size, location, creation and modification dates, and more.

The Windows equivalent, the Properties dialog box, offers the same sort of information. To open it, right-click an icon and choose Properties (Alt-Enter).

Depending on the type of icon, though, the information provided by the Properties dialog may go well beyond the basics. For instance, the Properties dialog boxes of applications feature a separate tab for version information, and Microsoft Word documents add Summary, Statistics, Contents, and Custom tabs (see Figure G-1), some of which are editable, much like the Comments field in the Mac OS's Get Info window.

If you select multiple icons and then choose File → Properties, Windows presents you with a single Properties dialog box that summarizes information about the selected items. (On the Macintosh, a similar action would result in multiple Get Info windows.)

GIF
In Windows: GIF

GIF, which stands for Graphics Interchange Format, is a standard bitmapped graphic file

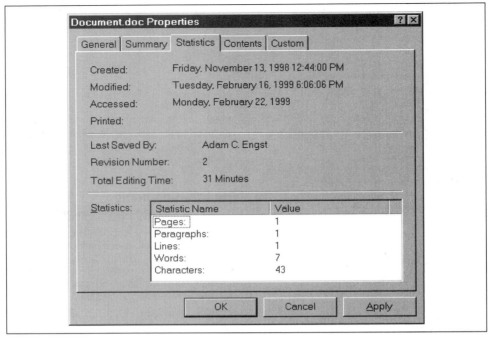

Figure G-1. Properties dialog box for Word document

format. Its most notable features are its small size, its limit of 256 colors per file—making it inappropriate for photos, but great for logos and cartoons—and its widespread use on the Web. Fortunately, GIF files are completely cross-platform, so you can transfer GIF files between PCs and Macs with no trouble at all. (Be sure to add the suffix *.gif* to such files before moving them to the PC, however.)

Graphing Calculator
In Windows: None

Windows offers no equivalent to the Mac's glamorous 3-D Graphing Calculator program.

Grow Box
In Windows: Resizing Windows

See **Resizing Windows**.

H

Hard Disks

In Windows: Hard Disks

Although hard disk technology is essentially the same on both Macs and PCs, there are a number of differences.

IDE versus SCSI. You can attach a SCSI hard disk to a PC, but SCSI drives are less common than in the Macintosh world, where SCSI was once the standard. To attach a SCSI-based hard disk to a PC, you need either a SCSI host adapter card or a built-in SCSI connector on the motherboard, which isn't common. For more information, see **SCSI**.

Most PC hard disks, like all Macintosh internal hard disks today, are IDE (Integrated Drive Electronics) drives, which merely means that the hard disk controller is integrated with the drive. The better term is ATA (AT Attachment), which is a specific type of IDE drive. ATA-IDE hard disks are popular because they're fast and cheap. However, you can put only two ATA-IDE controllers, each with only two disks, in a PC, so the possibilities for expansion are more limited than with SCSI.

ATA-IDE drives are generally cheaper and slightly faster than the equivalent drive mechanism using SCSI, simply because the SCSI controller chip adds some overhead. However, because each SCSI drive has its own controller chip, multiple SCSI drives attached to the same computer can all work simultaneously. In contrast, the two ATA-IDE drives on a single controller cannot operate simultaneously, which means that copying files between two such disks can take longer.

Boot disks. You're probably used to being able to start up a Macintosh from any kind of disk—a floppy disk, Zip drive, external

hard disk, or the CD-ROM that came with the Macintosh, for example. On the other hand, PC models from only a few manufacturers can start up from any disk other than the built-in C: hard disk and the A: floppy drive. (Check the manual or call the manufacturer to find out.) For more information, see **Boot Disk**.

Hard drive icon positioning. The first time you use a Windows machine, you may be alarmed to discover that no hard disk icon appears in the upper-right corner of your screen, where would appear on a Macintosh. That's because all hard disk icons appear in a central window—the one that opens when you double-click the My Computer icon in the upper-left corner of your screen.

It's easy enough to simulate the Macintosh approach, however—just drag the desired icons (including CD-ROM, Zip, and floppy) out of the My Computer window and onto your Desktop in the traditional positions. You've just created shortcuts (aliases) of your drives, which you can now rename in the usual way (see **Filenames**).

The icons will always be present, even when there's no corresponding floppy, CD, or Zip inserted in the machine. That may throw you if you're used to the Macintosh way, in which icons only appear on the Desktop if the corresponding disks have actually been inserted. Still, the shortcuts-on-the-Desktop trick is one of the most efficient means of becoming comfortable with working in Windows.

Internal versus external. Thanks to the two-drive limit of ATA-IDE hard disk chains, it's relatively uncommon to see PCs with external hard disks attached. It's technically possible to attach certain external parallel-port hard disks to a PC, but they're extremely slow, especially when compared with SCSI hard disks.

As on the Macintosh, if you plan to attach a SCSI hard disk to your PC (after equipping the computer with the SCSI card, for example), use high-quality SCSI cables. Cheap SCSI cables may not be sufficiently shielded, which can lead to strange disk-related errors such as files being corrupted or crashes while reading files. In addition, turn any external hard disks on before you turn the PC on and turn them off after turning the PC off.

Compression. Although drive compression programs were once marketed for the Macintosh, they've all fallen by the wayside as hard disk sizes increased and prices dropped. However, in the PC world, those technologies remain popular—in fact, Microsoft includes one, called DriveSpace, with Windows. Use DriveSpace (Start → Programs → Accessories → System Tools → DriveSpace) to compress a PC hard disk to free up some space—at the expense of speed. To save even more disk space, you can use Compression Agent (in the same location) to compress files even further. Compression Agent compresses files quite slowly, though, so you'll probably want to set it up as a scheduled task (see **Macros**).

Disk maintenance. Although hard disks may last for many years, it's important to perform routine disk maintenance to keep the data structures (such as directories and lists of bad blocks) up to date. If you don't, your disk may suffer an increasing level of data corruption, which could cause crashes or even data loss.

For more information about performing routine disk maintenance, see **Disk First Aid**.

Disk formats. With Mac OS 8.1, Apple introduced HFS Plus, which saves space by using small block sizes even on very large hard disks. The Windows 98 equivalent is FAT 32, a 32-bit filesystem that's more efficient than the previous FAT 16 and supports larger hard disks.

Just as HFS Plus-formatted disks aren't accessible by Macs running Mac OS 8.0 or earlier, so too FAT 32 disks aren't accessible on machines running Windows versions earlier than Windows 98.

Converting a Windows hard disk from FAT 16 to FAT 32 is easier than converting a Macintosh hard disk from HFS to HFS Plus. Just run the program called Drive Converter, found in Start → Programs → Accessories → System Tools → Drive Converter. After you've converted your drive, it's a good idea to run Disk Defragmenter (available in the same location).

Reformatting. As on the Macintosh, you'll rarely need to reformat (erase) a Windows hard disk. There are two levels of formatting: quick and full. Quick formatting, which corresponds to "initializing" on the Macintosh, just wipes the directory information. Full formatting, which compares with "formatting" on the Macintosh, actually erases the surface of the disk. Needless to say, a quick format is considerably faster than a full format.

To format a PC hard disk, follow these steps:

1. If your PC can start up Windows from any disk other than the internal C: hard disk, boot from another disk. (If, like most PCs, yours can start up only from the internal hard disk or a floppy disk, see the following instructions.)

2. Right-click the hard disk icon, and then choose Format.

3. In the Format dialog box, choose Quick or Full, and specify whether you want to copy system files (which you do if you want the disk to be bootable).

You can also reformat your hard disk when you start up the machine from the System floppy disk that came with it. Unfortunately, such a floppy starts up your machine in DOS mode, not the more familiar Windows.

After the machine has started up, you'll see this on the screen:

```
C:\>
```

At this point, you should type:

```
format c: /s
```

and then press Enter to reformat your hard disk. (Replace C: with the appropriate drive letter for the hard disk you want to format.)

Checking free space. When using a PC for the first time, you might want to see how large its hard disk is and how much of that space is free. To do so, open the My Computer window and then click the hard disk icon; you'll see its capacity and free space statistics at the bottom of the window. You can also view a graph of the hard disk's free space by right-clicking its icon and then choosing Properties → General (see Figure H-1).

Drive letters. On the Macintosh, every disk has a name, and you can give multiple disks the same name. In Windows, however, every disk is referred to by a drive letter, although disks can also have labels that you make up yourself.

In general, floppy disks are called A: and B:, your main hard disk is known as C:, and your CD-ROM drive is D:. If other hard

disks are attached to the PC, they'll have higher drive letters. It's also possible to give a shared folder or disk from the network its own drive letter, so don't assume if you see an M: drive, for instance, that there's another hard disk attached to the PC.

Help
In Windows: Help

As on the Macintosh, Windows offers a Help menu in almost every program. Also as on the Macintosh, however, the kinds of help commands you'll find in this menu vary depending on the program you're using. You may encounter three help formats: Windows Help, ToolTips, and context-sensitive help in dialog boxes.

Windows Help. Using Windows Help is similar to using the Help Viewer in Mac OS 8.5. In Windows 95 and applications of its era, each help topic appears in its own separate window, forcing you to switch between

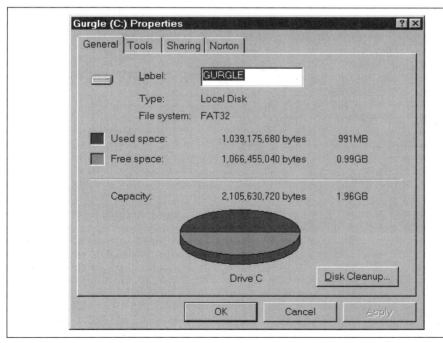

Figure H-1. Determining disk size and free space

windows as you search. In Windows 98, the help mechanisms improved, eliminating much of this window-switching. The trickiest part of using Windows Help is that Help-menu items don't have standard names. The primary help command may be called: Help Topics, Contents, Index, or even Info Desk.

Windows 98 help tips. The left pane in Windows 98 Help lists the contents or index entries, or search results, and the right pane displays the information associated with the topic you select (see Figure H-2). If you want, you can hide the left pane entirely, though that eliminates the entire advantage of the two-pane interface.

Some index entries are associated with more than one topic. When you double-click one of those entries, Windows Help displays a dialog box containing the available topics. Double-click one to display it in the right pane.

When you see words underlined, much as in a web browser, clicking them either provides a pop-up note that defines the underlined term or performs some action, such as opening a control panel. Unfortunately, Windows Help can't coach you through performing a task nearly as well as Apple Guide can.

ToolTips. ToolTips are something like balloon help on the Macintosh. When you point to some window control, button, or other interface element, a tiny rectangle appears, offering a label for the item you're pointing to.

ToolTips occasionally provide more than a simple label for a button or icon. Point to the Start button, for example, and the ToolTip tells you "Click here to begin." (It's not clear what you're beginning, of course, and don't get confused by the fact that you also click the Start button to end a session.) More useful is the ToolTip that appears when you move your mouse over the clock, which then tells you the day and date (see Figure H-3).

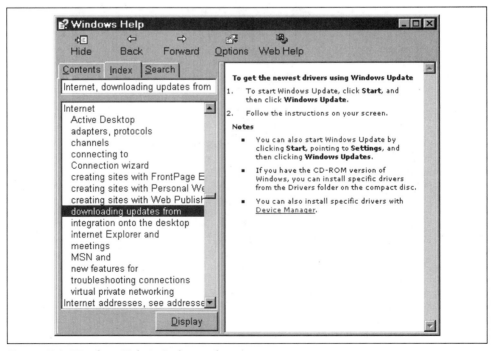

Figure H-2. Windows Help in Index mode

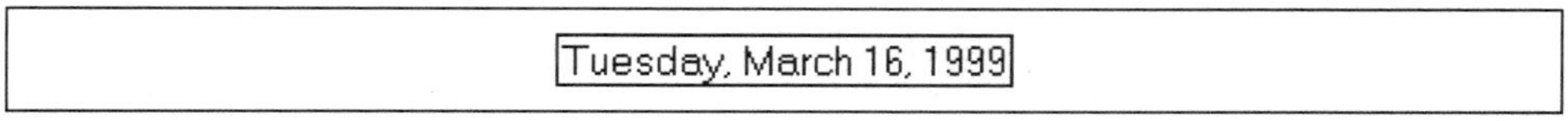

Tuesday, March 16, 1999

Figure H-3. Day and date ToolTip

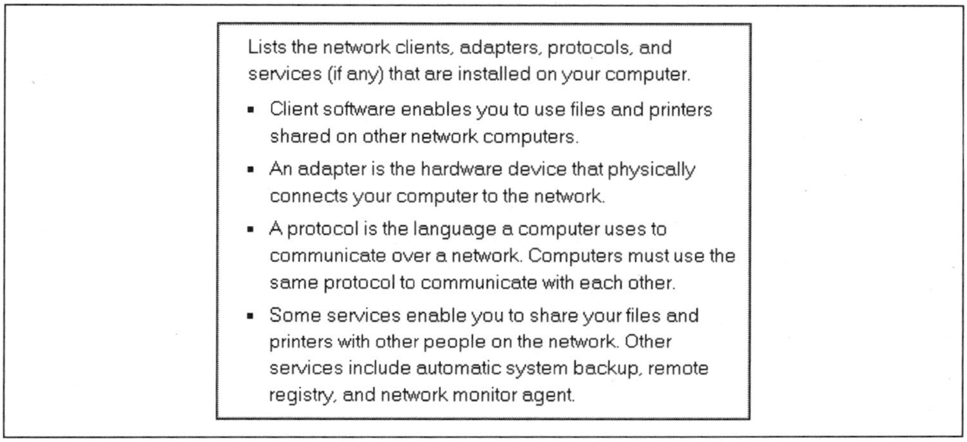

Lists the network clients, adapters, protocols, and services (if any) that are installed on your computer.

- Client software enables you to use files and printers shared on other network computers.
- An adapter is the hardware device that physically connects your computer to the network.
- A protocol is the language a computer uses to communicate over a network. Computers must use the same protocol to communicate with each other.
- Some services enable you to share your files and printers with other people on the network. Other services include automatic system backup, remote registry, and network monitor agent.

Figure H-4. Network control panel's context-sensitive help

Context-sensitive help. The context-sensitive dialog-box help in Windows is even more like the Mac's balloon help than Tool-Tips. When you're in a dialog box, there's often a question mark button in the upper right corner, next to the Close button. When you click it, your cursor turns into an arrow with a question mark. Then click on any item (button, field, list, whatever) in the dialog box; if there is help available for that item, Windows displays it in a box that looks like a Post-It note. For instance, Figure H-4 shows the context-sensitive help for the list of components in the Network control panel.

As with everything else in Windows, there are several other ways to access this context-sensitive help in dialog boxes. If you right-click an item in a dialog box, a What's This? button appears; click it and the help message appears. Alternatively, move your mouse over the item in question and then press F1 to reveal the help message.

HFS, HFS Plus
In Windows: FAT 16, FAT 32

HFS and HFS Plus are the schemes the Macintosh uses to store files on hard disks in systems before and after Mac OS 8.1, respectively. The exact analogues in Windows are called FAT 16 and FAT 32; for details, see **Hard Disks**.

Hiding Applications
In Windows: Minimizing Windows

It's common practice on the Macintosh to hide applications when you wish to clear the screen to work in another program. The Hide command in the Application menu works well for this purpose, instantly hiding all windows belonging to the frontmost program. In contrast, in Windows, the windows of many applications—Internet Explorer and Outlook Express, for example—operate independently of the application itself, and there's no way to hide all of them at once.

Instead of the Hide command, therefore, in Windows, you use the Minimize button (in the upper-right corner of every document and application window) to achieve the same effect. Clicking this button makes the window collapse to the size of a single icon on your taskbar at the bottom of the screen. For more information, see **Collapsing Windows**.

In Windows 98, you can hide all windows of all applications in a single click, as though you had switched to the Macintosh Finder and then used the Hide Others command in the application menu. To do so, summon Windows 98's Quick Launch toolbar (right-click the Taskbar and choose Toolbars → Quick Launch) and then click the Show Desktop button (see Figure H-5). To restore all the windows in their original locations, click Show Desktop a second time.

In both Windows 95 and 98, you can press WIN key-M to perform the same stunt.

Figure H-5. Show Desktop button on Quick Launch toolbar

I

Icons

In Windows: Icons

Both Windows and the Macintosh make heavy use of icons to represent disks, files, and folders on the computer. Using the View menu, you can specify how you'd like the icons in a particular window to appear.

On the Macintosh, the icon displayed on a certain file is determined by its invisible Type and Creator codes. In Windows, however, document icons are associated with filename extensions—a file with the extension *.doc*, for example, gets the Microsoft Word icon.

Custom icons. Changing a Windows icon isn't as easy as it is on the Macintosh. You're free to replace only three kinds of icons: those that represent certain Desktop items, such as the Recycle Bin; the icon displayed on any shortcut; and the icon that appears on a certain kind of document, such as Word documents. But Windows offers no means of replacing the icon of one file or folder (without using third-party utility programs).

Changing the icon associated with a certain document type. To change the icon associated with a filename extension, follow these instructions:

1. Choose View → Folder Options → File Types.
2. Select the file type that you want to change. If you know the first few letters of its name, type them to scroll the list.
3. Click Edit → Change Icon.
4. Select an icon from the list shown (see Figure I-1), or click the Browse button if you'd like to copy the icon from another file on your hard disk.

When you click the Browse button, you're offered the chance to navigate your hard disk on a quest for files whose icons you'd like to swipe. Here are a few files that contain ready-to-use icons:

- *\Windows\System\shell32.dll*
- *\Windows\System\pifmgr.dll*
- *\Windows\moricons.dll*
- *\Windows\System\rnaui.dll*
- *\Windows\progman.exe*
- *\Windows\System\user.exe*

Changing the icon on a shortcut file. To change the icon associated with a shortcut, follow these steps:

1. Right-click the shortcut and choose Properties → Shortcut → Change Icon.
2. Select an icon from the list shown, or click the Browse button to find another file containing icons, as described in the previous tip.

Changing the icons of Desktop items. To change the icons for various items on your Desktop, do this:

1. Open Control Panel → Display → Effects.
2. Select one of the icons, then click Change Icon.
3. Select an icon from the list shown, or click the Browse button to find another file containing icons, as described in the prior tip.

Rebuilding Desktop icons in Windows 98. If you notice that some of the items on the Windows Desktop have lost their original icons, you can direct Windows to delete and then rebuild the ShellIconCache file, which is the Windows equivalent of the

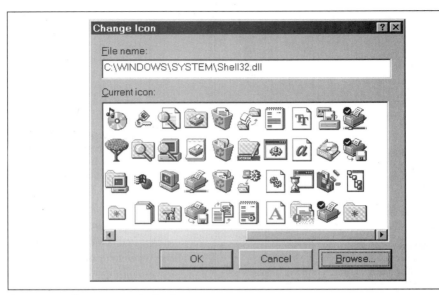

Figure I-1. Change Icon dialog box

Mac's invisible Desktop files. Follow these steps:

1. Install TweakUI by installing the Windows 98 Resource Kit Tools Sampler on the Windows 98 CD-ROM at *Windows 98\tools\restkit\setup.exe*. If you use Windows 95, you can download TweakUI from *http://www.microsoft. com/windows95/downloads/default.asp*.

2. Open Control Panel → TweakUI → Repair → Rebuild Icons.

3. Click Repair Now.

IDE
In Windows: IDE

For information about IDE hard disks in PCs, see **Hard Disks**.

Installing Hardware
In Windows: Add New Hardware

Connecting a new peripheral, such as a printer or Zip drive, to a Windows-based PC isn't nearly as simple as it is on the Macintosh. In Windows, every gadget you add to your PC must have a corresponding soft-

ware driver on the hard disk—and it's your job to hope that this driver is up-to-date, bug free, and compatible with all your other drivers.

With the advent of Windows 95, this driver chaos has improved considerably, thanks to the built-in collection of drivers Microsoft calls "Plug and Play" technology. This system permits Windows to recognize most popular hardware add-ons and install the proper driver automatically. Unfortunately, peripherals that Windows doesn't yet know about continue to cause headaches.

In the event that you want to connect a device that Windows doesn't recognize automatically, you need to use Control Panel → Add New Hardware. Add New Hardware is a wizard that walks you through the process of installing the necessary driver software. Before you run Add New Hardware, make sure you've properly attached the new peripheral. Then, make sure the device is turned on, if it has its own power switch. Windows won't be able to detect devices that are turned off.

Add New Hardware first scans for Plug and Play-compatible devices. If it doesn't find your new accessory device in its list, Windows gives you a choice: you can identify the device in a list Windows shows you, or you can let Windows scan the PC for devices that aren't Plug and Play-compatible (a process jokingly called "Plug and Pray"). For best results, choose the latter option—Windows can sometimes figure out what device you've plugged in.

If Windows fails to identify the device correctly, then identify it yourself—select it from the Windows list, or click Have Disk and insert the floppy disk provided with the add-on device. (The manufacturer of the add-on generally provides instructions along these lines.)

The Add New Hardware wizard makes it emphatically clear that you should restart your PC manually should it freeze during the detection phase. (When Microsoft gets the time, perhaps it will rewrite the wizard to avoid these crashes rather than simply displaying warning messages.)

Installing Software
In Windows: Add/Remove Programs

Installing new software programs in Windows isn't as simple as on the Macintosh. Windows applications often require the installation of many different files in different places, making subsequent removal difficult, to say the least. You can't install many Windows programs by simply dragging them to your hard disk, either, as you can on the Macintosh.

Because of these considerations, most Windows applications come in the form of an installer. This installation program can both install and, when the time comes, uninstall your new program (using the Control Panel → Add/Remove Programs function).

Installing applications. Most applications come with installation instructions, but the general installation procedure follows one of these courses:

- Insert the software CD-ROM to run the installation program (which is generally called *Setup.exe*). Follow the instructions on screen.

- Open Control Panel → Add/Remove Programs → Install/Uninstall, click the Install button, and follow the instructions on the screen. (Behind the scenes, this wizard does little more than locate the software's manufacturer-supplied installer program.)

- Occasionally, you're required to run *Setup.exe* (the installation program on the software CD or disk) manually, which you can do as though it were any other application. See **Opening Files** for the various different ways of opening an application, and see **Find** for instructions on how to find *Setup.exe* if it's not visible.

- If you've downloaded the program from the Internet, you may need to expand a compressed Zip file before running an installation program. (See **StuffIt** for more information about dealing with Zip files.) After you've expanded the downloaded file, look for a file called something like "Read Me" for installation instructions.

Uninstalling applications. The uninstall portion of Add/Remove Programs is more useful, though not always effective. Good installers include uninstall routines when they install applications, and they register themselves with the Add/Remove Programs control panel so you can uninstall the program easily. You can uninstall anything listed in the Install/Uninstall tab's scrolling list by selecting it, then clicking the Add/Remove button (see Figure I-2). Windows asks if you're sure you want to do remove all traces of the program from your computer, and if you agree, it tries to do so. It doesn't always succeed, so you may have to delete shortcuts and other remnants of the application manually.

One piece of advice: If Windows ever asks you if you want to delete a file that it claims no program is using, say "No!" in a firm voice (and click the No button). Windows isn't very smart about this kind of thing sometimes, and has been known to delete files that are not only necessary, they're in fact used by Windows itself. Play it safe and leave those files be—at worst they'll clutter a folder slightly.

H–M

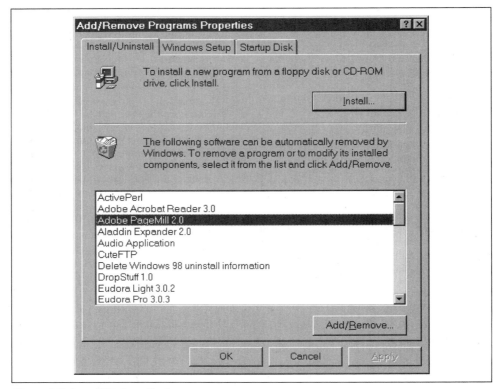

Figure I-2. Install/Uninstall tab

Adding and removing parts of Windows.
When you installed Windows itself, you
may not have installed all the optional components you wanted, or you may have
installed some that you no longer want,
because they're wasting disk space you
need. The second tab in the Add/Remove
Programs control panel lets you add and
remove Windows components. Installed
components are marked with a checkmark;
if the checkbox is shaded, only part of the
component has been installed (see
Figure I-3). (Again, if Windows ever asks
you if you want to delete a file that it claims
nothing is using, do not delete the file.)

To mark a component for installation, click
the box to add a checkmark. To remove a
component, click so that the checkmark disappears. To select specific parts of a component, select the component name and
then click the Details button—or double-
click the component name—to summon a
list of the individual parts of the compo-

nent, which you can add and remove in the
same way. When you're finished, click OK.
Insert any disks that Windows asks for (it's
likely to require the Windows CD-ROM).

Internet
In Windows: Internet

The rise of the Internet is the most significant change in the computer world over the
last few years. One important aspect of this
sea change is that the Internet has brought
Windows and the Macintosh closer together.
Since the Internet is essentially platform-
agnostic, the world's programmers have put
a great deal of work into open standards
that work on both Windows and the Macintosh. That's why you can receive Internet
email, or browse the Web, equally well on
either a Macintosh or a PC. Aspects of Internet use are covered throughout this book;
refer to the following list for some of the
main entries:

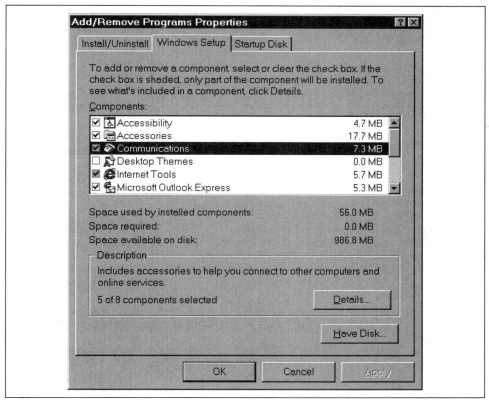

Figure I-3. Windows Setup tab

- For information about connecting a Windows-based PC to the Internet via a modem, see **Remote Access Control Panel** and **Modems**.

- For information about connecting a Windows-based PC to the Internet via a network, see **TCP/IP Control Panel**.

- For information about cross-platform Internet email programs, see **Eudora** and **Microsoft Outlook Express**.

- For information about cross-platform web browsers, see **Internet Explorer** and **Netscape Navigator/Communicator**.

- For a list of Internet-related applications that exist in both Macintosh and Windows flavors, see **Cross-Platform Applications**.

- For information about file formats you might encounter on the Internet, see **File Types**.

- For information about transferring files from a Macintosh to a Windows-based PC over the Internet, see **Transferring Files to Windows**.

- For information about searching the Internet, see **Find**.

- For information about running a personal web server, see **Web Sharing Control Panel**.

- For a list of useful web sites, see **Web Sites for Windows Software and Information**.

Internet Config
In Windows: Internet Control Panel,
Individual Application Preferences

For more information about the equivalent
to Internet Config in Windows, see **Internet
Control Panel**.

Internet Control Panel
In Windows: Internet Control Panel,
Individual Application Preferences

You'll find a control panel called Internet on
both Windows and Macintosh, but the two
control panels aren't very similar. The Mac's
Internet control panel lets you set up preferences for a variety of Internet applications
in Mac OS 8.5 and later, but the Windows
Internet control panel duplicates only the
preference panels in the Internet Explorer
web browser. The other equivalent settings
from the Macintosh Internet control panel
are scattered among various Windows programs:

Personal, Email, News. In Windows, specify
your email, newsgroup reader, and personal account settings in your actual email
and newsgroup reader programs—there's
no centralized location or control panel, as
on the Macintosh.

Web. The Web tab of the Macintosh Internet control panel stores your home page
and search page locations, a location for
saving downloaded files, and settings for
colors and links. In the Windows Internet
control panel, the General tab lets you specify a home page location (though not a
search page) and General → Colors lets you
control the various colors used in your web
browser. The option to underline links, however, is located in Advanced → Browsing.

Advanced. Of the various panels in the Macintosh Internet control panel's Advanced
tab, only two have any correspondence to
the Windows Internet control panel: Helper
Apps and Firewalls. The Programs tab of the
Windows Internet control panel closely
resembles the Mac's Helper Apps panel, and
its Connection tab → Proxy server section

corresponds to the proxy entries in the Macintosh Internet control panel's Advanced →
Firewalls tab.

The remaining options in the Mac's
Advanced panel correspond to Windows
like this:

File Transfer, Hosts
You can't select default FTP servers or
hosts in Windows.

Fonts
The font settings on the Macintosh side
take effect in applications like email
programs and newsreaders. In Windows, you select fonts individually in
each such application.

File Mapping
On the Macintosh, this database lets
you associate downloaded Windows
files with the programs you'd like to
open them—according to the filename
extensions of the downloaded files. For
example, you might decide to have
sound files whose names end with *.aiff*
and *.wav* opened in the Mac's Movie
Player program.

There's no corresponding Windows
feature, since Windows already knows
which filename extension launches
which application. For more information, see **File Types**.

Messages
In Windows, you make this kind of setting—email and news quoting characters and email/new signatures—within
your email and newsreader programs,
not in a centralized control panel.

Internet Explorer
In Windows: Internet Explorer

Internet Explorer, Microsoft's free web
browser, is available for both the Macintosh
and Windows, and works essentially alike
on each platform. You can learn more about
the Macintosh version of Internet Explorer
and download a copy from Microsoft's web
site at *http://www.microsoft.com/windows/ie/
default.htm*.

J

Java

In Windows: Java

Java is a cross-platform programming language developed by Sun Microsystems. It's used primarily on the Internet for small programs, called applets, that can be downloaded and run from web pages.

On Windows, you don't need to think much about Java. When you encounter a Java applet on a web page, it should download and run automatically, requiring no input from you—and often more smoothly than it would on the Macintosh.

JPEG

In Windows: JPEG

JPEG, which stands for Joint Photographic Experts Group, is a graphics compression format that's commonly applied to photographic images. Almost every photograph you find on the World Wide Web, for example, is stored in JPEG format (and bears the suffix *.jpg* or *.jpeg* on its name). In Windows, you can open JPEG files with any web browser.

JPEG files are 100 percent cross-platform—you can easily transfer JPEG files between Macintosh and Windows machines with no conversion. Remember, however, to add the suffix *.jpg* to any Macintosh JPEG file you intend to transfer to a Windows machine. If you don't, double-clicking the file may not open it correctly.

H–M

K

Key Caps

In Windows: Character Map

On the Macintosh, you're probably used to using the Key Caps desk accessory when determining the keystrokes necessary to generate special characters like the trademark or yen symbols. In Windows, you use the Character Map program instead, accessible in Start → Programs → Accessories → System Tools → Character Map (see Figure K-1).

To insert a special character into a word processing document, follow these steps in Character Map:

1. Choose the appropriate font from the Font menu.

2. Double-click the desired special character in the character grid.

If the character is too small to identify, hold down the mouse on it to see a magnified version. Dingbat fonts (in which each character is a tiny graphic) benefit the most from this feature.

3. Click the Copy button.

4. Switch to your word processing document, and then choose Edit → Paste to paste the special character.

If you find the prescribed method of inserting special characters clumsy, note the Alt keyboard shortcut in the lower right corner of the Character Map window. If you make a note in of this keystroke, you'll later be able to reproduce the special symbol by typing the appropriate number while pressing the Alt key. When you release the Alt key, the character appears.

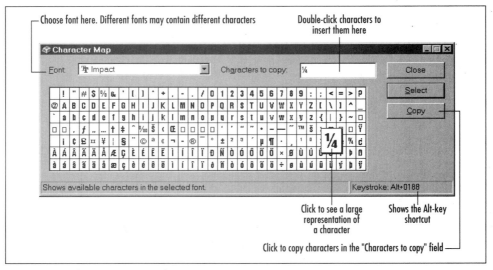

Figure K-1. Character Map utility

Keyboard

In Windows: Keyboard

Apple has created a number of different keyboard layouts over the years, starting with the early Macintosh Plus keyboard and gradually adding keys. At some point, Apple more or less standardized on a keyboard that's similar to the 104-key keyboard common in the PC world. You won't have much trouble using a PC keyboard if you're used to a Macintosh keyboard, but you will run across some unfamiliar keys that have specialized functions. Refer to Table K-1 for an overview.

Keyboard Control Panel

In Windows: Keyboard Control Panel

The controls in Mac's Keyboard control panel govern various aspects of the keyboard; you'll find exactly the same options on Windows, although they aren't all in the same places.

Key Repeat Rate, Delay Until Repeat. These settings let you specify how soon a key begins repeating when you hold it down (to type XXXXX, for example), and how quickly

the key repeats once it starts. To find the same controls in Windows, open Control Panel → Keyboard → Speed. (See Figure K-2.)

Keyboard Layouts. On the Macintosh, you use this list to choose from among several different keyboard layouts corresponding to the keys frequently used in various languages. The same feature is available on Windows: open Control Panel → Keyboard → Language.

If you plan to switch your keyboard to a single alternative language layout, click Properties, choose the layout from the pop-up menu, and then click OK.

If you frequently switch among different keyboard layouts, however, follow these steps:

1. Click the Add button, choose a language from the pop-up menu that appears, and then click OK. Repeat until all the layouts you plan to use are visible in the Keyboard control panel's Language tab. You may be asked to insert the Windows CD-ROM as Windows loads the desired language's keyboard layout.

Table K-1. Keys Unique to PC Keyboards

PC Keyboard Key	Function / Equivalent
Application key (has an image of a cursor selecting a menu item)	Simulates clicking the right mouse button; no Macintosh equivalent.
Insert key	In some text-editing programs, this key switches the keyboard from the usual Insert mode (in which new typing pushes any existing text to the right) and Overwrite mode (in which new typing types over existing text to the right of the insertion point—a mode that's unavailable on the Macintosh).
Pause / Break key	Used in the occasional terminal emulation program to stop and start text scrolling; no Macintosh equivalent.
Print Screen / SysRq key	Copies the image of the screen—or, if you also press the Alt key, the image of the active window—to the Clipboard, ready for pasting into a graphics program as a screen illustration. (On the Macintosh, the equivalent keystrokes are Control-Command-Shift-3 and Control-Caps Lock-Command-Shift-4; see **Screen Capture**.) (The SysRq function, whose label appears on the same key, is unused today—it was reportedly added to support an IBM operating system that never shipped.)
Scroll Lock key	No longer used on either Macintosh or Windows.
WIN key (has a Windows logo on it)	Opens the Start menu and offers some preset keyboard shortcuts; no Macintosh equivalent.

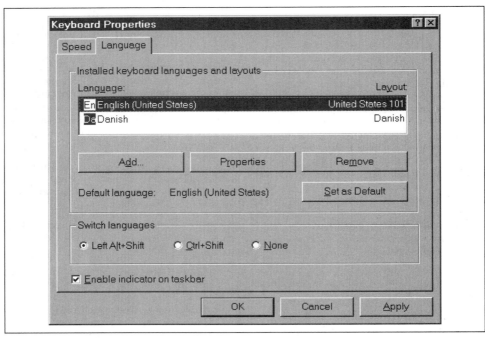

Figure K-2. Keyboard control panel

2. Specify a keyboard shortcut for switching languages, if desired. Make sure that the "Enable indicator on taskbar" checkbox is selected.

3. Click OK to close the Keyboard control panel.

4. In the Tray area on the Taskbar, note that an icon has appeared, representing the currently active language layout. That icon is actually a menu; click it to choose a different language.

As on the Macintosh, Windows doesn't only switch between different foreign-language keyboard layouts—it can also be configured to an alternate English layout, such as the Dvorak layout. To do so, choose Control Panel → Keyboard → Language → English (United States) → Properties → United States-Dvorak.

L

Labels
In Windows: None

On the Macintosh, you can label icons with a color or text label as a quick and easy means of categorization. There's no equivalent in Windows.

Launcher Control Panel
In Windows: None

The Mac's Launcher control panel creates a Desktop window that stores the icons of frequently used files, folders, disks, and servers. A single click on one of these buttons opens the corresponding icon, saving you the effort of burrowing through your nested folders to find the original item. The Launcher can have multiple "pages" filled with icons in particular categories.

Windows has no precise equivalent. However, you can easily create a toolbar that's loaded up with icons to which you'd like easy access. For more information on creating toolbars, see "Toolbars in Windows 98" in **Application Menu**.

List Views
In Windows: List Views

When you're examining your files and folders in a Desktop window, the Macintosh and Windows both offer a list view—a compact display of a window's contents. (The alternative Icon view is better suited for windows containing only a few files or folders.)

However, you, the experienced Macintosh user, may be alarmed at first to discover that the Windows list view arranges your icons in multiple columns, forcing you to scroll both vertically and horizontally to get through the list. You'll probably feel much more at home with the view Windows calls Details view, which is almost exactly like the Mac's list view. (Choose View → Details View in any Windows window; see Figure L-1.) Now, as on the Macintosh, you can click the heading above a column (where it says Size, for example) to sort the list by that criterion; click again to reverse the sorting order.

Also as on the Macintosh, you can adjust column widths in Details view by dragging the tiny divider line between column headings. You can't rearrange the columns in a Windows list view, however, as you can Mac OS 8.5 and later. (Nor can you specify which columns appear in a particular window, as you can on the Macintosh.)

Separate folder lists. You may also be disoriented by the fact that Windows maintains two separate alphabetical clusters in each list view: first folders, and then individual files are listed. On the Macintosh, folders sort within the list of files, rather than separately, as in Windows.

Disclosure triangles. The final difference between the Windows and Macintosh list views: Windows doesn't have what are called *disclosure triangles*, the tiny triangle buttons beside each folder name. In Windows, there's no way to view an indented list revealing the contents of a folder without opening a new window, as the Mac's disclosure triangle does. The closest approximation Windows offers is its two-pane Explorer window mode; for more information, see **Finder**.

LocalTalk
In Windows: Direct Cable Connection

LocalTalk was a significant development for the Macintosh. Using this technology, you

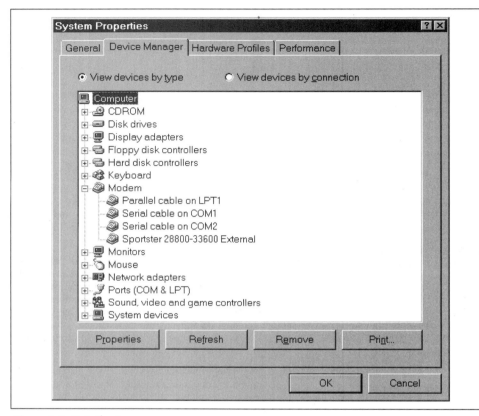

Figure L-1. Details view

could connect Macs and printers in an office using little more than ordinary telephone wire, so that their users could share printers and transfer files among machines.

Today, of course, Ethernet is a far faster and more reliable networking method, if slightly more expensive. See **Networking** for more information on connecting Macs and PCs.

On Windows, there's no inexpensive, standard equivalent to the Mac's LocalTalk system. However, you're not stuck without an inexpensive way to share files and resources between two PCs running Windows, thanks to the Direct Cable Connection.

Direct Cable Connection lets you designate one computer as a host and the other as a guest. Once you've set up the connection, the guest computer can access shared files

on the host computer, including any files on a network connected to the host computer. You can also print on printers connected to the host computer.

You have three options for physically connecting the computers. The easiest is infrared. However, infrared ports are relatively uncommon, particularly on desktop PCs, and can be difficult to configure. The best option, therefore, is a bidirectional parallel cable, which connects the computers' parallel ports. It's faster than the third option, a null modem serial cable, which connects the computers' serial ports and is thus more likely to conflict with modems or mice. These are both special cables—make sure you buy the right type at a computer store. Windows Help recommends cables from Parallel Technologies at *http://www.lpt.com/*.

Follow these steps once you have the appropriate cable:

1. Ensure that both Network control panels (Control Panel → Network → Configuration) have the "Client for Microsoft Networks" client component and the "File and printer sharing for Microsoft Networks" service component installed, along with the NetBEUI protocol component. See **AppleTalk Control Panel** for more information.

2. Go to Control Panel → Network → Identification and give each PC a unique name. Share your files by selecting Control Panel → Network → Configuration → File and Printer Sharing → "I want to be able to give others access to my files." Now open Start → Programs → Accessories → Communication → Direct Cable Connection on both PCs. If this option is not installed, install it from Control Panel → Add/Remove Programs → Windows Setup → Communications → Details → Direct Cable Connection. Set one as the host and the other as the guest.

3. Select the appropriate port on both machines. Both must be using the same type of cable. Finally, share a folder on the host (for more information, see **File Sharing**).

4. Once the connection is made, click the View Host button on the guest machine to see shared folders on the host. If that fails, open Start → Find → Computer and enter the name of the other computer to find it on the network.

If you have trouble, check the Direct Cable Connection troubleshooter located within Start → Help → Contents → Troubleshooting. Also be sure to check out the Windows 95 Direct Cable Connect Problem Page, at *http://www.tecno.demon.co.uk/dcc.html*, for a vast amount of useful information. Frank Kime's Direct Cable Connect Win 95 to Win 95 page at *http://www.cs.purdue.edu/homes/kime/directcc/directcc95.htm* is also helpful.

After you've run the Direct Cable Connection setup wizard once, you won't have to do so again; it remembers your settings.

Location Manager Control Panel
In Windows: Hardware Profiles, System Control Panel, My Locations, Telephony Control Panel, User Profiles, Users Control Panel, Passwords Control Panel

The Mac's Location Manager control panel and related components let you switch many control panel settings at once—time zones, network configurations, Internet settings, speaker volume, and much more—with a single click. This feature is extremely valuable to laptop owners who travel from office to office, but can also be useful to desktop Macintosh owners who switch among, for example, multiple Internet accounts.

There's no direct Windows equivalent of the Mac's Location Manager. However, you can use three different features of Windows to simulate aspects of the Mac's Location Manager: hardware profiles, user profiles, and dialing locations.

Hardware profiles. One side effect of the way Windows automatically detects hardware and installs the necessary drivers is that at every boot, Windows checks to see what hardware you've attached to your PC and adjusts software configurations—such as network settings—correspondingly. The reverse is also true—it checks to see what you've removed and tries to act appropriately. Most of the time, this comes into play with laptops, of course, since it's likely that you would have different setups at work and home or at work and on the road.

So, to make your PC laptop realize that it has a new configuration, shut it down in the old configuration, add or remove hardware, then start it back up again. Some configuration changes may be detected when you wake up a laptop from Standby mode, but a full boot works best.

Windows can memorize these hardware configurations as hardware profiles. Most of the time, Windows automatically creates and switches between hardware profiles. However, you can create and switch between hardware profiles manually, and more important, you can edit existing hardware profiles.

H–M

To do so, open the System control panel's Hardware Profiles tab (Control Panel → System → Hardware Profiles) or right-click My Computer and choose Properties → Hardware Profiles). In the Hardware Profiles tab, you can create, rename, and delete profiles. To switch between them, you must restart the machine—as Windows begins to load at the next startup, you'll be asked to choose a profile from a text menu.

Once you've booted with a profile, you can edit it (to remove devices, for example) in Control Panel → System → Device Manager (see Figure L-2). Find the appropriate device, double-click it, and in its Properties window, check either "Disable in this hardware profile" or "Remove from this hardware profile." Use the former option if you might want to restore that device to the pro-file later; use the latter to eliminate the device from the profile forever.

My Locations. When traveling, you may want to change the phone number you dial to connect to the Internet. The Mac's Location Manager is ideal for this task, letting you store predefined sets of Internet settings and switch among them using a menu.

Windows stores a single system-wide set of phone numbers, but provides numerous places to access that set. The easiest in Windows 98 is Control Panel → Telephony → My Locations. Alternatively, if you're using Windows 95, you can choose Control Panel → Modems → Dialing Properties, or you can summon the same control panel from within most communications programs.

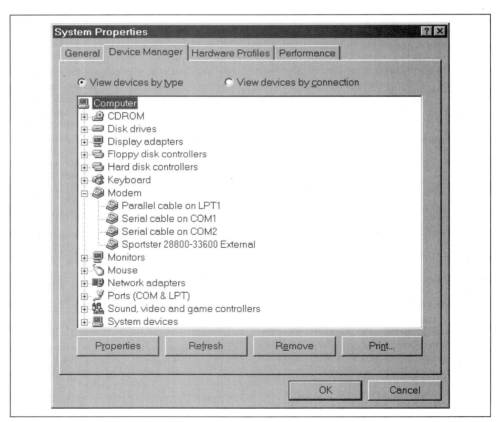

Figure L-2. Device Manager

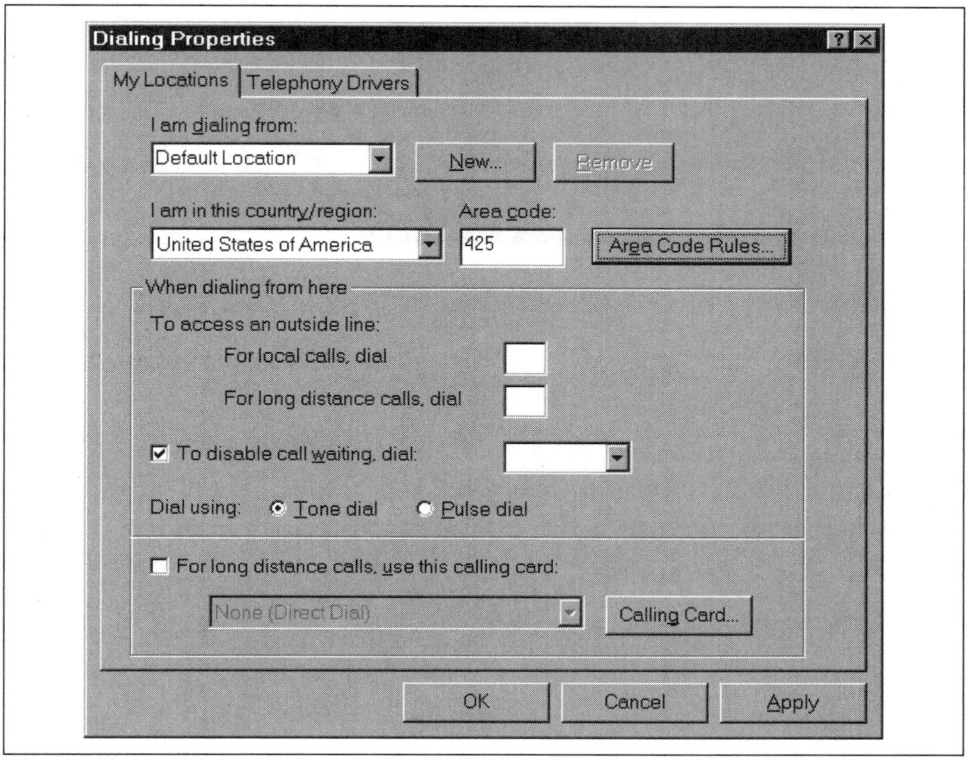

Figure L-3. My Locations

In the My Locations tab, you can define multiple locations, each with its own area code, dialing rules, and options for getting outside lines (see Figure L-3). An additional dialog box lets you enter calling card details.

User profiles. It's easy for several people to share a single Windows PC; thanks to the User Profiles feature, each person will encounter his or her own customized Windows environment. You can coopt some of these options in the Users control panel (Control Panel → Users) to make a traveling laptop easier to use (see Figure L-4). Items you can personalize include:

- Desktop folder and Documents menu
- Start menu
- Favorites folder
- Downloaded web pages
- My Documents folder

To set up a user profile, choose Control Panel → Users; the wizard will walk you through the process.

For instance, if you're switching from a large monitor to a relatively small LCD display, you may wish to logon as a different user and switch the contents of the Desktop. You may also decide to set up have different Favorites for use when traveling. After you've set up profiles in the Users control panel, be sure to turn on multiple user support in Control Panel → Passwords → User Profiles.

H–M

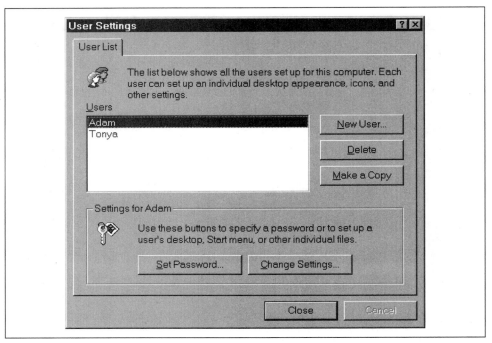

Figure L-4. Users control panel

M

Mac OS Easy Open Control Panel
In Windows: Open With Dialog Box

In Mac OS versions before 8.5, when you double-click a document whose parent application isn't on the hard disk, Mac OS Easy Open presents you with a list of alternate applications that can open the document. Windows does the same when you try to open a document that lacks a filename extension, or one whose extension isn't included in the Registry.

Double-clicking such an unknown document type summons the Open With dialog box, which lets you choose an application to open the file (see Figure M-1). The "Always use this program to open this type of file" checkbox lets you create a permanent association between the application and file type as indicated by the filename extension.

You can bring up the Open With dialog box even for files that Windows does recognize, which might be handy if you want to open an HTML file in Notepad rather than Internet Explorer, for instance. To do so, Shift-right-click the file, and then choose "Open with" from the contextual menu.

Mac OS Help
In Windows: Windows Help

The HTML-based Windows Help, accessible from Start → Help, is extremely similar to the Mac OS Help system introduced in Mac OS 8.5. For more information, see **Help**.

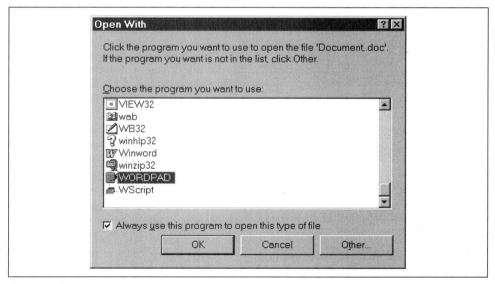

Figure M-1. Open With dialog box

Macros
In Windows: Macros, Scheduled Tasks

Macro programs let you record or script actions—mouse clicks, menu commands, type phrases, and so on—and then play them back with a single keystroke or click. Because a macro program can also be used to reassign keystrokes to other functions, you might find them especially helpful in making your PC behave more like the Macintosh you're used to.

For more information on commercial macro utilities, visit the following web sites. (Of the following products, QuicKeys is likely to be the most familiar to you, since it's also the most popular Macintosh macro program.)

- QuicKeys (CE Software): *http://www.cesoft.com/quickeys/qkhome.html*

- Aim Tools (AimSoft Development): *http://www.aimtools.com/aimtools/index.cfm*

- Aim Keys (AimSoft Development): *http://www.aimtools.com/aimkeys/index.cfm*

- AutoMate (Unisyn): *http://www.unisyn.com/Automate/automate.htm*

- EZ Macros (American Systems): *http://www.americansys.com/ezmacros.htm*

- MacroMagic (Iolo Technologies): *http://www.iolo.com/macromagic/*

- ShortCuts (Kiss Software): *http://www.kissco.com/html/shortcuts_product_page.html*

Scheduled tasks. Although Windows has no built-in macro capability, Windows 98 can launch a particular program on a repeating basis via Scheduled Tasks (accessible via My Computer → Scheduled Tasks). This feature is most useful for running disk utility programs like ScanDisk (for more information, see **Disk First Aid**) or Disk Defragmenter, but you could also theoretically schedule a task to do something such as connect to the Internet and retrieve your email, or perhaps print a weekly report automatically.

To create a scheduled task, follow these steps:

1. Open My Computer → Scheduled Tasks → Add Scheduled Task.

2. Select a program to run from the list, or click the Browse button if you want to choose a document or a program that's not listed.

3. Set how often the task should run and when it should run.

Once you've set up a task, right-click it in the Schedule Tasks folder, and then choose Properties to modify the schedule, details about the task, and other settings, including whether it should wait until the computer is idle (see Figure M-2).

Map Control Panel
In Windows: Date/Time Control Panel

The Map control panel (in the Control Panels folder until Mac OS 8.5; in the Apple Extras folder thereafter) lets you look up the latitude, longitude, and time zone of any place on the planet. It can also be used to specify your current time zone (a function also available in the Date & Time control panel).

In Windows, you set your local time zone in Control Panel → Date/Time → Time Zone (see Figure M-3). Unfortunately, although the Date/Time control panel displays a map of the world, you can't click to specify your current location (except in the initial release of Windows 95); you must select a time zone from a menu.

Windows offers no equivalent of the latitude and longitude finding capabilities, or the Time-zone comparison feature, of the Map control panel.

Memory Control Panel
In Windows: Virtual Memory Dialog Box

Because of the way Windows handles memory, you don't need to perform as much configuration as you do on the Macintosh. In most cases, you don't need to change the default settings at all.

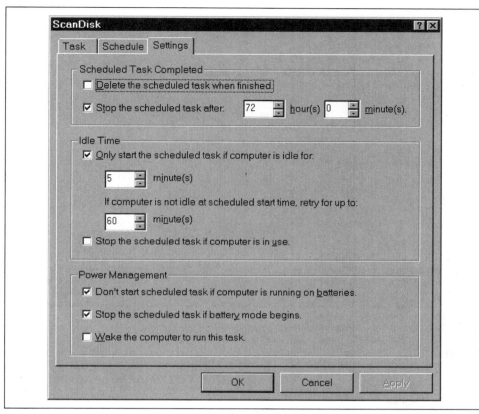

Figure M-2. A scheduled task's Properties dialog box

Virtual memory. To modify the virtual memory configuration in Windows, right-click the My Computer icon and choose Properties → Performance → Virtual Memory. You can specify which hard disk contains the swap file and how small and large it can grow. After you restart the machine and return to the Virtual Memory dialog box, the setting will seem to have reverted to letting Windows handle virtual memory. That's normal—Windows is handling virtual memory, but now using the settings you provided.

Disk cache. Windows handles its own disk cache automatically, too, although here again, you can modify it to increase speed slightly.

1. Right-click My Computer. From the pop-up menu, choose Properties →

Performance → File System → Hard Disk.

2. From the "Typical role of this computer" menu, choose "Network server." Doing so forces the computer to *cache*, or memorize for speed, more directory paths and filenames.

This setting consumes 30K more memory than the "Desktop computer" setting, but makes windows and some menus appear faster when opened.

Also make sure that the settings in the CD-ROM tab match the speed of your CD-ROM drive, which is probably a quad-speed or faster drive. Unless the PC has less than 12 MB of RAM total, set the supplemental cache size to the largest setting, 1238K, using the slider.

H–M

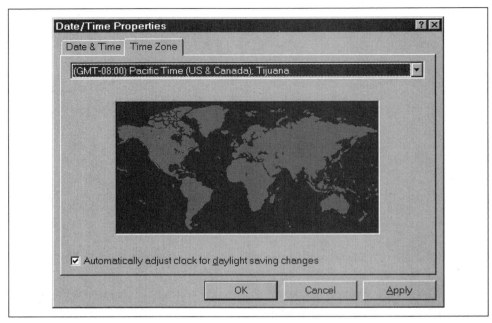

Figure M-3. Choosing a time zone in the Date/Time control panel

RAM disk. Windows offers no equivalent to the Mac's built-in RAM disk capability.

Memory Usage

In Windows: My Computer Properties; Virtual Memory

To find out how much RAM your PC has, right-click the My Computer icon. From the pop-up menu, choose Properties. Look at the bottom of the dialog box to see how much RAM is installed.

If you're familiar with how the Macintosh manages memory—where each application claims a certain chunk of memory, which it then relinquishes when quitting—you'll appreciate how memory generally works in Windows: for the most part, automatically.

Virtual memory is always turned on in Windows, exactly as on the Macintosh. In Windows, however, the amount of hard disk space used by this memory-optimizing scheme constantly changes according to the demands your work places on the PC's memory. You can change some of its settings, such as the hard disk that Windows

uses for virtual memory; right-click My Computer and choose Properties → Performance → Virtual Memory (see Figure M-4). Otherwise, however, it's best to let Windows manage your virtual memory with no intervention from you.

As on the Macintosh, virtual memory on a PC uses empty hard disk space as temporary artificial memory when you run out of RAM. It's important, therefore, to avoid letting your hard disk fill up. If you run low on disk space, Windows has more trouble swapping information to the hard disk and performance may suffer badly. Worse, you may experience random problems before Windows complains about being out of memory.

When your disk starts to fill up, you can use Disk Cleanup in Windows 98 to remove unnecessary files; a message may even warn you that your disk is getting full. Disk Cleanup is located at Start → Programs → Accessories → System Tools → Disk Cleanup. In older versions of Windows, just delete some files or uninstall applications using Control Panel → Add/Remove Programs.

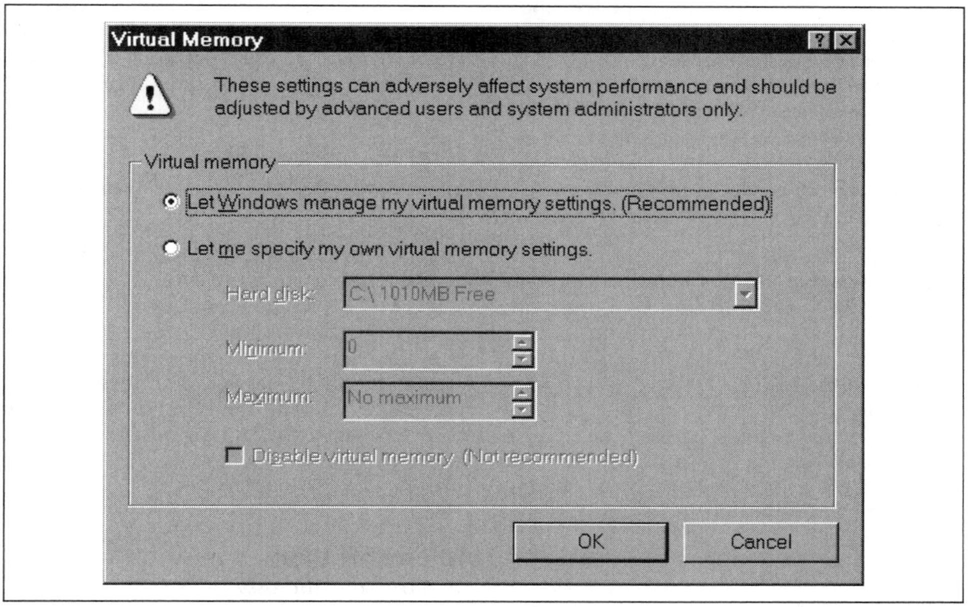

Figure M-4. Virtual Memory dialog box

Menu Bar
In Windows: Menu Bar, Taskbar

As a Macintosh user, you're accustomed to seeing a single menu bar at the top of the screen. Windows is totally different—in Windows, you'll see a menu bar at the top of every single window.

The closest interface element Windows has to the Mac's top-of-screen menu bar is the Taskbar, the strip of icons at the bottom of the screen. If you're trying to make the Windows Desktop feel more familiar, consider moving the Taskbar to the top of the screen—just drag it by any unoccupied gray area.

Doing so makes the Start menu, now located at the top-left corner of the screen, simulate the Apple menu. It also makes the Tray (the collection of icons on the right side of the Taskbar) emulate the right side of the Macintosh menu bar, which generally holds the clock and various utility menus. (See **Control Strip** for details on the Tray and Taskbar.)

If you're a keyboard-shortcut lover, you may be pleased to discover that you can open Windows menus without using the mouse—you can actually pull down the menu with a keystroke so that you can survey its contents. See **Menus** for details.

Menus
In Windows: Menus

Menus are one of the primary interface elements of both Windows and the Mac OS. As on the Macintosh, you can click once on a menu to open it, after which it stays down, even if you release the mouse button. (In Windows, however, the menu doesn't close automatically after 15 seconds, as on the Macintosh—it stays open until you make a selection or press Esc.)

If you're used to older Macintosh operating systems, in which menus don't stay down when clicked, you can still use Windows menus in the traditional way—by keeping the mouse button depressed continuously as you open the menu and drag down to the command you want.

H-M

One of the first things you'll notice about Windows menus is that one letter of each menu name is underlined. If you open a menu, you'll see that each menu command also has such an underline. These are *keyboard accelerators*—keyboard shortcuts that let you open menus and make selections from them without using the mouse.

The key to mastering these underlined commands is the Alt key. For example, you might notice that the first menu in your program is called File, and the Save command is in that menu. Without using the mouse, then, you could press Alt-F (to open the File menu) and then Alt-S (to use the Save command). Eventually, after you've had some practice, many Windows users fall into the practice of pressing F and then S in rapid sequence while pressing Alt, thus opening the menu and choosing the command in a single step.

Microphones
In Windows: Microphones

Most Macs come with a microphone jack, and many also include either a built-in or external microphone for recording sounds. In the PC world, however, equipping your machine with a sound card (if your computer doesn't include one) and microphone is generally left up to you. Refer to the sound card's documentation for details on what sort of microphones it supports.

Microsoft Excel
In Windows: Microsoft Excel

If you use Microsoft Excel 98 on the Macintosh, you can use Microsoft Excel 97 in Windows without having to learn anything new. Even the file format is identical—you can email or otherwise transfer Excel files between the two platforms without having to convert them.

Microsoft Outlook Express
In Windows: Microsoft Outlook Express

As with the other programs included in today's Microsoft Office, the email program Outlook Express is nearly identical on Macintosh and Windows. Outlook Express for Windows is a free download from *http://www.microsoft.com/ie/ie40/oe/*; it also comes with Windows 98 and Internet Explorer.

Microsoft PowerPoint
In Windows: Microsoft PowerPoint

PowerPoint, the leading presentation/slide show software on the Macintosh, is also available in a nearly identical version on Windows. It's included with Microsoft Office 97 for Windows, and is also sold separately. As with the other programs in today's Microsoft Office, PowerPoint files are 100 percent cross-platform: you can email (or otherwise transfer) a PowerPoint file back and forth between Windows and Macintosh with no conversion necessary.

Microsoft Word
In Windows: Microsoft Word

The level of your comfort using Microsoft Word in Windows (known as WinWord by the insiders) depends on the version you're accustomed to using on the Macintosh. Word 98 on the Macintosh is nearly identical to Word 97 for Windows, for example; the documents produced by these two programs share the same file format, and can be freely exchanged with no conversion necessary. Likewise, Word 6.0 on the Macintosh is equivalent to Word 95 in Windows. Earlier versions of the program weren't identical, however, and file translators downloaded from the Microsoft web site may be necessary to convert their files.

Modem Control Panel
In Windows: Modems Control Panel

In Windows, you probably won't have to fiddle with modem settings, provided Windows detects your modem properly. However, if you do need to configure your modem, the Modems control panel provides all the options you need. It's accessible from Control Panel → Modems.

General tab. In the General tab, you can add and remove modem information and modify modem settings. You can also modify dialing properties such as location and area code, plus options for accessing outside lines, disabling call waiting, and using credit cards for long distance calls.

To modify settings for a modem, click its name in the list, and then click Properties. Another dialog box appears, with a General tab and a Connection tab.

The General tab contains the basic options for choosing a serial port, setting speaker volume, and setting maximum speed. The more powerful settings are in the Connection tab, where you can change both connection and call preferences. You shouldn't need to change the connection preferences since almost everything uses eight data bits, no parity, and one stop bit. The call preferences might be more useful; for instance, not waiting for a dial tone can be useful when traveling in countries with different dial tones.

The truly tweaky settings such as flow control and modulation type live in the Advanced Connection Settings dialog box (see Figure M-5). Pay special attention to the Extra settings field, since you can use it

to override the default modem initialization string that Windows uses. You might need to do this to change the initialization string to connect with weird modems or for other unlikely situations.

The Diagnostics tab of the Modems control panel provides technical information about the driver your modem uses and internal modem settings. Click More Info to see the internal settings; that information might be useful for serious troubleshooting, but it's not light reading.

Modem Port
In Windows: Serial Port

PCs generally come with two serial ports, called COM1 and COM2, although one is often taken up by an internal modem. The occasional PC may also have an additional serial card that provides two more serial ports, called COM3 and COM4. You can plug much more than just external modems into these jacks—you can also connect a mouse, printer, PalmPilot HotSync cradle, and similar add-ons to COM ports.

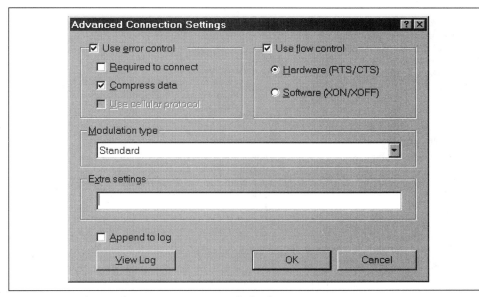

Figure M-5. Advanced Connection Settings dialog box

Figure M-6. PC serial ports

PC serial ports use either DB-25 or DB-9 jacks (see Figure M-6).

In general, Windows serial ports are dramatically more complex than those on the Macintosh; persuading a knowledgeable guru to help you with such configurations is almost always a good idea. For example, inside the PC, your COM ports get the CPU's attention by making an interrupt request—an IRQ. Because the PC has a limited number of channels over which these requests can take place, some COM ports (such as COM1 and COM3) are designed to share an IRQ channel. If action takes place on these two ports simultaneously, the result is the common Windows headache known as an *IRQ conflict*. Whatever was plugged into those two COM ports—a modem and a mouse, for example—is temporarily disabled. In such an event, you have no choice but to call the PC manufacturer's help line.

You can learn more about how a serial port is configured by right-clicking My Computer and choosing Properties → Device Manager → Ports (COM & LPT) → Communication Port (COM1) → Properties. Don't

change the low-level port settings unless you know what you're doing.

Modems

In Windows: Modems

In general, modems work exactly alike on Macs and Windows. In fact, you can sometimes move the identical modem between platforms, provided you overcome the incompatibility of connections and driver software. Refer to Table M-1 for information about modem cross-platform compatibility.

Once a modem connected to a PC, Windows automatically detects it and tries to install the correct drivers. If Windows can't identify the modem, or the modem won't connect with the default settings, you might have to modify settings in Control Panel → Modems → General → Properties. In addition, you can access the useful Windows 98 Modem Troubleshooter from Control Panel → Modems → Diagnostics → Help.

For more information about configuring a modem, see **Modem Control Panel** and **Remote Access Control Panel**.

Table M-1. Modem Cross-Platform Compatibility

Modem Type	Compatibility Notes
Macintosh external modems	Generally compatible with PCs, once you add a PC serial cable. A few external Macintosh modems (such as Global Village models) come with nonstandard cabling that can't easily be adapted for the PC. Finding a Windows modem driver for a Macintosh modem shouldn't be a problem for most well-known brands.
Macintosh internal modems	Both connector and software driver problems make these modems incompatible with PCs.
Macintosh-oriented PC Card modems	Generally compatible with PC Card-capable PC laptops, but verify Windows modem driver availability with the manufacturer.

Figure M-7. PC monitor port

Monitor Port

In Windows: Video Connector

All PCs sold today come with standard 15-pin video connectors (see Figure M-7), often called VGA connectors—precisely the same monitor jack found on today's Macs. (Very old PCs might have 9-pin connectors for older video standards such as EGA or CGA, but you shouldn't see those on any modern PC.) The happy result is that you can freely move monitors between Macs and PCs without buying so much as a single adapter.

Monitors

In Windows: Monitors

Most monitors sold today are *multiple frequency* monitors (also called *multisync* monitors), which means, among other things, that they'll work with both PCs and Macs. Better yet, all Macintosh models today feature standard PC-style VGA monitor connectors on the back panel. (When installing an older Apple monitor onto your PC, you may need an inexpensive adapter, available from an electronics shop or online mail-order web site, for the video connector.)

If you have Windows 98 or later, you can connect multiple monitors to your PC; the additional monitors act as an extension of the primary monitor's Desktop. Setting up such a configuration isn't, however, anywhere near as simple as doing so on the Macintosh. For example, in Windows, you must define one monitor as your primary monitor, which is always fixed in the upper-left corner of the virtual Desktop. The primary monitor can be connected to almost any video card, but each secondary monitor requires one of a small set of video cards, such as the ATI Mach 64, Rage I, and Rage II. Be sure to check this capability before buying a video card for use with a secondary monitor.

In addition, the BIOS (roughly equivalent to the Macintosh ROM chips that store low-level instructions on how the machine works) on your PC must correctly identify which video card is driving the primary monitor. If the BIOS doesn't let you select which video card is the primary one, it decides based on the order of the PCI slots in the machine. In this case, install the primary video card in the highest priority PCI slot—the easiest way of determining this is probably through trial and error, starting with the PCI slots on the ends.

Monitors & Sound Control Panel

In Windows: Display Control Panel's Settings Tab, Sounds Control Panel, Multimedia Control Panel

In Windows, you make the settings for your monitors, sounds, and speakers in separate control panels; there's no direct equivalent to the Mac's centralized Monitors & Sound control panel.

Monitor tab. On the Macintosh you specify the resolution and color settings for your monitor by clicking the Monitors icon in Monitors & Sound. In Windows, you make the settings in Control Panel → Display → Settings (see Figure M-8). The options for number of colors are essentially the same as on the Macintosh, although the terms are different. In Windows, "High Color (16 bit)" corresponds to the Macintosh "Thousands" setting, and "True Color (24 bit)" is the same as the Mac's "Millions." The available screen resolutions are accessible from the Screen area slider; the options here depend on your video card model. Similarly, clicking Advanced brings up the Properties for your specific video card.

Although Windows 95 can't work with more than one monitor, Windows 98 supports up to nine of them, and the "Extend my Windows Desktop onto this monitor" checkbox

H-M

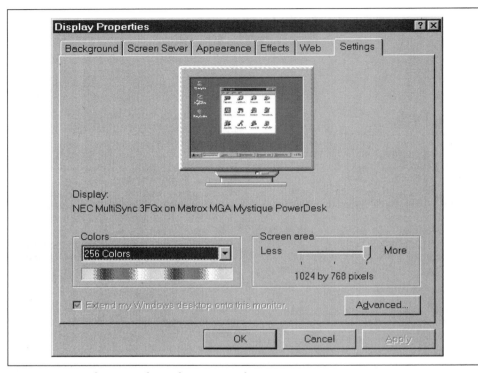

Figure M-8. Display control panel's Settings tab

lets you create a large Desktop, as is the default on the Macintosh. (If that checkbox is unchecked, you see the same image on all monitors.)

The primary monitor is always fixed in the upper-left corner of the virtual Desktop; the secondary monitors can be arranged as you like.

Sound tab. The Sound panel of Monitors & Sound lets you adjust your speaker volume and identify what sound source you'd like to record from (CD-ROM, microphone, and so on).

In Windows, you use the Multimedia control panel for the same purpose (Control Panel → Multimedia). Just drag the Volume slider to adjust your overall speaker volume. To fine tune your speaker sound, you can also use the Volume Control application, available at Start → Programs → Accessories → Multimedia → Volume Control (see Figure M-9); on some systems, a corre-

sponding icon is available at the right side of your Taskbar, as described in **Control Strip**.

The Multimedia control panel also lets you specify the sound source for recording your own sounds in Windows, exactly as on the Macintosh. The Preferred Device corresponds to the Mac's Sound Monitoring Source pop-up menu, and the Preferred Quality pop-up menu corresponds to the Mac's Sound Output Quality pop-up menu.

Alerts. To specify what sound effect you'd like Windows to use as its error beep, choose Control Panel → Sounds. You'll discover here that Windows can play a different beep sound to each error event—one sound when a program quits unexpectedly, another when an error message appears, and so on—as well as many non-error events, such as opening or closing a window. To use this control panel, click the name of an event in the list. Then, using the

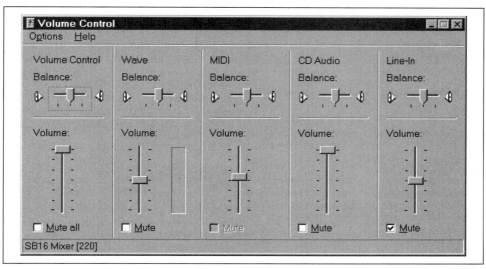

Figure M-9. Volume Control window

Name pop-up menu below the list, choose the sound effect you want to associate.

Motherboards
In Windows: Motherboards

Macintosh users don't think about swapping motherboards because Apple motherboards aren't interchangeable among different models. However, in the PC world, you might very well want to speed up your machine by installing a faster motherboard. Although doing so isn't a task for a novice, various books can walk you through the process; visit a bookstore and browse through the PC hardware section to find one you like. You can also upgrade the CPU chip itself in many PCs, provided your motherboard is designed to accommodate a faster chip.

Mouse
In Windows: Mouse

Using a mouse in Windows is almost exactly the same as using one on the Macintosh, with one major exception. The standard Macintosh mouse has only a single button, whereas a PC mouse sports two. The left PC mouse button corresponds to the Macintosh mouse button; the right PC mouse but-

ton generally does what Control-clicking something does on the Macintosh. In addition to summoning contextual menus, right-clicking in Windows may also bring up contextual help (see **Help**) and options for moving files and copying files.

Many modern PC models come with a Microsoft IntelliMouse—easily identified by the small rubber roller wheel nestled between the two mouse buttons. In many programs, rolling this wheel with your index finger does nothing at all. In Microsoft programs and some others, however, rolling this wheel scrolls the current window or list, saving you a trip to the scroll bar.

When you want to scroll in more dramatic increments, push down on the roller wheel as you drag upward or downward. Using this power-scrolling method, you can zoom all the way to the top or bottom of a document with only a single mouse gesture—but without much precision, of course.

Mouse Control Panel
In Windows: Mouse Control Panel

The Macintosh Mouse control panel lets you choose the speed of the mouse tracking (how fast the cursor moves when you move

H–M

the mouse) and the double-click speed (how quickly you must click twice for the computer to register a double-click instead of two separate clicks). The Mouse control panel in Windows provides the same settings, plus a few more.

In the Buttons tab, you can swap the two mouse buttons, which is handy if you're left-handed. The Motion tab lets you turn on pointer trails, which could conceivably be useful on laptops with lousy LCD screens. (Macintosh PowerBook laptops offer the same feature.)

The Windows Mouse control panel even lets you choose from among different mouse pointer shapes. (Click the Pointers tab to see your choices.) You can choose "schemes" (sets of related pointers), or you can change any individual pointer by clicking Browse and then selecting a different cursor file.

Movie Player

In Windows: Media Player, Active Movie Control

On the Macintosh, you use the Movie Player or QuickTime Player program to view digital QuickTime movies. If you're trying to find a similar program in Windows, look no further than Media Player, located in Start → Programs → Accessories → Entertainment [or Multimedia] → Media Player.

Media Player can play a wide variety of multimedia files, including ActiveMovie files, Video for Windows, sound files, MIDI files, and CD audio (although playing audio CDs is better done with CD Player). Media Player's interface resembles a CD player or VCR (see Figure M-10). Media Player can also show you the scale in time, frames, or tracks and play selections from a file. You can even include a multimedia file in a document by opening it in Media Player, choosing Edit → Copy Object, and then pasting it into your document.

Moving Files

In Windows: Moving Files, Copying Files

There's little to moving files and folders on the Macintosh—you just drag the file or folder's icon from one window to another on the same disk. The situation is much more complicated in Windows, where there are multiple ways to move files and folders around. Note that Windows doesn't offer a "spring-loaded folder" feature, as in Mac OS 8 and later.

Here are a number of different ways you can move a file from one location to another:

- Drag any file icon (except that of an application) or folder icon from one window to another on the same disk, exactly as on the Macintosh.

- Drag any file or folder from one disk to another, holding down Shift after you start dragging.

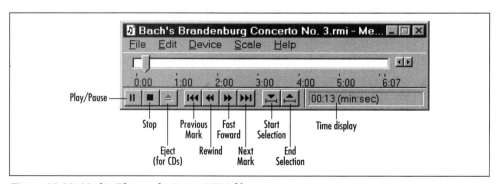

Figure M-10. Media Player playing a MIDI file

- Right-drag any file or folder from one window to another on any disk, and then choose Move Here from the contextual menu that appears.

- Select one or more files or folders, and then choose Edit → Cut. (Alternatively, right-click one of the selected items and choose Cut.) Then switch to another window and choose Edit → Paste. Using this technique, you can even "paste" files onto a different disk.

A few aspects of moving files in Windows may catch you by surprise:

- If you drag an application, Windows makes a shortcut (alias) in the destination instead of moving the actual application. The cursor shape lets you know what's about to happen: if you see a tiny curved arrow on your cursor, Windows is about to make a shortcut (see Figure M-11). For more information about shortcuts, see **Alias**.

- You can change a move into a copy by pressing Ctrl while dragging. However, there's no way to turn a move action into a shortcut creation action.

- Once you've begun to drag an icon, you can change your mind—making

the icon snap back to its original location—by clicking the other mouse button or by pressing Esc.

- You cannot move a file into or out of the My Computer window. Anything you drag out of this window becomes a shortcut.

- Moving files in Explorer windows works just like moving them in Desktop windows; you can drag files or folders from the left pane to a folder in the right pane. (See **Finder** for details on Explorer windows.)

Multitasking
In Windows: Multitasking

Despite the online battles waged by proponents of each platform, you won't notice much difference between the multitasking schemes used by the Macintosh and Windows. On either platform, you can download a file from the Internet while retrieving your email, browsing the Web, and writing in a word processor. For information about switching between different applications in Windows, see **Application Menu**.

Figure M-11. Curved-arrow badge on cursor when making a shortcut

N

Netscape Navigator/ Communicator

In Windows: Netscape Navigator/ Communicator

The Macintosh and Windows versions of Netscape Navigator and Communicator are even more alike than the corresponding versions of Microsoft Internet Explorer. Better yet, the Windows versions of Netscape's browsers seem to have been designed first on the Macintosh, so they're among the easiest Internet programs to use on both platforms. You can learn more about the Windows version of Netscape Communicator and download a copy from Netscape's web site at *http://www.netscape.com/ computing/download/index.html*.

Network Browser

In Windows: Network Neighborhood

In Mac OS 8.5, Apple introduced Network Browser, which helps you find and connect to file servers on your network. The corresponding program in Windows is called Network Neighborhood. (If it doesn't show up on your Windows Desktop, you can add it from Control Panel → Network → Config-

uration → Add → Client → Microsoft → Client for Microsoft Networks.)

Using Network Neighborhood to browse for, and connect to file and print servers on your network is simplicity itself. Double-click the Network Neighborhood icon, and then double-click the icon for the server you want to access. The process works exactly like opening folders in Windows, with three exceptions:

- In the main Network Neighborhood window, you'll see an icon for Entire Network, along with icons for servers in your local workgroup. If your network includes multiple workgroups, double-click Entire Network to move up a level to view other workgroups.

- If you view the Network Neighborhood window in Details view (View → Details), the Comment column may provide useful information about specific servers (see Figure N-1). Comments aren't available in other views.

- When you double-click a server icon in the Network Neighborhood window, you'll see a folder icon for each shared folder, and a printer icon for each

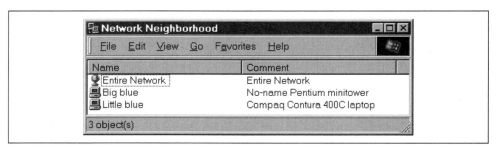

Figure N-1. Network Neighborhood in Details view

shared printer. Printers otherwise show up only in My Computer → Printers.

Note

If your network includes many servers, you may prefer to search for a particular server instead of browsing for it manually. To do so, right-click Network Neighborhood and then choose Find (or choose Start → Find → Computer). Then enter the name of the computer you want to find; click the Find button. Matching computers are displayed in a list below the search field; double-click to open any of them.

Simplifying access. After you've located and connected to either a shared folder or printer, you can simplify the process of connecting to that resource again in the future.

As a Macintosh user, your first reaction might be to create a shortcut to the resource, just as you'd create an alias to a shared folder on an AppleShare server. This trick works well in Windows, too. However, you can also map a shared folder to a drive letter, after which the shared folder appears in My Computer just as though it were another disk.

Networking Macs and PCs together. Thanks to some ingenious software tools, Macs and PCs can exist on the same network, sharing hard disks and printers as though there were no OS difference whatsoever.

Consider, for example, the Macintosh-side software known as DAVE (*http://www. thursby.com/*). It adds Windows' NetBIOS networking protocol, which permits the Macintosh to connect to Windows machines (versions 3.1, NT, or whatever). DAVE requires no installation on the PC side—a relief to Macintosh fans who can continue using their favorite machine without bothering the company's tech staff. Once DAVE is running, PC users see Macs and Macintosh printers through the standard Network Neighborhood program; Macintosh users see PC volumes through the Chooser or Network Browser.

DAVE is great for introducing a Macintosh minority to a larger PC network. If you're in the opposite situation, adding a few Windows machines to a predominantly Macintosh network, buy PC MACLAN instead (*http://www.miramarsys.com/*). It lets a PC access the network's Macintosh printers and hard disks through the standard Network Neighborhood program. In fact, if you launch the included AppleShare Server software on the Windows machine, the PC can also become available to the Macs on the network—using the same Chooser or Network Browser software the Macintosh users would ordinarily use to access other networked Macs.

Network Control Panel
In Windows: Network Control Panel

Before the release of the AppleTalk control panel several years ago, the Mac OS included a Network control panel that let you specify which kind of physical network (LocalTalk, Ethernet) you wanted to use. In Windows, you use the Network control panel for that task; see **Networking** for the basics of Windows networking and **AppleTalk Control Panel** for the details of using the Network control panel.

Networking
In Windows: Networking

Configuring your network on Windows is quite a bit different from doing so on the Macintosh.

Windows networking basics. The Mac OS separates networking resources by protocol and task, providing you with AppleTalk and TCP/IP control panels to set up your network configuration and the File Sharing control panel to configure file sharing. In Windows, on the other hand, everything is bundled together into the Network control panel (Control Panel → Network). Within the Network control panel, Windows provides four types of network components:

Client
> Client components help you connect to servers on your network. If you want to access files on a remote server, you

N–R

need the appropriate client software installed. The most common is "Client for Microsoft Networks." The Macintosh equivalent is the AppleShare extension.

Adapter

Adapter components let you configure the physical network interfaces, such as Ethernet cards. You must have a software adapter for each card type. If you have a modem, you'll need a Dial-Up Adapter as well. For the most part, you don't configure adapters, although the Bindings tab in the Properties dialog box for each one lets you specify which protocols the adapter will use. For instance, you might not want your Dial-Up Adapter to use NetBEUI, just TCP/IP. On the Macintosh, you specify adapters in the "Connect via" pop-up menu in the AppleTalk and TCP/IP control panels.

Protocol

Protocol components let the PC speak specific protocols, or network languages. For communication to take place, all the computers involved must be configured to use the same protocol using the same type of adapter (protocols are "bound" to adapters, which means that that adapter uses that protocol). Most of your networking configuration takes place at the protocol level, especially if you're using a protocol like TCP/IP that can require a fair amount of manual configuration. The Macintosh equivalents are the AppleTalk control panel and TCP/IP control panel.

Service

Service components let you share folders and printers with other people on your network. If you want to set up your computer as a server for others to access for file or printer sharing, you must install and configure the appropriate service, the most common of which is "File and printer sharing for Microsoft Networks." On the Macintosh, you'd use the File Sharing control panel and the Printer Share extension. See **File Sharing** and **Printer Sharing** for more information.

Procedures. To install a new networking component in the Network control panel, click Add, choose the component type, and then choose the appropriate component. Make sure you have your Windows CD handy, since Windows will almost certainly need to install some new files.

To remove a networking component because you're not using it, select it in the list and click Remove. Keep notes on what you've done, since if something stops working after removing a component, you should reinstall it.

To modify the configuration for a component, either double-click it or select it and then click Properties. Windows opens a tabbed Properties dialog box offering configuration choices. Configuration possibilities break down like this:

- Client components primarily offer logon options.

- With adapter components, you're most likely to want to choose which protocols to bind in the Bindings tab; you can also fiddle with advanced settings if you know what you're doing.

- Protocol components also offer bindings and advanced options, plus any standardized options necessary for that protocol. For instance, TCP/IP requires an IP address, gateway, and DNS configuration, all of which you set in different Properties tabs (see **TCP/IP Control Panel** for help).

- Service components offer various settings appropriate to that service.

Other networking related entries. In today's networked world, large portions of both the Mac OS and Windows are linked to networking. The following entries should get you started in networking on Windows. For Internet-specific references, see **Internet**.

- For information about sharing files in Windows, see **AppleShare** and **File Sharing**.

- For information about sharing printers in Windows, see **Printer Sharing**.

- For information about configuring PCs to see each other on a network, see **AppleTalk Control Panel**.

- For information about connecting a Windows-based PC to the Internet via a modem, see **Remote Access Control Panel** and modems.

- For information about connecting a Windows-based PC to the Internet via a network, see **TCP/IP Control Panel.**

- For information about transferring files from a Macintosh to a Windows-based PC via a network, see **Transferring Files to Windows.**

Note Pad
In Windows: Notepad, WordPad

On the Macintosh, the Note Pad desk accessory holds short notes. There's no direct equivalent in Windows, though you can just create text files in either Notepad (Start menu → Programs → Accessories → Notepad) or WordPad (Start menu → Programs → Accessories → WordPad), just as you might in SimpleText on the Macintosh.

For the record, the primary difference is that Notepad creates pure text files without any formatting. WordPad can not only create files with fonts, sizes, and type styles, but also read and save Microsoft Word documents.

NuBus Slots and Cards
In Windows: PCI Slots and Cards

Over the years, Macs have sported a number of different types of expansion slots. From 1989 to 1995, the most common Macintosh expansion slot was the industry standard NuBus specification. Although a standard, it wasn't used in the PC world, and in 1995, Apple switched to using the higher performance PCI (Peripheral Component Interconnect) bus for expansion slots.

In the Windows world, expansion cards today come in the PCI format, exactly as on all Macs made since 1995. For details, see **PCI Slots and Cards.**

Numbers Control Panel
In Windows: Regional Settings Control Panel

The Mac's Numbers control panel lets you choose among a variety of settings that relate to how numbers are displayed in different countries.

Windows provides more control over number display in the Regional Settings control panel. In Control Panel → Regional Settings → Number, you can specify how numbers should appear (see Figure N-2). And in Control Panel → Regional Settings → Currency, you can choose how currency numbers should appear.

Most people in the U.S. don't need to change the defaults. If you live in a part of the world were numbers are written differently, changing the settings is merely a matter of choosing the appropriate options from the drop-down menu.

Whether on Macintosh or Windows, you won't see the effects of your changes except in a couple of out of the way places: the currency setting affects Microsoft Excel, and large-number punctuation may appear in the Size column of your Desktop list views.

Num Lock Key
In Windows: Num Lock Key

Older PC keyboards lacked separate cursor keys; in those days, a press of the Num Lock key turned the number keypad into its alternate function as cursor keys.

That workaround is no longer necessary in this age where every keyboard has a separate bank of cursor keys. Even so, the Num Lock key still appears on most PC keyboards; it's virtually useless except in certain Microsoft programs. For example, in Microsoft Word, pressing this key performs its time-honored function of turning the number keypad into cursor keys.

N-R

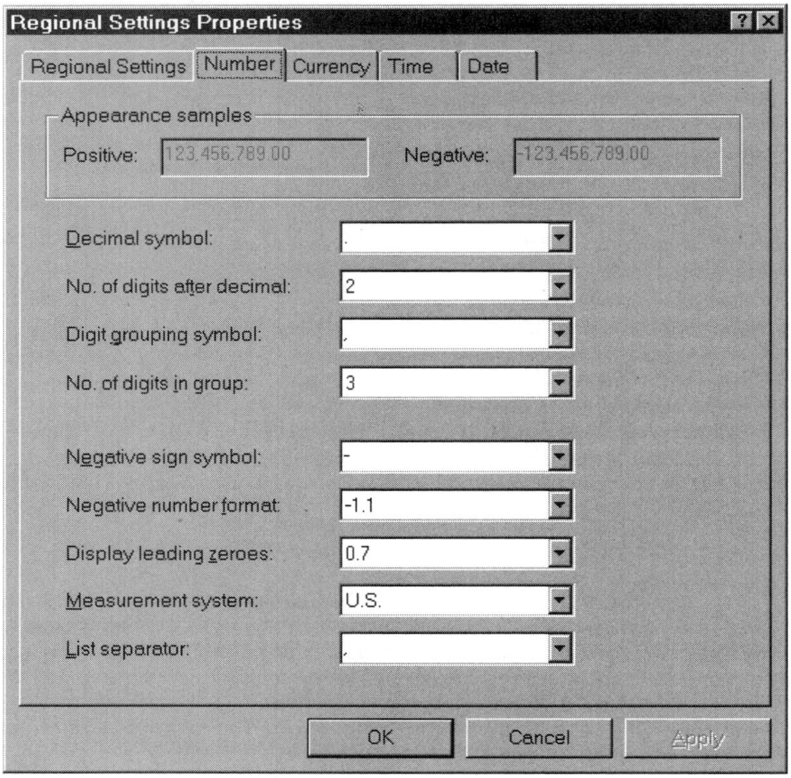

Figure N-2. Regional Settings control panel's Numbers tab

O

OLE

In Windows: OLE

Object Linking and Embedding, or OLE, is Microsoft's technology for embedding live, self-updating copies of one kind of data—such as spreadsheet data—in another kind of document, such as a word processing document. OLE is fairly similar to the Mac's Publish and Subscribe technology.

You can insert OLE data from one program, such as a spreadsheet, into another program, such as Word, in one of two ways: as *linked* data, which updates automatically when you change the source material, and as *embedded* data, which, like a standard piece of pasted data, maintains no link to any extra document. (Use File → Insert and then turn on "Link to file" to create a self-updating link.) Consult the application's manual for details on how to link or embed objects appropriately.

Opening Files

In Windows: Opening Files

The basics of opening files are similar in both Macintosh and Windows, but the preferred methods of working differ.

Documents and applications. As on the Macintosh, there are quite a few possible ways of opening documents and applications in Windows, including these:

- Double-click the icon (or a shortcut to it).
- Right-click the icon and then choose Open from the contextual menu.
- Right-click a document's icon; choose Quick View from the contextual menu. This option isn't available for all documents and doesn't open the document in the application that created it, but instead in a separate Quick View window.
- Drag a document's icon onto the icon of an application that can open it.
- Drag a document's icon to a window of an application that can read the document. This works primarily when dropping icons into web browser windows.
- Select the icon (in a window, not on the Desktop), and then choose File → Open or press Enter.
- Open an application that can read the document, and then choose File → Open from within that application.
- Choose a document from Start → Documents if you've worked with the document recently. See **Recent Documents Menu** for more information.
- In a Windows 98 window, select a document or program icon and then choose Favorites → Add to Favorites. Then choose the item from the Favorites menu in a window or from Start → Favorites. See **Favorites Menu**.
- Drag an icon to the Windows 98 Start menu; without releasing the mouse button, navigate down until you can drop the icon in the StartUp folder at Start → Programs → StartUp. Doing so ensures that every time Windows starts up, that document or program will open automatically. For more information, see **Startup Items Folder**.
- Choose an application's name from Start → Programs. This is the most common way of opening applications in Windows.
- Choose Start → Run, type the name of the application, and press Enter.

Folders and disks. Use the following methods to open folders or disks:

- Double-click the folder's icon or a shortcut to the folder.

- Right-click the folder's icon and then choose Explore to display the two-paned Explorer window. Click the plus sign next to the folder's name in the left pane to reveal nested folders inside it, or click the folder's name to display its contents in the right pane.

- In a window, select the folder icon and then choose Favorites → Add to Favorites. Then choose the folder from the Favorites menu in a window or from Start → Favorites. See **Favorites Menu**.

- Select the folder's icon (only in windows, not on the Desktop) and then choose File → Open or File → Explore.

- Drag the folder's icon to the Windows 98 Start menu. Without releasing the mouse button, navigate down until you can drop the icon in the StartUp folder at Start → Programs → StartUp. Doing so ensures that every time Windows starts up, that folder will open automatically. For more information, see **Startup Items Folder**.

Option Key
In Windows: Alt Key

In Windows, the Alt key is similar to the Mac's Option key. Its common functions in Windows include the following:

- In applications, you can use the Alt key followed by a sequence of letter keys to access menus from the keyboard. For instance, instead of choosing Exit from the File menu with the mouse you could press Alt, release the key, press F, release the key, and then press X. (You know which keys to press because you noticed which letter is underlined in each menu name and menu command.) You can also keep the Alt key depressed continuously as you press the keyboard shortcuts, but doing so isn't necessary.

- In dialog boxes, you can click buttons and access pop-down menus using the Alt key simultaneously with letter keys. As with menus, the appropriate letter is underlined. For instance, in the Shutdown dialog box, to restart the PC press Alt; while holding it down press R and then O.

- When typing text you can use the Alt key plus a four-digit number to enter characters (such as accented characters) that you can't normally type from the keyboard. For instance, to type a paragraph mark, press Alt, and then type 0182. Obviously, this technique requires looking up the appropriate numeric code for each character in each font; it's easier to use the Character Map utility in the Accessories folder's System Tools folder (see **Key Caps** for more information).

Along with these generic uses for the Alt key, Windows offers a number of keyboard shortcuts that rely on the Alt key, as listed in Table O-1.

Table O-1. Keyboard Shortcuts Using the Alt Key

Keyboard Shortcut	Function
Alt-*	In the Explorer, pressing Alt-* expands all the branches in the folder hierarchy. (Use the * on the keypad.)
Alt-Enter	Alt-Enter displays the Properties dialog box for the currently selected item. See **Get Info Command**. If you're using a DOS program, pressing Alt-Enter toggles between displaying DOS in a window and in full-screen mode.
Alt-Esc	Pressing Alt-Esc switches you to the next active application without showing the list of active applications and open folders, exactly like the Mac's Command-Tab keystroke. See **Application Menu**.

Table O-1. Keyboard Shortcuts Using the Alt Key (continued)

Keyboard Shortcut	Function
Alt-F4	No matter where you are in Windows, pressing Alt-F4 closes the active application window, which has the effect of quitting some applications, like Microsoft Word. If no windows are active, Alt-F4 displays the Shut Down Windows dialog box. See **Shut Down**.
Alt-Print Screen	If you press Alt-Print Screen, Windows copies the active window to the clipboard (Print Screen alone copies the entire Windows Desktop to the clipboard). See **Screen Capture**.
Alt-Spacebar	Pressing Alt-Spacebar is the same as clicking the system menu icon (the tiny icon to the left of the File menu in most programs). Once the system menu is visible, you can use Alt plus letter keys to access any of the menu items.
Alt-Tab	Pressing Alt-Tab makes a list of active applications appear. Press the keystroke repeatedly to cycle through the active applications' icons—when you release the keys, you jump to the highlighted program. See **Application Menu**.
Alt-Tab-click	If you're in a full-screen DOS program, press Alt-Tab and click either mouse button to display the Windows Desktop.

N-R

P

Page Setup

In Windows: PageMaker

As on the Macintosh, the Page Setup command is available in almost every Windows program's File menu. It offers a dialog box where you can specify page size, margins, and other program-specific options related to printing. The individual options in this dialog box vary widely from Windows program to Windows program, but the idea is the same.

PageMaker

In Windows: PageMaker

If you're accustomed to using PageMaker on the Macintosh, you should have little trouble switching over to PageMaker on Windows. Moving files between platforms may be more complicated, most often because the fonts may not be identical on the two platforms.

Keep in mind that your Windows version of PageMaker can open documents created by the same-numbered Macintosh PageMaker version, but can't open older (or newer) Macintosh PageMaker documents.

For more information about PageMaker and its successor, InDesign, visit *http://www. adobe.com/*.

Note

To open a Macintosh PageMaker 6.0 document in PageMaker 5.0 for Windows, you must first save the file in Macintosh PageMaker 5.0 format. You should now be able to open the document on the PC.

Password Security Control Panel

In Windows: Passwords Control Panel

Macintosh PowerBook users may be used to relying on the security offered by the Password Security control panel, which is available only on PowerBooks. The same basic feature is offered by the Windows control panel called Passwords (Control Panel → Passwords), although this security is much more easily circumvented.

The Windows Passwords control panel has three tabs relating to different password uses:

Change Passwords. In the Change Passwords tab, you can change the Windows password, which is the one that appears at every startup. However, it offers little true security: pressing Esc dismisses the login dialog box, and entering a new username and password creates a new user profile.

Since the Windows password exists primarily to thwart the idle pair of prying eyes, you may wish to shut it off entirely so you don't have to enter a password every time the PC starts up. To eliminate the login dialog box, check these conditions:

- Your Windows password must be blank in Control Panel → Passwords → Change Passwords → Change Windows Password.

- You must disable user profiles by selecting Control Panel → Passwords → User Profiles → "All users of this computer use the same preferences and desktop settings."

- You must set Windows so your primary network logon is Windows Logon, which you do by choosing Control Panel → Network → Configuration → Windows Logon.

If you wish to use user profiles, or to log onto your local network automatically at startup, you'll have to endure having to enter your password on each startup.

Remote Administration. In the Remote Administration tab, you specify whether you want to permit remote administration of your files and printers from other computers. Unless your network administrator tells you to turn this on, leave it off.

User Profiles. The User Profiles tab controls whether you use User Profiles. Here, you can specify which aspects of Windows will be included in the user profiles. Once you've turned on user profiles here, use the Users control panel (Control Panel → Users) to create and set up accounts for new users.

Paste
In Windows: Paste

The Windows Paste command (Ctrl-V) works exactly as it does on the Macintosh (Command-V). On Windows, however, it offers an additional feature: you can actually cut and paste file icons for the purpose of moving them to another window, as described in **Edit Menu**.

PC Cards
In Windows: PC Cards

PC Cards, originally known as PCMCIA cards, are credit card-sized expansion cards commonly used to provide modem or network features to laptops that otherwise lack them. Other uses of PC Cards include hard-disk storage, RAM expansion, ISDN adapters, and even systems that use the Global Positioning System (GPS) satellites to locate your exact position on the planet.

There are three types of PC Cards. Type I cards were designed to be only memory expansion cards; they're 3.3mm thick. Type II cards have many more functions, but are the same size. Type III cards, usually hard disks, are 10.5mm thick. Each type is backward compatible, so you can insert a Type I card into a Type II or Type III slot. Better yet, most Macintosh and PC laptops offer a pair of Type II slots on top of one another;

the advantage of this arrangement is that you can insert either two Type I or Type II cards, or a single Type III card.

Using PC Cards in Windows is much like using them on the Macintosh; you can insert and remove them without having to turn off the computer.

On the other hand, no icon appears on Windows Desktop when you insert a PC card, as it would on the Macintosh. Furthermore, beware: on a Windows PC, you must "stop" a card before ejecting it. To do so, open Control Panel → PC Card, select the PC Card you want to eject, click Stop, and then eject the card manually (by pressing the eject button).

Despite the fact that the PC Card specification is a standard, PC Cards require driver software. Windows comes with a huge database of drivers, and can therefore recognize many PC cards automatically, but you can't assume that a PC Card sold for use on the Macintosh will work with Windows. If your PC doesn't automatically recognize a Macintosh PC Card when you insert it, contact the card's vendor to see if Windows driver software is available.

PC Exchange Control Panel
In Windows: None

The PC Exchange control panel lets Macs read PC-formatted disks and offers some translation capabilities. No equivalent is built into Windows, although you can buy programs like Macintosh Drive 98 for Windows (*http://www.media4.com/*), Conversions Plus and MacOpener from DataViz (*http://www.dataviz.com/*), or MacSEE from Reevesoft (*http://www.reevesoft.com/macsee_info.htm*) that serve the same purpose. For more information, see **File Exchange Control Panel** and **Transferring Files to Windows**.

PCI Slots and Cards
In Windows: PCI Slots and Cards

Over the years, Macs have sported different types of expansion slots. Starting with the Macintosh II, the most common slot was called NuBus. In 1995 and later Macintosh models, Apple substituted the faster PCI (Peripheral Component Interconnect) expansion slots. Today's PCs also contain PCI slots.

Although PCI slots are universal on today's desktop Macintosh models, the PC world evolves more slowly. As a result, although most modern PCs include PCI slots, they also often include the older ISA or EISA slots to support older cards. If you have a choice, always use the PCI version of a card.

Installing a PCI card in a PC is essentially the same as installing one in a Macintosh. The only difficulty you may encounter is the struggle to open your PC's case, depending on its design. Refer to the PC's manual for instructions on opening the case and installing the PCI card.

Don't assume that you can use a PCI card sold for use in a Macintosh. That arrangement may be possible, but check with the card's manufacturer to make sure Windows drivers for the card are available.

PCMCIA
In Windows: PCMCIA

The PCMCIA (Personal Computer Memory Card International Association) specification for credit card-sized expansion cards was considered far too difficult to remember or say (wags claimed it stood for "People Can't Memorize Computer Industry Acronyms"), so PCMCIA cards are now officially known as *PC Cards.*

PDS (Processor Direct Slot) Slots and Cards
In Windows: PCI Slots and Cards

Exactly as on the Macintosh, the expansion slots found in Windows computers have varied over the years—ISA, EISA, and VESA each preceded the current kind of slot, known as PCI. Those are the rough equivalents of the various Macintosh slot types: PDS, NuBus, and today's PCI. See **PCI Slots and Cards.**

Photoshop
In Windows: Photoshop

Adobe Photoshop has become the standard program for photo editing and image production for both Macintosh and Windows users. The program is identical on both platforms, and you can exchange Photoshop files—as well as GIF, TIFF, EPS, and other graphics files, of course—without any conversion. For additional information about Photoshop, visit Adobe's web site at *http:// www.adobe.com/.*

PICT
In Windows: Bitmap

The standard graphics file format on the Macintosh is called PICT and can hold either object-oriented graphics or bitmapped graphics. In general, a bitmapped graphic is composed of a specific arrangement of dots, and the image can be edited only by adding or removing dots. In contrast, object-oriented images contain objects, such as squares and circles, and you can edit them by modifying the object.

In Windows, the most common graphics file format is the bitmap (*.bmp*) file. You encounter this kind of file in a number of situations:

- You can copy the image of the active window or of the entire screen in bitmap format—thus making what's known as a screen capture—by pressing Alt-Print Screen or Print Screen. To paste the image into a document, choose Paste from the Edit menu.

- You can use Paint (or any of many other graphics applications) to create and edit bitmap images.

- You can cover the background of your Desktop with "wallpaper" made of any bitmap image. To do this, open the Display control panel, click the Background tab, and then, in the wallpaper area, click the Browse button. Select any bitmap (or GIF or JPEG) image, and then finally click OK or Apply.

If you need to open a Windows bitmap file on the Macintosh, you can use Picture

Viewer, the free program on every modern Macintosh hard disk (which you can also download as part of the QuickTime software suite from *http://www.apple.com/quicktime/*). You can also use any standard graphics program, such as Photoshop or the shareware GraphicConverter.

Power Key
In Windows: Power Switch

You turn most Macs on and off by pressing the Power key on the keyboard. Every Windows machine, however, is different, but few have keyboard power switches.

Instead, you must generally push a physical switch on the front of the machine to turn it on. And to shut down a Windows PC, choose Start → Shut Down, and then click Shut Down in the dialog box that appears. If you have a relatively modern PC—one that supports the Advanced Power Management specification—the machine then shuts down completely; if it doesn't, you have an older machine that must then be manually switched off using the same power switch.

PPP Control Panel
In Windows: Dial-Up Networking

For information about connecting a PC to the Internet by modem, see **Remote Access Control Panel**.

PRAM (Parameter RAM)
In Windows: None

When the Mac's control panel settings—especially mouse, network, and monitor settings—seem to go awry, the veteran Macintosh user immediately thinks of zapping the PRAM. This troubleshooting trick involves pressing the Command, Option, P and R keys while the Macintosh starts up; after two or three repetitions of the startup chime, the keys are released, and the Macintosh resets all of its control panel settings to their factory defaults.

There's no equivalent in Windows. When mouse, network, and other peripherals begin to act up, your troubleshooting

thoughts should turn to software driver updates and other Windows techniques.

Preferences Folder
In Windows: Registry

On the Macintosh, most applications store their settings and preferences files in the Preferences folder. Windows has no equivalent folder for storing individual configuration files; instead, it relies on a single, preference-collecting database file called the Registry.

Applications (or their installers) can create and modify entries in the Registry, just as applications on the Macintosh manage their own preferences files.

The existence of the Registry explains why you generally can't copy an application to a different PC and expect it to work—without the Registry components created by the original installer, many programs can't run.

As you probably know, you can't manually open a Macintosh preference file to make changes. In contrast, the Windows Registry is, technically speaking, editable, provided you have the Registry Editor program and a great deal of expertise. Registry entries are cryptic, and making a mistake could cripple an application or even Windows itself. Don't mess with the Registry unless you have specific instructions for performing a task.

Printer Port
In Windows: Parallel Ports, Serial Ports

Most inexpensive printers in the Macintosh world connect to the printer port of older Macintosh models, which is technically known as an RS-422 serial port. (There's no printer port on any modern Macintosh at all, of course; USB has replaced the serial port technology of older models.) For more information about serial ports on PCs, see **Modem Port**. In Windows, however, most inexpensive printers connect to the parallel port, which doesn't exist on the Macintosh.

Parallel ports (often called LPT ports) send data on eight lines simultaneously, making them significantly faster than serial ports.

N-R

That's why they're also good for accommodating network adapters, low-speed storage devices, and direct file transfer with other PCs.

A number of different types of parallel ports have appeared over the years, including the original *unidirectional parallel port* (which could only send information), the *bidirectional parallel port* (which could send and receive data and is sometimes referred to as *Standard Parallel Port*, or SPP), the significantly faster *Enhanced Parallel Port* (EPP), and another high-speed variant called the *Enhanced Capabilities Port* (ECP). In modern PCs, you're likely to have combination ECP/EPP ports.

No matter what type of parallel ports the PC sports, the connectors are the same. On the computer, you'll find the DB-25 D-shell connector; on peripherals with parallel ports you'll find 36-pin Centronics connectors that look like SCSI connectors (see Figure P-1).

You can learn more about how a parallel port is configured by right-clicking My Computer and choosing Properties → Device Manager → Ports (COM & LPT) → ECP Printer Port (LPT1) → Properties. Don't change the low-level port settings unless you know what you're doing.

Along with connecting printers to PCs, the most common use of parallel ports is for the Direct Cable Connection; for more information, see **LocalTalk**.

Printer Sharing
In Windows: Printer Sharing

Because of the prevalence of LocalTalk- and Ethernet-compatible printers in the Macintosh world, many Macintosh users don't realize they can also share serial StyleWriter inkjet printers. But you can, thanks to the Printer Share extension. Windows lets you share printers attached directly to a PC in much the same way you share folders on the PC's hard disk.

Note that you can't share a printer attached to a PC with a Macintosh on the same network.

Configuring file and print sharing. To turn on file and print sharing in Windows, follow these steps:

1. Open Control Panel → Network → Identification. Fill in a name, workgroup, and description for your computer.

2. In Control Panel → Network → Configuration's list of network components, make sure you have the same protocol used on both the PC sharing the files and the PC you want to be able to access the files. TCP/IP or NetBEUI work fine.

3. In Control Panel → Network → Configuration's list of network components, make sure you have the "File and printer sharing for Microsoft Networks" service component. If you don't see it

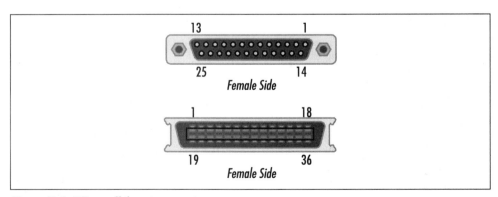

Figure P-1. PC parallel port connectors

in your list, add it by clicking Add → Service → Microsoft → File and printer sharing for Microsoft Networks. Service icons look like little computers with a hand under them.

4. Also in the Network control panel, click the "File and Print Sharing" button, and check "I want to be able to allow others to print to my printer(s)" (see Figure P-2).

5. Open My Computer → Printers, right-click the printer you want to share, and then choose Sharing from the contextual menu.

6. In the Properties dialog box's Sharing tab, click Shared As, enter a name for the shared item, type a comment others will see in the Network Neighborhood, and enter a password (see Figure P-3). Be careful with your password, especially if other people on the network can access your PC or if you have a permanent Internet connection via a cable modem or DSL connection.

7. When you close the Properties dialog box, Windows asks you to confirm your password.

That's all there is to turning on printer sharing in Windows.

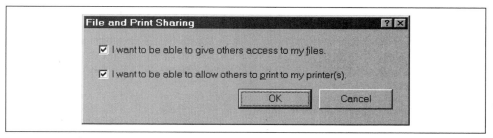

Figure P-2. File and Print Sharing dialog box

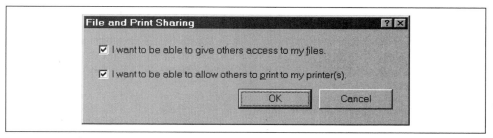

Figure P-3. Printer Properties Sharing tab

Accessing shared printers. To connect to a shared printer, follow these steps. For more information, see **Network Browser**.

1. In Control Panel → Network → Configuration's list of network components, make sure you have the same protocol used on both the PC sharing the printer and the PC you want to be able to access the printer. TCP/IP or NetBEUI work fine.

2. In Control Panel → Network → Configuration's list of network components, make sure you have the "Client for Microsoft Networks" client component. If you don't see it in your list, add it by clicking Add → Client → Microsoft → Client for Microsoft Networks. Client icons look like little computers.

3. Double-click the Network Neighborhood icon on your Desktop. For extra information about the shared computers, switch to Details view by choosing View → Details.

4. Double-click the icon for the computer whose printer you want to access, and then double-click the printer you want to access.

5. If this is the first time you've accessed this printer, Windows prompts you to set up the printer. Doing so involves installing the appropriate drivers and creating an icon for the printer in My Computer → Printers.

6. You can print to the shared printer as you would to any other printer. But the first time you print, Windows prompts you to enter the password. You can choose to have the password remembered in your password list, which can be a security risk. Once the password is accepted, your document prints on the shared printer.

Printing Files

In Windows: Printing Files

Once properly configured, printing in Windows works almost exactly the same way it does on the Macintosh. For information about setting up Windows printers, see **Desktop Printers**, **Page Setup**, and **Printer**

Sharing, and for information about font handling in Windows, see **Fonts**.

As on the Macintosh, you can print from Windows in a number of different ways:

- From within an application, choose File → Print (Ctrl-P). The Print dialog box appears, where you can choose which printer to use, which pages to print, how many copies to print, and any other application-specific options (see Figure P-4).

- Drag one or more document icons to either a printer icon in My Computer → Printers or to an open print queue window (accessed by double-clicking a printer icon). When you do this, Windows launches the necessary application and prints the document without displaying the Print dialog box.

- You can print some kinds of documents by right-clicking their icons and then choosing Print from the contextual menu. This command has the same effect as dragging the document icon to the printer icon. Trial and error is the only way to determine which kinds of documents you can print in this way.

Windows can print in the background, exactly as on the Mac OS.

Publish and Subscribe

In Windows: OLE

With System 7, Apple introduced a technology called Publish and Subscribe, which is a lot like Copy and Paste, except that the pasted material can be automatically updated when the original changes.

Microsoft's Object Linking and Embedding technology, or OLE, accomplishes much the same thing. OLE exists both on the Macintosh (in Microsoft applications and a few others) and in Windows. It gives OLE-savvy programs two features: linked objects and embedded objects.

A linked object is a living copy of material whose original sits in another document. Changes to the original object are reflected in the copy, exactly as in Publish & Subscribe. As an example, imagine inserting an

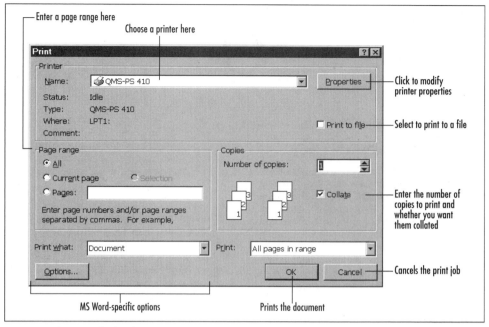

Enter a page range here

Choose a printer here

Click to modify printer properties

Select to print to a file

Enter the number of copies to print and whether you want them collated

Cancels the print job

MS Word-specific options

Prints the document

Figure P-4. Print dialog box

Excel spreadsheet with yearly data into a corporate report created as a Word document. You want changes to the data to be reflected in the corporate report, so when you insert the file into Word (via Insert → File), you'd make sure to select the "Link to file" checkbox.

In contrast, an *embedded* object has no link back to the original object—it's a copy that doesn't change if changes are made to the original. For example, you might want to insert a logo graphic into a Word document, but since you're unlikely to change your logo, there's no reason to maintain a link between the original and the copy.

Not all Windows applications offer OLE features, although most Microsoft applications do. Consult your application's manual for details on how to link or embed objects.

Q

QuarkXPress
In Windows: QuarkXPress

If you use QuarkXPress on the Macintosh, your skills will translate to the Windows version. Transferring Quark files themselves between a Macintosh and a PC may not always go smoothly, thanks to both technological differences and font implementation differences. For more information, check out Quark's web site at *http://www.quark.com/* and especially the tech notes at *http://www.quark.com/tech/technotes.html.*

Quicken
In Windows: Quicken

Quicken on the Macintosh isn't identical to the Windows version, but the basic idea is the same. If anything, you'll probably be pleased to find that some features, particularly those related to the Internet, exist only in the Windows version. For more information about the Windows version of Quicken, visit *http://www.intuit.com/.*

The Quicken Support web pages also offer information on converting Macintosh Quicken files for use with the Windows version of Quicken—it's not a trivial process, so check the current recommendations.

QuickTime
In Windows: QuickTime

Most people probably think of QuickTime as a way of playing movies on the Macintosh, but the various QuickTime players and plug-ins can also display pictures and play sounds. QuickTime 4 even offers real-time streaming of audio and video over the Internet—great for people who like to listen to the radio via the Internet or watch live "webcasts" of important events. QuickTime can also be a useful file-format conversion utility for use by other applications, including web browsers and email programs.

Apple put a great deal of effort into making QuickTime a cross-platform standard. Many Windows applications rely on QuickTime technology to display graphics files or to play audio and video. QuickTime is often bundled with applications that require it (such as the Windows version of Eudora Pro), and you can download QuickTime from Apple's web site for free. For about $30, you can upgrade the free copy of QuickTime to QuickTime Pro, which contains tools for creating and editing QuickTime movies.

For more information about QuickTime in Windows, visit *http://www.apple.com/quicktime/.*

Quitting Applications
In Windows: Exiting Programs

You quit a Windows program the same way you quit a Macintosh program—with two differences. First, you don't use the Quit command in Windows; you use the Exit command (although the keystroke is sometimes the same as it is on the Macintosh, Ctrl-Q). Second, when you close the last window in a Windows application, the application quits, which doesn't happen on the Macintosh. Here, then, are the ways you can quit a Windows application.

- Choose File → Exit from within the application you want to quit.

- Press Alt, then F, and then X. In most programs, doing so opens the File menu and then chooses the Exit command.

- Choose Start → Shut Down → Restart (or → Shut Down). Windows first quits all the open applications before restarting or shutting down the PC.

- Press Ctrl-Alt-Delete to display the End Task dialog box, then select the application you want to quit and click Close Program. Using this method of quitting an application is recommended only when the application is frozen or otherwise refusing to quit normally. See **Force Quit**.

N–R

R

RAM Upgrades

In Windows: RAM Upgrades

If you've bought RAM for a Macintosh recently, you already know the basics of buying and installing RAM in a PC. But when it comes time to buy the actual RAM upgrade, you'll discover that choosing the kind of upgrade to buy is dramatically more complicated in Windows than on the Macintosh.

For information on how Windows manages memory, see **Memory Usage**.

What kind of RAM to buy. Since the time when PCs used the 80386 processor, PCs have accepted *SIMMs* (Single Inline Memory Module) and *DIMMs* (Dual Inline Memory Module), just as Macs do. Depending on the age of your PC, you may need to buy RAM upgrade boards known as 30-pin SIMMs, 72-pin SIMMs, or the modern DIMM boards. In general, you can install DIMMs one at a time, but you must install SIMMs in pairs.

In buying RAM upgrades, you may also encounter such terms as DRAM, FPM RAM, EDO RAM, and so on. For definitions, see the sidebar "The RAM Upgrade Glossary." The bottom line: call your PC's manufacturer to find out what kind of memory chips to order if you've decided to buy a memory upgrade.

How much RAM to buy. How much memory you'll want for your PC is another question. As on the Macintosh, more is always better, and successive versions of Windows require ever more RAM. Use Table R-1 as a quick reference for how much you'll need.

Buying the right RAM. You can determine what RAM to buy in a number of ways, including looking through the PC's system documentation, calling the original vendor, or calling a reputable RAM supplier. To research the situation ahead of time, visit the Peripheral Enhancements, Inc. web site at *http://www.peripheral.com/*, which features an On-Line Memory Guide. The "Memory Configurator," as Peripheral calls it, contains information about different PC models and their RAM requirements.

Installing RAM boards. After you've purchased your RAM boards, installing them works precisely as it does on the Macintosh. Open the computer's case, search the motherboard (the large circuit board) for corresponding slots, and snap the new RAM boards in. Today's RAM slots are designed so that you can't install an upgrade board improperly—they only snap in when facing the correct direction. Tiny plastic clips at each end of each board snap inward to secure the board's ends.

Table R-1. Suggested PC RAM Configurations for Windows 95 or 98

Use	Amount of RAM
Basic productivity applications	32 MB minimum, 64 MB to 96 MB recommended
Games	64 MB and up
Graphics applications	64 MB to 256 MB
Server applications	64 MB to 256 MB, depending the number of server applications running

---

The RAM Upgrade Glossary

There are several commonly used types of DRAM (dynamic RAM, the type computers use for main memory): FPM RAM (Fast Page-Mode RAM), EDO RAM (Extended Data Out RAM), and SDRAM (Synchronous DRAM). SDRAM is faster than EDO RAM, and EDO RAM is faster than FPM RAM, and although many modern motherboards can handle all three types, speed requirements may require either EDO RAM or SDRAM. Prices aren't significantly different between the types, so it's always worth getting the newest and fastest—SDRAM—if your PC's motherboard supports it. See "Buying the right RAM" for where to turn for help figuring out which RAM you need.

When buying RAM, you may also be asked what speed you want. Faster would seem to be better, but not always. If you're replacing 70 nanosecond SIMMs with 60 nanosecond SIMMs, everything should work fine and slightly faster (although probably imperceptibly so). However, putting RAM that's too fast into a machine can cause crashing problems, so make sure your motherboard can handle the faster RAM. Mixing speeds does no harm, although the system runs at the speed of the slowest RAM installed.

Some PCs support a technique called parity checking that involves an additional chip on each SIMM or DIMM to detect (but not correct) temporary memory errors. Parity checking can also help identify a defective SIMM or DIMM. Parity errors cause freezes, but when you reboot, the BIOS detects the error and provides additional diagnostic information.

Unfortunately, many PC motherboards sold in recent years don't include BIOS (ROM) support for parity checking, in large part because the additional chip and circuitry required for parity checking increases RAM costs by 10 to 15 percent. This trend may be reversing; most Pentium Pro, II, and III motherboards now support not just parity checking, but also error correcting code (ECC), which can correct many temporary errors on the fly.

In short, if your motherboard supports parity checking, you can buy either parity or non-parity RAM, depending on whether you want to spend more or risk the occasional unexplained freeze. If your motherboard doesn't support parity checking, there's no point in buying the more expensive parity RAM.

RAM Usage
In Windows: RAM Usage

See **Memory Usage**.

Recent Applications Menu
In Windows: Programs Menu

Studies have shown that Macintosh users use more applications than Windows users, and that fact may explain a difference in philosophy. Macintosh users are used to being able to launch recently used applications from the Recent Applications menu in the Apple menu. The obvious parallel in Windows is the Programs menu in the Start menu, but there's an important difference. Recent Applications tracks only your most recently used applications, whereas the Pro-grams menu in Windows holds nearly all your applications.

Because the items in the Programs menu are actually shortcuts (aliases), you can easily add, remove, rename, and rearrange them to suit your preferred style of working. Right-click the Start menu, and then choose either Open (to open a folder window) or Explore (to open a two-pane Explorer window; see **Finder**). Then navigate to the Programs folder and customize to your heart's content. For more information, see **Apple Menu Options Control Panel**.

Recent Documents Menu
In Windows: Documents Menu

The Windows Documents submenu (in the Start menu) tracks the 15 most recently used documents; you can't adjust this number, as you can for the Mac's Recent Documents submenu (using the Apple Menu Options control panel). Furthermore, the Windows Document submenu tracks only documents that you open by double-clicking at the Desktop level—if you open a document from within a program, the Documents menu doesn't get updated.

On the Macintosh, the Recent Documents menu relies on aliases in a Recent Documents folder; the Documents submenu in Windows uses a similar technique. Its shortcuts are stored in the *C:\Windows\Recent* folder; you can delete them if you like. However, since that folder is a hidden folder, you need to turn on Show All Files in View → Folder Options → View to see and work with it.

If you don't want anyone to see what you've been working on, you can use the TweakUI control panel to set Windows to clear the Document submenu on every restart (check the Paranoia tab). For more information about TweakUI, see **ResEdit**. For more information on the Documents submenu, see **Apple Menu Options Control Panel**.

Recent Servers Menu
In Windows: None

Most Macintosh users aren't on a network with multiple servers and thus have probably never worked with the Recent Servers menu. Nonetheless, this automatically updating Apple submenu can be useful for people who regularly need to mount different servers. It lists the network hard disks to which you've most recently connected. If you find yourself using a Windows machine on a large network, unfortunately, there's no equivalent to the Recent Servers menu in Windows.

You can, however, duplicate the effect of the Recent Servers menu in Windows by creating a folder in your Start menu and populating it with shortcuts to the servers you frequent. For more information, see **Alias**, **Apple Menu**, and **Chooser**.

Remote Access Control Panel
In Windows: Dial-Up Networking

To configure a Macintosh to connect to the Internet via a modem, you must configure two control panels: TCP/IP, where you set up your TCP/IP configuration, and the Remote Access control panel (or the PPP control panel prior to Mac OS 8.5). In this control panel, you specify the dialing aspects of the connection. In Windows, the corresponding setup takes place in the Dial-Up Networking program (accessible from My Computer → Dial-Up Networking).

For information about connecting a Windows-based PC to the Internet using a network, see **TCP/IP Control Panel**.

Using Dial-Up Networking is fairly easy. Indeed, many Internet service providers give you an installation program that configures the settings for you, in which case you can use the following instructions to check what they've done.

Configuring Dial-Up Networking. To configure a PC to connect to the Internet using a modem, here's what you do. See Figure R-1 for additional information.

1. Check the Control Panel → Network control panel's list of network components for the presence of something called Dial-Up Adapter. If you don't see it in your list, add it by clicking Add → Adapter → Microsoft → Dial-Up Adapter. Adapters have icons that look like little PCI cards.

2. See if the TCP/IP protocol is included in the list of installed components in the Network control panel. Protocols have icons that look like network wires. If the TCP/IP protocol is not present, add it by selecting Add → Protocol → Microsoft → TCP/IP. If TCP/IP is present in the list but isn't followed by the words Dial-Up Adapter, try adding TCP/IP again.

3. Close the Network control panel, and then restart your PC.

4. Open My Computer → Dial-Up Networking → Make New Connection. Doing so runs the Make New Connection wizard.

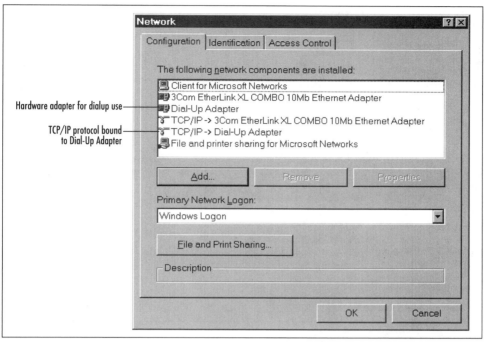

Figure R-1. Network control panel's parts and pieces

5. The Make New Connection wizard requests a name for the connection, the modem you want to use to connect, and your local Internet access phone number.

6. Assuming that the Internet service provider you're calling uses standard PPP and doesn't require a login script, that's all you must do other than provide your username and password on your first connection attempt.

Using Dial-Up Networking. Your new Internet connection appears in the Dial-Up Networking folder with any other connections you've created. To open a connection, double-click it. (As on the Macintosh, email programs, web browsers, and other Internet programs generally save you this step.) Finally, click Connect. You may be asked to enter your username and password the first time you dial, but Windows can remember them for future connections (see Figure R-2). On subsequent connects, you can simply right-click the connection icon in Dial-Up Networking, then choose Connect.

While a connection is in place, a connection icon that looks like two small computers appears in your Tray (the right side of the Taskbar) with connection statistics. To see the status dialog box (see Figure R-3), double-click the icon in the Tray, double-click the connection icon in Dial-Up Networking, or right-click the connection icon and then choose Status.

When you're done using the connection, disconnect by clicking Disconnect in the status dialog box. Alternatively, right-click the connection icon in Dial-Up Networking and choose Disconnect.

Other options. You can modify the details of any connection by right-clicking it in Dial-Up Networking, and then choosing Properties. The Properties dialog box offers four tabs: General, Server Types, Scripting, and Multilink.

General
Use the General tab to modify the connection's telephone number or modem model.

N–R

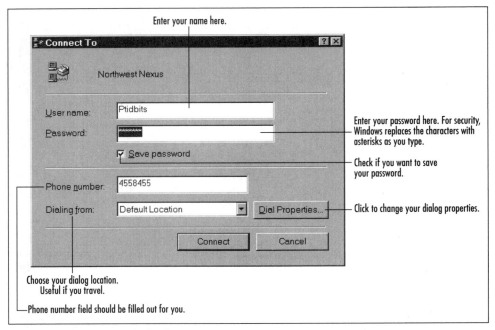

Figure R-2. Connect to dialog box

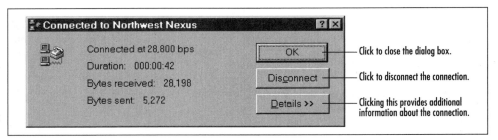

Figure R-3. Status dialog box

Server Types

The Server Types tab lets you switch types of dial-up servers (CSLIP, NRN, PPP, SLIP, or Windows for Workgroups), set several advanced options, and choose which network protocols are carried over the connection. Only TCP/IP is necessary for Internet access.

Scripting

A few rare Internet service providers require you to run a script to log into their systems. If so, choose the login script file from the Scripting tab. You can create your own login script if you know how; otherwise contact the ISP for help.

Multilink

If you, an extremely technically savvy user, combine multiple modems or ISDN adapters to double the bandwidth of your Internet connection, check the Multilink tab. You're a very lucky individual.

Renaming

In Windows: Renaming

Renaming icons in Windows works the same as on the Macintosh, although it requires an additional click. To rename a file in Windows, follow these steps:

1. Click once on the file to select it.
2. Click again on the icon's name to enter editing mode.
3. Make your changes.
4. Press Enter or click elsewhere to exit editing mode.

You can also right-click an icon and choose Rename to select the name for editing. However, you cannot select an icon and press Enter, as you would on the Macintosh, because pressing Enter when an icon is selected opens it.

Although you can use most characters in Windows filenames, several are off-limits (compared to one on the Macintosh—the colon). Characters you cannot use, mostly because they still have specific uses in DOS, include the following:

$ % < > | * . \ / " ~ : ? = ;

Restrictions. You can't rename the Recycle Bin, although you can rename just about everything else on the Windows Desktop. Be careful about renaming cryptically named items—Windows requires many system files to maintain their precise, unhelpful names. Renaming the wrong file or folder could cause trouble.

To rename a disk in the My Computer window, right-click it, choose Properties → General, and enter a new name in the Label field.

Also, don't change the three-letter suffix at the end of filenames. Doing so changes the type of the file as well, so a *.doc* file that used to open in Microsoft Word won't open properly if you change its extension to *.txt.*

ResEdit

In Windows: TweakUI, Registry Editor

Sophisticated Macintosh users can modify menus, dialog boxes, and other aspects of their favorite programs using Apple's free resource editor, ResEdit. There's no direct equivalent in Windows. However, the TweakUI utility from Microsoft lets you fiddle with a number of otherwise inaccessible settings. You can install TweakUI from the Windows 98 CD-ROM by installing the Windows 98 Resource Kit Tools Sampler *Windows 98/tools/restkit/setup.exe.* If you're using Windows 95, you can download TweakUI from Microsoft at *http://www. microsoft.com/windows95/downloads/ default.asp.*

For more information about using TweakUI to remove icons from your Desktop, see **Desktop**.

Along the same lines, the Windows Registry Editor, which lets you modify your Registry directly, is another ResEdit relative. If you plan to use the Registry Editor, however, be certain you have good instructions to follow; making a mistake with the Registry Editor can cripple your computer even more drastically than a mistake with the Mac's ResEdit can. For more information about the Registry, see **Preferences Folder**, as well as O'Reilly's *Inside the Windows 95 Registry*, by Ron Petrusha.

Reset Switch

In Windows: Ctrl-Alt-Delete Keystroke, Reset Switch

When you experience a crash on the Macintosh that freezes the keyboard, you have little choice but to turn to the "three-fingered salute"—the Control-Command-Power keystroke, which restarts most frozen machines. In Windows, the Ctrl-Alt-Delete keystroke summons the End Task dialog box, which accomplishes almost the same thing.

If you find that the Ctrl-Alt-Delete keystroke does nothing, your next course of action is to press the Reset switch on the computer itself. Not all PCs have reset switches, and some of them, particularly laptops, may require strange combinations or actions; refer to your owner's manual for details.

N-R

Resizing Windows

In Windows: Resizing Windows

On the Macintosh, you resize a window by dragging the resize handle in the lower-right corner. Windows has exactly the same resize handle in that location, and it works in exactly the same way.

However, you can also resize a Windows window by dragging any edge. When you drag the edge of a window, the window changes shape only in one dimension, which can be handy for making a window taller, for example, without making it wider.

For information about changing the size of windows with a single click, see **Collapsing Windows** and **Zooming Windows**.

Restart

In Windows: Restart

After installing new software, or when you're experiencing problems and want to start afresh, you restart your Macintosh. The same situation applies to Windows.

To restart Windows manually, choose Start → Shut Down → Restart. The "Shut down now?" dialog box appears, featuring a Restart option. (In Windows 98, you can double-click the Restart radio button rather than clicking it once and then clicking OK.) If any documents require saving, you'll be asked if you want to save them, and just like the Macintosh, if you click Cancel when

asked to save a document, that cancels the restart process.

You can restart a Windows PC from the keyboard, too, exactly as on the Macintosh. Press Alt-F4 repeatedly; with each press, another window or application closes. (Alternatively, click the Desktop, then press Alt-F4 only once.) Finally, a dialog box appears in which you're offered the opportunity to shut down or restart. Type the letter R (which corresponds to the underlined Restart option) and then press Enter to restart the computer.

If your PC is frozen, you can perform an emergency restart, too: press the famous Ctrl-Alt-Delete keystroke twice. And if even that doesn't work, try pressing your PC's manual power button or reset switch, if it has one—or just unplug the machine.

Return Key

In Windows: Enter Key

PC keyboards have two identical Enter keys, one set in the main typing area and one on the numeric keypad. This quirk may catch Macintosh users by surprise; Macintosh keyboards have one Return key and (on the numeric keypad) one Enter key, which occasionally perform different functions.

In Windows, the two Enter keys operate precisely alike, and can perform the tasks shown in Table R-2.

Table R-2. Keyboard Shortcuts Using the Enter Key in Windows

Shortcut	Function
Enter	Activates the highlighted choice—the heavily outlined button, for example, in dialog boxes. Also opens selected icons on the Windows Desktop and in Explorer windows.
Alt-Enter	Opens the Properties dialog box for the selected item. (Tip: If you select multiple items and press Alt-Enter, the Properties dialog box tells you how many items you selected and the total space they occupy.)

S

Saving Files

In Windows: Saving Files

You save documents in Windows exactly the way you do on the Macintosh: by choosing File → Save or by pressing, in the Windows case, Ctrl-S.

Only a few differences are worth noting:

- When naming a file for the first time, remember that most punctuation is off-limits (see **Filenames**).
- When the Save As dialog box appears, as shown in Figure S-1, Windows 98 offers a Desktop button (the folder button that contains an asterisk). To get the same kind of directory overview in Windows 95, choose Desktop from the Save In pop-up menu, or click the tiny "next level up" folder icon repeatedly.
- You can adjust the look—the equivalent of the Desktop View setting—of the Save As dialog box by clicking the icons in the upper right. These icons correspond to List view (see **List Views**), Details view (which resembles the Macintosh list view), and the special Properties view. In Properties view, single-click a file on the left side of the window to view an information pane on the right side.
- You can switch to another application even while the Save box is still on the screen. See **Dialog Boxes** for details.

- You can move the Windows Save dialog box around on the screen by dragging its title bar.

Scrapbook

In Windows: Scraps

Apple's Scrapbook program lets you store text, graphics, or sounds for use in other applications. Windows has no equivalent, but Windows 98 features scraps (see **Clipping Files**) that serve much the same purpose.

Screen Capture

In Windows: Screen Capture

For writers of computer books, magazines, and manuals, the screen capture, or screen shot, is a vital tool: it's a graphics file that captures what was on the screen at a precise moment. On the Macintosh, you create screen shots by pressing various key combinations, such as Command-Shift-4. In Windows, too, you press specified keyboard keys to create screen shots, as outlined in Table S-1.

As on the Macintosh, more powerful screen capture utilities can do things such as saving snapshots in different file formats. One popular example of these utilities is SnagIt (TechSmith Corporation, *http://www.techsmith.com/products/snagit*).

Table S-1. Screen Capture Options in Windows

Key Combination	Function
Print Screen (sometimes abbreviated Prt Sc)	Takes a picture of the entire screen and copies it to the clipboard, ready for pasting into a graphics program
Alt-Print Screen	Takes a picture of the currently active window and copies it to the clipboard

Z–S

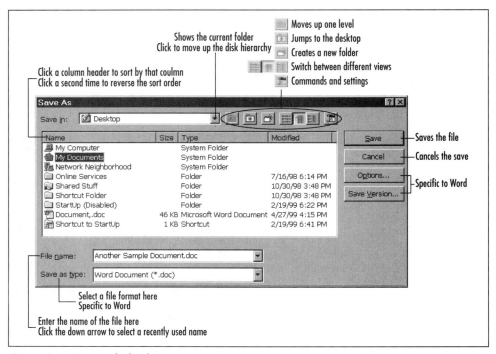

Figure S-1. Save As dialog box

Screen Savers

In Windows: Screen Savers, Power Management Control Panel

Windows has a built-in screen saver, saving you the trouble of buying a commercial one like After Dark for Windows. Better yet, Windows can also shut the monitor off after a specified period of inactivity, which saves the screen far more effectively than a screen saver ever could (see **Energy Saver Control Panel**).

To set up the screen saver in Windows, follow these steps:

1. Open Control Panel → Display → Screen Saver.

2. From the pop-up menu, choose a screen saver module. A small preview appears (see Figure S-2).

3. Click Settings; in the dialog box, modify the options for the selected screen saver, if desired.

4. If you want to see a full size preview of the screen saver, click Preview.

5. If you want to assign a password that must be entered to stop the screen saver, select "Password protected" and enter a password.

6. Set the time before activation—the amount of time since you last used your computer before the screen saver kicks in—in the Wait field.

7. Click OK or Apply to save your settings.

The Windows screen saver's password option offers only minimal security. Simply restarting the computer is enough to bypass it.

Script Editor

In Windows: Notepad

Script Editor is a small text editor specifically designed for editing AppleScript scripts. There's no direct equivalent in Win-

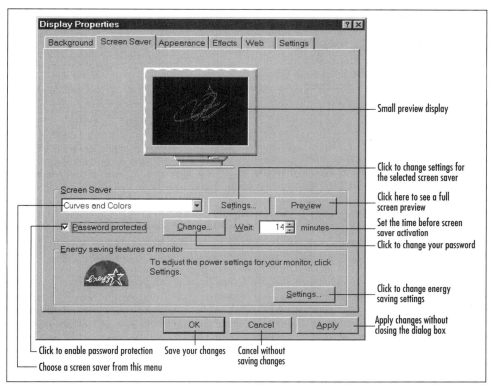

Figure S-2. Setting up a screen saver

dows, though most Windows users would use Notepad to edit batch files. For more information about scripting in Windows, see **AppleScript**. For information about Notepad, see **SimpleText**.

SCSI

In Windows: SCSI

The basic rules for SCSI on a PC are much the same as they are for the Macintosh: Each SCSI device requires its own unique ID number, the first and last devices on a SCSI chain require terminator plugs, and so on.

Unfortunately, SCSI on the PC can be quite confusing for a Macintosh user—for one thing, SCSI isn't a standard feature on most PCs, as it was on the Macintosh for many years. In general, you have to buy a SCSI card and install it into your PC if you plan to attach SCSI devices to it. (Zip drives sometimes come with low-end adapters, but this inexpensive card may not let you attach multiple SCSI devices, as a real SCSI card would.) If you experience SCSI problems—your SCSI gadgets don't work, for example—follow the same steps you would on a Macintosh. Start by checking SCSI IDs and termination. Use high-quality cables—cheap and poorly shielded cables can cause strange problems.

Then reduce the SCSI chain to a single device and test again. If that configuration works, add another device and test again. Repeat this process, adding devices slowly and testing after each one.

S-Z

Sherlock

In Windows: Find

Sherlock is Apple's name for its beefed-up Find program, which made its debut in Mac OS 8.5. For information about finding files and folders in Windows, and searching the Internet, see **Find**.

Shift Key

In Windows: Shift Key

As on the Macintosh, the Shift key does far more in Windows than simply produce capital letters:

- Hold down Shift when booting the PC to prevent items in your StartUp folder from launching, as on the Macintosh.

- When selecting multiple icons in a Desktop window, or when selecting multiple items in a list, Shift-click to select all the items between the first selected item and the one on which you're clicking. (This isn't the same effect you get when Shift-clicking items on the Macintosh, where each additional click adds only a single item to the selection. To produce that effect in Windows, Ctrl-click each item.)

- Press Shift-Del to delete a file immediately—without sending it to the Recycle Bin. (You won't be able to recover the file later, as you would if it were stored in the Recycle Bin.)

- Shift-double-click a folder to open it in a two-pane Explorer window.

- In situations where the Tab key is used for navigation (to move between fields in a dialog box, for example), adding Shift reverses the direction of the navigation, exactly as on the Macintosh.

Shut Down

In Windows: Shut Down

As with the Macintosh, you shouldn't shut down a Windows PC simply by cutting its power. If you do so, Windows complains at the next startup and encourages you to run the ScanDisk disk repair program to check for any hard disk corruption that your rash action may have caused.

Instead, to shut down a Windows machine, follow these steps:

1. Choose Start → Shut Down, or click the Desktop and press Alt-F4.

2. In the Shut Down dialog box, select Shut down (or type the letter S).

3. Click OK.

Windows quits all running programs, prompting you to save any changes in unsaved documents. Then, if your PC supports Advanced Power Management, it shuts off completely; if not, it prompts you to turn off the power manually.

Shutdown Items Folder

In Windows: None

When you shut down a Macintosh, anything in its System folder → Shutdown Items folder is automatically opened (a backup program, for example) before the shut down process wraps up. Windows has no equivalent feature.

SimpleSound

In Windows: Sound Recorder

SimpleSound, the simple sound-recording program in the Mac's Apple menu, looks positively Spartan next to its Windows equivalent, Sound Recorder (available from Start → Programs → Accessories → Entertainment → Sound Recorder). (Of course, neither program is suitable for professional audio processing.)

The basics of using Sound Recorder are easy, provided you have an audio input device—a microphone, for example—connected to your PC. To record a sound, click Record. When you're finished recording, click Stop. Save your file by choosing File → Save As.

To play a sound file, choose File → Open, open the sound file you want to play, and then click the Play button. See Figure S-3 for descriptions of the various buttons.

That's only the beginning of Sound Recorder's features. Choose Help → Help Topics for details on using the following features:

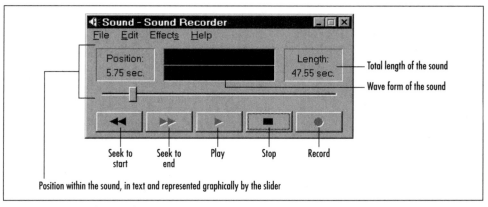

Figure S-3. Sound Recorder

- Delete parts of sound files
- Change the speed of a sound file
- Change the volume of a sound file
- Play a sound file in reverse (great for those Beatles songs!)
- Add an echo to a sound file
- Change the quality of a sound file
- Change the format of a sound file
- Mix sound files

SimpleText
In Windows: Notepad, WordPad

SimpleText is the free, stripped-down word processor—ideal for Read Me files—that comes with the Mac OS. Windows provides a pair of text-processing utilities, one less powerful than SimpleText, the other more powerful.

Notepad. Notepad (Start → Programs → Accessories → Notepad) is the older of the two Windows text editors; its feature set is truly basic. You can open only a single text file at a time, and only files smaller than 32K. Notepad offers only a single font for the entire document. Its concept of advanced features are a Word Wrap command that wraps the text to the current size of the window—without it, and when you resize the window, text scrolls past the right edge of the window—and a Time/Date command that inserts the current time and date at the insertion point. You can also search for text in a file, which is occasionally handy when reading a long ReadMe file.

Notepad is the default application for opening text files, so you'll probably see a fair amount of Notepad when reading ReadMe files. The program is also good for editing configuration text files, which you may occasionally encounter in Windows.

WordPad. WordPad (Start → Programs → Accessories → WordPad) steps past Simple-Text's features with a few basic word processing features. WordPad is also limited to opening a single file at a time, but it can open text files, RTF (Rich Text Format) files, Microsoft Word files, and Windows Write files. (In View → Options, you can specify how WordPad displays files of each type). WordPad can display graphics stored in Word files, and it's handy for reading Word files without launching—or even owning—Word.

WordPad sports the basic trappings of its big brother, including a toolbar, formatting bar, ruler, and status bar. They work as you'd expect in a word processor; if any of the icons throw you, hold the cursor still over the icon in question to see a ToolTip that explains the cryptic graphic.

You can format your WordPad text with fonts, sizes, and styles, along with bullet styles, paragraph formatting, and tab settings. Like Notepad, WordPad can insert the time and date into the document; it can also

S-Z

accept pasted graphics. Also like Notepad, WordPad can find text in a document, but it can also replace found text strings.

Sleep
In Windows: Stand By, Suspend

Every recent Macintosh model offers a sleep mode. In sleep, the computer requires less power, yet springs fully back to life when you press a key. Windows and recent PCs offer a similar feature, called Stand by in Windows 98 or Suspend in Windows 95. The command appears in Windows only if your PC supports the technology called *Advanced Power Management* (APM). Some Windows programs don't react well when the PC is awakened from sleep; otherwise, though, the Suspend or Stand by mode of your PC can save you electricity, money, and wear and tear.

To put a Windows 95 PC into standby mode, choose Start → Suspend. In Windows 98, choose Start → Shut Down; in the Shut Down dialog box, click "Stand by" and then click OK. To wake up a PC that's in standby mode, press any key or move the mouse.

You can also configure your PC go into standby mode automatically, much as you would schedule a Macintosh to go to sleep in the Energy Saver control panel. Options to turn off the monitor, spin down the hard disks, and put the entire PC in standby mode are available in the Control Panel → Power Management control panel.

Sorting Files
In Windows: Sorting Files

When you're faced with a folder containing a large number of files, sorting the files makes it easier to find the one you want. For more information on sorting files in Desktop windows, see **View Menu**.

Details. Details view in Windows is much like the Mac's list views; to sort files in a Details View window, click the name of the appropriate column at the top of the window. For instance, to sort the files alphabetically by name, click the Name column

header, exactly as on the Macintosh. To reverse the direction of the sort, click the column header again.

You can also choose a sorting criterion from View → Arrange Icons, but clicking column headers is easier.

Large icons, small icons, or list. In the three Windows icon views, you can arrange the icons in four ways: by name, type, size, or modification date. Just choose the appropriate item from View → Arrange Icons, almost exactly as on the Macintosh. To clean up a poorly arranged window, choose View → Line Up Icons. And if you're sick of lining up the icons, choose View → Arrange Icons → Auto Arrange, which works just like the Keep Arranged feature in Mac OS 8.5 and later.

Special Menu
In Windows: Contextual Menus, Start Menu

The Finder's Special menu offers a grab-bag of commands related to the Trash, disks, and the Macintosh itself. The equivalent Windows commands are equally useful—if you can find them.

Empty Trash. Because the Windows Recycle Bin empties itself automatically when it becomes full, you don't need to empty it yourself. If you prefer to do so, however, right-click the Recycle Bin; from the contextual menu, choose Empty Recycle Bin. For more information, see **Trash**.

Eject. In Windows, you can generally summon the Eject Disk command for particular disk—a Zip, floppy, or CD, for example—by right-clicking the disk icon itself (in the My Computer window). Most Windows users, however, don't bother with such menu commands, preferring instead to simply press the physical eject button on the front panel of every kind of removable-disk drive. For more information, see **Ejecting Disks**.

Erase Disk. To reformat a disk in Windows, right-click its icon and then choose Format. For more information, see **Erase Disk**.

Sleep. To put a PC into standby mode (the equivalent of sleep on the Macintosh), choose Start → Suspend (Windows 95) or Start → Shut Down → Stand by (Windows 98). See **Sleep** for more information.

Restart. To restart a PC, choose Start → Shut Down → Restart. For details, see **Restart.**

Shut Down. To shut a PC down, choose Start → Shut Down → Shut down. For more information, see **Shut Down.**

Speech Control Panel
In Windows: None

Thanks to Apple's MacinTalk speech synthesis technology, the Mac OS can read text out loud in a variety of voices. The most helpful use of this feature is the Talking Alerts option in the Speech control panel, which reads the text of dialog boxes aloud.

There's no built-in speech synthesis technology in Windows.

Speech Recognition
In Windows: Speech Recognition

One happy discovery you may make as you move into the Windows world is the variety of speech-recognition software. Programs like ViaVoice (IBM), Naturally Speaking (Dragon Systems), and Voice Express (L&H) let you actually dictate to your computer. You wear a headset microphone; as you speak normally, at full speed, the software turns your spoken words into typed words.

Dragon Systems (*http://www.dragonsys.com*), one of the major companies in the speech recognition field, purchased Articulate Systems, and Power Secretary has disappeared. Dragon concentrates on its Windows program Naturally Speaking, which not only accepts dictation, it does so with continuous speech recognition, so you can speak, well, naturally.

Spring-Loaded Folders
In Windows: None

Spring-loaded folders, a feature of Mac OS 8 and later, are a great way of navigating quickly through a hierarchy of closed windows.

Windows has no equivalent to spring-loaded folders. If you're seeking a faster way of navigating through closed folders in Windows, you should try the two-pane Explorer view (see **Finder**).

Startup Disk Control Panel
In Windows: None

Although a Macintosh can start up from any hard disk that contains a System Folder, you can use the Startup Disk control panel to specify which such disk you'd like to start up the Macintosh (if more than one is available).

Only a few PCs can start up from a disk other than the internal hard disk, so Windows offers no standard means of specifying a startup disk. Refer to your PC's manual for information on how to go about specifying alternate boot disks, if such a thing is possible on your model. See **Boot Disk** for more information.

Startup Items Folder
In Windows: StartUp Folder

The Windows StartUp folder (in *C:/ Windows/Start Menu/Programs*) is almost exactly the same as the Mac's Startup Items folder: when you turn on the computer, any document, shortcut or program inside this folder is automatically launched. You can add items to or remove them from the StartUp folder in any of several ways.

The easy method. Follow these steps to add a file to the StartUp folder:

1. Find the icon for the program or document you want to put in your StartUp folder. There's no need to make a shortcut—Windows will do so automatically.

2. Drag the icon to Start → Programs → StartUp. When you see a thick black line between items in the StartUp menu listing, release the mouse. This action may feel alien to you, because you can't drag an icon into a menu on the

Macintosh. Windows creates a shortcut to the icon in the StartUp folder. The next time you boot the PC, that file will open automatically.

Removing an item from the StartUp menu is similar, if equally unfamiliar for a Macintosh user:

1. Open Start → Programs → StartUp.

2. Drag an item in the StartUp menu to a new location, such as the Desktop. Once removed from the StartUp menu, the file won't launch the next time you boot the PC.

The Macintosh-like method. If dragging icons in and out of menus feels too bizarre, follow the steps below to add and remove items from the StartUp folder just as you'd do it on the Macintosh:

1. Open *C:/WindowsStart Menu/Programs/ StartUp.* As an alternate method of navigating from the My Computer window, right-click the Start menu, choose Open, open the Programs folder, then open the StartUp folder.

2. Drag icons into, or out of, the StartUp window to enable or disable them as startup items.

Stationery
In Windows: None

Via the Get Info window, you can turn any Macintosh document into a "stationery pad"—a special file that when double-clicked generates a new, untitled copy of the original file. Windows itself has no equivalent feature.

Stickies
In Windows: None

The Mac's Stickies desk accessory lets you create and edit little pastel-colored Post-It–style notes on your Mac's Desktop. There's no equivalent built into Windows.

StuffIt
In Windows: Zip

The standard compression and archiving format on the Macintosh is StuffIt, a proprietary format created by Aladdin Systems. Although Windows PCs can create and open StuffIt archives (using the Aladdin DropStuff and Aladdin Expander utilities), the primary compression and archiving format in Windows is the Zip format. You can identify a Zip file by the letters *.zip* at the end of its name, just as the letters *.sit* identify a StuffIt file.

Because StuffIt is a proprietary format, most of the software available for working with StuffIt archives comes from Aladdin, whereas numerous companies produce utilities for working with Zip archives. The best-known companies in this field, along with Aladdin Systems, are PKWARE and Nico Mak Computing. You can download PKWARE's PKZIP from *http://www.pkware. com/* and Nico Mak's WinZip from *http:// www.winzip.com/.* Aladdin Expander and Aladdin DropStuff are available from *http:// www.aladdinsys.com/.*

Expansion. Macintosh users using Windows will find comfort in using the free Aladdin Expander in Windows; it can expand both Zip files and many common Macintosh file formats. To expand a Zip file with Aladdin Expander, drag the file onto the Aladdin Expander icon. (Many people leave Aladdin Expander, or a shortcut to it, on the Desktop for this purpose.) Even easier: right-click the Zip file's icon, and then choose Extract from the contextual menu.

The most popular shareware Windows Zip utilities, PKZIP from PKWARE and WinZip from Nico Mak Computing, work the same way.

Compression. To compress a file in Windows, consider the shareware Aladdin DropStuff, which can create either StuffIt or Zip files. You can drag the files onto the Aladdin DropStuff icon, just as you'd do on the Macintosh, or you can right-click the icons and then choose an appropriate action from the DropStuff menu.

PKZIP and WinZip resemble the full-featured StuffIt Deluxe on the Macintosh—

they not only create Zip archives, but also let you add files to and remove files from those archives. Because they're shareware applications, you're free to try both before choosing one.

If you decide to try multiple applications to work with Zip archives, be aware that since Windows assigns file types by filename extension, the different utilities may fight over the right to "own" the *.zip* filename extension.

System Folder
In Windows: Windows Folder

The most important folder on the Macintosh is the System Folder, which holds all the files the Mac OS needs to make your Macintosh work. In Windows, the equivalent folder is the Windows folder, which sits right in your main hard disk window.

The Windows folder contains hundreds of cryptically named files and folders, and there's no way to identify each one. Don't feel bad—most Windows users can't tell you what those files and folders are, either. In other words, your PC will run best if you avoid deleting, moving, or renaming any of these files.

On the other hand, a number of folders within the Windows folder are worth knowing about. See Table S-2 for details.

Table S-2. Interesting Folders in the Windows Folder

Folder	Contents
Command	Contains DOS programs that are still useful on PCs running Windows.
Cookies	Stores cookies created on your PC by web sites you've visited.
Cursors	Holds standard and optional cursor graphics.
Desktop	Files and folders that appear on the Desktop are actually stored in this folder, exactly the way the Macintosh stores Desktop icons in the invisible Desktop folder. See **Desktop**.
Favorites	Stores your web pages and folders. See **Favorites Menu**.
Fonts	Contains fonts, just as on the Macintosh. See **Fonts**.
Help	Stores help files used by Windows, just as on the Macintosh. See **Help**.
History	Contains shortcuts to web pages you've visited recently.
Options	May contain .cab files (archive files for the Windows installer). They're stored here so that the Windows CD-ROM isn't necessary when you want to add and remove parts of Windows.
Recent	Holds shortcuts to recently used documents, which Windows displays in the Start → Documents menu. Equivalent to the Recent Documents folder on the Macintosh.
Sendto	Contains shortcuts and folders that appear in the Send To menu.
Start Menu	Shortcuts and folders here appear in the Start menu; see **Apple Menu**.
Start Menu → Programs	Contains shortcuts and folders found in the Start → Programs menu.
Start Menu → Programs → StartUp	Shortcuts or other files here open automatically when Windows boots. Equivalent to the Mac's Startup Items folder.
System	Contains a vast number of important drivers and other system files. Roughly equivalent to the Mac's Extensions folder or its System suitcase.
Web	Stores files related to the Active Desktop and channels.

S-Z

T

Tab Key

In Windows: Tab Key

In addition to its traditional function—moving the insertion point to the next Tab stop in a word processor, or advancing to the next cell on a spreadsheet—the Tab key has several special functions in Windows, just as it does on the Macintosh:

- Press Tab to cycle the "focus" (highlighting) from one set of controls in a dialog box to the next—buttons and pop-up menus, for example. Press Shift-Tab to cycle backward through dialog box items. When an item is highlighted, pressing Enter or Spacebar is the same as clicking that item.

- In tabbed dialog boxes, press Ctrl-Tab to cycle through the different tabs. Press Ctrl-Shift-Tab to cycle backward through the tabs.

- Press Alt-Tab to switch to the last window you used. Hold the Alt key down and press Tab repeatedly to cycle through open windows.

- In Desktop windows, Explorer windows, and any other window divided into fields or panes, press Tab to navigate between fields or panes. For instance, if you have the Address bar showing in Desktop windows, press Tab to switch between the file list and the Address bar.

TCP/IP Control Panel

In Windows: Network Control Panel

To configure a Macintosh to connect to the Internet via a network, you work in the TCP/IP control panel, where you choose how you're connecting and set up your TCP/IP configuration. To accomplish the

same task in Windows, you use the Network control panel. For information about connecting a Windows-based PC to the Internet using a modem, follow steps 1 and 2 in the following directions, and then go to **Remote Access Control Panel**.

The Windows Network control panel, and especially the TCP/IP Properties dialog box, can be intimidating to the Macintosh user. If you haven't used the Network control panel in Windows before, read **Networking**, and then return to this entry for specifics on TCP/IP.

To configure a PC to connect to a TCP/IP-based network such as the Internet, follow these steps. See Figure T-1 for additional information.

1. Open Control Panel → Network. In the Network control panel's list of network components, look for the name of the hardware device that connects you to the network. If you're using a modem, you'll use the Dial-Up Adapter. If you don't see the correct hardware device listed, add it to the list by clicking Add → Adapter and picking from the lists that appear.

2. If you don't see an icon for the TCP/IP protocol in the list, add it by selecting Add → Protocol → Microsoft → TCP/IP. This step causes Windows to create network components for TCP/IP for each hardware adapter. If TCP/IP appears in the list but isn't followed by the name of your modem or hardware card, try adding TCP/IP again.

3. If you're connecting to the Internet via a modem, see **Remote Access Control Panel** to find out how to configure Dial-Up Networking connections in Windows. If you're connecting by some

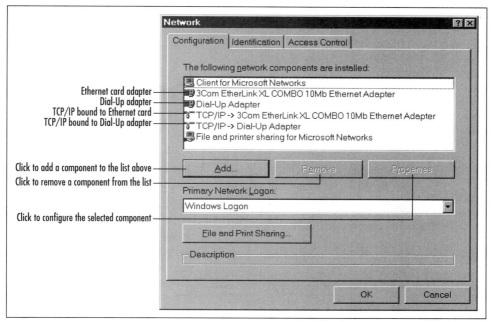

Ethernet card adapter
Dial-Up adapter
TCP/IP bound to Ethernet card
TCP/IP bound to Dial-Up adapter

Click to add a component to the list above
Click to remove a component from the list

Click to configure the selected component

Figure T-1. Network control panel's parts and pieces

other means, such as by Ethernet network, continue with these steps.

4. Double-click the TCP/IP item in the list, or select it and then click Properties. The TCP/IP Properties dialog box opens, with the IP Address tab active (see Figure T-2).

5. In the IP Address tab, click either "Obtain an IP address automatically" or "Specify an IP address." If you choose the latter option, enter an IP address and subnet mask—specialized network numbers that your consultant or network administrator can provide. Obtaining an IP address automatically requires a server on your network to assign it to you upon request, probably through the DHCP protocol; again, contact your network guru for advice.

6. Click the Gateway tab, enter the IP address of your gateway—once again, a number that only the person who maintains your office network knows—and then click Add (see Figure T-3).

7. Click the DNS Configuration tab, where you choose whether or not you want to enable DNS (domain name service), which is necessary if you're connecting to the Internet. If you do want to enable DNS, enter your host name and domain name in the appropriate fields. Enter the IP address of your primary domain name server, click Add, enter the IP address of your secondary domain name server, and click Add again. Finally, enter your domain again in the Domain Suffix Search Order field and click Add. Yet again, query your network administrator for this information, and see Figure T-4 for details.

8. Don't worry about the Bindings, Advanced, NetBIOS, or WINS Configuration tabs unless your network administrator directs you to configure them.

9. Click OK in the TCP/IP Properties dialog box.

10. Click the OK button in the Network control panel, after which Windows installs any necessary files from the Windows CD-ROM and asks you to reboot the PC.

T-Z

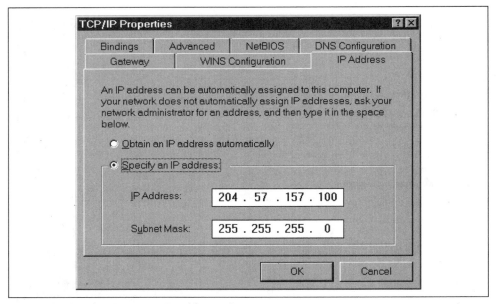

Figure T-2. TCP/IP Properties IP Address tab

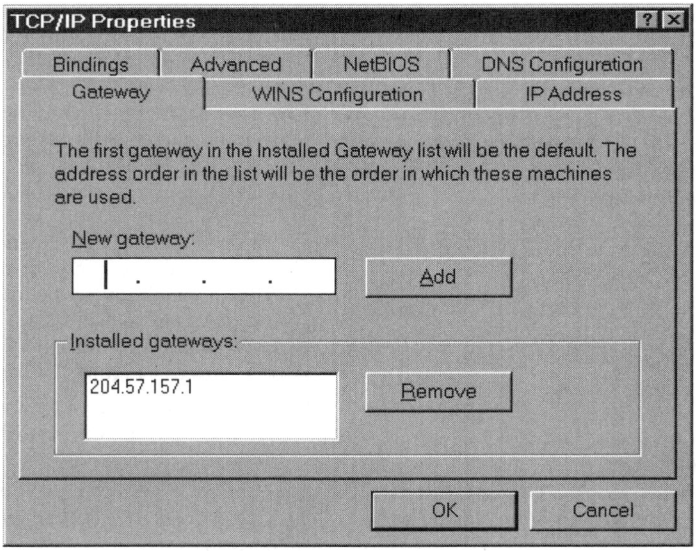

Figure T-3. TCP/IP Properties Gateway tab

After configuring TCP/IP and rebooting the PC, test the connection by launching an Internet program like a web browser. If you can visit different web sites, you're all set. If not, return to the Network control panel, double-click the TCP/IP component for your network adapter, and double-check your settings. It's worth checking the advanced

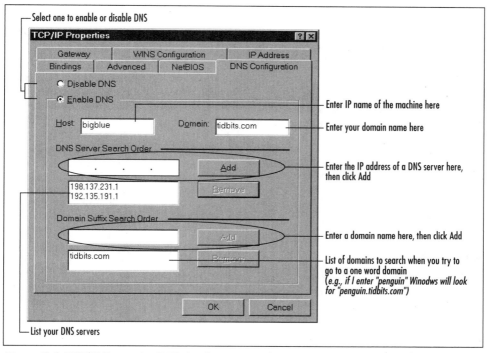

Figure T-4. TCP/IP Properties DNS Configuration tab

settings for your network adapter's component—the occasional PC Card Ethernet adapter, for example, requires you to specify the type of Ethernet cabling in the Advanced tab.

Text

In Windows: Text

The most common file format on all computer platforms is text, also known as ASCII text after the American Standards Committee for Information Interchange. Text files contain only the characters you can type from the keyboard, without formatting, graphics, sounds, or any other form of binary data. In short, text files are the lowest common denominator between computers, which is why the Web's HTML documents are straight text documents that use specific codes. Any computer can read text files, so basing HTML on text files makes HTML a universally readable format.

Of course, text files are slightly different between platforms. For instance, on the Macintosh, the end-of-line character (such as you get when you press Return) is a carriage return, whereas in Windows, text files use a carriage return/linefeed pair of characters, and Unix text files use a single linefeed character to end each line. The upshot of this is that when you transfer text files from a Macintosh to a Windows-based PC, you must make sure that the end-of-line characters are translated properly. Most programs that you would use to transfer files between the two systems automatically convert the end-of-line characters appropriately, but if the text file doesn't look right on the other platform, you may have to do a search-and-replace to insert the proper end-of-line characters. Alternatively, use a utility like the Macintosh program Add/Strip, available at *http://hyperarchive.lcs.mit.edu/HyperArchive/Archive/text/add-strip-322.hqx*, or the Windows program MacSEE, available at *http://www.reevesoft.com/macsee_info.htm*.

T-Z

Text files can differ in one other way between platforms. Only the first 128 characters of the ASCII character set, generally called the lower ASCII characters, are truly standardized, and the Macintosh and Windows may disagree about some of the characters in the upper 128 characters of the ASCII character set. This is seldom a big deal, but occasionally, if someone has relied heavily on characters like the British pound character or the Japanese yen symbol, it might not appear correctly on the other platform. The only solution is to perform a search-and-replace in a word processor.

Text files on the Macintosh seldom have a filename extension, but in Windows they have a *.txt* extension.

Text Control Panel

In Windows: Regional Settings

The Mac's Text control panel lets you choose between different text behaviors—sorting order, typing direction, and so on—based on WorldScript kits you've purchased from Apple. There's no equivalent in Windows. (But see **Numbers Control Panel** and **Date & Time Control Panel** for more on international options in Windows.)

Title Bar

In Windows: Title Bar

If you've just been plopped in front of a Windows PC, you'll have little trouble using the controls in each window's title bar. They're similar in both operating systems—for example, you can move a window by dragging its title bar, exactly as on the Macintosh. (See also **Windows**.)

The basic elements of a Macintosh title bar are the close button, the name of the window, the zoom button, and in Mac OS 8 and later, the collapse button.

The controls at the top of a Windows window perform most of the same functions. Moving left to right, they are the System Menu, the name of the window, the minimize button, the maximize/restore button, and the close button (see Figure T-5).

The Windows close button works much like it does on the Macintosh. (Note, however, that closing the last window in a Windows application often quits the application, which catches many Macintosh users by surprise.)

The Windows maximize and Macintosh zoom buttons are also relatively similar (see **Zooming Windows**), and the Windows minimize button serves the same purpose as the Mac's collapse button (see **Collapsing Windows**).

Note that while double-clicking a title bar on the Macintosh is the same as clicking the collapse button (if you turn this option on in the Appearance control panel), double-clicking a title bar in Windows maximizes (or restores) the window.

In Windows, you can't Command-click a window title to view a pop-up menu showing the folder's complete hierarchy, as you can on the Macintosh. On the other hand, Windows windows offer the System menu. Located where the close button would be on a Macintosh window, the System menu offers menu-command versions of the minimize, maximize/restore, and close buttons, along with Move and Size commands.

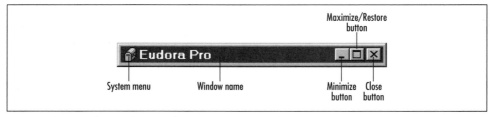

Figure T-5. Windows title bar

You can access the System Menu from the keyboard (press Alt-Spacebar), choose Move or Size (M or S), and then either move or resize the window using the arrow keys. For example, if a maximized window's title bar ends up hidden under the Taskbar, you can use the keyboard shortcuts to move, resize, or restore the window.

Trackpad Control Panel
In Windows: Trackpad Control Panel

PowerBook users use the Trackpad control panel to change the tracking and double-click speed for the PowerBook's built-in trackpad. The situation in Windows laptops varies—some come with software that lets you adjust the trackpad behavior, and others require you to use the Mouse control panel, which doesn't provide as precise control over your trackpad settings.

Transferring Files to Windows
In Windows: Transferring Files to the Macintosh

The painful process of transferring files to a PC from a Macintosh has become significantly easier over the years. You can use various methods, depending on the hardware and software you have available: disks, networks, FTP by Internet, or email. This entry covers only the physical transference of files; for more information about opening or converting the files once you've moved the file, see **File Translation**. There you'll find a reminder, for example, to include the appropriate three-letter suffix at the end of each file's name before sending it to a Windows machine.

Disks. Floppy disks, Zip disks, and similar disks are useful low-tech means of transferring files, especially if the PC and the Macintosh are near one another, or when the computers aren't connected to a network or the Internet.

PCs and Macs use different floppy disk formats; fortunately, the Mac's PC Exchange or File Exchange control panel lets the Macintosh accept disks from Windows PCs, and even format fresh disks for use on a PC.

To create a PC disk, follow these steps:

1. Put a disk in the Mac's floppy drive.
2. Choose Special → Erase Disk → DOS 1.4 MB.
3. Enter a name for the disk.
4. Click OK to format the disk.

The Special → Erase Disk command on the Macintosh can't create PC-formatted Zip or Jaz disks—only floppy disks. Fortunately, the Iomega Tools program that accompanied your Zip or Jaz drive offers reformatting commands that let you specify which format prefer when erasing a disk.

You can identify a PC-formatted floppy disk or Zip disk on your Macintosh by its distinctive icon. In addition, the Mac OS adds several invisible files to the disk—Desktop files, Finder information, and a folder for Macintosh resource forks, and so on—that often show up on the disk when you insert it into a PC.

If you prefer to use Macintosh disks in your PC, you'll have to buy an add-on program, such as MacDrive 98 for Windows (*http://www.media4.com/*), Conversions Plus and MacOpener from DataViz (visit *http://www.dataviz.com/*), or MacSEE from Reevesoft (*http://www.reevesoft.com/macsee_info.htm*).

Both PC Exchange/File Exchange and its commercial Windows equivalents work with any removable media—floppies, Zip disks, and so on.

Networks. Although both Windows and the Mac OS support networking and can be connected to the same Ethernet network, they don't understand the same network protocols (think of it as a language barrier). Windows uses "File and printer sharing for Microsoft Networks," whereas the Macintosh uses AppleShare. Getting the Macintosh and the PC to speak the same network protocol requires additional software. You have several options:

• Install software like TSSTalk from Thursby Software Systems (visit *http://www.thursby.com/*) or PC MACLAN from Miramar Systems (visit *http://www.miramarsys.com/*). These programs let your PC connect to an AppleShare

S-Z

server (such as an everyday Macintosh with file sharing turned on). Then copy files from the PC to the AppleShare server, and if necessary, from the AppleShare server to another Macintosh. (In this arrangement, you bring the Mac's hard disk onto your PC's screen.)

- Use PC MACLAN to run an AppleShare server on a PC. Then connect to the PC MACLAN AppleShare server from the Macintosh, and use the Macintosh to copy files from the PC to the Macintosh. (In this arrangement, you bring the PC's hard disk onto your Mac's screen.)

- Use DAVE from Thursby Software Systems (visit *http://www.thursby.com/*), which provides bidirectional file sharing between Macs and PCs running Windows, although it doesn't use AppleTalk. You install DAVE on both the PC and the Macintosh.

- Install Netopia's Timbuktu Pro (visit *http://www.netopia.com/*) on both the PC and the Macintosh, and then use Timbuktu Pro's built-in file transfer service to move files back and forth. (In this arrangement, you can also view and manipulate one computer's screen in a window on the other computer's screen.)

- If you have a NetWare network, install AppleTalk Filing Protocol on the NetWare server and install MacIPX (which comes with NetWare) on the Macintosh. Doing so lets the Macintosh copy files from the NetWare server, so that you can put a file on the server from a PC, and then copy it down using the Macintosh. For more information, visit *http://www.novell.com/* or talk to a NetWare consultant.

- If you have a Windows NT-based network, install support for Apple File and Print Services. Doing so lets the Macintosh copy files from the NT server, so that you can put a file on the server from a PC, and then copy it down using the Macintosh. For more information, talk to an NT consultant.

- Install Apple's AppleShare IP 6.0 or later (visit *http://www.apple.com/*

appleshareip/) on a Macintosh, and then turn on Windows File Sharing, which uses the SMB (Server Message Block) protocol supported by Windows with no additional software. Once you turn on Windows File Sharing in AppleShare IP, the AppleShare IP server appears in the Network Neighborhood like any other Windows server. (In this arrangement, you bring the Mac's hard disk onto your PC's screen.) See **Network Browser** for additional information.

Internet. Transferring files via FTP has two big advantages over the methods just described. First, the PC and the Macintosh don't have to be near each other or on the same network. Second, doing so doesn't require buying any additional software (although some freeware or inexpensive shareware can simplify the process).

To make this work, you need access to an FTP (File Transfer Protocol) server. You may have one already without even knowing it: most Internet accounts include several megabytes of FTP space. Ask your ISP for details.

If your PC and Macintosh are on the same network, you can run an FTP server on one and connect to it from the other using an FTP client or web browser. Running your own FTP server isn't worth the effort for a single file every now and then, but it might be if you frequently want to transfer files via FTP.

Once you have access to an FTP server, follow these steps:

1. From the Macintosh, run your FTP client and connect to the FTP server.

2. Upload the file from the Macintosh to the FTP server.

3. On the PC, run a web browser (web browsers can download from FTP servers) or the Windows FTP client. You can access the Windows FTP client from a DOS shell (Start → Programs → Ms-Dos). In the DOS window type `ftp` followed by the domain name of the server.

If you're using a web browser and need to enter a username and password to

> **Note**
>
> FTP transfers files in either text or binary mode. The Windows FTP client starts in text mode by default. To change to binary mode, type "binary" after you're connected to the FTP server but before you've started the file transfer.

access the FTP server, build them into an FTP URL that looks like this:

```
ftp://username:password@ftp.domain.
com/pub/users/tmp/
```

This single address identifies the username, password, machine name for the FTP server, and path to the directory that holds your files.

For instance, if I've uploaded a file to my FTP server in the */pub/tidbits/issues/ 1998* directory, then you would have to type the following URL into your web browser to . see a list of files in that directory: *ftp://ftp.tidbits.com/pub/tidbits/ issues/1998/*. If you need to enter a username and password to download files from the remote FTP server, you must instead enter something like: *ftp:// username:password@ftp.tidbits.com/pub/ tidbits/issues/1998/*.

Either way, once you have a directory list, click any filename to download the file—you may need to select where it will appear on your hard disk.

4. Download the file to the PC from the FTP server.

The Mac OS doesn't come with a built-in FTP program. If you don't want to use your web browser, you can download an FTP client from *http://tucows. cyberspacehq.com/mac/ftpmac.html*; we recommend either Anarchie (Stairways Software) or Fetch (Dartmouth College). If you want to set up an FTP server on the Macintosh, check out the shareware NetPresenz from the same company that makes Anarchie—it's at *http://www.stairways.com/*.

In addition to Windows' primitive FTP client, many dedicated FTP programs are available for Windows, some of which are freeware or shareware. For a

list of them (including the shareware FTP server ExpressFS FTP), visit *http:// www.winfiles.com/apps/98/ftp.html*.

Email. Email often proves to be the easiest method of sending a file from a Macintosh to a PC. The PC and the Macintosh don't have to be near one another, nor do they have to be connected to an office network. Email often works better than disks, too, because it's much faster.

In practice, however, as any veteran can tell you, not every Macintosh/Windows email file attachment emerges at the other end intact. The reasons are very technical, but they boil down to four problems: encoding differences, Macintosh resource fork problems, incompatibilities with MIME file splitting, and StuffIt compression.

Problem one: encoding differences. Any binary components of an email message will be encoded as text. Here's why. Internet email only guarantees 7-bit transfers, so 8-bit files (anything but straight text files) must be encoded to avoid damage. Think of the encoding format as an envelope that protects the file. For this process to succeed, both the sending and receiving program must understand the encoding format used.

Problem two: the resource fork. Many Macintosh files consist of two software chunks bundled together: a data fork and a resource fork. But PCs understand only data forks. That's why pure data files, such as Microsoft Word or Microsoft Excel files, generally arrive on a PC intact—but software that relies on the resource fork, such as applications, arrive in damaged and unusable form on a Windows PC.

Some attachment-encoding formats do indeed preserve the resource forks of Macintosh file attachments, the better to ensure their safe arrival on other Macs. Unfortunately, since PCs can't make head nor tail of resource-fork data, some encoding formats transmit unreadable files to Windows PCs. Refer to Table T-1 for information about the different attachment encoding formats; inspect your email program's file-attachment options to see which of the formats in Table T-1 are available.

Table T-1. Attachment Encoding Formats

Format	Use
AppleDouble	Best for sending files to both Windows and Macintosh users. Creates separate MIME parts (described later in this section) for the data fork and resource fork, allowing Windows email programs to ignore the resource fork. The receiving Windows email program must be MIME-savvy for this to work properly. Older email programs don't understand the MIME format; America Online doesn't interpret MIME files correctly.
AppleSingle	Useful only for sending files to Macintosh users; combines the data fork and the resource fork before sending. For the most part, avoid AppleSingle.
Base64	Encodes only the data fork of a file. Very reliable, but only for sending files to Windows users, particularly those with modern email programs.
BinHex	Combines both forks of the file before encoding; ideal for sending files to Macintosh users. Some Windows email programs, such as Eudora, can decode BinHex attachments, so this format may work when sending files to Windows users.
uuencode	Encodes only the data fork; useful only for sending files to Windows users. Since uuencode is the least common denominator, it's the best fallback option if AppleDouble isn't offered by your email program.

For more information about these file formats, see "Macintosh Internet File Format Primer," available at *http://db.tidbits.com/getbits.acgi?tbart=05066.*

Problem three: the MIME format. The third problem with Macintosh/Windows email attachments is that many email programs split outgoing mail into several chunks, one of which is the attachment. This special formatting system is called MIME, which stands for Multipurpose Internet Mail Extensions. Unfortunately, older email programs may not be MIME-savvy; they may put the encoded attachment in the body of the message instead of recognizing it as an attachment. You, the unlucky recipient, must extract the text and manually decode it, which seldom works.

Problem four: StuffIt compression. Finally, some Macintosh email programs, including America Online and Claris Emailer, automatically compress outgoing files in the StuffIt format for faster transmission. That's an admirable goal, but you're better off turning off such compression before sending a file to a PC. (When sending multiple files attached to a single America Online email message, you're not offered the choice of turning off StuffIt compression; you must therefore send one noncompressed file per email message when sending to your Windows friends.) Few Windows users have Aladdin Expander, the free program necessary to expand StuffIt files on Windows (it's available at *http://www.aladdinsys.com/expander/expander_win_login.html*).

Finding the proper combination of settings when sending Macintosh files to Windows by email, therefore, is a process of trial and error. Experiment with your email program's settings by sending a small file from your Macintosh to your PC, or vice versa, by email using each of the following settings in turn:

1. AppleDouble
2. Base64
3. uuencode
4. BinHex

If you receive an email in Windows that's little more than garbled text, ask the sender to resend it using a different attachment encoding format. If this happens repeatedly, consider upgrading your email program to a newer version.

The best email programs to use for reliable transmission of files to Macs from PCs are those that exist on both platforms, such as Qualcomm's **Eudora** and **Microsoft Outlook Express**.

Trash

In Windows: Recycle Bin

The most well-known part of the Macintosh interface may be the Trash can in the lower-right corner of the screen. The Trash provides a holding place for files and folders before they're deleted for good, giving you a chance to recover a file before it's too late.

Microsoft picked up on this idea, but since Windows 95 came out so much later than the Macintosh (over ten years later, in fact), Microsoft chose a more politically correct name for its unwanted file purgatory, calling it the Recycle Bin. The Windows Recycle Bin works much the same way as the Trash, although Microsoft couldn't resist adding a few additional features.

Deleting items. You can move icons into the Recycle Bin in a number of different ways:

- Drag one or more icons from a Desktop window or Explorer onto the Recycle Bin icon.

- Select one or more icons in a window or Explorer and then press the Del key.

- Press Shift-Del to delete selected icons instantly rather than sending them to the Recycle Bin.

- Select one or more items in a window or Explorer and then choose File → Delete.

- Select one or more items in a window or Explorer, right-click one of them, and then choose Delete from the contextual menu.

Note

When you delete an item using either the File menu or the contextual menu, Windows asks if you really want to delete the item (it doesn't warn you if you drag an item into the Recycle Bin). To turn off that warning, right-click the Recycle Bin, choose Properties, and then uncheck Display delete confirmation dialog box in the Global tab.

Recovering items. You can recover items from the Recycle Bin much as you do in the

Mac's Trash. Double click the Recycle Bin, and then drag one or more items out to another location.

When in Details view, the Recycle Bin's window displays special columns for Original Location and Date Deleted (see Figure T-6). Knowing the original location of a file is handy—you can also right-click a file and then choose Restore to restore it to its original location.

Finally, you can select icons in the Recycle Bin window and then choose File → Restore.

Emptying the Recycle Bin. When you decide to recover the space wasted by unnecessary files in your Recycle Bin, you have several options. First, you can manually empty the Recycle Bin by right-clicking it, and then choosing Empty Recycle Bin. (Alternatively, open the Recycle Bin and choose File → Empty Recycle Bin.)

You don't have to empty the entire Recycle Bin at once. If you open the Recycle Bin and select several files by Ctrl-clicking them, you can delete just those files by choosing File → Delete.

However, you can also set up the Recycle Bin to empty itself automatically. Once the Recycle Bin's contents reach a specified size, Windows deletes the files it contains, oldest first, to maintain the size you've set. To modify the size of the Recycle Bin, follow these steps:

1. Right-click the Recycle Bin, and then choose Properties → Global (see Figure T-7).

2. Set the slider bar to a percentage of the total space on each drive. If you prefer, each drive can have different settings.

3. Click OK to save your changes.

If you don't want the protection that the Recycle Bin offers, you can check "Do not move files to the Recycle Bin. Remove files immediately when deleted." There's no good reason to do away with the safety net provided by the Recycle Bin unless you're concerned about someone poking around sensitive deleted files.

S–Z

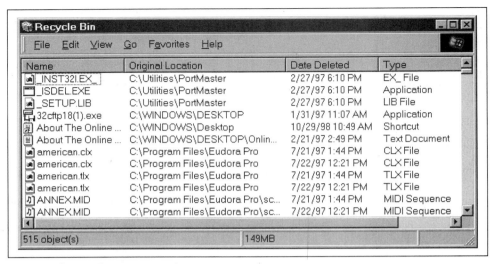

Figure T-6. Recycle Bin in Details view

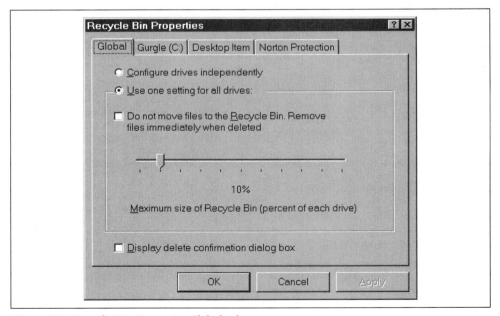

Figure T-7. Recycle Bin Properties Global tab

Caveats. As a Macintosh user, you're used to any file remaining in the Trash until you choose Empty Trash. In Windows, however, only files on your hard disks stay in the Recycle Bin. If you drag a file from a floppy, Zip disk, network drive, or other external drive to the Recycle Bin, Windows deletes the file instantly. Be careful!

If you drag the icon of a floppy disk to the Recycle Bin, Windows deletes all the files on that disk—a distinctly confusing behavior for Macintosh users used to ejecting disks by dragging their icons to the Trash. Be especially careful not to drag the icon of a hard disk to the Recycle Bin, since Windows will promptly delete all the files on it!

Because some components of the Windows interface aren't actually files or folders, Windows doesn't let you delete everything on your Desktop. If you can't drag an item into the Recycle Bin to delete it, try right-clicking the item and choosing Delete. If that fails, check out the TweakUI control panel's Desktop tab. For more information about TweakUI, see **Desktop**.

Troubleshooting
In Windows: Troubleshooting

One of the hardest parts of switching from the Macintosh to Windows is learning how to deal with problems; your Macintosh experience may not always be helpful.

For a complete discussion of troubleshooting Windows, consult a web site like PCGuide at *http://www.pcguide.com/* or books like *Windows 98 Optimizing and Troubleshooting Little Black Book* from The Coriolis Group.

However, your first stop should always be the troubleshooting information built into Windows Help—it provides a good deal of useful information. After that, and for more serious problems, look first at driver conflicts, especially video drivers. For more information, see **Drivers**.

Generic troubleshooting technique. If you find yourself at sea when faced with a Windows problem, take a deep breath and remember that the process of troubleshooting a problem is similar on the two operating systems. There are five steps you can take to solve most computer problems:

1. *Read the error message.* Windows is generally good about providing error dialog boxes when problems occur, so make sure to read those error messages carefully. Even though they're sometimes cryptic (and error numbers are seldom helpful), the messages often contain clues to the problem. It's a good idea to write down the error mes-

sage if it seems unusual, since a technical support representative may need to know exactly what the message said.

2. *See if the problem recurs.* Many problems with computers are single occurrences. That can be annoying, but if a problem happens only once, it's not something you have to put much work into solving.

One caveat here. If the problem seems serious and you're working on important files, make sure to create a backup before doing anything else. Regular backups will protect you from most problems, but it never hurts to have multiple backups of your most important files.

3. *Isolate the cause of the problem.* This is the hard part, but there are two basic approaches you can take that generally work. First, think about recent changes you've made to the computer. Have you installed new software or added a new expansion card? Also think about any unusual situations that might have caused a change to the computer without your intervention—perhaps the machine took a lot longer to boot than normal or made funny noises while booting. Second, try to narrow the problem down. For instance, if you can't open a file stored on a CD-ROM, the problem could be that particular file, the program you're using to open the file, the CD-ROM disk, the CD-ROM drive, or even the CD-ROM driver software. You can isolate each variable by trying alternate approaches. In this case, try opening a different file on the same CD-ROM, opening the same file with a different program, opening a file from a different CD-ROM disk, or copying the file to your hard disk. There are no hard and fast rules here, but if you try to think about the dependencies, you can often isolate the cause of the problem.

4. *Get help.* Once you've identified the problem or at least isolated a number of possibilities that have not caused the problem, it's time to look for more help. Useful sources of help include online help, manuals, savvy friends,

web sites and mailing lists (see **Web Sites for Windows Software and Information**), reference books, and technical support engineers. Work your way through each source of help in turn to avoid being told by people on a mailing list, for instance, to read the manual.

5. *Fix the problem*. After getting the answer to your problem, you need to implement the fix. In many cases, the answer will come in the form of a number of options to try, because it can be difficult to know exactly what will solve any given problem. Work through the fixes in order from easiest to hardest, keeping track of what you've done in case none of them work (at which point, return to the previous step and get more help).

TrueType
In Windows: TrueType

TrueType is an outline font technology developed by Apple and cross-licensed to Microsoft in exchange for a PostScript clone called TrueImage. Apple got the short end of that deal, since TrueType has become the standard outline font technology in both the Mac OS and in Windows, whereas nothing much ever happened with TrueImage.

You can convert Macintosh TrueType fonts to Windows using the shareware utility TT FontConvert, available at *http://www. netmagic.net/~evan/shareware/*. To convert Windows TrueType fonts for use on the Macintosh, check out TTconverter, available at *ftp://members.aol.com/raymarkcd/ ttconverter.hqx*.

For more information about fonts in general, including where to store the font files, see **Fonts**.

Type Codes
In Windows: Registry Extension Mapping

Every Macintosh file, behind the scenes, is assigned two four-character codes. The creator code identifies the application that created the file (such as Photoshop), and the type code specifies what sort of file it is (JPEG, GIF, PICT, and so on). Together, these codes define what file icons look like and what happens when you double-click a file in the Finder.

The closest equivalent in Windows is the three-letter filename extension on every Windows file. The document called *Letter. doc*, for example, opens in Word; *Letter.wri*, on the other hand, opens in Microsoft Write. The relationships between these filename suffixes and applications to which they correspond are established in the Windows Registry—an important behind-the-scenes Windows database file—in the HKEY_ CLASSES_ROOT section. Through a complex set of interrelated keys, the Registry defines a variety of different attributes for files with a given extension. For more information about the Registry, see **Preferences Folder**.

U

Undo

In Windows: Undo

The Windows Undo command, available from Edit → Undo, works exactly like the Mac's. Even its keystroke is equivalent: Ctrl-Z.

At the Desktop level, in fact, the Windows Undo command does even more than it does on the Mac: it can undo actions like moving files, copying files, and deleting files. Better yet, it remembers multiple actions, so you can undo more than just the last action. (The Windows Undo command doesn't work while you're renaming a file, however—it doesn't actually work until you've finished the renaming.)

Uninstalling Applications

In Windows: Add/Remove Programs Control Panel

You must uninstall applications properly in Windows (rather than just dragging their folders and related files to the Recycle Bin). See **Installing Software** for details, since the Add/Remove Programs control panel handles both installing and uninstalling.

USB

In Windows: USB

USB, or Universal Serial Bus, is an increasingly popular technology for connecting slow or medium-speed devices to computers. USB connectors and cables can transfer data at up to 12 megabits per second, which makes them useful for gadgets like keyboards, mice, graphics tablets, joysticks, floppy disk drives, Zip drives, scanners, and digital cameras. By attaching an inexpensive USB hub to an available USB port on the computer, or even stringing one USB hub to another, you can theoretically connect up to 127 printers, scanners, hard disks, and other devices to a single computer.

Although USB has been available for years in the Windows world, the typical Windows-world chaos of competing drivers and incompatible standards has caused instability in the USB racket, which in turn dissuades users and vendors from adopting USB with more enthusiasm. Still, you may see a USB port or two on the back of your PC, right next to all the older standard jacks such as the keyboard, mouse, serial, and parallel ports.

For more information about USB itself and availability of USB-based peripherals, visit *http://www.usb.org/*.

Users & Groups Control Panel

In Windows: Access Control Control Panel

To restrict access to a Macintosh over a network, you use the Users & Groups control panel to define users—individuals with their own passwords. Users can be collected into groups, and you then assign separate access privileges for any folder to the owner, a user or group, and guests.

Windows offers two types of access control for shared resources: share-level and user-level, both of which you set up in Control Panel → Network → Access Control. User-level access control works along the same lines as the Mac's Users & Groups control. However, you can't set up this information on your PC, as you would on the Mac—a master list of users and groups must reside on a network server. In short, don't use user-level access control without the cooperation of your network administrator. (If you don't have a network administrator, don't use this feature at all.)

Share-level access control works differently. Whenever you share a folder or a printer over the network (see **File Sharing**), you specify a password that restricts access to that item. To open the Sharing dialog box, right-click the folder or printer, and then choose Sharing from the contextual menu (see Figure U-1).

Printers can have only a single password that provides complete access, but folders can have two passwords: one that provides read-only access (other people on the network can see the files inside it, but can't change them), and another that provides full access.

Uuencode

In Windows: uuencode

Uuencode is a method of converting 8-bit binary files into 7-bit text files. It's used mostly for Internet email attachments, since Internet email guarantees only 7-bit transfers. Uuencode is little used in the Macintosh world other than for emailing files to Windows users, but it's more commonly used when sending files between Windows machines. For more information on when to use uuencode for email attachments, see the email section of **Transferring Files to Windows**.

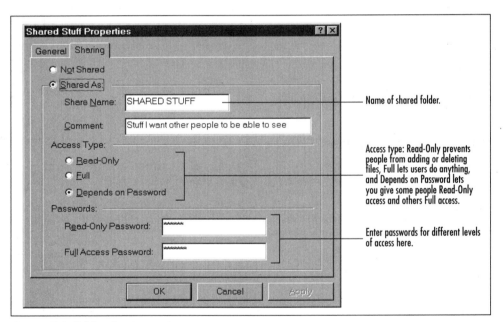

Figure U-1. Folder sharing settings

V

View Menu

In Windows: View Menu

As on the Macintosh, you can view the icons in a Windows window in several different ways. Most of the commands you're used to seeing in the View menu (or the contextual menu for any window) have close relatives in Windows, as follows:

As icons, as list. The Mac OS offers views of the files in a window: Icon, Button, or List. The Windows Large Icons and Small Icons views (available in the View menu) duplicate the Mac's Icon view, and the Windows Details view matches the Mac's List view.

Although Windows offers a List view, it has little in common with the Mac's List view; instead, the Windows List view shows multiple columns of small icons, which frequently requiring horizontal scrolling. See Table V-1 for a summary of how the different views compare.

As buttons. Windows has no built-in equivalent of the Button View found in Mac OS 8 and later, in which a single click on any enlarged icon "button" opens the corresponding file. Still, if you miss this aspect of the Macintosh interface, you can simulate it on your PC if you have Windows 98 or later:

1. Open the window in question. Using the View menu, set the view to either Large Icons or Small Icons.
2. Choose View → Folder Options → Custom → Settings to open the Custom Settings dialog box (see Figure V-1).
3. In the bottom set of options, click "Single-click to open an item (point to select)."

Once you've done that, icons work much like they do in Button view on the Macintosh, except that you can drag icons to move them. (In the Mac's Button view, you must drag icons by their names to move them.)

As pop-up window. Windows has no equivalent of the pop-up windows that debuted in Mac OS 8.

Clean Up. When you're in Icon view on the Macintosh, View → Clean Up makes the icon snap onto an invisible grid in neat alignment. In Windows, the identical command is View → Line Up Icons.

Arrange and sort list. On the Macintosh, you can sort an Icon view or Button view by name, modification date, creation date, size, kind, or label. And through View → View Options → Keep Arranged, you can specify that the sorting is permanent, even when the window shape changes or more icons are added to the window.

Table V-1. View Comparisons

Macintosh View	Windows View
Icon (either large or small, depending on size setting in View → View Options)	Large Icons or Small Icons
List	Details
Button	See the preceding instructions
Small Icon view, with "Keep arranged by name" turned on in View → View Options	List

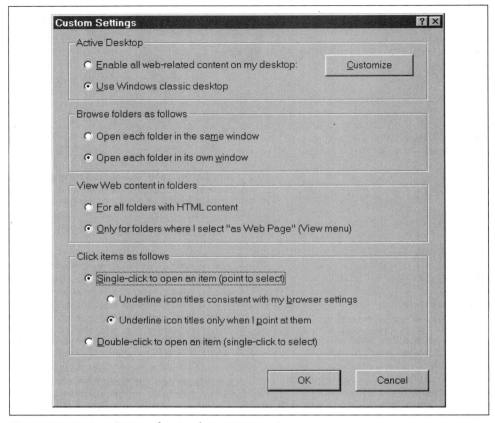

Figure V-1. Custom Settings for simulating Button view

Windows is more limited, offering only options to arrange by name, date, type, and size, all of which are accessible from View → Arrange Icons. To keep a Windows window arranged, make sure View → Arrange Icons → Auto Arrange is checked.

While the wording of the Mac's View menu changes—from Arrange to Sort List—depending on whether the open window is displayed in icon view or list view, Windows makes no similar change—the command is always called Arrange Icons.

Reset Column Positions. In Mac OS 8.5 and later, you can rearrange the columns of a List view by dragging the column titles horizontally. The Reset Column Positions command restores the original configuration of columns.

You can't rearrange the columns in the Windows 95; although you can in Windows 98, there's no equivalent in Windows to the Mac's View → Reset Column Positions command.

View Options. The View Options dialog box for a Macintosh window (View → View Options) lets you set a variety of options for each view. Windows has no equivalents for the options accessible in View Options—except the option to keep icons permanently sorted (View → Arrange Icons → Auto Arrange) and the choice of large or small icons in Icon view (View → Large Icons and View → Small Icons). Windows doesn't offer options for relative dates, calculating folder sizes, keeping icons aligned with an invisible grid as you move them, multiple icon sizes in Details view, or a choice of which columns display for each window.

Web-browser mimicry. On the other hand, the Windows View menu offers a number of unique options of its own, especially in Windows 98. Many of these commands pertain to Windows 98's Active Desktop option, in which you view the contents of your hard disk in a web browser-like interface; you're offered the chance to turn on a variety of toolbars, view individual windows as web pages (icons appear as though they were in a web page), customize each folder's web page look, and in View → Folder Options, switch all your windows to use the full web-style interface. Most Macintosh users find the hard disk-as-web-browser concept extremely disorienting.

Folder Options. View → Folder Options → View (just Options in Windows 95) lets you customize how files and folders look. (Note, however, that the Folder Options affect all windows, not just the active one.) The most important one is the "Hide file extensions for known file types" checkbox. Although it might seem more Mac-like to hide filename extensions (the three-letter suffixes on all Windows filenames), you may find their absence disconcerting and confusing; for example, you might add a filename suffix to an icon, unaware that one already exists (because Windows is hiding it). You'll probably find that turning off this "Hide file extensions" checkbox results in a much more comprehensible computing environment.

View → Folder Options → File Types provides an interface to the association of documents to applications. On the Macintosh, you never have to worry about which document was created by which application; but in Windows, you must explicitly tell a GIF image to open in Internet Explorer by giving it a *.gif* extension. In the File Types tab, you can change that to open in, for example, a graphics program.

On the Macintosh, you might double-click one GIF file that opens into Photoshop, and another that opens into GraphicConverter; thanks to the Mac's behind-the-scenes creator codes, every document on your Macintosh remembers which program originally created it.

Windows files don't have creator codes, however. File extensions are absolute in Windows—all *.gif* files will open in only one program.

In general, installation programs add new file extensions automatically, so you should never need to add a new one. However, you may occasionally wish to modify one that has been "taken over" by the installation of a new program. For example, when you install Netscape Navigator it will try to "take over" the opening of all HTML documents, even if you had previously installed Internet Explorer; similarly, Microsoft's installer "stole" the file extension *.doc* from WordPerfect when Windows was first released, forcing all WordPerfect documents to open into Microsoft Word when double-clicked.

Virtual Memory
In Windows: Virtual Memory

For details on virtual memory in Windows, see **Memory Usage.**

Viruses
In Windows: Viruses

The virus problem is far more serious in the PC world than in the Macintosh world; according to some sources, there are over 40,000 viruses and virus variants written for Windows. Worse, PC viruses tend to be far more malevolent than Macintosh viruses, actively deleting files and damaging hard disks. If you're using a PC, you must have an anti-virus program, and you must keep it up to date with new virus definitions.

Symantec and Network Associates dominate the PC antivirus market. Both offer a number of products, including Symantec's Norton AntiVirus and VirusScan from Network Associates. You can find more information about Norton AntiVirus and about viruses in general at *http://www.symantec.com/avcenter/*. For information about the various Network Associates anti-virus products, visit *http://www.nai.com/products/antivirus/*.

Z-S

Word macro viruses, macros written in WordBasic that propagate by infecting Word documents, are another increasing threat today. Word files are ubiquitous in the business world, and some macros run when the document is opened; as a result, these viruses can spread quickly. (They affect both PC and Macintosh users of Microsoft Word.) Fortunately, most anti-virus programs can help find and eliminate Word macro viruses. Furthermore, whenever you open a document containing Word macro files, Word 97 or later offers to disable macros in documents when you're opening them—a convenient solution that rules out any possibility that the document you're about to open will infect your system.

W

Web Sharing Control Panel
In Windows: Personal Web Server

The Web Sharing control panel, included with Mac OS 8 and later, lets any Macintosh become a low-volume web server. Windows's Personal Web Server software is similar. It's not part of a standard installation, but it's on the Windows 98 CD-ROM (and with Internet Explorer 4.0 when installed on Windows 95).

To install Personal Web Server, follow these steps (note that you can't install Personal Web Server from Control Panel → Add/Remove Programs → Windows Setup → Internet Tools):

1. Insert the Windows 98 CD-ROM.

2. Choose Start → Run.

3. Type `x:\add-ons\pws\setup.exe` in the dialog box (where *x* is the letter of your CD-ROM drive), and then click OK. (To find out the letter of your CD-ROM drive, double-click the My Computer icon; you'll see an icon, with the appropriate letter identified, representing the CD-ROM drive.)

4. Follow the directions in the Personal Web Server Setup program, making sure to note the folder where you place HTML files to be served.

Once you've installed Personal Web Server, open Start → Programs → Internet Explorer → Personal Web Server → Personal Web Manager to configure your web server. Five icons down the left side provide access to the Personal Web Server's options (see Figure W-1).

Of these different sections, the Main icon corresponds most directly to the Mac's Web Sharing control panel. It provides a Start/Stop button, tells you the address of your web site, and lists your shared folder. You're also shown the current number of connections and basic access statistics.

The Publish and Web Site icons provide access to wizards that walk you through putting basic content on your web site. The Web Site icons leads to the Home Page wizard, which, after you've answered a few questions, creates a rudimentary home page. The Publish icon leads to the Publishing Wizard, which lets you put links to your documents on your home page. You'll also find the Tour icon, which suggests different ways you can use Personal Web Server.

Instead of using the Publishing Wizard, you may prefer to drop your finished web page documents onto the Publish icon that Personal Web Server puts on your Desktop. When you do so, Personal Web Manager runs, filling in the necessary information in the Publishing Wizard for you.

Finally, the Advanced icon lets you change folders, identify default documents, save activity logs, and turn on directory browsing, which is akin to the Macintosh Web Sharing control panel's Personal NetFinder feature.

In the Mac's Web Sharing control panel, you can control who has access to which web pages by setting up accounts in the Users & Groups control panel. But Personal Web Server offers no such security.

Web Sites for Windows Software and Information
In Windows: Web Sites for Macintosh Software and Information

The Web is full of useful Windows software and information; here are some of the best sites.

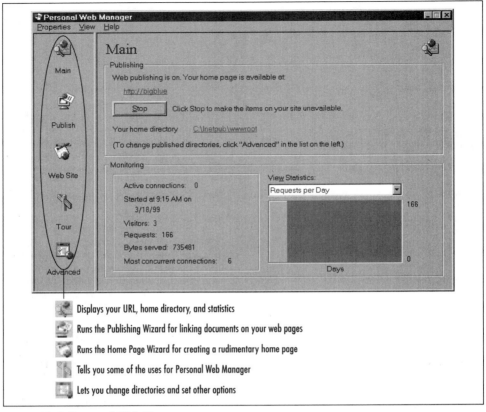

Figure W-1. Personal Web Manager

MacWindows. The MacWindows web site is the most appropriate for readers of this book, because it focuses on information of interest to people using both Macs and Windows-based PCs—or switching from one platform to another. See *http://www.macwindows.com/*.

Microsoft Support Center. If you're having trouble with Windows or another Microsoft product, your first stop should be Microsoft's online support resources. Especially useful are the online troubleshooters and Microsoft's support newsgroups, where you can post questions and read answers. See *http://support.microsoft.com/*.

PCWin Resource Center. The PCWin Resource Center offers downloadable freeware and shareware files, plus tips and tricks, a discussion area covering networking and hardware issues, and—in case you didn't think Windows programmers had a sense of humor—a list of Easter Eggs. See *http://pcwin.com/*.

Stroud's Consummate Winsock Applications. If you need an Internet-related program for Windows, check out Stroud's Consummate Winsock Applications list. This web site features nothing but Internet utilities, making it easy to navigate. See *http://cws.internet.com/home.html*.

Windows FAQ. FAQ stands for Frequently Asked Questions; this site collects those questions and provides answers. It may take some time to find the section that matches your question, but it's worth looking. See *http://www.orca.bc.ca/win95/*.

Windows 95 Annoyances. *Windows Annoyances,* which is both a book from O'Reilly and a web site, offers information on how to cope with Windows, ways of customizing the operating system, dealing with networking, and more. As a Macintosh user in a Windows world, you're probably having no difficulty finding annoyances about Windows; this web site can help you work around them. See *http://www.annoyances.org/win95/.*

WinFiles.com. WinFiles.com provides explanations, software, and information about Microsoft Windows. WinFiles.com is especially useful if you're looking for a freeware or shareware utility. See *http://www.winfiles.com/.*

Windows

In Windows: Windows

Mac OS windows are relatively Spartan, concentrating on what's in the window. In Windows, particularly in the Desktop windows of Windows 98 however, you can choose to view all sorts of window dressing (see Figure W-2) by choosing items from the View menu (alternatively, right-click the window's menu bar to add or remove toolbars).

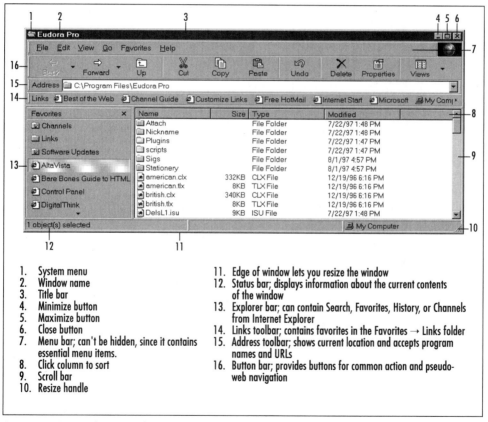

1. System menu
2. Window name
3. Title bar
4. Minimize button
5. Maximize button
6. Close button
7. Menu bar; can't be hidden, since it contains essential menu items.
8. Click column to sort
9. Scroll bar
10. Resize handle
11. Edge of window lets you resize the window
12. Status bar; displays information about the current contents of the window
13. Explorer bar; can contain Search, Favorites, History, or Channels from Internet Explorer
14. Links toolbar; contains favorites in the Favorites → Links folder
15. Address toolbar; shows current location and accepts program names and URLs
16. Button bar; provides buttons for common action and pseudo-web navigation

Figure W-2. Windows window, with all the trimmings.

You can find extensive information on manipulating and understanding Windows windows in the sections **List Views**, **Collapsing Windows**, **Zooming Windows**, **Title Bar**, **Resizing Windows**, and **View Menu**. In the meantime, here's a crash course on windows in Windows:

- Move a window by dragging its title bar, exactly as on the Macintosh.

- Close a window by clicking the X in the upper-right corner.

- Resize the window by dragging the lower-right corner—or enlarge it only vertically or only horizontally by dragging the thin gray window edge.

- You can *maximize* a window, making its edges expand until they merge with the edges of the screen, by clicking the middle icon of the three in the upper-right corner. To turn it back into a free-floating rectangle, click the same button again (even though the button has changed shape).

- You can hide the window by clicking the leftmost of the three icons in the upper-right corner. Doing so is called *minimizing* the window—in effect, the window collapses into a single icon on the Taskbar at the bottom edge of your screen. Click that icon again to restore the window to full size.

- Use the View menu in a Desktop window to do the same kinds of things you would do on the Macintosh—change to a list view (called Details View in Windows), icon view, and so on.

Z

Zooming Windows

In Windows: Maximizing Windows

The Windows maximize button (see Figure Z-1) is similar, but not identical, to the Macintosh zoom button. When you click the Windows maximize button, the window expands to fill the entire screen (instead of growing only as large as necessary to show the entire contents, as on the Macintosh). If you maximize a Web browser or word processor window on a large screen, therefore, you may end up with long and hard-to-read lines of text.

Because Windows is window-centric, rather than application-centric, like the Macintosh, many Windows users work with all applications maximized at all times. As a result, they see only one window at a time, and use the Taskbar or Alt-Tab to switch between applications.

When you click the maximize button, its icon changes to what's called a restore button. Click it to restore the window to its original size.

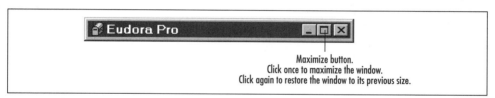

Maximize button.
Click once to maximize the window.
Click again to restore the window to its previous size.

Figure Z-1. Maximize button

Introduction

The Macintosh and Windows are the most popular computer platforms on earth. But the relationship between them, and the people who use them, has never been smooth. For years, Macintosh fans felt robbed by Microsoft, who, they felt, stole the best features of the Macintosh when designing Windows. And Windows users, for their part, often resented what they perceived as the excessive enthusiasm Macintosh fans felt for their underdog platform.

Today, much of the anger has subsided. Microsoft, it turns out, is enthusiastic in its support of the Mac OS, happy to support its sole competitor (if only to show the U.S. Justice Department that Microsoft is no monopoly). The Macintosh, moreover, benefits greatly by Microsoft's Macintosh software division, whose Office suite and Internet tools rank among the most popular Macintosh applications. Meanwhile, Apple has helped itself to some of the best ideas from Windows in the latest versions of the Mac OS, bringing the two systems even closer together.

Bilingual Education

As a result, we now live in an era of unprecedented shifts from one operating system to another. During Apple's financial slump of 1995 to 1997, thousands of Macintosh fans reluctantly started using Windows out of fear that their favorite computer maker might not be around to support the Macintosh for long. Then, during Apple's subsequent recovery, thousands of frustrated Windows users embraced the simplicity and style of Apple's smash-hit iMacintosh computer. It's increasingly common for someone to use a Macintosh at home, but Windows at work; Windows in Accounting, but a Macintosh in the art department; Macs for the kids, Windows for their parents. And among computing professionals—network administrators, consultants, and web page designers—familiarity with both platforms is becoming ever more important.

With all the emotion clearing like smoke, one fact becomes clear: whether at Apple or Microsoft, the designers of an operating system must solve the same set of challenges. They need to offer you, the user, a means of interacting with your files and folders; access to preference settings to tailor the operating system to your purposes; a system of printing and going online; and so on. Sometimes Apple and Microsoft solved these puzzles in similar fashions, other times they took drastically different approaches, but the problems themselves are the same. Once you study both platforms, the parallels become crystal clear: a Windows shortcut is essentially identical to a Macintosh alias; the Windows Recycle Bin matches the Mac's Trash can; the Windows Network Neighborhood and the Mac's Network Browser both access other computers on your network; and so on.

But knowing one set of terminology isn't much help in figuring out the other. Who would guess that a shortcut and an alias have the same function? And more important, when you're plopped in front of the platform you don't know, how can you figure out the important differences between shortcuts and aliases, for instance?

This book is the answer. It's designed like a foreign-language translation dictionary. For instance, if you're a Windows user trying to use a Macintosh and you want to create an shortcut, you look up *shortcut* to find out it's an *alias* on the Macintosh. Like a French-English/English-French phrasebook, this one is split in half; one set of alphabetical entries is written for the person who's switching to Windows, and this set is written for people going to Macintosh.

How to Use This Book

Crossing Platforms assumes that you already know your native computer; it makes no attempt to start from such basics as pointing, clicking, or how RAM and hard disks work. Its mission is to make you operational on the less familiar platform as efficiently as possible, to help minimize your groping for important controls in an unfamiliar vehicle.

The key to using this book is simple: Turn to the appropriate half of the book—"For Windows Users Learning Macintosh" or "For Macintosh Users Learning Windows." Then look up the term you already know.

If you're a Windows user, you're reading the correct half of the book. Look up such Windows-specific terms as *Alt key, Network Neighborhood,* and *Recycle Bin,* or generic computing terms like *file sharing, moving files,* and *printing files*. Either way, you'll find out exactly what the equivalent component is on the Macintosh, and you can read about how it differs from the one you already know. Words in **boldface** are cross-references—other related terms in this same half of the book that you can look up.

As you become increasingly familiar with the Mac OS, you'll likely recognize more and more familiar landmarks. Eventually, you'll grasp the stylistic differences of the world's two most famous system software companies, and maybe you'll even anticipate where Apple stashed things. At that point, you won't need this book as often, and you'll have attained a most impressive status—as a truly bilingual computer user. When that time comes, you won't even bat an eye when taking what was once an inconceivable leap: crossing platforms.

Operating System Versions

Both Apple and Microsoft update their operating systems constantly. This book covers the most widely used versions of each: Windows 95 and 98, and Mac OS 8.0 through 8.6. The book doesn't explicitly cover Mac OS 9, but almost all of this book's Macintosh discussions should apply equally well to the newer Mac OS.

The Ten Most Important Macintosh Differences

This entire book is dedicated to documenting the differences between Windows and the Mac OS. But if today is your first day in front of a Macintosh, here are the ten difference most likely to trip you up:

1. **Turning the machine on and off.** Every modern Macintosh—laptop or desktop—has a power key on the keyboard. It's marked by a triangle or, on recent models, by a circle with a vertical line in the middle. Push this button to turn the Macintosh on; push it again to summon the "Are you sure you want to shut down?" dialog box.

2. **Mouse buttons.** The Macintosh mouse's single button corresponds to the left mouse button on a Windows PC. To summon pop-up contextual menus—the right mouse button's traditional job—you Control-click something on the Macintosh.

3. **Menu bars.** On the Macintosh, a single menu bar appears at the top of the screen at all times. The commands in it change as you switch from one application to another. You won't find a separate menu bar inside every window, as you do in Windows.

4. **Keyboard shortcuts.** Most keyboard shortcuts are the same on the Macintosh as in Windows—except that you should substitute the Command key (which has clover leaf and Apple logos on it) for the Ctrl key, and the Option key for the Alt key.

5. **Window controls.** To close a window, click the tiny square in the upper-*left* corner of a Macintosh window. To move a window, drag the title bar as usual. And to resize it, drag the lower-right corner, exactly as you would in Windows. (Dragging the fat edges of a window moves the window instead of resizing it, as it would in Windows.) The two squares in the upper-right corner of the Macintosh window are the *zoom box* (makes the window exactly large enough to reveal all of its contents) and the *collapse box* (makes the window vanish into its title bar).

6. **The Application menu.** The Macintosh has no Taskbar. Instead, you switch from one application to another using the Application menu, which appears at the far right of the menu bar and is marked by the icon of the current application. If you're running Mac OS 8.5 or later, this menu may also display the *name* of the current running application; you can switch from one application to another by pressing Command-Tab.

7. **Application windows.** Quitting a Macintosh application (by choosing Quit, the Macintosh equivalent of Exit) closes all of its windows. No stray windows remain on the screen, as they sometimes do in Windows. Also, closing the last window in an application generally won't quit the application, as happens with some Windows programs.

8. **The Apple menu.** The Apple menu, whose icon appears at the top-left corner of the screen, resembles the Start menu in many ways. You should know about a few important differences, however: first, only the most recently used applications appear in the Recent Applications submenu; the Macintosh offers no complete list of every application on the hard disk. Second, adding new documents, applications, disks, or even networked servers to the Apple menu is extremely easy. See **Start Menu** in this half of the book for step-by-step instructions.

9. **Disks.** The Macintosh has no My Computer icon. The hard disk icon always appears at the upper-right corner of the screen; icons for other kinds of disks—floppies, CDs, or Zip disks, for example—don't appear on the Desktop until you insert such a disk into the machine. Ejecting a disk is also very different on the Macintosh: there's no manual-eject button on the front panel for most kinds of disk drives. Instead, eject a disk by highlighting its icon and then choosing Special → Eject Disk. Or use the time-honored Macintosh shortcut: drag the disk's icon onto the Trash can (the equivalent of the Recycle Bin). Doing so does not erase the disk! Instead, the disk pops out of the drive.

10. **Emptying the Trash.** The Mac OS never removes files from the Trash automatically, as Windows does with files in the Recycle Bin. To remove files from the Trash manually, choose Special → Empty Trash.

11. **Bonus Difference: Troubleshooting.** Troubleshooting on the Macintosh is generally a do-it-yourself affair—partly because Apple's free technical support period is only 90 days long, and partly because most Macintosh problems are easy to fix. For example, every Macintosh comes with a startup CD that can be used to boot, run, and troubleshoot the computer, even when the hard disk is damaged or missing. See **Troubleshooting** in this half of the book for some starting points.

A

About This Program

On the Macintosh: About This Program

In Windows, when you want to find out more information about the current program, you're probably used to looking for the About This Program command at the bottom of the Help menu. When using a Macintosh, though, look at the first item in the Apple menu in the upper left of the screen—it's always About for the current application.

When you're in the Finder (click the Desktop to be sure), that command is About This Computer; it provides information about your version of the Mac OS, the memory configuration of your Macintosh, and infor-mation about whatever programs you're running at the moment (see Figure A-1).

Accessibility Options

On the Macintosh: CloseView

The Accessibility Options control panel in Windows is designed to make using the PC easier if you're disabled. Its features include:

Keyboard tab, Mouse tab. Features like Sticky Keys and Filter Keys can make using the keyboard easier if you can only type with one hand. For example, you can con-figure Windows so that a modifier key like Ctrl can be pressed before its accompany-ing keystroke, instead of simultaneously.

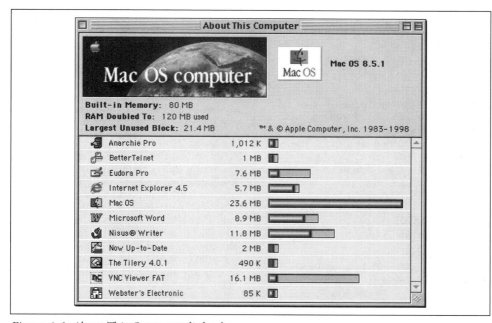

Figure A-1. About This Computer dialog box

The Mouse tab contains options that let you move the cursor by pressing the keys on the numeric keypad.

The equivalent features on the Macintosh are in the CloseView control panel. This software isn't a part of the standard system-software installation, however—you must install it yourself, using the Custom option of any Macintosh system-software installer, System 6 and later.

Sound tab. This Accessibility Options tab makes the Windows screen blink instead of beeping when it wants your attention. To achieve the same effect on the Macintosh, open Apple menu → Control Panels → Monitors & Sound, click Alert Sound, and set the volume to zero. Now, whenever it would otherwise beep, the Macintosh blinks its menu bar.

Display tab. The Macintosh has no one-click checkbox that enlarges text and enhances text clarity through the use of high-contrast colors. But the Fonts tab of the Appearance control panel in Mac OS 8.5 and later lets you create the same effect, and the previously described CloseView control panel can double the entire screen image. For less severe sight problems, consider simply setting a lower resolution for your monitor, such as 640×480, using the Monitors & Sound control panel. Doing so enlarges the display without dramatically changing the landscape.

General tab. This final pane of Accessibility Options governs how Windows lets you know that one of these accessibility features has been turned on or off. The Mac's CloseView control panel produces special chirps and sounds by default when you turn mysterious features on or off.

Active Desktop
On the Macintosh: None

Active Desktop—available in Windows 98, or in Windows 95 with Internet Explorer 4.0 —is a means of viewing your Windows Desktop with a web-browser (Internet Explorer) interface. This scheme lets you place HTML-based objects on your Desktop that might display frequently updated sports

scores, news headlines, weather reports, stock prices, and so on.

There's no equivalent on the Macintosh—if you want to view content from the Web, you'll have to use a web browser.

ActiveMovie Control
On the Macintosh: Movie Player

Windows 95 provides ActiveMovie Control for you to play a variety of multimedia files—digital movies, digitized sounds, and so on. In Windows 98, though, that task is handled by Media Player, and on the Macintosh, Apple provides the Movie Player application. For more information on Movie Player, see **Media Player**.

Add New Hardware Control Panel
On the Macintosh: No Equivalent—New Hardware Works Without Special Setup

In theory, you should be able to plug any add-on device (scanner, printer, mouse, and so on) into your PC; when you start up, Windows should recognize the new gadget, install the appropriate drivers, and proceed to work perfectly. In practice, of course, the tremendous variety of hardware available for the PC often makes this much-touted "plug and play" scheme more like "plug and pray." This, then, is the purpose of Windows' Add New Hardware control panel; it lets you manually ask Windows to detect any newly added gear and install the necessary software from the accompanying disks.

The Macintosh doesn't require an "Add New Hardware" application; in almost all cases, the computer automatically recognizes newly attached gadgets and configures itself to work with them. Adding a mouse, track-ball, keyboard, memory card, video card, and even SCSI device to a Macintosh requires little more than connecting it (although SCSI requires some knowledge; see **SCSI**). Networkable printers work the same way—no special software installation is required.

A few Macintosh add-ons, however, require that you install the provided driver software; graphics tablets and inkjet printers fall into this category. (Installing drivers is generally a matter of running an installer program and rebooting the Macintosh.)

Add/Remove Programs Control Panel
On the Macintosh: Individual Installers

When you install a new Windows program, your installer generally places myriad files, including cryptically named DLLs (Dynamic Link Libraries), onto your hard disk—and makes changes to the Registry. Fortunately, most Windows installers register themselves with the Add/Remove Programs control panel; thereafter, you can uninstall your programs—including the assortment of associated support files that the installation sprayed into your computer.

There's no similarly coherent way of uninstalling applications on the Macintosh; on the other hand, doing so is generally unnecessary. Macintosh application installers (except those from Microsoft) usually install many fewer components than Windows programs, and those components are generally confined to predictable locations. So, if you install a Macintosh application and later wish to delete it, you seldom have to do more than drag the application's folder to the Trash. A few applications may put files in the Extensions, Control Panels, or Preferences folders in the System Folder, but such files are generally easily identifiable by name. In addition, many installers provide the capability to remove what they've installed.

Since the Macintosh has no Add/Remove Programs control panel, you may be wondering how to create a startup disk on the Macintosh (since creating a Windows startup disk is a function of Add/Remove Programs). There's no need to bother; every Macintosh comes with a startup floppy disk or CD-ROM.

Adobe Acrobat
On the Macintosh: Adobe Acrobat

Adobe Acrobat is a cross-platform program (versions exist for Windows, the Macintosh, and Unix) that lets you see documents on-screen as they were meant to be seen on paper, complete with graphics, typography, and original layout. You can also print these documents without loss of quality, even if you lack the documents' original fonts.

Some companies choose to distribute online in Acrobat format—more accurately called PDF or Portable Document Format—because of this guarantee of display quality. Other uses of Acrobat include sending proofs of documents to people who may lack both the necessary program and the necessary fonts to view the original file, and distributing forms such as the IRS tax forms, which must be printed out accurately.

Adobe put a lot of effort into making Acrobat files totally cross-platform. If you create an Acrobat file using Acrobat Distiller in Windows, you can send that file to a Macintosh user who can read and print it using the free Acrobat Reader—and vice versa.

You can find much more information about Adobe Acrobat on Adobe's web site at *http://www.adobe.com/*.

Alt Key
On the Macintosh: Option Key

As with the Alt key in Windows, you can use the Mac's Option key to enter hidden characters that don't normally appear on your keyboard, such as ¢ and £.

Many of these are clever maps: where Shift-4 produces the $ character, Option-4 creates a ¢ symbol. To look up the full set of available characters, open Apple menu → Key Caps, and then press the Option key to view which symbols hide behind which keys.

Accented letters require a different technique. The U, N, I, E, and tilde (~) keys are so-called "dead" keys when used with the Option key—that is, typing Option-U doesn't do anything until you type another character to create the accented character. For instance, type Option-U, then O to create an O with an umlaut. Table A-1 lists the five possibilities.

Modified behavior. The Mac's Option key, like the Alt key, can also produce a random assortment of special productivity effects in daily Macintosh use, as summarized in Table A-2.

Table A-1. Accented Characters Available via the Option Key

Option Key Combination	Result (Typed Over an O)
Option-E	acute accent (ó)
Option-I	circumflex (ô)
Option-N	tilde (õ)
Option-Tilde	grave (ò)
Option-U	umlaut (ö)

Table A-2. Optional Behaviors Using the Option Key

Modified Behavior	Function
Option-click to switch programs	Pressing Option as you switch to another program (by choosing its name from the Application menu, or by clicking in its window) hides all windows of the first program—a handy housekeeping trick.
Option-Empty Trash	The Mac OS deletes locked files in the Trash instantaneously, bypassing the usual confirmation warning.
Option-drag an icon in the Finder	Option-dragging an icon creates a duplicate of the original file.
Option-Clean Up (System 7 only)	Pressing Option while choosing Special → Clean Up arranges icons on an invisible grid and sorts them at the same time.
Option-click a window's close box	Clicking the close box while pressing Option closes all visible windows in the current application (especially on the Desktop).
Option-double-click a folder	Opening a folder while pressing Option automatically closes the previous window (that is, the one that contains the folder you're double-clicking).
Option-drag text	In most word processing and email programs, Option-dragging text into a new location duplicates the original highlighted phrase.

ATM (Adobe Type Manager)

On the Macintosh: ATM (Adobe Type Manager)

Adobe Type Manager, commonly known as ATM, is a font utility designed to display clear, sharp characters of any size onscreen and on non-PostScript printers. ATM works with Type 1 PostScript fonts; TrueType fonts, which exist for both Windows and the Macintosh, don't require ATM to perform the same feat. (Without ATM, PostScript fonts often look jagged on the screen and on inkjet printouts.)

ATM is available for both Windows and the Macintosh, but you're more likely to see it on the Macintosh, since a limited version of ATM is installed with the Macintosh version of Adobe Acrobat's free Acrobat Reader. A commercial product with additional type manipulation capabilities, ATM Deluxe, is available for both Windows and the Macintosh. See *http://www.adobe.com/* for more information.

B

Backspace Key
On the Macintosh: Delete Key

The Backspace key is near and dear to the hearts of editors everywhere. Standard keyboards from Apple call the same key "Delete."

In Mac OS 8 and later, the Delete key has one additional function that's extremely welcome. You can move files to the Trash by selecting their icons and then pressing Command-Delete. Doing so is exactly the same as selecting a file in Windows and pressing Delete. On the other hand, there's no way on the Macintosh to delete a file completely without sending it to the Trash first (Shift-Delete in Windows).

Background
On the Macintosh: General Control Panel, Desktop Patterns Control Panel, Desktop Pictures Control Panel, Appearance Control Panel

In Windows, you can change the appearance of your Desktop background by applying either a graphics file (wallpaper) or a pattern to it. You can do the same in the Mac OS as well, although they've moved around over different versions of the operating system.

- In versions of the Mac OS prior to System 7.5, the General Controls control panel (Apple menu → Control Panels → General Controls) let you switch between a number of built-in Desktop patterns.

- With System 7.5 and 7.6, Apple included the Desktop Patterns control panel (accessible from Apple menu → Control Panels → Desktop Patterns) to let you switch between different Desktop patterns.

- Mac OS 8.0 and 8.1 featured the Desktop Pictures control panel, described later in this entry, which let you apply both patterns and pictures to your Desktop. Desktop Pictures is located in Apple menu → Control Panels → Desktop Pictures.

- In Mac OS 8.5, Apple incorporated the Desktop Pictures control panel into the Appearance control panel, accessible from Apple menu → Control Panels → Appearance → Desktop (see Figure B-1). It works the same way as Desktop Pictures.

To apply a pattern to your Desktop, follow these steps:

1. Open Apple menu → Control Panel → Appearance → Desktop.
2. Select a pattern from the Patterns list.
3. Click Set Desktop.

Applying a picture to the Desktop is slightly more complicated. Apple included some sample pictures in Macintosh HD → System Folder → Appearance → Desktop Pictures, but you can use any picture you like if it's in the GIF, JPEG, Photoshop, or the Macintosh-only PICT file format.

1. Open Apple menu → Control Panel → Appearance → Desktop.
2. Click Place Picture, then find the desired picture on your hard disk. Alternatively, from the Finder, drag the picture file's icon into the preview monitor in the Appearance control panel.
3. If you wish, choose a position from the Position menu under the Place Picture button.
4. Click Set Desktop.

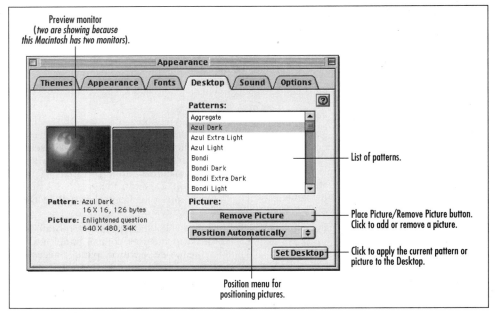

Preview monitor (*two are showing because this Macintosh has two monitors*).

List of patterns.

Place Picture/Remove Picture button. Click to add or remove a picture.

Click to apply the current pattern or picture to the Desktop.

Position menu for positioning pictures.

Figure B-1. Appearance control panel's Desktop tab

Batch Language
On the Macintosh: AppleScript

Many Windows users, particularly those who grew up using DOS, know that you can create collections of commands called *batch files*. Although batch files are primarily used to automate what you could do manually from the DOS command line, a variety of other commands in the batch language provide looping, conditionals, and other programming constructs. Batch files aren't important or heavily used in Windows, but they can still prove useful on occasion for automated processes. In Windows 98, Microsoft introduced the Windows Scripting Host, which lets you write and execute scripts written in a variety of scripting languages, including Microsoft's VBScript and JScript, along with JavaScript, Perl, PerlScript, Python, and TCL.

The Macintosh has no command-line underpinnings, so a batch language *per se* has no meaning in the Macintosh world. Instead, you can use AppleScript to control many Macintosh applications, including the

Finder. AppleScript is a full-featured scripting language, and those who know it well can make it do impressive things, ranging from automating desktop publishing layout production to creating scripts that enhance web servers.

If you want to write a script, it's most easily done in a simple program that comes with the Mac OS called Script Editor. More capable AppleScript editors are available from third parties.

Scripts can be saved in several different formats, which is useful to know because other people may send you scripts. Scripts might be text files, compiled scripts, applications, or run-only applications. Double-clicking text files and compiled scripts opens them in Script Editor, where you can edit the AppleScript code and run the script by clicking the Run button. Applications and run-only applications act like any other applications on the Macintosh; the only difference between them is that Script Editor can open and edit applications, but not run-only applications.

You can extend AppleScript's capabilities with files called *scripting additions* (they're also sometimes informally referred to as "osaxen"). Scripting additions belong in System Folder → Scripting Additions.

The Mac OS comes with a number of useful sample scripts—you'll find them in Apple menu → Automated Tasks.

BinHex
On the Macintosh: BinHex

You may be a bit perplexed when receiving email attachments on the Macintosh in BinHex format, or when trying to download software from the Internet for the Macintosh in BinHex format, since BinHex isn't commonly used in Windows.

BinHex is a bit of an anomaly on the Macintosh—it's both a binary packaging format that lumps the two Macintosh file forks together and a transfer encoding format that converts the resultant 8-bit file into 7-bit ASCII text for transmission via email or downloading from FTP or web sites. Unfortunately, as with all transfer encoding formats, the file size grows when encoded.

Most Macintosh files downloadable from the Internet are stored in BinHex format still, even though it's no longer the necessity it once was. The reasons are mostly historical, although some people on the Internet are still using older programs or hardware devices that can't handle 8-bit communications. In cases where 8-bit data paths are guaranteed, MacBinary is more efficient, since it solves the multiple fork problem without increasing the file size.

You can identify BinHex files by their filename extension of *.hqx.* You should need to create a BinHex file only if you're planning to upload a file; email programs encode attachments in BinHex format automatically. Similarly, email programs decode binhexed attachments automatically, but not all Macintosh web browsers and FTP programs do; you may need to decode the file by using a utility like Aladdin's StuffIt Expander (see **Zip**). Aladdin also makes the shareware program DropStuff and the com-

mercial StuffIt Deluxe, both of which can create BinHex files.

Some, but not all, Windows email programs can encode and decode BinHex files. If you find yourself with a binhexed file, to decode it you'll need StuffIt Expander from Aladdin Systems. You can download it from *http://www.aladdinsys.com/.*

For more information, see **Transferring Files to the Macintosh.**

BIOS
On the Macintosh: ROM or ROM File

The Macintosh has no exact equivalent to the tiny, hardware-based kernel of Windows boot-up information known as the BIOS (Basic Input Output System). The Mac's much larger, more complete ROM file (found in the System Folder of iMacs and other modern models) or the ROM chip (on older Macs) performs similar under-the-hood functions, such as providing the fundamental bootstrap code necessary for the computer to turn on before its actual operating system software loads. But you can't edit the Mac's ROM files, and the Macintosh ROM constitutes far more of an OS component than the BIOS code on a PC.

Bitmap (.bmp) Files
On the Macintosh: PICT Files

A bitmapped graphic, often created by what are called paint programs, is an image composed of a specific arrangement of dots; you can edit the image only by adding or removing dots. In contrast, object-oriented images (created by drawing programs) contain objects, such as squares and circles, which you can edit as discrete objects.

More to the point, in Windows, bitmap is a specific graphic file format, typically signified by a filename with a *.bmp* extension. The comparable Macintosh format is PICT, which can be composed of either bitmapped or object-oriented graphics. The principal uses for PICT files are as screen captures and file icons.

Note

Although PICT files are the Mac's main graphics file format, they're not well suited to desktop publishing. Professional printing equipment frequently chokes on such graphics—whenever possible, save your graphics files in such cross-platform file formats as TIFF. Be careful when working with images if you care about the file format, since copying an image generally copies it as a PICT, which may not be what you expected.

Boot Disk
On the Macintosh: Boot Disk

Most PC users are accustomed to being able to boot a PC only from an A: floppy disk or C: hard disk drive, although many recent PCs support booting from alternate drives in the BIOS.

On the Macintosh, any disk can boot the computer if it contains a valid System Folder. This capability is tremendously handy for troubleshooting, since you can use any hard disk, CD-ROM, or removable disk to boot a Macintosh.

The order in which the Macintosh checks to see which disk to use can be helpful to know:

1. If there is a floppy disk containing a System Folder in the floppy drive, the Macintosh boots from the disk. Remember that Macs automatically eject floppies when you choose Special → Restart, so you may have to insert the floppy disk again if it was in before restarting.

2. If you hold down the C key on most modern Macs, the Macintosh boots from the internal CD-ROM drive, again assuming a CD with a System Folder (such as the system CD that comes with every Macintosh) is in the drive.

3. If you aren't holding down the C key, the Macintosh looks for the hard disk (or partition) selected in the Startup Items control panel. If that hard disk includes a System Folder, the Macintosh boots from it.

4. If the hard disk (or partition) selected in the Startup Items control panel lacks a System Folder, the Macintosh continues to look for another hard disk or partition from which to boot. If the Macintosh can't find any valid boot disk, it flashes a question-mark icon on the screen until you insert a disk containing a System Folder.

Briefcase
On the Macintosh: PowerBook File Assistant, File Synchronization

Working with multiple computers—such as a laptop and your desktop PC—raises the thorny issue of tracking different versions of the same file on different computers. The obvious solution is to copy files to the laptop before a trip, and back to the desktop on return. Unfortunately, if you're not careful, you could end up with modifications in both copies of a file.

Microsoft addressed this problem with the Briefcase in Windows, which lets you carry files between computers and synchronize them when you return. The Mac's File Synchronization program (formerly known as PowerBook File Assistant) performs roughly the same function.

Note

Although File Synchronization works fine on desktop Macs as well as PowerBooks, your system installer doesn't install it by default unless you have a PowerBook. To install File Synchronization onto a desktop computer, perform a custom installation of Mac OS 8.5 and select File Synchronization from the list of Control Panels.

File Synchronization is simpler to understand than the Windows Briefcase. You simply identify pairs of folders—one on the laptop, one on the desktop, for example—to synchronize. When you ask it to perform a synchronization, File Synchronization compares the modification dates of all the files in the synchronization pairs and copies files back and forth as necessary.

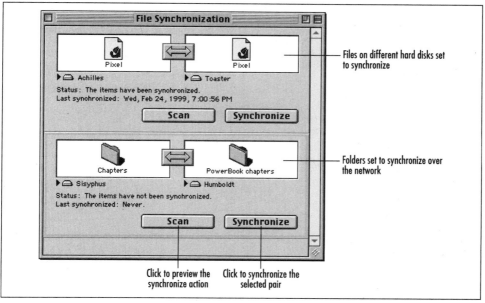

Figure B-2. Synchronizing files and folders using File Synchronization

To synchronize two folders (which don't have to have the same name), follow these steps.

1. Open Apple menu → Control Panels → File Synchronization.

2. In the Finder, drag the source folder into one side of the file pair (see Figure B-2) and the destination folder into the other side.

3. Then, if you want changes made in either folder to be reflected in the other, make sure the arrow pointing between the two is double-headed. Otherwise, if you only want changes in one folder to be reflected in the other, click the arrow until it points from the source to the destination.

4. When you're ready, click the Scan button to see what File Synchronization plans to do, or click the Synchronize button to synchronize the files without prior verification.

Synchronizing a pair of files requires exactly the same steps, but when selecting a source and destination, the files must have the same name.

Once you've become comfortable with what File Synchronization does, you may want to set certain file or folder pairs to automatic synchronization (select the pair, then choose Synchronize → Automatic). That way, whenever you open File Synchronization, it will synchronize that pair without your intervention. For even more automation, consider putting an alias to File Synchronization in your Startup Items folder so it runs at startup. Then, when you insert a disk or mount a server that contains half of a synchronization pair, the synchronization happens immediately.

Button
On the Macintosh: Button

Along with menus, buttons are one of the most common elements of a graphical user interface. Buttons are generally rectangular in Windows and rounded rectangles on the Macintosh.

As in Windows, when a button has an outline around it (heavier and darker in Macintosh dialog boxes), it's the default button—press Return or Enter to "click" it. You can also trigger a Macintosh Cancel button from the keyboard—press the Esc key or Command-period.

If you're used to Windows, where you can trigger any button in any dialog box from the keyboard, you may be disappointed on the Macintosh. Only a few programs—notably those from Microsoft and the former Claris—offer the ability to "click" buttons with keystrokes.

C

Calculator

On the Macintosh: Calculator

Using its View menu, you can switch the Windows calculator between its basic four-function and scientific modes. The Mac's Calculator desk accessory (Apple menu → Calculator) can't do anything more than basic four-function math. At the high end is the Mac's Graphing Calculator (Apple menu → Graphing Calculator), which can solve and graph complex equations.

For a reasonable calculator in between those two extremes, you'll have to turn to a third party calculator, such as the freeware Calculator II, available from the web site *http://hyperarchive.lcs.mit.edu/ HyperArchive/Archive/sci/calc/calculator-ii-15.hqx.*

CD Drives

On the Macintosh: CD Drives

CD drives for accessing CD-ROMs and audio CDs are standard equipment on Macs and PCs today, with the notable exception of laptop computers that lack room for a CD drive. For the most part, using CDs on a Macintosh is similar to using them on Windows, with a few caveats.

Inserting and removing CDs. You insert a CD into a Macintosh just as you do on a PC—press the eject button on the drive, insert the CD, and press the button again (or push the tray gently) to close the tray. (On newer models, such as the late-1999 iMac, there's no tray; you insert the CD directly into the slot.) CDs on the Macintosh appear on the Desktop like any other disk; once a disc's icon appears, you use it exactly like any other disk (except that you can't write data to a CD, of course).

Removing the CD from a Macintosh may throw you at first—you can't just press the CD-ROM button to make the disc pop out, as you can in Windows. Instead, use one of the three onscreen methods: Control-click a CD's icon, then choose Eject from the contextual menu; click the CD's icon, and then choose Special → Eject; or drag the CD's icon to the Trash. In all three cases, the CD slides out.

AutoPlay on CD insertion. Some CDs for both the Macintosh and Windows come pre-programmed to launch a program—often an installer—automatically when you insert the CD. Although many Windows CDs take advantage of this feature, you'll rarely see it in action on the Macintosh. In part, this is due to the fact that a recent Macintosh virus exploited this auto-launch feature. Many Macintosh users turn off CD-ROM AutoPlay (Apple menu → Control Panels → Quick-Time Settings → AutoPlay) to avoid being infected with this virus, and we recommend that you do the same.

On the other hand, there's little downside to leaving the audio CD AutoPlay feature turned on (in the Mac's QuickTime Settings control panel), so that music CDs you insert start playing automatically.

CD Player

On the Macintosh: AppleCD Audio Player

AppleCD Audio Player, the Macintosh equivalent of CD Player in Windows, offers all the controls you normally see on a music CD player, including shuffle, repeat, and program modes; stop, play, eject, and forward and back buttons; and a volume control. The display includes the current track number and an elapsed time indicator, which can show either elapsed time for the disc or remaining time for the disc or the track.

Note

Every CD can be uniquely identified through a checksum, which is how AppleCD Audio Player identifies CDs after you've named them. Unfortunately, the information you enter exists only in the CD Remote Programs file; if you have another computer, AppleCD Audio Player won't recognize CDs you've annotated in this way. As a simple workaround, copy the CD Remote Programs file to the Preferences folder on your other Macintosh. As an alternative, check out the shareware TitleTrack CD Player, which can download information about your CDs from an Internet database containing details of 230,000 CDs. You can find Title-Track CD Player at *http://www.titletrack.com/*.

What sets AppleCD Audio Player apart from a run-of-the-mill CD player are its hidden controls and options. Click the tiny downward-pointing triangle on the left side of the window to expand the display. Now you see the name of the CD, the name of each track, and the length of the CD and of each track (see Figure C-1). Double-click a track number to play that track. Initially, the CD and track titles are all generic—"Audio CD" and "Track 1," for instance. However, you can edit the names; AppleCD Audio Player stores them in a file called "CD Remote Programs" in your System Folder's Preferences folder, so that the next time you insert the CD, Audio Player will display its name and names of the songs on it..

Character Map
On the Macintosh: Key Caps

Figuring out the keystrokes necessary to generate special characters like the trademark symbol or the copyright symbol requires the use of the Character Map utility in Windows. The Macintosh equivalent is called Key Caps (Apple menu → Key Caps).

Although Key Caps looks somewhat different from the Character Map utility, it works similarly (see Figure C-2)

To insert a special character in a word processing document, follow these steps in Key Caps:

1. Choose the appropriate font from the Key Caps menu.

2. Press Shift, Option, Control, or combinations of these keys to see how they affect the symbols that will appear when you type. For example, pressing the Option key makes the normal alphabet keys produce a range of useful symbols, such as ¢ and £.

3. Click the desired special character in the character grid to place it in the text field at the top of the window.

4. Select the character, choose Edit → Copy (Command-C), switch to your word processing document, and choose Edit → Paste (Command-V) to paste the special character.

5. If the character you wanted doesn't exist in the font you're using in the word processing document, select the character you just pasted, and then choose the font you had chosen in Key Caps.

This method of inserting special characters is clumsy. If you find yourself having to repeat the procedure for certain common symbols, you can save time by simply memorizing the necessary key combination. For instance, if you want a registered trademark symbol (®), your experiments in Key Caps will show you that Option-R is the right combination.

In short, whereas in Windows you're used to typing Alt plus a four-digit number to access special characters, on the Macintosh, you instead use modifier keys in conjunction with the alphanumeric keys. (As in Windows, however, different fonts contain different sets of available symbols.)

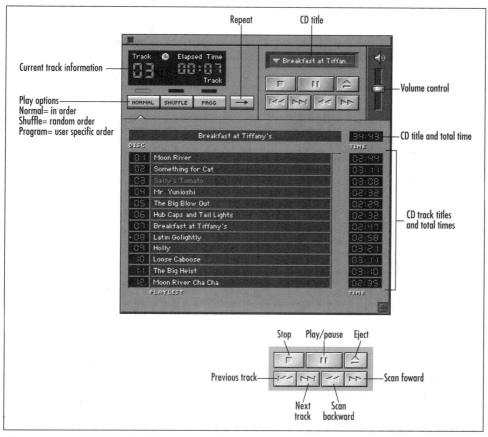

Figure C-1. AppleCD Audio Player controls

Clean Install

On the Macintosh: Clean Install

Like the Windows installer program, the Mac OS installer is designed to replace only those components of the operating system that need updating, as a convenience to you. Unfortunately, that means that if a system file is corrupted, it stays corrupted. The only way to guarantee a virginal, all-new System Folder (on the Macintosh) or Windows folder (on Windows) is to perform a clean install.

Fortunately, on the Macintosh, a clean install isn't anywhere near as complex, serious, and time-consuming an affair as it is on Windows. On a Macintosh, you can simply replace the System Folder itself; all of your

data and applications can remain where they are on the hard disk. A clean install on the Macintosh is a terrific troubleshooting technique, since it performs a surgical strike, wiping out every conceivable problematic system file and replacing it with a spotless, perfect new one—in about 15 minutes.

The method for doing a Macintosh clean install depends on which operating system version you have.

Mac OS 8.5 and later (also System 7.6): Run the Installer. Click Continue on the welcome screen. Click Options on the next screen. Turn on the "Perform a clean installation" or "Create additional System Folder" checkbox, and then install normally.

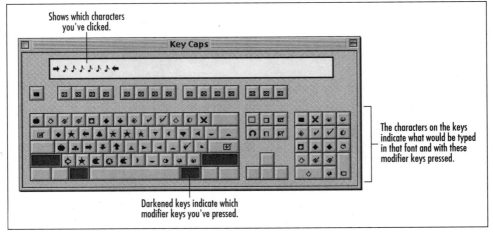

Shows which characters you've clicked.

The characters on the keys indicate what would be typed in that font and with these modifier keys pressed.

Darkened keys indicate which modifier keys you've pressed.

Figure C-2. Key Caps

Mac OS 8 and 8.1: Run the Installer. Click Continue on the welcome screen. Now turn on the checkbox called "Perform a clean installation," and then install normally.

System 7.5: Insert your system CD (or the first Installer disk). Double-click the Installer icon. Click Continue. At the main installation screen, where you'd normally click the Install button, press Command-Shift-K. You'll be asked which you want: a brand-new System Folder, or just an updated existing System Folder. You want the whole new one. Click your choice, click OK, click Install, and then follow the directions.

When the installation is over, you'll be asked to restart the Macintosh. You're now running from a duplicate, fresh System folder. Your old, messed-up one is deactivated and automatically renamed Previous System Folder.

Client for Microsoft Networks
On the Macintosh: AppleShare

On Windows, to access remote servers on your network you need the Client for Microsoft Networks installed in your Network control panel. On the Macintosh, you need the AppleShare extension in your Extensions folder. For additional information on how to mount an AppleShare server, see **Network Neighborhood**.

Clipboard
On the Macintosh: Clipboard

Windows and the Macintosh offer similar clipboard features. In essence, you can cut or copy information from one program to an invisible clipboard storage area, and then switch to another application to paste that information.

On the Macintosh, however, you can't copy and paste a file icon as you can in Windows—only highlighted material within your application windows can be pasted.

On the Macintosh, you don't need a special program like the Windows Clipboard Viewer to see what you've cut or copied; that feature is built into most programs' Edit menus. Choose Edit → Show Clipboard at any time to see what's in the clipboard.

Clock
On the Macintosh: Clock

In Windows, a clock appears in the Tray at the right side of the Taskbar. The Mac's clock lives in a similar location on the right side of the menu bar. The Windows clock displays the date if you hover over the time display; the Macintosh clock shows the date temporarily if you click the time.

The Macintosh clock offers a great deal of customization. If you click Apple menu →

Note

The new System Folder doesn't have any of the extensions, fonts, control panels, Apple menu items, and sounds you may have added to your original System Folder. It also lacks any preference files your software has created over the years.

After you've confirmed that the clean reinstall successfully restored your Macintosh to health, you can put those add-on components back into the new System Folder. Open the System Folder and the Previous System Folder side-by-side, in tall, skinny windows, and compare their contents. Check these folders for elements missing from your new System Folder: Apple Menu Items, Extensions, Control Panels, Fonts, and Preferences. If you find items in the old System Folder that aren't in the new System Folder, drag them into the corresponding locations in the new System Folder to reinstate them. Alternatively, use the commercial program Conflict Catcher (*http://www.casadyg.com/*) to automate this process.

Yet you don't want to reintroduce whatever problem you were having to begin with. Where possible, therefore, reinstall this material from original master disks, not from your problematic previous System Folder. Preference files are tricky; you can usually get away with dragging them out of your old System Folder's Preferences folder into the new one, but remember that corrupted preference files are a leading cause of Macintosh glitches within particular programs. If you can limit your Preferences file-dragging to the programs you've spent the most time customizing (such as your web browser's Favorites or Bookmarks files), you may spare yourself yet another round of troubleshooting.

Control Panels → Date & Time → Clock Options, you can change a variety of display options, the font and size used for the clock display, and even periodic chimes (see Figure C-3).

For more information about time on the Macintosh, see **Date/Time Control Panel**.

Closing Windows
On the Macintosh: Closing Windows

The standard method of closing a window in Windows is to click the close button in the title bar. Furthermore, if you Shift-click a window's close button, Windows closes that window and all of its parent windows (the windows above it in the hierarchy).

Closing windows works similarly on the Macintosh. Click in the close box (the Macintosh term) in the upper-left corner to close the window (see Figure C-4). Alternatively, choose File → Close (Command-W). Option-clicking a close box (Command-Option-W) closes all open windows. (This trick works in most, but not all applications.)

Although the Macintosh has no equivalent to right-clicking an icon in the Windows Taskbar and choosing Close to close a minimized window, quitting a Macintosh application also closes all associated windows. Contrast this with such Windows applications as Internet Explorer, where each window is a separate task, and closing one doesn't affect the others. Applications like Microsoft Word, which put documents in child windows inside a main parent window, work more like the Macintosh in this respect. See **Windows** for more details.

For more information about closing windows by minimizing them, see **Minimizing Windows**.

Command Line
On the Macintosh: None

Although Windows is a primarily graphical operating system, you can launch programs on a command line—a place where you type the name of the program, then press Enter to execute it. You can do this either using Start → Run or by using the Address toolbar on the Taskbar.

There's no equivalent on the Macintosh, which is a fully graphical operating system.

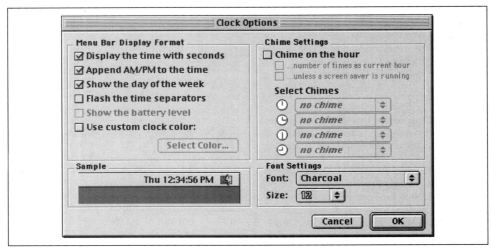

Figure C-3. Clock Options dialog box

Figure C-4. Close box

Contextual Menus
On the Macintosh: Contextual Menus

In Windows, contextual menus—the pop-up menus that appear when you right-click various interface elements—get heavy use. Although Mac OS 8.0 introduced contextual menus, accessible by Control-clicking items, contextual menus are still new to Macintosh users. In addition, most Macintosh contextual menus duplicate commands in the normal menus, so Macintosh users haven't been forced to use contextual menus.

As in Windows, you can add items to the default Macintosh contextual menus by installing add-on software. In this case, you drop such contextual menu plug-ins into the Contextual Menu Items folder (Macintosh HD → System Folder → Contextual Menu Items). If you drop a contextual menu plug-in on the System Folder, it routes the file to the Contextual Menu Items folder automatically. You may need to restart before a newly installed contextual menu plug will be available.

Control (Ctrl) Key
On the Macintosh: Control Key, Command Key

In Windows, the Ctrl key is the primary modifier; though every Macintosh keyboard has a Control key, it's used primarily for triggering contextual menus. Instead, the

Mac's Command key is the equivalent of the Windows Ctrl key. The Command key is labeled with an apple and a cloverleaf and sits immediately to the left (and right, on full size keyboards) of the Spacebar.

See Table C-1 for a list of the common uses of the Command key, and Table C-2 for the uses of the Control key.

Table C-1. Keyboard Actions Using the Command Key

Keyboard Shortcut	Function
Command-A	Select All
Command-B	Makes selected text bold in most applications, though not the Finder.
Command-Delete	Moves the selected icons to the Trash. See **Recycle Bin**.
Command-C	Copy to clipboard. Doesn't work with files on the Macintosh—only highlighted material within an application window.
Command-click items in a list like the Open File dialog box	Selects multiple discontinuous items.
Command-Control-Power	Restarts the Macintosh after a lockup.
Command-D	Duplicates Finder icons. (May have other functions in other applications.)
Command-drag an icon in the Finder	Makes a dragged icon snap into position on an invisible grid.
Command-E	Ejects the selected disk.
Command-F	Brings up the Find File or Sherlock window for searching. See **Find**.
Command-I	Displays the General Information window for the selected item. In text-oriented applications, italicizes the selected text.
Command-M	Makes an alias of the selected item.
Command-N	Makes a new Untitled folder. In most applications, creates a new document.
Command-O	Opens the selected items. In most applications, displays the Open File dialog box for opening documents.
Command-Option-drag an icon in the Finder	Makes an alias. See **Shortcuts**.
Command-Option-Esc	Forces the current application to quit, even if it's crashed. See **End Task**.
Command-P	Prints the selected files. In most applications, opens the Print dialog box.
Command-Q	Quits the application.
Command-R	Displays the original item for a selected alias. See **Shortcuts**.
Command-S	Saves the current document.
Command-T	In many applications, removes all styles from styled text.
Command-U	In text-oriented applications, underlines the selected text.
Command-V	Paste from clipboard. Doesn't work with files on the Macintosh, only cut or copied material from application windows.
Command-W	Closes the current window. See **Closing Windows**.

Table C-1. Keyboard Actions Using the Command Key (continued)

Keyboard Shortcut	Function
Command-X	Cut to clipboard. Doesn't work with files on the Macintosh—only highlighted material within application windows.
Command-Y	Moves an icon back to its previous location after a move to the Desktop or the Trash.
Command-Z	Undo. Doesn't undo icon manipulation in the Finder.
Command-. (period)	Universal "stop" command. Equivalent to Esc.

Table C-2. Keyboard Actions Using the Control Key

Keyboard Shortcut	Function
Control-click	Displays a contextual menu appropriate to the clicked item.
Control-Command-Power	Restarts the Macintosh after a lockup.

Most Macintosh application menus show Command key shortcuts next to the corresponding menu items, so you don't have to remember them.

Control Panel
On the Macintosh: Control Panels

You configure the various parts of Windows using the programs in the Control Panel folder, which you can access by choosing Start → Settings → Control Panel. Windows users tend to think of the Control Panel as a single entity even though it contains multiple items (probably because Microsoft made the folder name singular, unlike Printers or Scheduled Tasks). On the Macintosh, the concept and procedure is almost exactly the same: choose Apple menu → Control Panels to view a window full of individual control-panel applications.

Useful facts about the Macintosh Control Panels include:

* Unlike Windows control panels, Macintosh control panels are normal files that you work with just like any other files. For instance, you can delete a control panel by dragging it to the Trash, which isn't possible in Windows.

* Each Macintosh control panel lets you configure something, whereas some Windows control panels are simply shortcuts to folders (such as Fonts and Printers), or wizards (like Add New Hardware).

* You can access some Windows control panels in multiple ways. For instance, you can open the System control panel by right-clicking My Computer and choosing Properties. Control panels on the Macintosh are more discrete objects; the closest thing you'll find to that sort of system-wide integration on the Macintosh is the linkups among some control panels (such as the Remote Access menu item that opens the TCP/IP or DialAssist control panels).

* The Mac's Control Panels folder is a special folder. If moved or deleted, the Mac OS creates a new one automatically on the next restart.

* Some Macintosh control panels (and extensions) modify the way the Mac OS works, which can cause conflicts. To help manage control panels and extensions, Apple provides a control panel called Extensions Manager, which lets you turn control panels off and on. (See Figure C-5 and the sidebar "Mastering the Extensions Manager" in the **Troubleshooting** entry of this book.)

Copy
On the Macintosh: Copy

The Mac's Copy command (Command-C) works exactly the same way as it does on Windows—it transfers highlighted text or graphics onto the invisible clipboard, ready for pasting into another document or another part of the same document.

Only one aspect of the Mac's Copy command may throw you: you can't use it to copy files (in preparation for pasting them into a different window, for example).

If you select an icon and choose Edit → Copy, the Finder copies the name of the

> **Note**
>
> You can also use the Mac's Copy command to transfer the image of a file's icon onto another. Open the General Information window for an icon with File → Get Info (Command-I), and then select and copy the file's icon. Use the Get Info command on the target icon, click its icon in the resulting window, and paste.

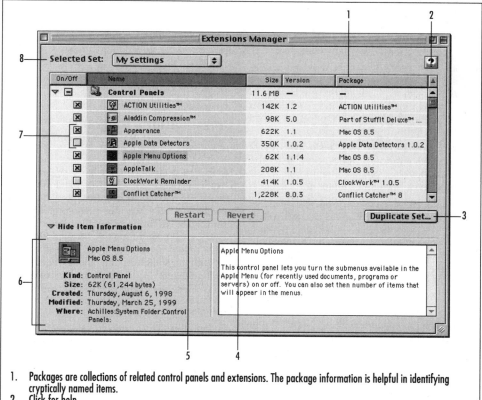

1. Packages are collections of related control panels and extensions. The package information is helpful in identifying cryptically named items.
2. Click for help.
3. Duplicates the current set.
4. Click to revert to the previously saved configuration.
5. Click to restart the Mac.
6. Full information about the selected item.
7. Items with checks are on; unchecked items are off.
8. Current set. You can make and switch between sets. This menu contains some permanent sets of Mac OS base extensions.

Figure C-5. Extensions Manager

icon. If you select multiple icons and choose Edit → Copy, the Finder copies a list of icon names to the clipboard. That can be a useful feature when, for example, you want to email a list of filenames to somebody.

Copying Files

On the Macintosh: Copying Files

Windows offers a number of ways to copy files; the situation on the Macintosh is sim-

pler. (See also **Moving Files**.) When you're drag-copying a file in Mac OS 8.5, the mouse cursor acquires a small plus character badge (see Figure C-6).

Figure C-6. Plus badge on cursor when copying

- To copy files between disks, drag their icons to a window on another disk.

- To copy files to another window on the same disk, Option-drag the icons to the new location. (This technique is akin to Control-dragging in Windows.) If you don't hold down the Option key, the files will be moved instead.

- To copy a file to the Desktop from its original window, Option-drag it to the Desktop. If you have multiple disks mounted, doing so creates the copy on the Desktop of the startup disk.

- If the original file was stored on a locked disk (like a locked floppy disk or CD-ROM) or on an AppleShare server, dragging it to the Desktop copies it rather than moving it. Option-dragging isn't necessary in such cases.

- To duplicate a file within the same window, select the file and choose File → Duplicate (Command-D). The duplicate has the same name as the original, with "copy" appended.

- To cancel a copy in progress, press Command-period.

Spring-loaded folders. Mac OS 8 and later versions offer a feature called "spring-loaded folders" that can make it easier to copy or move files. When you drag an icon on top of a folder or disk icon, but keep the mouse button pressed for a few seconds, the folder or disk window pops open. You can continue to drag the icon deeper and deeper into nested folders—just don't let up on the mouse button. When you've reached your desired location, release the mouse

button. The file you were dragging now appears in its new, deeply nested location. The Mac OS automatically closes all of the intermediate windows that have opened during this process.

Cross-Platform Programs

On the Macintosh: Cross-Platform Applications

In the past, the hardest part of switching between Windows and the Macintosh was that you had to use completely different applications. Today, the most popular programs are available in nearly identical Windows and Macintosh versions. Plus, it's likely that the two versions share the same file format, which is important when moving back and forth between the two platforms. Here are some of the most popular:

Database

- AppleWorks (Apple Computer): *http://www.apple.com/appleworks/*

- FileMaker Pro (FileMaker): *http://www.filemaker.com/*

Graphics and illustration

- Adobe Illustrator (Adobe Systems): *http://www.adobe.com/prodindex/ illustrator/main.html*

- Adobe PhotoDeluxe (Adobe Systems): *http://www.adobe.com/prodindex/ photodeluxe/main.html*

- Adobe Photoshop (Adobe Systems): *http://www.adobe.com/prodindex/ photoshop/main.html*

- Adobe Streamline (Adobe Systems): *http://www.adobe.com/prodindex/ streamline/main.html*

- AppleWorks (Apple Computer): *http://www.apple.com/appleworks/*

- Bryce (MetaCreations): *http://www.metacreations.com/*

- Canvas (Deneba): *http://www.deneba.com/*

- CorelDRAW (Corel): *http://www.corel.com/products/ graphicsandpublishing/draw8/ index.htm*

- DeBabelizer (Equilibrium): *http://www.equilibrium.com/*

- FreeHand (Macromedia): *http://www.macromedia.com/software/ freehand/*

- Kai's Photo SOAP (MetaCreations): *http://www.metacreations.com/*

- Kai's Power Tools (MetaCreations): *http://www.metacreations.com/*

- Painter (MetaCreations): *http://www.metacreations.com/*

- Ray Dream Studio (MetaCreations): *http://www.metacreations.com/ products/rds/studio.html*

Internet

- America Online (America Online): *http://www.aol.com/*

- Eudora (Qualcomm): *http://www.eudora.com/*

- Microsoft Internet Explorer (Microsoft): *http://www.microsoft.com/*

- Microsoft Outlook Express (Microsoft): *http://www.microsoft.com/*

- Netscape Communicator (Netscape Communications): *http://www.netscape.com/*

Multimedia

- Adobe After Effects (Adobe Systems): *http://www.adobe.com/prodindex/ aftereffects/main.html*

- Adobe Premiere (Adobe Systems): *http://www.adobe.com/prodindex/ premiere/main.html*

- Macromedia Director (Macromedia): *http://www.macromedia.com/software/ director/*

Page layout and publishing tools

- Adobe Acrobat (Adobe Systems): *http://www.adobe.com/prodindex/ acrobat/main.html*

- Adobe FrameMaker (Adobe Systems): *http://www.adobe.com/prodindex/ framemaker/main.html*

- Adobe InDesign (Adobe Systems): *http://www.adobe.com/prodindex/ indesign/main.html*

- Adobe PageMaker (Adobe Systems): *http://www.adobe.com/prodindex/ pagemaker/main.html*

- QuarkXPress (Quark): *http://www.quark.com/*

Personal finance

- Quicken (Intuit): *http://www.intuit.com/*

- Kiplinger TaxCut (Block Financial): *http://www.taxcut.com/*

Spreadsheet

- AppleWorks (Apple Computer): *http://www.apple.com/appleworks/*

- Microsoft Excel (Microsoft): *http://www.microsoft.com/office/*

Web graphics and authoring

- Adobe GoLive (Adobe Systems): *http://www.adobe.com/prodindex/ golive/main.html*

- Adobe ImageReady (Adobe Systems): *http://www.adobe.com/prodindex/ imageready/main.html*

- Adobe ImageReady (Adobe Systems): *http://www.adobe.com/prodindex/ imageready/main.html*

- Adobe PageMill (Adobe Systems): *http://www.adobe.com/prodindex/ pagemill/main.html*

- Home Page (FileMaker): *http://www.filemaker.com/*

- Macromedia Dreamweaver (Macromedia):

*http://www.macromedia.com/software/
dreamweaver/*

- Macromedia Flash (Macromedia):
  *http://www.macromedia.com/software/
  flash/*

- Macromedia Fireworks (Macromedia):
  *http://www.macromedia.com/software/
  fireworks/*

- Macromedia Generator (Macromedia):
  *http://www.macromedia.com/software/
  generator/*

- Macromedia ShockWave (Macromedia):
  *http://www.macromedia.com/
  shockwave/*

- NetObjects Fusion (NetObjects):
  http://www.netobjects.com/

Utilities

- Aladdin DropStuff (Aladdin Systems):
  http://www.aladdinsys.com/dropstuff/

- Aladdin Expander (Aladdin Systems):
  http://www.aladdinsys.com/expander/

- Norton AntiVirus (Symantec):
  http://www.symantec.com/

- Norton Utilities (Symantec):
  http://www.symantec.com/

Word processing and presentation

- AppleWorks (Apple Computer):
  http://www.apple.com/appleworks/

- Corel WordPerfect (Corel):
  *http://www.corel.com/products/
  wordperfect/index.htm*

- Microsoft PowerPoint (Microsoft):
  http://www.microsoft.com/office/

- Microsoft Word (Microsoft):
  http://www.microsoft.com/office/

Cut

On the Macintosh: Cut

The Mac's Cut command (Command-X) works exactly as it does on Windows—it removes highlighted text or graphics from an application window, placing it onto the invisible clipboard ready for pasting into as different place.

The Mac's Cut command can't be used to move files in conjunction with Paste, however, as it can in Windows.

D

Date/Time Control Panel

On the Macintosh: Date & Time Control Panel

The Windows Date/Time control panel lets you set your date, time, and time zone. You can do all that and more in the Macintosh Date & Time control panel (Apple menu → Control Panels → Date & Time).

The Date Formats and Time Formats buttons let you modify the way the Macintosh displays dates and times; in Windows, these settings are in the Regional Settings control panel.

Both Windows and Mac OS 8.5 (or later) can automatically adjust your computer's clock for daylight savings time (see Figure D-1). In all previous versions of the

Mac OS, you must check a Daylight Savings Time checkbox to make the Mac OS adjust the time.

Another welcome feature that appeared in Mac OS 8.5's Date & Time control panel is time synchronization over the Internet. Few computer clocks are completely accurate on their own; and by leaving this setting on, you can be sure that the Mac's clock is always accurate to within fractions of a second.

Finally, you can turn the menu bar clock on and off from the Date & Time control panel, set a wide variety of clock options, including display format, chimes, and font settings.

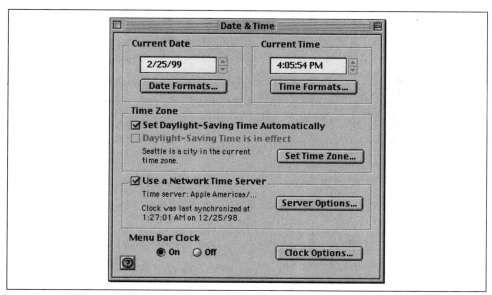

Figure D-1. Date & Time control panel

Note

Consider turning on the Date & Time control panel's option to display the seconds ticking by on its menu clock. That way, you'll be able to tell at a glance whether or not a program has crashed.

Delete Key
On the Macintosh: Del Key

The Delete key on PC keyboards is generally grouped with the Insert, Home, End, Page Up, and Page Down keys. On most Macintosh keyboards, the same key is labeled Del, and it's usually called the "forward delete key." (The modern Apple keyboard, such as the one provided with the iMac, iBook, and Power Macintosh series, don't have this key at all—a good argument, among power users, for buying a replacement USB keyboard.)

Unlike the Mac's Delete key and the Backspace key in Windows, which delete the character to the left of the insertion point, the Del key deletes the character to the right—thus the "forward" delete. (When you're using a graphics or layout program, on the other hand, the Del and Delete keys behave identically, deleting the selected object.)

Deleting Files
On the Macintosh: Deleting Files

The most basic method of deleting files and folders on the Macintosh is the same as in Windows—just drag them to the Trash. However, you can delete items on the Macintosh in several additional ways, though not as many as in Windows. For a full list, see **Recycle Bin**.

Desktop
On the Macintosh: Desktop

The desktop metaphor in Windows was one of the most significant moves toward the Macintosh style of working. Like the Windows Desktop, the Macintosh Desktop is, behind the scenes, actually a folder that contains files and other folders that appear on the backdrop, the Desktop, when you first turn on the computer. Anything you'd do on the Windows Desktop is likely to work on the Macintosh Desktop: renaming files, opening folders, dragging icons, and so on.

The Macintosh Desktop displays icons for all the accessible disks, the Trash, available printers (in Mac OS 8 and later), and any other items you might have dragged or saved to the Desktop. In new installations of the Mac OS, a variety of additional icons—mostly aliases that you can delete if you wish—are on the Desktop by default.

Here are the differences between the Windows and Macintosh Desktops:

- The Windows Desktop holds files and folders only from the C: drive, whereas every Macintosh disk has its own invisible Desktop Folder. So, if you drag a file from a floppy disk window to the Macintosh Desktop, it remains on the floppy disk but appears on the Desktop.

- Windows printer icons appear in My Computer → Printers, whereas Mac OS 8 Desktop Printer icons appear on the Desktop.

- In Windows, the Network Neighborhood icon shows up on the Desktop; in Mac OS 8.5 and later, the equivalent Network Browser is in Apple menu → Network Browser. In earlier versions of the Mac OS, the Chooser (Apple menu → Chooser) is the only way to find servers on the network.

- In contrast to Windows, where it can be difficult to remove some items from the Desktop without using the TweakUI control panel, only two kinds of icons must remain on the Macintosh Desktop: disk icons and the Trash. To remove an icon from the Macintosh Desktop, drag it to the Trash or to another folder.

- The Macintosh Desktop has only one feature that's even vaguely similar to the web browser-like Active Desktop in Windows: Button view, where a single click, not a double-click, opens any icon. (To turn on button view in any window or the Desktop itself, choose View → as Buttons.)

Note

If you find yourself seated at a Macintosh whose Desktop appears in Button view, you may wonder how you're supposed to move or copy Desktop icons. After all, clicking one opens it, so dragging is out of the question.

Solution: drag the file by its name, not by its icon.

The Finder Desktop versus Windows Desktop. The most significant difference between the Windows and Macintosh Desktops, however, is that the Macintosh Desktop "belongs" to the Finder, along with all other Finder windows. So, when you switch into the Finder (by clicking any visible Desktop area, for example), all Finder windows appear over whatever other application windows you have open.

Note

Some people, particularly novices, occasionally click the Macintosh Desktop by accident while working in another program—and are then confused by the sudden disappearance of the application windows, which are now concealed by Finder Desktop windows. If that syndrome affects you, uncheck "Show Desktop when in background" in the General Controls control panel; from now on, wayward clicks can't take you out of the current application—the Application menu, or the Quit command, is your only way out.

The fact that Finder windows appear over other windows when you click the Desktop exemplifies the different way the Macintosh and Windows handle tasks. In Windows, every window is a separate task that appears separately on the Taskbar. On the Macintosh, though, every application is a separate task that appears in the Application menu. Windows belonging to those applications are not separate tasks, and thus appear or disappear all at once.

For whatever reason, perhaps the differences in the way tasks are handled between Windows and the Macintosh, Windows users seem not to use the Desktop much. In contrast, Macintosh users often use the Desktop as a temporary storage spot for active documents, filing them when the project is done. Since you can drag-and-drop Macintosh document icons onto Desktop application icons, just as in Windows, many Macintosh fans also store aliases to their most frequently used programs on the Desktop for quick access.

Changing the Desktop pattern or picture. For information about changing the Macintosh Desktop's background, see **Background**.

Details view. If you're a fan of Details view in Windows, in which files are listed in a folder window database-style, with columns indicating each file's size, modification date, and so on, you'll feel right at home on the Macintosh. Choose View → as List in any Macintosh window to create the identical effect.

In Mac OS 8.5 and later, you can perform all the usual stunts in this view—click a column's name to sort the list by that criterion, drag the column dividers to make columns wider or narrower, and so on. (Note how cleverly the Date column rewrites itself as you shrink its space—first the Macintosh abbreviates, then eliminates the day of the week; as the column gets narrower, the dates are written in a shorter format [7/2/99]; and finally, the modification time is eliminated from the column display.)

In fact, the Macintosh even lets you rearrange the columns by dragging their names horizontally. (The Name column must always be the first column, however.)

Dialog Boxes
On the Macintosh: Dialog Boxes

In Windows, you're used to seeing dialog boxes in a wide variety of situations: changing settings, opening documents, printing, and so on. The Mac OS uses dialog boxes

Making the Macintosh Look Like Windows

If you're using the Macintosh for the first time, you needn't find the new look (and new window-control placement) disorienting. Take a couple of steps and install a couple of shareware add-ons, and your Macintosh screen will look almost exactly like Windows.

Kaleidoscope (*http://www.kaleidoscope.net/*) is a popular Macintosh shareware add-on that lets you change the look of the entire Macintosh interface: color scheme, button design, progress bars, dialog boxes, window shapes, accents, and so on. Inevitably, perhaps, somebody came up with add-on Kaleidoscope schemes that look exactly like Windows. (Different versions simulate the look of any version of Windows, from 2.0 through 98.) Download this surprisingly effective tool, and you'll find that even the controls in the title bar of the window are in the "correct" place.

Installing Kaleidoscope, however, only affects the look of your Macintosh; you still have no Taskbar at the bottom of the screen. To give your Macintosh a Start menu and a Taskbar, install GoMac (*http://www.actionutilities.com/site2/html/products/agm.html*). The resulting taskbar does everything the Windows version does, and much more—for example, you can install a new permanent "tile" onto this Taskbar just by dragging an icon onto it from your Desktop.

You'll find no shareware, alas, to solve the final disorienting aspect of the Mac's interface—the fact that it has no My Computer icon. Of course, you could make an alias of your hard disk icon and put it into a newly made My Computer folder in the upper-left corner of the screen. But because icons for the floppy disk, Zip, and CD-ROM don't appear on your screen until a corresponding disk is actually inserted, and because the Macintosh always puts these icons at the right side of your screen, there's no way to add them to your phony My Computer icon.

---

for similar tasks, but there are differences which you may find either confusing or helpful.

Modality. The Macintosh has two types of dialog boxes. First, there's the *application modal* type, which lets you work in other applications before closing the dialog box; this kind of box generally has a title bar, which you can drag to move the window. *System modal* dialog boxes, on the other hand, must be dismissed before you can return to work. (The Print and Save dialog boxes take this form.) These usually lack a title bar and can't be moved; if you click anywhere outside of such a window, the Macintosh rewards you with only a beep.

Most Windows dialog boxes, on the other hand, are application modal. Windows has only a few system modal dialog boxes, such as the Shut Down dialog box, which prevent you from doing anything else until you've closed the dialog box.

Dialog box title bar controls. Windows dialog boxes have two standard controls in their title bars—a help button and a close

button. Clicking the help button provides a pop-up window of information about the next thing you click in the dialog box, and clicking the close button is the same as clicking a Cancel button.

Macintosh dialog boxes lack these controls. You close a Macintosh dialog box by clicking OK or Cancel, and (in most Macintosh programs) you get help by choosing Help → Show Balloons and pointing at different items in the dialog box. See **Help** for more information.

Tabbed dialog boxes. Many Windows dialog boxes use tabs to separate different panels in a dialog box. (Examples include most Windows control panels, including Display and Accessibility Options.) That interface convention is becoming more common on the Macintosh as well, but it's not universal. In its place, Macintosh dialog boxes often feature a scrolling list of icons; click an icon to display the panel associated with it. Other dialog boxes let you change dialog box panels from a pop-up menu.

Dialog box buttons and keyboard shortcuts. In many Windows dialog boxes, an Apply button saves the changes you've made without closing the dialog box, as clicking OK would do. Settings dialog boxes on the Macintosh seldom have an Apply button (except for some Microsoft programs), so you must click OK to save your changes and close the dialog box.

As in Windows, pressing Return or Enter in a Macintosh dialog box is the same as clicking the default button. Also as in Windows, you can usually press Esc (or Command-Period) as the equivalent of clicking Cancel. See **Button** for more detail on keyboard operation of dialog-box elements.

Dial-Up Networking Folder

On the Macintosh: PPP Control Panel, Remote Access Control Panel

The Dial-Up Networking folder in Windows contains a wizard that helps you create new connections for dialing up Internet servers, connecting two computers via Direct Cable Connection, and more. Dial-Up Networking requires the appropriate configuration in the Network control panel—for instance, if you want to connect to an Internet service provider using Dial-Up Networking, your TCP/IP settings in the Network control panel must be correct. The situation is relatively similar on the Macintosh, though the details are different.

On the Macintosh, you use the Remote Access control panel (Mac OS 8.5 and later) or the PPP control panel (Mac OS 8.0 and 8.1) to enter the settings for an Internet service provider. And exactly as in Dial-Up Networking, you must configure various other control panels for connections to work. See **Network Control Panel** for instructions on configuring the Mac's TCP/IP control panel to provide an Internet connection. This is necessary before continuing with the Remote Access control panel.

Configuring a connection. Configuring the Remote Access control panel (or the older PPP control panel) is easy. You enter your username, password and the telephone number to dial, and decide whether you want the software to save your password (see Figure D-2). Click the Options button to view a tabbed dialog box that offers some optional settings—none are essential.

From the Remote Access menu, you can open the various other control panels that you might need to configure for a connection, including AppleTalk (necessary for an

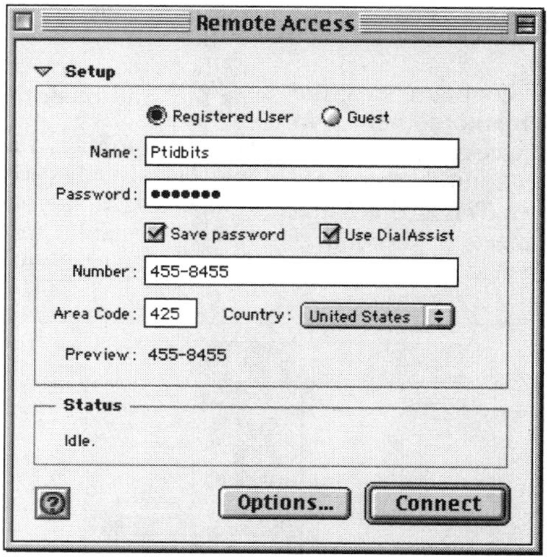

Figure D-2. Remote Access control panel

Apple Remote Access connection), Dial-Assist (useful if you're using a calling card), Modem (necessary no matter what), and TCP/IP (essential if you're calling an Internet service provider).

Just as with Dial-Up Networking, you can create and switch between multiple configurations, which is handy if you use different ISPs at home and work, or when you travel. Follow these steps:

1. In Remote Access, choose File → Configurations (Command-K).

2. With Default selected, click Duplicate, then give the new configuration a new name.

3. Click Make Active to switch to that configuration and close the Configurations dialog box.

4. Make appropriate changes to the settings, then close the Remote Access window, saving changes when it prompts you to do so.

Using Remote Access. Once configured, you open and close connections in one of two ways:

- You can open the Remote Access control panel, switch to the correct configuration (if you have more than one) using File → Configurations, then click the Connect button. When connected, the Connect button changes to Disconnect.

- If you have multiple configurations, the easiest way to switch among them is to use the Remote Access menu (see Figure D-3) on the Control Strip (for more information, see **Tray**). This same menu lets you connect or disconnect without having to open a control panel.

> **Note**
>
> Suppose each of your multiple Internet configurations requires different network settings. (That might be the case if, for example, your PowerBook connects to an Ethernet network at work, but a modem at home.) In such a situation, consider using the Location Manager control panel (Apple menu → Control Panels → Location Manager). It lets you create configurations for different locations, each with different network settings, Internet phone numbers, and so on.
>
> Thereafter, you can use the Location Manager menu on the Control Strip to switch quickly among them without even restarting the computer. Doing so is much easier than flipping between configurations in several different control panels before dialing out. For more information, see **User Profiles**.

Direct Cable Connection
On the Macintosh: LocalTalk, Ethernet, File Sharing Control Panel

The Windows Direct Cable Connection utility is useful for connecting two PCs that can't easily be networked in any other way. That's seldom a problem on the Macintosh, since every Macintosh has a LocalTalk (printer) port, Ethernet port, or both. LocalTalk and Ethernet, with the Mac OS's built-in file sharing software, are the preferred methods of connecting two Macs for sharing files and other network resources.

Connecting Macs via LocalTalk. To connect two Macs via LocalTalk, you need a pair of PhoneNet adapters, which are inexpensively available from any mail order or online retailer. You use standard telephone

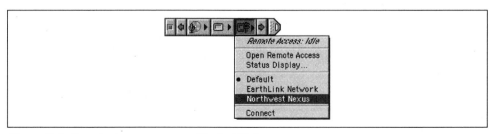

Figure D-3. Remote Access menu on Control Strip

cable to connect the two PhoneNet adapters. Once you have the necessary hardware, follow these steps:

1. Plug one PhoneNet adapter into each Mac's printer port.

2. Connect the adapters with the telephone cable.

3. Each adapter has two telephone-style jacks. Fill the empty one on each adapter with the terminator plug provided in each adapter package.

4. On one Macintosh, open the AppleTalk control panel. Make sure it says Printer port (or, on older PowerBook models, Modem/Printer port). Close the control panel and save changes, turning on AppleTalk if you're prompted to do so.

5. On the same Macintosh, use the File Sharing control panel to turn file sharing on. For more information, see **File Sharing** and **Printer Sharing**. Close the window and save changes.

6. On the other Macintosh, open the Chooser (Apple menu → Chooser), click the AppleShare icon, and then double-click the name of the server (the first Macintosh). If you're running Mac OS 8.5 or later, you can instead use the Network Browser, which works more like the Network Neighborhood in Windows.

7. Log in using the owner name and password of the first Macintosh (which you set either in Apple menu → Control Panels → File Sharing in Mac OS 8.5 and later, or in Apple menu → Control Panels → Sharing Setup for earlier versions of the Mac OS). An icon representing the first Mac's hard disk appears on the Desktop.

There's no reason to use LocalTalk networking to connect modern Macs, since iMacs, blue power Macintosh G3 models, and 1999-and-later PowerBooks don't even have the necessary printer port. These modern models should be connected with Ethernet, described later in this section.

If you must add a modern Macintosh to a network of older Macs that don't have

Ethernet jacks, however, an adapter like the Farallon iPrint LT will bail you out. It plugs into a USB ports and provides a standard older-Macintosh printer port, which can then accept your standard PhoneNet adapter. For information, visit *http://www. farallon.com/*.

Connecting Macs via Ethernet. All current Macs, and many older models, have built-in Ethernet jacks. That's fortunate, since Ethernet is many times faster than LocalTalk.

You set up an Ethernet network among Macs exactly as you would among Windows PCs—by buying an Ethernet hub, connecting it to the computers, and so on. But for quick connection between two Ethernet-equipped Macs (á là Direct Cable Connection), you can use an inexpensive Ethernet crossover cable instead. (Such a cable is available for about $10 from computer superstores or mail order outfits.) Once you have the crossover cable, follow these steps:

1. Connect the crossover cable from one Mac's Ethernet port to the other's.

2. Open Apple menu → Control Panels → AppleTalk.

3. From the pop-up "Connect via" menu, choose Ethernet. Close the control panel and save changes.

4. On one Macintosh, use the File Sharing control panel to turn file sharing on. For more information, see **File Sharing** and **Printer Sharing**.

5. On the other Macintosh, open the Chooser (Apple menu → Chooser), click the AppleShare icon, and then double-click the name of the server (the first Macintosh). If you're running Mac OS 8.5 or later, you can instead use the Network Browser, which works more like the Network Neighborhood in Windows.

6. Log in using the owner name and password of the first Macintosh (which you set either in Apple menu → Control Panels → File Sharing in Mac OS 8.5, or in Apple menu → Control Panels → Sharing Setup for earlier versions of the Mac OS). An icon representing the first Mac's hard disk appears on the Desktop.

For more information about iMac connections, read the article at *http://db.tidbits.com/getbits.acgi?tbart=05085*.

Directories

On the Macintosh: Folders

This terminology issue is a "tomato/tomahto" problem: in Windows, people call the file-folder icon a directory; on the Macintosh, the identical entity is called a folder. They're one and the same.

For more information about what you can do with directories, see **Folders**.

Disk Defragmenter

On the Macintosh: Third-Party Utilities

Windows's Disk Defragmenter utility program defragments your hard disk, moving the portions of files that are scattered around the disk into contiguous chunks.

Disk defragmentation programs are available for the Macintosh, but Apple has never bundled one with the Mac OS. In part, that may be because disk defragmentation isn't as much a performance problem as it used to be when hard disks were much slower. In addition, you can easily defragment a Macintosh hard disk the homemade way: back up your entire hard disk, reinitialize it with Drive Setup, and restore your files.

Most people never defragment their hard disks, since the almost imperceptible performance gain doesn't seem worth the time for the risk of having a program touch every file on your hard disk. If you want to defragment your hard disk, however, consider the following Macintosh utilities:

* Norton Utilities for Macintosh (Symantec): *http://www.symantec.com/*
* DiskExpress Pro and PlusOptimizer (Alsoft): *http://www.alsoft.com/*

Disk Space

On the Macintosh: Window Info Strip, Get Info

To find out how much space is available on a Macintosh disk, open its window (or open any folder on that disk). The information strip just below the title bar shows exactly how much space is available.

The info strip, however, doesn't tell you how big a disk is, nor how much is in the disk already. To find that out, highlight the disk's icon. Choose File → Get Info. The resulting window shows the disk's capacity, as well as how much data is on the disk (and how much is available).

Disks

On the Macintosh: None

The Macintosh has no equivalent of the My Computer window, where icons for all your disk drives appear. In fact, the Macintosh doesn't display permanent icons for your disk drives at all.

Instead, icons appear on the right side of the Desktop screen only when a disk—floppy, Zip, CD-ROM, or whatever—is actually inserted into the machine. (If you insert a disk and no corresponding icon appears, then the Macintosh lacks the necessary software to read it. You may be inserting a Windows floppy disk on a Macintosh lacking the File Exchange control panel, a CD-ROM when the Mac's CD-ROM extensions are turned off, or a Zip disk when the Iomega software hasn't been installed.)

Ejecting disks. Ejecting disks is different on a Macintosh, too. You'll quickly discover that pushing the eject button on a Macintosh disk drive accomplishes nothing at all—a safety feature designed to protect the unwary from ejecting a disk while it's being accessed. Instead, you must eject a disk by highlighting its icon on the screen, and then performing one of these steps:

* Drag the disk icon to the Trash. Alarming as this may feel it first, this action doesn't actually trash the disk—ejecting it instead.
* Choose Special → Eject Disk (in Mac OS 8.5 and later).
* Choose File → Put Away (in earlier Mac OS versions).
* Control-click the icon and choose Eject from the contextual pop-up menu that appears (Mac OS 8.5 and later).

A-D

Erasing disks. To erase a disk, highlight its icon on the screen and then choose Special → Erase Disk. If you have the File Exchange control panel installed, and you're erasing a floppy disk, you'll be asked whether you want the disk formatted for Macintosh or DOS (Windows). See **Formatting Disks** for more information.

Renaming disks. You can rename a Macintosh disk just as you'd rename any file: Click once on its name, and then type away. If this doesn't work, try turning off File Sharing first.

Display Control Panel
On the Macintosh: Appearance Control Panel, Energy Saver Control Panel, Monitors & Sound Control Panel

In Windows, the Display control panel is positively bristling with features, spread out among seven tabs in the dialog box. On the Macintosh, most of the same features are scattered among several different control panels. Here they are, corresponding to each of the Display control panel's seven tabs:

Background. On the Macintosh, you choose a picture to use as your Desktop background with either the Appearance control panel or the Desktop Pictures control panel, depending on your OS version. For more information, see **Background**.

Screen Saver. The Mac OS doesn't include a built-in screen saver, although a variety of third party utilities can do the job. However, the Mac's Energy Saver control panel (Apple menu → Control Panels → Energy Saver → Sleep Setup) provides controls for putting the monitor to sleep, a state that not only blacks the screen—therefore preserving its phosphor coating far more effectively than an animated "screen saver" could—but also consumes far less power. For more information, see **Power Management Control Panel**.

Appearance. The Mac's Appearance control panel (Apple menu → Control Panels → Appearance) controls the system-wide look of your Macintosh, much like the Windows Display control panel's Appearance tab. The

Appearance control panel looks significantly different between Mac OS 8.0 and Mac OS 8.5, but the Mac OS 8.5-and-later version is a superset of previous versions.

- In the Themes tab, you can choose a predefined groups of settings, much as you select appearance schemes in Windows.

- The Appearance tab provides pop-up menus for choosing a highlight color, which applies to selected text, and a variation color, which tints scroll bars, menus, progress, bars, and so on.

- The Fonts tab lets you choose large and small system fonts, plus a font for lists and icons (see Figure D-4).

Effects. The Effects tab in the Windows Display control panel controls a number of unrelated visual effects, and it also lets you change Desktop icons.

On the Macintosh, you can change any icon (except Desktop Printers or the Trash) by pasting a new icon over the old one. To do so, Control-click an icon, choose Get Info → General Information, click the icon in the Get Info window to select it, and then paste the graphic you want to use as the replacement icon.

Of the other options, the Macintosh has equivalents only for "Use large icons" and "Smooth edges of screen fonts." To default to large icons, choose Edit → Preferences → Views → Icons and click the large icon radio button. And to smooth fonts, open Apple menu → Control Panels → Appearance → Fonts, select "Smooth all fonts on screen," and choose the point size above which the Mac OS starts smoothing fonts.

Web. The Macintosh has no equivalent to the Windows Active Desktop, which you control from the Display control panel's Web tab.

Settings. The Settings tab of the Windows Display control panel lets you set the resolution and color depth of your monitor; on the Macintosh, use the Monitors & Sound control panel (Apple menu → Control Panels → Monitors & Sound → Monitors) to perform the same tasks (see Figure D-5).

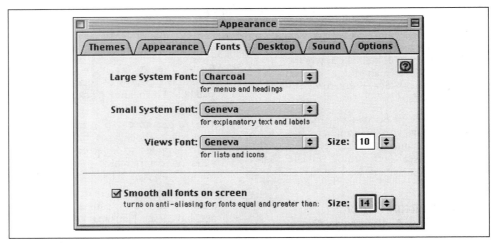

Figure D-4. Appearance control panel's Fonts tab

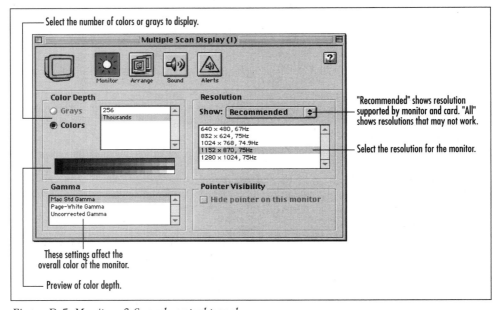

Figure D-5. Monitors & Sound control panel

If you have multiple monitors connected to your Macintosh (a highly recommended productivity enhancement), you can arrange them in Apple menu → Control Panels → Monitors & Sound → Arrange (see Figure D-6).

DLL Files

On the Macintosh: Shared Libraries

On the Macintosh, files whose names end with the letters *lib* are probably shared libraries, which fulfill the same purpose as

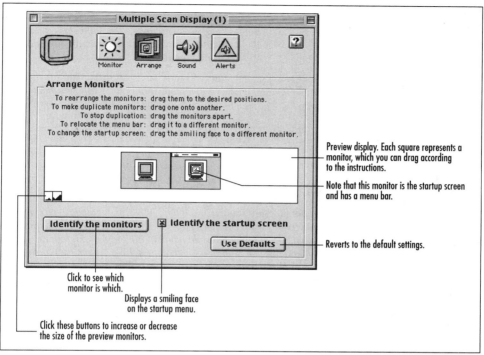

Figure D-6. Arranging multiple monitors

DLL files on Windows. You may find shared library files in the System Folder → Extensions folder, or in the same folder as an application that requires them.

Fortunately, shared libraries are completely invisible and forgotten on the Macintosh—the Macintosh user is never asked to install newer versions, for example. Microsoft programs, moreover, are smart enough to auto-install any shared libraries that you may have moved or deleted.

Documents Menu
On the Macintosh: Recent Documents

If you want to work with a document that you've been using recently in Windows, you can choose it from Start → Documents. On the Macintosh, choose your recently used document from Apple menu → Recent Documents. Although the Windows Document menu is restricted to 15 recently used documents, on the Macintosh you can specify how many documents you want tracked. To

do so, use the Apple Menu Options control panel (Apple menu → Control Panels → Apple Menu Options).

Another advantage of the Mac's Recent Documents menu is that it tracks all the documents you open. The Windows Document menu, on the other hand, includes only documents you open from an Explorer or a folder window—in other words, not documents you open from within an application.

To clear items from your Recent Documents command, you have two alternatives. First, you can just wait until they go away automatically, since Recent Documents tracks only the most recently used documents. Second, you can open the System Folder → Apple Menu Items → Recent Documents folder and throw away the aliases you find there. (Although the TweakUI control panel in Windows 98 lets you make Windows clear the Documents menu every time you restart, there's no equivalent on the Macintosh without writing a custom AppleScript script.)

DOS
On the Macintosh: Third-Party Utilities

Despite Microsoft's claims, Windows is built on top of DOS and continues to work with DOS. The Mac OS has no such underpinnings in a command-line based operating system.

If you're wondering how you can run DOS (or Windows) programs on a Macintosh, see **Emulators**.

Drivers
On the Macintosh: Drivers, Extensions

Drivers are small programs that let a computer, either a Macintosh or a PC, communicate with some piece of hardware, be it a printer, modem, or scanner. Drivers are a much bigger deal in the PC world than in the Macintosh world for two reasons:

- Since there are many more manufacturers of hardware for PCs, the possibilities for problems and conflicts are much greater.

- Apple often writes generalized drivers that work for an entire class of hardware devices, which relieves manufacturers from having to create their own drivers. For instance, most laser printers use Apple's LaserWriter driver, and many USB devices can use Apple's generic USB driver.

As a result, you're less likely to encounter conflicts or confusions with drivers for Macintosh hardware. Plus, just as with the PC, a custom driver comes with any peripheral that requires one, and updates are often available from the manufacturer's web site. Updates are far less frequently required on the Macintosh, too.

Many drivers, such as those for the mouse, keyboard, monitor, hard disk, speakers, and so on, are invisible and built into the Macintosh ROM. Other drivers are included in the form of Macintosh extensions. You'll find them in Macintosh HD → System Folder → Extensions.

DriveSpace
On the Macintosh: None

DriveSpace is a disk-compression product included with Windows to create compressed disks, saving space and making room for more files (at the expense of speed).

Although numerous Macintosh products have existed for compressing entire disks, they've all faded away as hard disks have grown in size and dropped in price. The tradeoffs of reduced speed and greater chance for lost data in the event of disk corruption caused the Macintosh market to reject these programs several years ago.

In part, these disk-compression products may have survived in the PC world because it's more difficult to add additional hard disks to a PC than to a Macintosh. If you need more disk space on a Macintosh, it's easy to attach an external hard disk, Zip disk, or other disk drive.

E

Edit Menu
On the Macintosh: Edit Menu

The Edit menu in most Macintosh programs is almost identical to the one in almost every Windows program. Most of the menu items—Cut, Copy, Paste, and so on—have the same names and keyboard shortcuts as in Windows, except that you use the Command key instead of the Ctrl key.

The commands in the Macintosh Edit menu work exactly as they do in Windows—you can cut, copy, or paste highlighted material in your applications. On the Macintosh, however, you can't use the Cut, Copy, and Paste commands on Desktop icons themselves, to move for copy actual files to other windows.

For information on the main commands in the Edit menu, Cut, Copy, Paste, and Undo, see their respective entries. Among the other Edit menu items are:

Paste Shortcut. Since the Mac's Paste command can't paste a file, there's no Paste Shortcut command.

Select All. The Select All command (Ctrl-A) in Windows is identical to the Mac's Select All command (Command-A)—with one exception. In Windows, Select All highlights all the icons in a window. But if you're editing a file's name, Select All doesn't select all the text in the name; the Ctrl-A keyboard shortcut doesn't work at all. On the Macintosh, Select All highlights text if you're editing a filename, and highlights all icons in the window if you're not.

Invert Selection. The Invert Selection command, which highlights all the files in a window that aren't already selected, has no equivalent on the Macintosh.

EISA Slots and Cards
On the Macintosh: PCI Slots and Cards

See **PCI Slots and Cards**.

Ejecting Disks
On the Macintosh: Ejecting Disks

On a PC, most people eject disks by pushing the manual-eject button on the front panel of every floppy, Zip, CD, and other drive. On the Macintosh, the manual-eject button doesn't work at all when a disk is in the machine. Instead, you eject a disk using a menu command or by dragging a disk icon to the trash. You can eject a Macintosh disk in any of these ways:

- Highlight the disk, and then choose Special → Eject (Command-E).

- Highlight the disk, and then choose File → Put Away (Command-Y).

- Drag the disk's icon to the Trash. In Windows, this would erase all the files on the disk, but on the Macintosh, doing so ejects the disk.

- Choose Special → Restart or Special → Shut Down to restart or shut down the Macintosh, which ejects the disk in the process. (There are some exceptions: CD-ROMs generally remain in the machine when you shut down or restart, and so do Zip or Jaz disks you've configured, using the Iomega software, to remain in their drives.)

- If a floppy disk is in the drive before you turn the Macintosh on, you can eject it on startup by holding down the mouse button. If the disk doesn't have a System Folder on it, though, even that action isn't necessary, because the Macintosh ejects the disk automatically once it realizes it can't boot from the disk.

Note

When the standard software methods of ejecting a Macintosh disk don't work—when the disk is jammed, for example—you can eject it manually. Insert a straightened paperclip into the small hole next to the floppy slot, CD-ROM, or Zip drive slot. Push straight in to activate the manual eject button.

Email attachments

On the Macintosh: Email Attachments

One of the best ways to transfer files from a PC to a Macintosh is by attaching the files to an email message. Unfortunately, although this technique can work extremely well, it's fraught with problems. For more information on how to transfer files successfully, see the "Email" section of **Transferring Files to the Macintosh**.

Emulators

On the Macintosh: Emulators

This book assumes that you have access to a physical PC or a physical Macintosh. However, several third-party programs let you run Windows—and Windows software—on the Macintosh; there are even programs that let you run Macintosh programs, in a limited way, on a PC.

Running Windows on the Macintosh.

Virtual PC (Connectix)
Virtual PC has an excellent reputation. One advantage of Virtual PC over Soft-Windows (described next) is that it emulates an entire PC, not just Windows. Thus, you can use Virtual PC to run PC-compatible operating systems other than Windows, such as Windows NT or even OS/2. You can learn more about Virtual PC at *http://www. connectix.com/html/connectix_virtualpc. html.*

SoftWindows (Insignia Solutions)
SoftWindows (and its predecessor, SoftPC) have been around for many years. Its price and feature list are very similar to Virtual PC's; one pleasant feature is TurboStart, which memorizes the state of your emulated Windows environment when you quit the program (Virtual PC has a similar feature). The next time you resume SoftWindows, it starts up in a fraction of the time an actual PC would take to start up. You can find more information on SoftWindows and other Insignia products at *http://www.insignia.com/.*

Whether emulation software makes sense for you depends on your proposed uses. Emulation works well if you need to run Windows programs only occasionally; you're more likely to encounter flakiness if you use the system heavily.

If you want to run Windows software on a Macintosh, but don't want to put up with the slow speeds of emulation software, many Macintosh fans look into an Orange Micro OrangePC. This PCI card includes a Pentium processor and the other circuitry found in a real PC, and can therefore run software at about the same speeds. You save considerable desk space and (if you have a fancy monitor, keyboard, and ergonomic setup) equipment cost.

On the other hand, compare prices—it may actually be less expensive to buy a PC. Furthermore, you may occasionally experience glitches when trying to move data back and forth between the two operating systems.

You can find more information about Orange Micro's products at *http://www. orangemicro.com/.*

Running Macintosh software on a PC. Software that lets you run Macintosh software on a PC is a much more difficult proposition, and attempts to write such a program have had decidedly mixed results. Such programs can't run many Macintosh programs because their creators can't legally copy necessary code from the Macintosh ROM chips. The most successful Macintosh emulator, called Executor, comes from a company called ARDI. You can learn more information about Executor (and find the compatibility list of software it can run) at *http://www.ardi.com/.*

End Task

On the Macintosh: Force Quit

If a program is behaving oddly in Windows and refusing to quit, you can press Ctrl-Alt-Delete to bring up the Close Program dialog box. From there, you can force the offending program to quit, although unsaved changes are lost in the process.

The Macintosh has a similar feature. If an application seems frozen, press Command-Option-Esc to bring up a dialog box asking if you would like to force the current application to quit. Make sure you're forcing the proper application to quit; due to the way the Macintosh multitasks, another application may in fact be "current" even though it's not frontmost. If the program named in the dialog box isn't the one you think is frozen, click Cancel, wait a few seconds, and press Command-Option-Esc again. Clicking the Force Quit button often jettisons the offending program, which gives you the opportunity to save your changes in any other running programs and then restart the computer to restore stability.

Unfortunately, exactly as in Windows, this emergency procedure doesn't always work. It sometimes results in a more severely frozen system; at this point, you have no choice but to restart the Macintosh.

Enter Key

On the Macintosh: Enter Key, Return Key

PC keyboards have a pair of Enter keys: one in the main typing area and one on the numeric keypad. The two are functionally identical.

On the Macintosh, however, the key in the main typing area is labeled Return, not Enter. Most of the time, Return and Enter have the same function, but in some programs, the two have different functions. In Excel, for example, pressing the Return key moves the input cell downward in a block of highlighted cells, and the Enter key moves across. Similarly, if you're using a macro program, you can assign macros independently to each key.

Esc Key

On the Macintosh: Esc Key

In Windows, the Esc (short for Escape) key has numerous functions. On the Macintosh, however, Esc has little purpose beyond its ability to cancel a dialog box or close an open menu. Macintosh users use the Command-period keystroke far more often, which performs the same functions and more, including canceling a lengthy procedure (such as downloading or copying files) in progress. (In the rare Macintosh program where Esc fails to close the dialog box, Command-period usually does the trick.)

The Esc key is also used on the Macintosh to force quit a frozen program—press Command-Option-Esc and then click the Force Quit button in the dialog box that appears. For more information, see **End Task**.

Ethernet

On the Macintosh: Ethernet

Ethernet is a networking protocol that's supported equally well by the Macintosh and Windows, so it's an excellent method of connecting a Macintosh and a PC to transfer files or share other network resources. For more information about moving files back and forth, see **Transferring Files to the Macintosh**.

Eudora

On the Macintosh: Eudora

Qualcomm's Eudora is one of the most popular Internet email programs for Windows, although it started life as a Macintosh program. It remains popular on the Macintosh, and the two versions are extremely similar, often down to the keyboard shortcuts. If you're used to Eudora Light or Eudora Pro in Windows, you should try it on the Macintosh, because it's easy to switch.

The other advantage of using Eudora in both Windows and the Macintosh is that you'll experience the fewest problems when sending attachments back and forth.

E-H

For more information, or to download a free copy of Eudora Light, visit *http://www. eudora.com/.* Also check out *Eudora 4.2 for Windows & Macintosh: Visual QuickStart Guide* (*http://www.tidbits.com/eudora/*).

Exiting Programs
On the Macintosh: Quitting Programs

There are two differences between quitting programs in Windows and in the Macintosh OS. First, the wording is different—on the Macintosh, you choose Quit, not Exit, from the File menu. Second, when you close the last window in a Macintosh program, the program remains running, whereas in Windows, it generally quits.

Explorer
On the Macintosh: Finder

Technically, the Windows Explorer is the program that creates and maintains the Desktop and many of the other visible aspects of Windows. However, you can also run the Explorer as a standalone application, at which point it displays a two-pane interface for navigating the hierarchy of your hard disk.

On the Macintosh side of things, the equivalent program is the Finder, which gives you the Macintosh Desktop, icons, and windows. However, the Finder doesn't offer a two-pane display like the Explorer; there's no way to have a window that lets you navigate the folder hierarchy in one pane and displays folder contents in the other.

That said, in List view (choose View → as List), the Finder offers "disclosure triangles" next to each folder. Click a triangle to view, outline-like, the contents of that folder (see Figure E-1). This feature lets you move around the hierarchy of your hard disk in much the same way you can in the two-pane Explorer view in Windows.

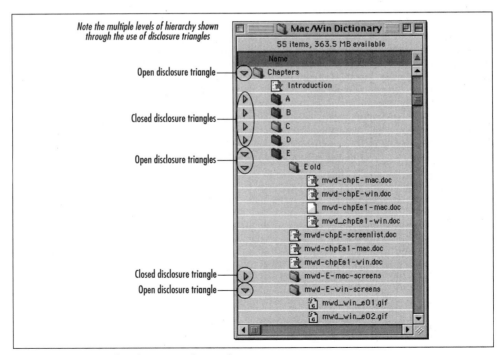

Figure E-1. Hierarchical views in the Finder's List view

Caveats and tricks. Keep a few things in mind when working with the Finder's folder triangles:

- You can view the contents of a folder either by clicking the disclosure triangle or by opening the folder into a window, but not both. If you click the triangle of an open folder, the folder's window closes; if you double-click a folder whose disclosure triangle is open (down), the triangle closes (points right), and the folder's contents appear in a new window.

- Because the contents of a folder are indented under the folder's name when you click the disclosure triangle, you may need to make windows wider to see the contents.

- You can Option-click a folder's triangle to expand the folder and all folders inside it, in effect clicking all the folder triangles, no matter how many folders deep. Option-click the triangle again to collapse the folder and all subfolders.

- You can also open (to one level) all folder triangles in a single window: choose Edit → Select All, and then press Command-right arrow. Press Command-left arrow to close them all again.

E–H

F

Fat 16, Fat 32
On the Macintosh: HFS, HFS Plus

Over time, both Apple and Microsoft have revamped the technical protocols used for storing files on your hard disk surface. The older schemes, which wasted large amounts of disk space, were called FAT16 in Windows or the Hierarchical File System, or HFS, on the Macintosh. The newer schemes are called FAT32 and HFS Plus (Mac OS Extended), respectively. After converting your PC's hard disk from one scheme to the other, you'll have many more megabytes free, especially if your hard disk contains many small files.

Just as Windows 98 is required to access FAT32 disks, only recent versions of the Mac OS recognize disks formatted with HFS Plus. For example, a Macintosh running Mac OS 8.0 or earlier doesn't recognize a disk formatted with HFS Plus. (When you look at such a disk—a Zip disk, for example—on an older Macintosh, you see nothing on the disk except a single text file called *Where_Have_All_My_Files_Gone?*.)

You can convert Macintosh disks from HFS to HFS Plus in one of two ways. The free way: erase it completely using the included Drive Setup application. The commercial way: use PlusMaker (*http://www.alsoft.com/*), which converts your Macintosh hard disk to HFS Plus without requiring erasure.

Favorites Menu
On the Macintosh: Favorites Menu

In Windows 98, Microsoft tried hard to merge the standard user interface with a web browser. The Favorites menu is a prime example of this. It can hold both shortcuts to web pages and shortcuts to folders; you can add either one by choosing Favorites → Add to Favorites from Inter-

net Explorer, an Explorer window, or a folder window. You can manage all your favorites at once by choosing Favorites → Organize Favorites.

Note

If you're using system software before Mac OS 8.5, you can use the Apple menu to perform roughly the same function as the Favorites menu. To do so, make an alias of the folder or file you want easy access to. Put that alias in the System Folder → Apple Menu Items folder. As soon as you do so, the item becomes available from the Apple menu. For more information, see **Shortcuts** and **Start Menu**.

Mac OS 8.5 and later has a Favorites command, too. It's in the Apple menu; it also shows up as a pop-up icon in the Save and Open dialog boxes of many programs. The main difference between the Macintosh Favorites menu and the Windows Favorites menu is that the Macintosh Favorites menu is designed to hold local items—Apple doesn't attempt to lump web pages and folders together.

To add a file, disk, or folder to your Favorites menu, highlight its icon and then choose File → Add to Favorites. (Alternatively, you can Control-click an icon in the Finder and choose Add to Favorites from the contextual menu that appears.) If you're using a modern program—technically, one that supports what Apple calls Navigation Services—you'll see the Favorites pop-up icon in the dialog box whenever you are opening or saving a file. (This icon looks like a folder with a bookmark on it.) You can also add an item to the Favorites menu by choosing Add to Favorites from this pop-up icon wherever you see it.

Faxing

On the Macintosh: Faxing

Any Macintosh equipped with a fax modem can send and receive faxes, just as you can on a Windows PC. However, Apple doesn't make fax software—no fax program is a standard part of the Mac OS, as it is on Windows. As a result, the instructions for sending and receiving faxes are different depending on the fax software that came with your fax modem.

The most common fax modem is the one built into every iMac, iBook, and most Power Macintosh and PowerBook G3 models. It comes with a third-party fax program called FaxSTF. Here's how it works:

To send a fax. Prepare the text of your fax in any Macintosh program, such as a word processor. While pressing the Option and Command keys, choose File → Fax. (The command that normally says Print changes to say Fax when you depress those special keys.) In the resulting dialog box, click Fax Numbers → Temporary Address. Now you can specify your fax recipient's name and fax number; click Send to send the fax. (You can build a permanent list of fax addressees using the Fax Browser program described next.)

To receive faxes. If you'd like your Macintosh to serve as a fax-receiving device, open the Macintosh HD → FAXstf folder, and then open the Fax Browser folder inside. Choose Edit → Settings → Fax Modem, and adjust the control that specifies how many rings should elapse before the computer answers the phone. (When a fax comes in, your Apple menu will blink. Launch Fax Browser to read, and, if you like, print the fax.)

Configuring your home or office so that the computer gets its own line is, of course, up to you.

File Menu

On the Macintosh: File Menu

There are two things to keep in mind about the File menu in Windows folder windows that are different on the Macintosh. First, the contents of the Windows File menu change

radically depending on what's selected—that's not true on the Macintosh, where menu items are grayed out when they aren't available. Also, programs can add menus to the File menu in Windows folder windows, which isn't generally true on the Macintosh. So, whereas you may have commands for adding files to Zip archives or using PGP (Pretty Good Privacy—an encryption program for protecting data from prying eyes) to encrypt or decrypt the selected files, those functions are handled in alternate ways on the Macintosh.

Explore. After highlighting a folder or disk icon in Windows, choosing File → Explore displays a two-pane Explorer interface. There's no equivalent on the Macintosh, although Finder windows can show the contents of nested folders in List views.

New (command). For certain types of documents, Windows puts a New item in the File menu; choosing File → New creates a new copy of the document type you choose. On the Macintosh, you instead select the file, choose File → Duplicate (Command-D), then double-click the newly created file to edit it.

New (menu). From File → New, Windows lets you create new folders, shortcuts, and a variety of documents, such as sound files and text files. The Mac's File menu offers equivalent commands only for New Folder (File → New Folder) and New Shortcut (File → Make Alias).

Quick View. There's no equivalent to Quick View on the Macintosh.

Send To. The commands in the Windows File → Send to menu let you copy the selected file to a floppy disk, or the Desktop as a shortcut, or to programs that register themselves as destinations. There's no equivalent menu command built into the Mac OS.

Create Shortcut. The Windows Create Shortcut command is essentially identical to File → Make Alias (Command-M) on the Macintosh. See **Shortcuts** for more information.

Delete. Choosing File → Delete in Windows is the same as choosing File → Move To Trash (Command-Delete) in Mac OS 8.5 and later. Most Macintosh users just drag files to the Trash or select the files and press Command-Delete. See **Recycle Bin**.

Rename. The Windows Rename command opens a filename's editing rectangle, which you can also accomplish by simply clicking the filename. The Mac OS has no specific Rename command—see **Renaming**.

Properties. The Macintosh equivalent to the Properties command is File → Get Info (Command-I), which opens the Get Info window for the selected items. Note that if you have multiple icons selected, the Mac OS opens one Get Info window for each, rather than treating them as a group, as Windows does. For more information, see **Properties Dialog Box**.

Work Offline. Since Work Offline is an artifact of the Windows 98 pseudo-web interface, there's no equivalent on the Macintosh.

File Sharing

On the Macintosh: File Sharing

With Windows 95, Microsoft added file sharing, which has been a feature of the Mac OS for years. With file sharing, you can mount a remote shared folder as a disk on your Desktop and use it just as you would any other disk.

Configuring file sharing. Configuring file sharing for your own use is easy, though it gets more difficult if you want to provide different access privileges to different users.

1. In Mac OS 8 and later, open Apple menu → Control Panels → File Sharing. If you're using Mac OS 7.6 or earlier, open Apple menu → Control Panels → Sharing Setup.

2. Enter an owner name (your name), an owner password (optional), and a name for the Macintosh (see Figure F-1).

3. Click the Start button to turn on file sharing. It may take a short while to start up, during which time the button changes to Cancel. When file sharing is on, the button turns to Stop. To turn off file sharing, click Stop. If you wish to share your entire hard disk and access it yourself from other locations on the network, you're done. If, however, you want to provide access only to specific folders, proceed as follows.

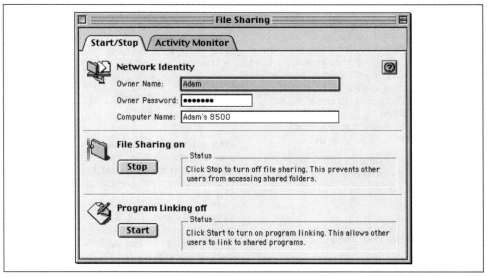

Figure F-1. File Sharing control panel

4. Open Apple menu → Control Panels → Users & Groups.

5. Click New User → Identity, and enter a user name and password for the coworker to whom you're giving access to your hard disk.

6. Close the Users & Groups control panel, and then select the disk containing the folder you want to share. Choose File → Sharing.

7. Click "Share this item and its contents," and then use the pop-up menus to assign an owner and users or groups, along with the desired privileges. Your options are Read & Write, Read only, Write only (Drop Box), or None. Repeat this step down through the hierarchy to the folder you want to share. The tricky part is that all folders down to the one you want to share must be shared, though they don't have to have any access privileges.

8. Once file sharing is on, open Apple menu → Control Panels → File Sharing → Activity Monitor to see who is connected to your Macintosh (Mac OS 8 and later). In Mac OS 7.6 and earlier, open Apple menu → Control Panels → File Sharing Monitor to achieve the same result.

Accessing files via file sharing, method 1. To connect to a machine running file sharing and access files, follow these steps in Mac OS 8.5 and later. For more information on using Network Browser, see **Network Neighborhood**.

1. Open Apple menu → Network Browser (see Figure F-2).

2. Either click the disclosure triangle next to a shared computer or double-click the computer's icon to display the login dialog box.

3. Enter your user name and password.

4. Double-click the disk in the Network Browser window to mount it as a disk on your Desktop.

Accessing files via file sharing, method 2. The instructions are slightly different for versions of the Mac OS prior to Mac OS 8.5, although they also still work in Mac OS 8.5 and later. For more information about the Chooser, see **Network Neighborhood**.

1. Open Apple menu → Chooser → AppleShare (see Figure F-3).

2. Select the desired server and click OK to display the login dialog box.

3. Enter your user name and password.

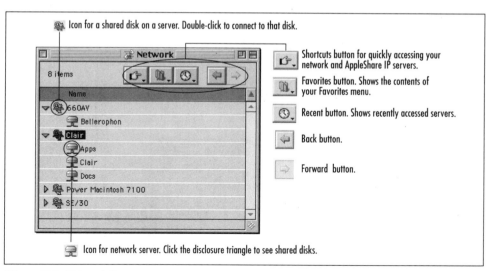

Figure F-2. Network Browser

4. In the dialog box that appears, select the disks you want to mount, and click OK. If you want to mount these disks on every startup, check the box next to them (see Figure F-4).

Simplifying access. There are several ways you can simplify the process of mounting shared disks over the network:

- Set them to mount at startup every time you turn on the Macintosh.

- Make an alias to the disk, or to a folder on the disk. Thereafter, when you open the alias, the Finder automatically connects to the shared disk, asks for your

password, and mounts the requested disk or folder on your Desktop.

Caveats. You should keep a few facts about network volumes in mind:

- To open a file that's sitting on the Desktop of a Macintosh you're accessing over the network, open the hard disk. In the main hard disk window is a folder called Desktop Folder—open it to view the files sitting on the Desktop.

- If you drag a file from a remote disk onto your own Desktop, you make a copy of it there.

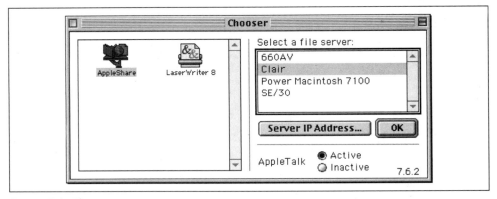

Figure F-3. Chooser

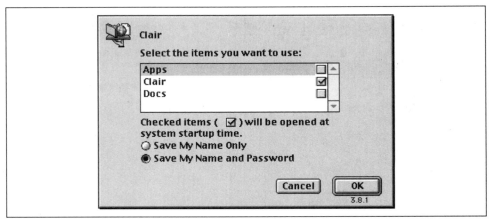

Figure F-4. Setting volumes to mount at startup

- To remove the icon of a shared disk from your Desktop, drag its icon to the Trash—or select it and then choose File → Put Away. You might want to do this to reduce the clutter on your Desktop.

- When you drag files from the remote disk to the Trash, you're actually putting them into an invisible Network Trash folder on the remote disk. As with any items in the Macintosh Trash, these items will remain there until you use the Special → Empty Trash command. Sometimes when you remove a disk from your Desktop, though, the Finder warns you that items you've deleted from the remote disk will be deleted permanently.

- Whenever you're accessing the remote disk, you can see the network access indicators flash in the upper-left of the menu bar, to the left of the Apple menu icon.

File Translation
On the Macintosh: File Translation

The most frustrating aspect of working with Macs and Windows-based PCs is file translation. It's hard enough to move files back and forth physically (see **Transferring Files to the Macintosh**), but trying to find the appropriate translator for them can be truly annoying. You have three options when trying to share Windows files with programs on the Macintosh: use cross-platform applications, rely on universal file formats, or use file-translation software.

Cross-platform programs. The easiest way to share files between Windows and Macintosh programs is to use programs that have almost identical versions on both platforms. Most Microsoft, Adobe, and Macintoshromedia applications fall into this category, as do many other popular programs. See **Cross-Platform Programs** for a list.

Note that you must generally use parallel versions of cross-platform applications for file formats to be similar. For instance, you might have trouble opening a Windows Word 97 document in Word 4 on the Macintosh.

Even when cross-platform applications don't share the same file format, they generally come with translators that let you read and write the appropriate formats. Sometimes, as with older versions of Microsoft Word, you may have to visit the company's web site to find the appropriate translators.

Universal file formats. Some file formats are sufficiently universal that most applications in the same category (graphics, word processors, etc.) can read them. For instance, any word processor can read a text file, and almost any word processor can read RTF (Rich Text Format) files. Similarly, any graphics program should be able to open a GIF or a JPEG file. For more details, see **GIF**, **JPEG**, and similar entries.

You can use these universal file formats to move data between programs that cannot otherwise read each other's files. But keep in mind that universal file formats don't offer as many features as proprietary file formats. In other words, if you save a file from Word 97 as RTF, and then try to open the resulting document in WriteNow on the Macintosh, you may lose some formatting in the process.

Note

When moving a file to the Macintosh, generally you don't need to add any three-letter suffix to its name, as on Windows. A Macintosh can identify, for example, an RTF file automatically, even if its name doesn't end with the *.rtf* suffix.

File translators. If you need to convert files from one format to another, you need a file-translation utility.

The best utilities for translating between PC and Macintosh file formats come from Data-Viz. This company's MacLinkPlus can convert most Windows word-processing and spreadsheet files to Macintosh equivalents, and Conversions Plus converts most Macintosh files in their Windows equivalents. (MacLinkPlus was included with the Mac OS until Mac OS 8.5.)

E–H

Both programs offer a long list of translators, plus tips on dealing with common formats for which DataViz has no translators. No file translation product can be perfect, but DataViz's products are among the best. For more information, visit *http://www.dataviz.com/*.

A number of older Macintosh programs supported an Apple technology called XTND, which could translate many popular file formats. XTND is moribund today, but you may still run into it on occasion, and it's worth trying if you don't have MacLinkPlus.

File Types
On the Macintosh: File Exchange Control Panel, File Types, Type Codes, Creator Codes

When it comes to figuring out which application opens when you double-click a document, the Macintosh and Windows work quite differently. Windows relies entirely on three-letter filename extensions, whereas the Mac OS uses hidden, four-letter type and creator codes for every file.

The creator code specifies the application that created the file (iBIM for Photoshop, MSWD for Microsoft Word, etc.). and the type code specifies what sort of file it is (JPEG, GIF, PICT, etc.). Together, these codes define what file icons look like and what happens when you double-click a file in the Finder.

Although shareware programs can change these type and creator codes, most Macintosh users don't bother, because you can generally open files of standard types in a variety of different programs as long as you use File → Open rather than double-clicking. For example, Microsoft Word can open any file, from text to graphics to web pages, in this way. Once you have the file open in the desired program, saving it changes its creator code, making it correspond to the program you most recently saved it from.

If you encounter documents that lack type or creator codes, here are several ways to open them automatically:

- Drag such an unidentified document icon onto the icon of the application.

For example, you can drop word-processing document icons onto Word 98's icon to open them.

- Map these files' Windows filename suffixes to the desired program in Apple menu → Control Panels → File Exchange → PC Exchange. For instance, if you transfer a Microsoft Word document from Windows to the Macintosh, but double-clicking the document doesn't open it in Word, add the *.doc* extension to the filename and try again. The File Exchange control panel should recognize the extension and open the file in Word.

- In Apple menu → Control Panels → File Exchange → File Translation, set up a translation to open files of a specific type in an application you choose. Click Add, select a representative document, and then choose your desired application from the dialog boxes that appear.

Filenames
On the Macintosh: Filenames

DOS and Windows 3.1 supported only the so-called "eight-dot-three" filenames: eight characters, a period, and then a three-letter extension. If you believe the brochures, Windows 95 radically increased the maximum length of filenames to 260 characters. Unfortunately, behind the scenes, the eight-dot-three system lurks as a parallel filename universe. Every Windows 95/98/2000 document still requires a three-letter extension, even though it's often hidden; moreover, you'll encounter thousands of files that retain the eight-dot-three convention in order to remain compatible with Windows 3.1 or even DOS.

In contrast, filenames in the Mac OS have always had a 31-character limit. You can add three-letter suffixes if you like, but they're merely cosmetic. Add the suffixes, though, if you plan to transfer these files to another computer platform, such as Windows or Unix. For instance, HTML, JPEG, and GIF files generally have *.html*, *.jpeg*, and *.gif* extensions.

Reserved characters. You're not allowed to use ?, >, :, /, or any of ten other symbols in Windows filenames. On the Macintosh, on the other hand, the only symbol you're not allowed to use in a filename is the colon (:). That's because on the Macintosh, a colon is essentially the separator to indicate directory structures, much like Windows uses the backslash. Whereas a path in Windows might look like this: *Windows\Multimedia*, the Macintosh internally stores paths like this: *Macintosh HD:System Folder:Preferences*. If you try to type a colon in a filename, the Finder replaces it on the fly with a dash.

Case sensitivity. Both Windows and the Mac OS are case insensitive—you can't create files called FILENAME and FileName in the same directory. That said, both systems preserve case in filenames, so you can use mixed case without fear of losing the capitalization.

Changing a file's name. To rename a Macintosh file, click once on its filename or click once on the icon and then press Return. Either way, a special editing rectangle appears; type the new name, or edit the existing name. Press Return or click elsewhere to confirm the new name.

Editing filenames. You can edit filenames using all the basic tools you'd expect in a text-editing environment, including the arrow keys; both the Delete key and (in Mac OS 8) the Del key; and Cut, Copy, and Paste.

Find

On the Macintosh: Find, Sherlock

In Start → Find, Windows provides utilities for finding files or folders on your computer, computers on your network, information on the Internet, and people (the last two are available only in Windows 98). On the Macintosh, you use Apple menu → Sherlock (Mac OS 8.5 and later) or Apple menu → Find (previous systems) to achieve the same purpose.

Files or folders. To search for a Macintosh file by its name, location, date, file type, or size, choose File → Find. Doing so opens the Find File tab of Sherlock (or the Find File window prior to Mac OS 8.5).

The Sherlock or Find File utility offers quite a bit of flexibility, letting you search all disks, local disks, local disks other than CD-ROMs, mounted servers, on the Desktop, only within a selected group of folders, or on a specific disk. Once you've chosen the location to search, you can use the criteria menu to search for files and folders by name, size, kind, label, creation date, modification date, version, comments, lock attribute, folder attribute, file type, and file creator. For each criteria, Sherlock/Find File provides appropriate variables and choices; for instance, if you choose to search for a file by size, you can then choose whether you want to find files whose size is greater than or less than a number you enter. You can also combine search criteria by clicking the More Choices button.

> **Note**
>
> Hold down the Option key when you click the criteria menu to reveal three additional options: name/icon lock, custom icon, and visibility.

Searching for files by size or date. Here's an example of how you would use Sherlock. Suppose you want to find a file larger than a megabyte that you created last year. See Figure F-5 for how the Sherlock window should look.

1. Choose Apple menu → Sherlock → Find File to open Sherlock.
2. Choose "on local disks" from the Find items menu.
3. Choose "size" from the criteria menu, "is greater than" from the next menu, and enter 1024 in the text field.
4. Click More Choices to add another set of criteria.
5. Choose "date created" from the second criteria menu, "is before" from the next menu, and enter January 1 of this year (you can either type or use the up/down arrows to change the numbers).
6. Click Find to perform the search.

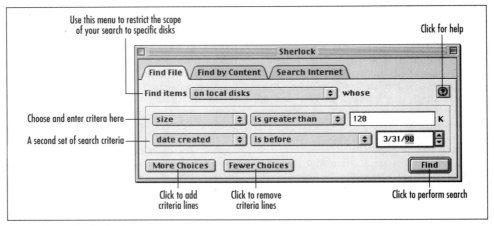

Figure F-5. Sherlock

Sherlock/Find File then opens a Results window that lists files matching your search criteria (see Figure F-6). The window works much like a Finder window—you can sort the list by clicking on the column headers, open a file by double-clicking it, or even drag a file icon to another open window to move or copy it. The pane at the bottom of the window, which can be expanded by clicking the disclosure triangle, shows the full path to the file; double-clicking any of the folders in the hierarchy opens that folder.

Searching for text within files. In Windows, you can search for text within your documents, but it's a straight brute-force search. In versions of the Mac OS prior to 8.5, you can do the same sort of straight text search by holding down the Option key, clicking the criteria menu, and choosing "contents."

In Mac OS 8.5 and later, Sherlock includes a smart text search. After first letting the program index your hard disk, cataloging every word in every document, you can perform impressively fast searches for words and ideas inside your documents—and enjoy such advanced features as relevance ranking.

To perform a content search in Sherlock, follow these steps:

1. Open Apple menu → Sherlock → Find by Content.

2. Click Index Volumes, and check the volumes you want to index. Indexes are big, and the indexing process is slow, so index only disks that contain useful content. Consider using the Schedule feature to let the Macintosh create its file indexes overnight.

3. Once your disks are indexed, enter text you want to find in the Words field, select which volumes to search, and click Find (see Figure F-7). You can also select files or folders in the Finder, and then click the "in the Finder selection" radio button to search just within the selected files or folders.

4. Sherlock presents a results window (see Figure F-8) sorted by relevance (the likelihood that the document is what you wanted). You can sort the window in other ways by clicking column headers.

Click Find Similar Files to perform a content search for files whose contents are similar to the file or files you have selected.

Computer. The Mac OS has no Find command for servers on a network. Of course, this is only a problem if you're on a huge network.

On the Internet. Microsoft's feature for searching on the Internet is really only a link to the web page you've defined as your search site; choosing Start → Find → On the

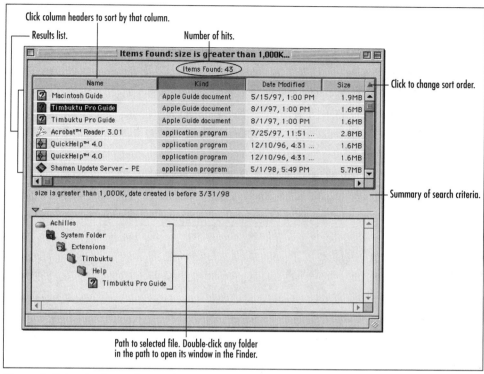

Figure F-6. Find File results window

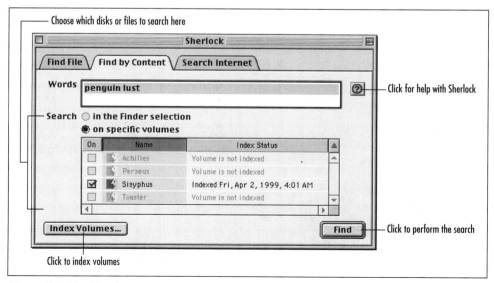

Figure F-7. Find by Content

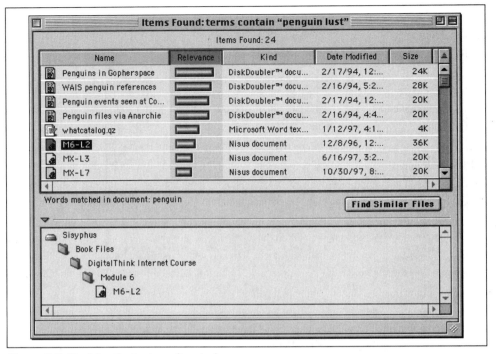

Figure F-8. Find by Content results window

Note

In Sherlock's Edit → Preferences dialog box, you can define a Finder label to apply to folders you don't want indexed. (Apply Finder labels by highlighting folders, and then choosing File → Label. Alternatively, Control-click a folder in the Finder, and then choose the appropriate label from the contextual menu that appears.)

Internet merely opens a web browser window to that page.

Mac OS 8.5 and later, on the other hand, lets you search a wide variety of Internet sites from within the Mac OS itself. Sherlock uses plug-ins, small files that communicate with specific search engines (such as Yahoo and Alta Vista); these files are stored in Macintosh HD → System Folder → Internet Search Sites. To install a new plug-in that you've downloaded from the Internet,

drop it on the System Folder; the Finder will place it in the Internet Search Sites folder automatically.

Note

Sherlock's Find by Content feature locates files according to "fuzzy logic," not by explicit phrases. That is, it tries to find documents that match your search terms in concept—you can't find documents that contain only the exact phrase "wombat migration patterns," for example.

You can find large collections of Sherlock plug-ins at various web sites, including the Apple-Donuts site at *http://www.apple-donuts.com/sherlocksearch/* and the Sherlock Collection at *http://moriarty.mit.edu/Sherlock/All.html.*

To search for information on the Web using Sherlock, follow these steps:

1. Choose Apple menu → Sherlock → Search Internet.

2. Enter your search terms in the Words field.

3. In the Search list, check the search sites you wish to search. Note that you can click the On column header to sort the list by the sites you have checked previously (see Figure F-9).

4. Click Search. Sherlock connects to each of the listed sites and performs the search. When it's done, Sherlock organizes and presents the results to you (see Figure F-10).

5. In the results window that appears, you can sort the results by name, relevance, and site by clicking the column headers. When you click a result, a summary appears below the list, complete with an icon identifying the site, a banner ad, and some of the text of the page.

6. When you've found a page that you want to read in its entirety, either double-click the result in the list, or click the page's title in the summary. Sher-

lock sends the URL to your web browser for display.

People. The Windows Find function can also find people (such as phone numbers and mailing addresses). This function relies on an Internet connection and a variety of directory web sites such as WhoWhere. The revamped Sherlock program in Mac OS 9 has a search icon dedicated to locating such personal data; previous versions, however, had no such built-in facility.

Fkeys
On the Macintosh: Function Keys

See **Function Keys (Fkeys)**.

Floppy Disks
On the Macintosh: Floppy Disks

Although floppy disks are becoming less important in both Windows and the Macintosh, they remain popular for transferring small files. Unfortunately, Windows and the Macintosh format floppy disks differently, so they cannot read each other's disks without special software. On the Macintosh side, that software is File Exchange, a control

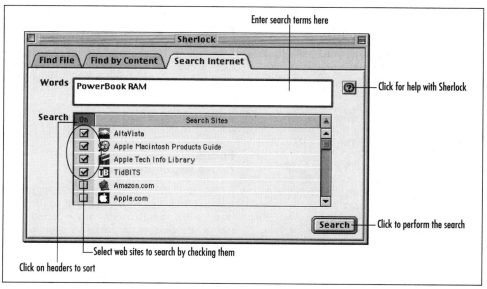

Figure F-9. Search Internet

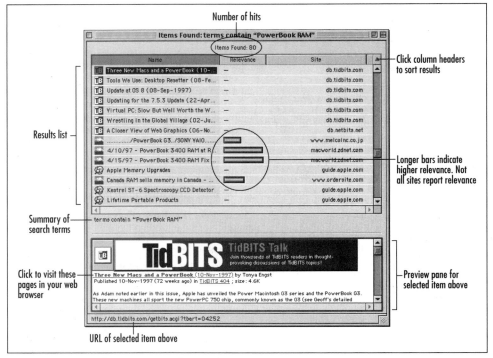

Figure F-10. Search Internet results window

panel that comes with the Mac OS. In Windows, various utility programs let you read Macintosh floppy disks; see **Transferring Files to the Macintosh** for details.

Inserting floppy disks. The Macintosh has no My Computer icon. Instead, disk icons appear on the screen only when a disk is actually inserted in the machine. Shortly after you insert the disk, you'll find its icon on the right side of the screen.

Formatting disks. Windows prompts you to format blank disks when you try to use them, and the Mac OS works similarly. However, since the Macintosh accesses disks as soon as they're inserted, the Mac OS prompts you to format the blank disk as soon as it's inserted. You can also reformat disks manually; see **Formatting Disks.**

Booting from floppy disks. Every Macintosh comes with a CD-ROM that can start up the computer, and that CD-ROM may contain the disk image of a Disk Tools disk that can also start up Macs with floppy drives. For

the different ways of booting a Macintosh from floppy or CD-ROM, see **Boot Disk**.

Ejecting a floppy disk. You'll quickly discover that a Macintosh doesn't have a disk eject button, as Windows machines do. To eject a disk, click its icon on the screen and choose either File → Put Away or Special → Eject Disk. (Or do what the Macintosh folk do—drag the disk's icon to the Trash to eject it.)

Focus
On the Macintosh: None

In Windows, focus is the subtle highlighting that indicates which element of the window or dialog box is currently selected. You frequently change the focus by pressing the Tab key, for example.

Macintosh dialog boxes don't use the focus mechanism, and no Macintosh user will know what you're talking about when you use the term focus; indeed, as described in

Dialog Boxes, you generally can't control Macintosh dialog boxes from the keyboard at all.

Still, the Macintosh displays subtle colored highlighting to indicate its version of focus in several circumstances. When you drag an icon into a Macintosh window at the Desktop, for example, you'll see a thin colored lining appear just inside the window borders to indicate that the Macintosh understands your gesture.

In these dialog boxes, the Tab key lets you switch focus subtle color cues tell you which area is highlighted. (You can change this highlighting color in the Appearance control panel.)

Folders
On the Macintosh: Folders

At their heart, folders are almost exactly the same in Windows and on the Macintosh—they're containers for holding files and other folders. You can move and copy folders just as you would files, but the two operating systems work slightly differently.

Special folders. Some folders have special functions on the Macintosh. You'll note that, especially in Mac OS 8.5 and later, they display specially designed icons to indicate that these are OS-created folders. For a list of those folders on the Macintosh, see Table F-1. Note that all of them are stored in the System Folder.

Table F-1. Special Folders on the Macintosh

Folder	Function
Apple Menu Items	Items in this folder appear in the Apple menu. See **Start Menu**.
Appearance	Stores sound effects and Desktop background pictures use by the Appearance control panel.
Application Support	Software companies can store support files for their applications in this folder, though few do currently.
ColorSync Profiles	Contains ColorSync profiles—files that describe, to the Mac's color software, various color printers, monitors, and scanners, in order to maintain color consistency throughout the color management system.
Contextual Menu Items	Items in this folder add entries to contextual menus accessed by Control-clicking. See **Right-Click**.
Control Panels	Contains control panels that let you configure the Mac OS. See **Control Panel**.
Control Strip Modules	Items placed in this folder add utilities to the Control Strip. See **Tray**.
Extensions	Holds extensions—start-up files that modify the operation of, or add features to, the Mac OS. See **Drivers**.
Favorites	Contains aliases to commonly used files and folders for quick access from the Favorites menu.
Fonts	Contains fonts.
Help	Contains help files for the Mac OS. See **Help**.
Internet Search Sites	Holds Sherlock plug-ins for searching Internet web sites. See **Find**.
Preferences	Stores user preferences for every application. See **Registry**.
PrintMonitor Documents	Contains temporary files while they're printing in the background. See **Printing Files**.
Recent Applications	Contains aliases to the most recent applications you've used.
Recent Documents	Stores aliases to the most recent documents you've used. See **Documents Menu**.
Recent Servers	Holds aliases to the most recent servers you've mounted onto the Desktop. See **Network Neighborhood**.

Table F-1. Special Folders on the Macintosh (continued)

Folder	Function
Scripting Additions	Contains scripting addition files, each of which adds a certain specialized function to AppleScript. See **Batch Language**.
Scripts	Stores AppleScripts that get triggered when you add items to, or just open, certain folders. See "Folder actions," later in this entry.
Shutdown Items	Contains applications, or aliases of them, that run when you shut down the Macintosh.
Startup Items	Stores files or folders, or aliases of them, that open when the Macintosh starts up. See **StartUp Folder**.

The most important Macintosh folder of all, of course, is the System Folder—the exact analog of the Windows folder on a Windows PC. It stores the operating system itself.

Folder actions. Mac OS 8.5 exposed a feature of the Mac OS that's been helpful for some time. If you drop a control panel on the System Folder icon, the Mac OS tells you that it's moving the file to the appropriate folder, Control Panels in this case. In essence, the System Folder recognizes certain types of files and can perform actions specific to them, such as route them to a specific folder.

Beginning in Mac OS 8.5, you can attach an AppleScript script to any folder as a folder action. Whenever somebody opens, closes, or drops a file into that folder, the folder action script runs—for example, printing out the newly deposited file and then automatically forwarding it to the executive editor. To assign an action to a folder, Control-click the folder, choose Attach a Folder Action, and choose a script. You can find some sample scripts in Macintosh HD → System Folder → Scripts → Folder Action Scripts. Once a folder action is attached to a folder, a small script badge is added to the folder icon. You can remove folder actions by Control-clicking the folder and choosing Remove Folder Action.

Folder icons. You may have noticed that many of the special folders mentioned above have custom icons. In fact, you can assign a custom icon to any folder other than the special folders. For more information, see **Icons**.

Fonts
On the Macintosh: Fonts

One of the most attractive aspects of working with graphical interfaces like Windows and the Mac OS is that they let you create documents using different fonts. Before graphical interfaces, fonts were specific to programs, rather than being accessible to any program.

Types of fonts. As on Windows, fonts on the Macintosh come in two varieties: TrueType and PostScript. Functionally, the two font technologies are similar, although they use different underlying mathematical algorithms. TrueType fonts are predominant on both Macintosh and Windows because they offer many advantages: for example, they appear smooth and attractive at any size, both on screen and when printed; furthermore, on the Macintosh, each TrueType font requires only a single font file in your System Folder, making font management simpler.

> **Note**
>
> Technically, there's a third kind of font format—bitmapped fonts. Bitmapped fonts are used on the Macintosh only for hand-tuned screen fonts at specific sizes.

PostScript fonts, on the other hand, are more frequently used in professional publishing and graphics, despite several drawbacks— each font requires numerous components to manage in your System Folder (separate files for the screen display and print out, for

---

The Mac's Spring-Loaded Folders

Macintosh folders do something Windows folders don't: they spring open. This peculiar and rapidly addicting feature is designed to eliminate one of the most frustrating aspects of windows-based interfaces like Windows and the Mac OS: window clutter as you try to move icons from one folder to another.

Suppose you want to drag an icon that's on the Macintosh Desktop into a folder that's nested three folders deep. You'd have to open the hard disk window; then open the first folder into a window; open the folder inside it; drag the icon into place; then close all the windows you've opened in the process.

In Mac OS 8.0 and later, however, you can simply drag an icon onto a folder (or the hard disk window). If you continue to press the mouse button, the hard disk window opens automatically. Now you can drag that icon on top of the next folder, and it, too, will spring open, so that you can drop it on its final, target folder destination. When you release the mouse, all the windows you've opened (except the final one) snap shut again.

You can also burrow into multiple nested folders even if you're not dragging an icon. (You might do so just to see what's in some nested folder, for example.) To do so, point to a disk or folder icon and do a click-and-a-half—that is, push the mouse button down-up-down, and leave it down. The window opens; keeping the button pressed, move the cursor over a folder icon in this window. You can continue opening window after window as long as you keep the mouse button down. When you arrive at the window you ultimately intended to reach, let go; all the windows except this innermost one snaps shut behind you.

You control how quickly a folder or disk window opens by choosing Edit → Preferences and adjusting the slider. Better yet, Mac OS 8.5 and later offer a shortcut: When you begin a spring-loaded drag, you don't have to wait for the folder beneath your cursor to open. Tapping the Spacebar makes the window spring open instantly, so that the timing of the opening is always within your control.

---

example), and these fonts can look jagged on the screen unless you've also installed Adobe Type Manager (ATM). Nonetheless, a wider variety of high-quality fonts are available in PostScript format, and most professional publishing equipment works better with PostScript than with TrueType fonts.

Identifying TrueType versus PostScript. To view the actual font files installed on a Macintosh, open System Folder → Fonts. Inside, double-click a font "suitcase" file (so-called because the file icon resembles a little briefcase) to examine its alphabet style. You can identify the different types of fonts by their icons—see Figure F-11 for the three different types. Also, screen fonts generally have a font size number in their names, and TrueType fonts may include styles in parentheses after their names.

Font suitcases. In Windows, if you look in the Fonts folder, you may see a separate font file for each font variant—Arial, Arial Black, Arial Bold, Arial Bold Italic, and so on. You may see the same situation on the

Macintosh, but more often, all the necessary software for a particular TrueType font is stored in a single font suitcase. PostScript fonts, on the other hand, may fill your Macintosh Fonts folder—these fonts require a suitcase file for the on-screen letter shapes, and a separate printer-font file for each style (bold, italic, bold italic, and so on).

Installing and removing fonts. Installing and removing fonts on the Macintosh is easy—just drag the font files into or out of the System Folder → Fonts folder. However, there are two caveats:

- You can install fonts by dragging them into the Fonts folder at any time, but these newly added fonts won't show up in the Font menus of any applications that are running until you quit and relaunch. (A message will tell you as much.)

- You can't remove fonts from the Fonts folder (or combine fonts into suitcases) while any applications other than the Finder are running.

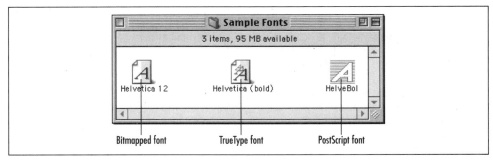

Figure F-11. Different font icons

Viewing fonts. To see what a font looks like, double-click it. A PostScript screen font suitcase opens to reveal a sample sentence in a single point size, whereas a TrueType font suitcase opens to display sample sentences in three sizes: 9 point, 12 point, and 18 point (see Figure F-12).

Choosing fonts. Using fonts in applications is easy—just choose a font from the Fonts menu. You can also choose among several Macintosh interface fonts—those used in menus, Windows, and so on—by choosing Apple menu → Control Panels → Appearance → Fonts; for details see **Display Control Panel**.

Font-size differences on Windows and the Macintosh. If you've ever viewed the same web page or Word document on both Windows and the Macintosh, you may have

> **Note**
>
> Another way to sample various fonts on the Macintosh is to choose Apple menu → Key Caps. Use the Font menu in the program that appears to specify the typeface you'd like to sample.

wondered why the two platforms seem to render the same fonts at different sizes. For instance, a web page that looks good in Windows has tiny text on the Macintosh, and a document that looks fine on the Macintosh has huge text in Windows.

The problem is related to the fact that the Mac OS assumes a screen resolution of 72 dpi, while Windows assumes a screen resolution of 96 dpi. For a detailed explanation

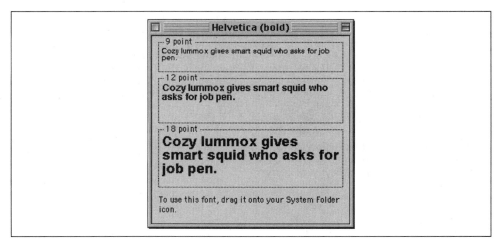

Figure F-12. TrueType font sample

of the problem, see Geoff Duncan's article on the issue in *TidBITS* at *http://db.tidbits. com/getbits.acgi?tbart=05284.*

Unfortunately, there is no easy way around the problem, although workarounds exist if you only run into the problem occasionally.

- On the Web, if you see a page whose text is way too small or too large, you may be able to increase or decrease the size of the text for that page, depending on your web browser. Look for Font or Text Size commands in the View menu.

- If you're using Microsoft Word, you can scale the document up for the Macintosh or down for Windows using the Zoom menu on the main toolbar. Or, if you must work in a style sheet-heavy document for a long time, you can redefine the main styles to use a larger or more readable font. For instance, when opening a Windows document that comes in Times 10-point type—a nearly unreadable style on the Macintosh—consider redefining the Normal style to the Mac's New York or Palatino 12-point font.

Formatting Disks

On the Macintosh: Formatting Disks

You can format Macintosh disks in several ways.

Floppy disks. To erase or format a floppy disk on the Macintosh, follow these steps:

1. Insert a disk. If it's brand-new and unformatted, you'll promptly be shown the dialog box illustrated in Figure F-13. If the disk has already been formatted and you'd like to erase it, select its icon and then choose Special → Erase Disk. The Finder displays the Erase Disk dialog box.

2. Give the disk a name.

3. Choose the desired format: Macintosh or DOS. (Ignore ProDOS, which is an Apple][format rarely used these days.)

4. Click Erase.

Zip and Jaz disks. You can use a Macintosh to reformat Zip and Jaz disks for use on a Windows machine, just as you can with floppies—but in this case, the Mac's Erase Disk command doesn't offer you the choice of Macintosh or Windows. Instead, you must use the Iomega Tools software to reformat a Zip or Jaz cartridge for use by a different operating system.

Hard disks. To reformat a Macintosh hard disk, you use the Drive Setup program that came with the computer. For details, see **Hard Disks.**

Function Keys (Fkeys)

On the Macintosh: Function Keys

Although every Macintosh keyboard has a row of function keys along the top, just like PC keyboards, only a few have functions in the Mac OS itself. (The ones that work are F1 through F4; they correspond to Undo, Cut, Copy, and Paste.) These keys have functions in only a few programs, especially cross-platform programs like those from Microsoft; otherwise, assigning these

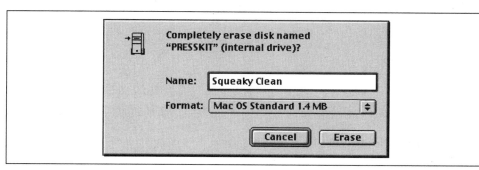

Figure F-13. Erase Disk dialog box

Fkeys to a useful purpose—such as launching your favorite programs—is up to you. If you have an iBook or late-1999 iMac model, just press one of the higher-numbered Fkeys to program it; the Macintosh asks what file you want associated with this Fkey from now on. On other Macintosh models, you need a macro program or a shareware program like QuickPop, which you can find at *http://www.northcoast.com/~jvholder/qpdesc.html.*

G

Game Controllers Control Panel

On the Macintosh: Individual game controller software

In Windows 98, you can configure and test joysticks using the Game Controllers control panel. Joysticks, foot pedals, and other customized game controllers are less common in the Macintosh world, so there's no standard control panel in the Macintosh OS for configuring them. Instead, each device comes with its own custom software.

GIF

On the Macintosh: GIF

GIF, which stands for Graphics Interchange Format, is a standard bitmapped graphic file format. (Its most notable features: small size, a maximum of 256 colors per file—making it inappropriate for photos, but great for logos and cartoons—and widespread use on the Web.) Luckily, GIF files are completely cross-platform, so you can transfer GIF files back and forth between PCs and Macintoshes with no trouble at all. Although it's common for GIF files to have a *.gif* extension even on Macintoshes, it's not required.

H

Hard Disks

On the Macintosh: Hard Disks

Although hard disk technology is essentially the same on both PCs and Macs, there are a number of differences.

Hard disk icon positioning. The first time you use a Macintosh, you may be alarmed to discover that no My Computer appears in the upper-left corner of your screen. On the Macintosh, there's no equivalent to the My Computer icon; instead, your disk icons appear individually at the right side of the screen—and only when disks (CD, Zip, floppy, and so on) are actually inserted into the machine. In other words, the absence of a CD icon doesn't mean that your Macintosh doesn't have a CD-ROM drive—only that no disc is inserted at the moment.

IDE versus SCSI. Most PC hard disks are IDE (Integrated Drive Electronics) drives, which merely means that the hard disk controller is integrated with the drive. The better term is ATA (AT Attachment), which is a specific type of IDE drive. ATA-IDE hard disks are popular because they're fast and cheap. Until the early 1990s, they were also limited to the PC world, since Macs had always come with SCSI-based hard disks instead. As Apple sought to lower prices, however, ATA-IDE became the standard internal hard disk format for all Macintosh models.

SCSI hard disks are less common in the PC world than on Macs. (Until 1998, every Macintosh model included a SCSI connector on the back panel, suitable for attaching external SCSI hard disks.)

ATA-IDE drives are generally cheaper and slightly faster than SCSI hard disks, simply because the SCSI controller chip adds some overhead. However, because each SCSI drive has its own controller chip, multiple SCSI drives attached to the same computer can all work simultaneously. In contrast, you can connect only two ATA-IDE drives (a master and a slave), and they can't operate simultaneously, which means that copying files between two such drives can take longer. Details on what is possible with different Macs vary; more information is available in a thread on TidBITS Talk, at *http://db.tidbits.com/getbits.acgi?tlkthrd=551.*

Boot disks. Some PCs can boot from disks other than the C: hard disk drive and the A: floppy drive. (This feature is BIOS-specific; many PC users don't even realize it's possible.) However, on the Macintosh, any disk, floppy, hard, or CD-ROM, can start up the machine. For more information, see **Boot Disk.**

Internal versus external. Thanks to the two-drive limit of ATA-IDE hard disk chains, it's relatively uncommon to see PCs with external hard disks attached. The fact that older Macintosh models had small internal hard disks and an available SCSI port on the back, on the other hand, makes external hard disks common on these older machines.

Compression. You might be accustomed to compressing your PC hard disk using Microsoft's DriveSpace program. Although drive compression technologies were once available for the Macintosh, they've all fallen by the wayside as hard disk sizes increased and prices dropped. The trade-offs of slightly reduced performance and greater chance for lost data in the event of disk corruption caused the Macintosh market to reject these programs years ago.

Disk maintenance. Although hard disks may physically last for many years, it's important to perform routine disk maintenance to keep the data structures (such as directories and lists of bad blocks) up to date. If you don't, your disk may suffer an increasing level of data corruption, which could cause crashes or even catastrophic data loss.

For more information about performing routine disk maintenance, see **Disk Defragmenter** and **ScanDisk**.

Disk formats. Just as Windows 98 marked the introduction of FAT 32, a more-efficient and capable disk format than the previous FAT 16 format, Mac OS 8.1 introduced Mac OS Extended format, commonly known as HFS Plus (the older Mac OS Standard format is known as HFS). You can tell how any Macintosh hard disk has been formatted by selecting its icon and then choosing File → Get Info (Command-I).

To understand the consequences of these different hard disk formats, it helps to understand the concept of a block—one individual "parking place" for data on the hard disk service. On Macintosh hard disks formatted using the older HFS scheme, these blocks were fairly large—64 K on a 2-GB disk, for example. Because each file on a hard disk consumes a minimum of a single block, even the tiniest text file would therefore take-up 64 K of space. Cumulatively, all of these small files wasted vast amounts of hard disk space.

In contrast, the blocks used by the HFS Plus formatting scheme (HFS Plus) are tiny—4 K. As a result, small files take up much less space, resulting in overall space savings.

You can convert an HFS hard disk to HFS Plus in two ways: by erasing and reformatting the drive or by using a program called PlusMaker from Alsoft. For more information, visit *http://www.alsoft.com/*.

Reformatting. You can initialize a standard Macintosh hard disk in one of two ways. Both methods require you to boot from another disk (such as the system CD-ROM that came with the machine), since you can't reformat the boot disk.

- Select the hard disk icon in the Finder, and then choose Special → Erase Disk. If you're running Mac OS 8.1 or later, you'll be offered a choice of Mac OS

Standard (HFS) format and Mac OS Extended (HFS Plus) format.

- Run Drive Setup (which comes with all Macs—on the system CD-ROM, for example), select the hard disk icon, and then click Initialize. Initializing takes only a minute or two.

Space questions. When using a Macintosh for the first time, you might want to see how large its hard disk is and how much of that space is free. In Mac OS 8, select the hard disk icon and then choose File → Get Info (Command-I). The Get Info window provides all the information you need (see Figure H-1), including total capacity, space available, and space used.

In versions of the Mac OS prior to Mac OS 8, the procedure is more complicated:

1. Open Apple menu → Control Panels → Views.
2. Turn on the "Show disk info in header." checkbox.
3. Close the Views control panel.
4. Open any window. The amount of space used and available appear at the top of the window. You must manually add them together to arrive at the total size of the disk.

Help
On the Macintosh: Help

To view the Mac's online help screens, open the Help menu. (If you're running system software before Mac OS 8, this menu looks like a question mark or light bulb at the right side of the menu bar.) Three forms of help may be available in the Help menu: balloon help, Apple Guide, and, in Mac OS 8.5 and later, Mac OS Help. (As in Windows, the presence of one form or another of help depends on the enthusiasm of the software company who created the program you're using.)

Balloon help. The concept behind balloon help is simple. After you choose Help → Show Balloons you point the cursor at some bewildering onscreen interface element or menu command and a cartoon speech balloon pops up to describe the element's

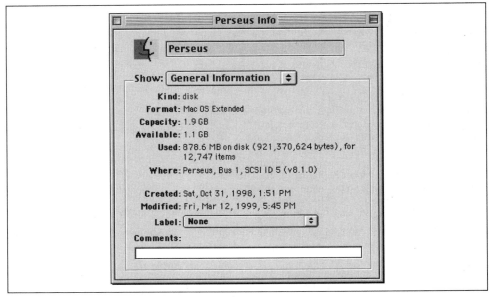

Figure H-1. Determining disk size and free space

function. Unfortunately, balloon help isn't available in every Macintosh program; when it's available, balloon help can be useful indeed (see Figure H-2).

When you've learned what you need to know, turn off balloon help by choosing Hide Balloons from the Help menu.

Apple Guide. Apple Guide provides online help for the Mac OS and many Macintosh applications. Apple Guide is more task-based than Windows Help—a typical entry in an Apple Guide index is: "How do I adjust the speaker volume?" Apple Guide, like some Windows Help entries, uses sequential help screens to walk you through common tasks; unlike Windows Help, Apple Guide offers bright-red, marker-like,

animated "coach marks" to draw your attention to certain menu items and buttons.

Although it can be an extremely helpful system, Apple Guide isn't, alas, available in many Macintosh programs. (Quicken, programs from the former Claris Corp., and the Mac OS itself are a few programs that include it.) Check the Help menu for a command called Guide—that's probably it. You can also press the Help key to bring up Apple Guide.

When you choose the appropriate Help command, the Mac OS displays the Apple Guide windoid (a special type of window that floats above all other windows that are currently open—see Figure H-3).

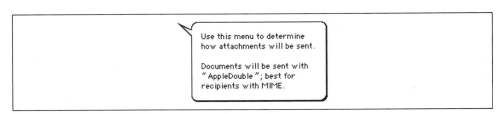

Figure H-2. Balloon help in Eudora on the Macintosh

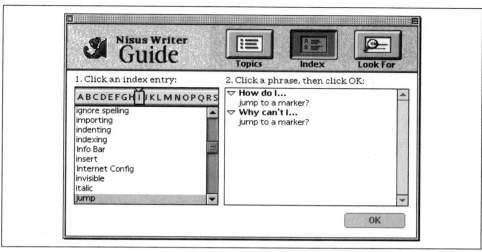

Figure H-3. Apple Guide windoid in Index mode

Just as in Windows Help, Apple Guide offers three ways of accessing help information. They're identified by buttons at the top of the Apple Guide window called Topics, Index, and Look For.

- Topics lists general topic areas. When you select an area by clicking it, the list of individual help entries appears in the right-hand scrolling list.

- Index lists terms alphabetically. Click a term to view corresponding help entries in the right-hand scrolling list.

- Look For lets you search the entire Apple Guide file. Type a search term and then click the Search button.

Once you've found a useful help entry, click its name and then click the OK button. Apple Guide opens a new instruction windoid that provides interactive instructions on performing the task at hand. If the help information isn't what you wanted, you can return to the main Apple Guide windoid by clicking the Up navigation arrow. When you're done, click the close box to close the windoid.

Mac OS Help. In part because Apple Guide doesn't make it easy to browse for information quickly, in Mac OS 8.5, Apple introduced a new Mac OS Help format, which uses a program called Help Viewer. Like Windows Help, Help Viewer provides a pane-based browser for navigating help information. The help screens can include text, graphics, and links, just as in a web browser (see Figure H-4). To access help for using the Mac OS, choose Help → Mac OS Help.

The left pane contains topics; double-clicking a topic reveals sub-topics in the right pane. Double-clicking a sub-topic opens yet another window for the help content; if you've chosen the wrong sub-topic, you must click the Back button and start over.

You can also type in the search field and then click Search to look through the entire Mac OS Help program. (The Help Viewer's search function uses Apple's Sherlock searching technology, so it ranks the results by relevance.)

On some Mac OS Help screens, you may even see a Show Me button. Clicking it opens up a page of the older Apple Guide help mechanism, which walks you through performing one task or another.

HyperTerminal
On the Macintosh: None

Windows comes with a simple terminal emulation program called HyperTerminal, which you can use to connect to old bulletin boards and for troubleshooting modem

Figure H-4. Mac OS Help

problems. There's no equivalent in the Mac OS, although you can download one like the shareware Zterm, which is one of the most popular. It's at *http://hyperarchive.lcs. mit.edu/HyperArchive/Archive/comm/term/ zterm-101.hqx*. Many other Macintosh fans use the Communications window of Claris-Works or AppleWorks, an integrated office suite that comes preinstalled with every iMac and some other Macintosh models.

If you're trying to connect to an Internet site using the PPP control panel in Mac OS 8.0 or 8.1, or the Remote Access control panel in Mac OS 8.5 and later, you can access a terminal window to log in manually, which can be a help when troubleshooting:

1. Open Apple menu → Control Panels → PPP (or Remote Access).

2. Click Options → Protocol.

3. Check "Connect to a command-line host" and "Use terminal window."

When you connect, you'll see a small terminal window for entering necessary login commands.

I

Icons
On the Macintosh: Icons

Both Windows and the Macintosh make heavy use of icons to represent disks, files, and folders on the computer. Using the View menu, you can specify how you'd like the icons in a particular window to appear.

In Windows, document icons are associated with filename extensions—a file with the extension *.doc*, for example, gets the Microsoft Word icon. On the Macintosh, however, the filename has nothing to do with the icon. Instead, every file on the Macintosh stores two invisible, four-letter codes—one that associates it with a particular application, and the other with the particular document type. (Without add-on shareware, there's no way to edit these codes.)

Custom icons. You can change any Macintosh icon except those used by special folders and the Trash. To give a file or folder a custom icon, follow these sample steps for giving your hard disk a new icon.

This example assumes that you've already created and copied a replacement icon, ready for pasting onto another Macintosh file icon. If you're handy with the graphics program, use it to create a picture no larger than 32 pixels square. Icons with a solid black or very dark border work best and prevent "Desktop color bleed-in" at the end of the process.

1. Select your hard disk's icon on the Desktop. Choose File → Get Info (Command-I) to open its Get Info window.

2. Click the hard disk's icon in the upper-left corner of the Get Info window. Choose Edit → Paste to paste the new icon over the default one. If you decide you don't like the new icon, click it and choose Edit → Cut (Command-X) to restore the hard disk's original icon.

Missing icons: Rebuilding the Desktop. Occasionally, you might notice that a number of documents and applications appear with corrupted or generic icons. Or you might install a new version of a program and notice that its document icons still look like documents from the previous version.

In both of these cases, the invisible Macintosh Desktop file—a database that associates icons with their parent applications—may have become corrupted. In such cases, you can perform a routine bit of Macintosh maintenance called rebuilding the Desktop. Follow these steps:

1. Restart the Macintosh by choosing Special → Restart.

2. Immediately press the Command and Option keys and hold them down until the Finder asks if you want to rebuild the Desktop.

3. Click OK to rebuild the Desktop database files.

It's not a bad idea to rebuild the Desktop on a relatively frequent basis—perhaps once every few months. Since the Desktop database files are constantly changing as you use the Macintosh, these files can grow large and cluttered. Rebuilding them purges unused icons and rearranges the Desktop files' contents for speedier access, which can improve the speed at which windows open in the Finder.

Installing Hardware
On the Macintosh: New hardware works without special setup

The Macintosh has always offered plug and play capabilities, so no special software steps are required when attaching a new monitor, hard disk, scanner, modem, and so on. See **Add New Hardware Control Panel** for more information.

Installing Software
On the Macintosh: Individual Installers

You won't encounter a standard software-installation interface on the Macintosh, along the lines of the Add/Remove Programs control panel on Windows. The Macintosh has no centralized Registry file that must be updated for each install or uninstall; when you install a Macintosh program, you're just adding files to the hard disk. Subsequent uninstalling is simply a matter of removing these files. Since Macintosh programs tend to have many fewer files than Windows programs and to install them in fewer locations, removing them manually isn't a serious chore. See **Add/Remove Programs Control Panel** for details.

Internet
On the Macintosh: Internet

The rise of the Internet is the most significant change in the computer world over the last few years. One important aspect of this sea change is that the Internet has brought Windows and the Macintosh closer together. Since the Internet is essentially platform-agnostic, the world's programmers have put a great deal of work into open standards that work on both Windows and the Macintosh. That's why you can receive Internet email, or browse the Web, equally well on either a Macintosh or a PC. Aspects of Internet use are covered throughout this book; refer to the following list for some of the main entries.

- For information about connecting a Macintosh to the Internet via a modem, see **Dial-Up Networking Folder** and **Modems**.

- For information about connecting a Macintosh to the Internet via a network, see **Network Control Panel**.

- For information about cross-platform Internet email programs, see **Eudora** and **Microsoft Outlook Express**.

- For information about cross-platform web browsers, see **Internet Explorer** and **Netscape Navigator/Communicator**.

- For a list of Internet-related applications that exist in both Macintosh and Windows flavors, see **Cross-Platform Programs**.

- For information about file formats you might encounter on the Internet, see **File Types**.

- For information about transferring files from a Windows-based PC to a Macintosh over the Internet, see **Transferring Files to the Macintosh**.

- For information about searching the Internet, see **Find**.

- For information about running a personal web server, see **Personal Web Server**.

- For a list of useful web sites, see **Web Sites for Macintosh Software and Information**.

Internet Control Panel
On the Macintosh: Internet Control Panel, Individual Web Browser Preferences

You'll find a control panel called Internet on both Windows and Macintosh, but the two control panels aren't very similar. The Windows Internet control panel duplicates the Internet Explorer preferences, whereas the Mac's Internet control panel (Apple menu → Control Panels → Internet) lets you set up preferences for a wide variety of Internet applications in Mac OS 8.5 and later.

The Mac's Internet control panel is the Apple front-end for a community-driven technology called Internet Config. Essentially, a group of developers got together and created a system-level database designed to hold Internet preferences—email address, passwords, preferred web home page, and so on—in one place; almost every Macintosh Internet application can then refer to these settings, thus saving you the effort of typing the same settings into every Internet application.

The Mac's Internet control panel settings are used by email programs, web browsers, Usenet newsreaders, FTP programs, and more. You can even switch between multiple sets of settings, so that different people using the same Macintosh can have different Internet settings. For more information, see **User Profiles**.

Fortunately, nearly all Macintosh Internet programs support Internet Config (and therefore the Internet control panel), including the browsers from Netscape and Microsoft. (You'll find the "Use Internet Config" checkbox in the Preferences commands of these programs.) In the following list of tabs from the Windows Internet control panel and their analogues on the Macintosh, therefore, remember that you'll have to create these settings independently if you use Netscape Communicator. Most other Macintosh Internet programs will inherit the settings automatically from the Internet/Internet Config software.

General. The General tab in Windows' Internet control panel lets you specify your home page location and settings for temporary files, history, colors, fonts, languages, and more. In the Macintosh Internet control panel, the Web tab lets you select home page, search page locations, a location for downloaded files, and color choices.

The remaining options in the Windows Internet control panel's General tab exist in the Preferences dialog boxes of individual Macintosh web browsers.

Security, Content. Each Macintosh web browser offers its own security and web-content settings; there are no such settings in the Mac's Internet control panel, as in Windows.

Connection. The Windows Internet control panel's Connection tab has options for proxy servers, connections, and automatic configuration. No Macintosh web browsers support automatic configuration, and Internet connections are handled by the TCP/IP control panel and the Remote Access control panel. (See **Dial-Up Networking Folder** for more information.)

Settings for proxy servers do exist in the Mac's Internet control panel, in Advanced → Firewalls.

Programs. The Windows Internet control panel's Programs tab lets you choose which programs you'll use for email, Usenet news, Internet calls, calendar features, and your contact list. The Mac's Internet control panel provides these and many more choices.

Click the E-mail, Web, or News tabs to choose the program you'd like to use for those Internet services. Then, in Advanced → Helper Apps, you can assign a helper application to any URL scheme. For instance, you can pick which application to use when you click on FTP URLs in an email message.

Advanced. The Advanced tab in the Windows Internet control panel sports a wide variety of semi-related settings, for which there is no consolidated equivalent on the Macintosh side. Make this kind of setting in your web browser itself.

Internet Explorer
On the Macintosh: Internet Explorer

Internet Explorer, Microsoft's free web browser, is available for both the Macintosh and Windows, and works essentially alike on each platform. You can learn more about the Macintosh version of Internet Explorer and download a copy from *http://www. microsoft.com/mac/ie/default.htm.*

IPX
On the Macintosh: MacIPX

IPX is a relatively common network protocol in Windows, one that's used on networks running Novell NetWare. Since Macs are second-class citizens in the world of NetWare, IPX is seldom used on the Macintosh. In fact, unless you use NetWare, you may have trouble even finding the IPX software. If you use a product that can support the IPX protocol, that product should come with a copy of MacIPX or information about how to get it. If IPX on the Macintosh is important to you, contact Novell at *http://www.novell.com/* for information about availability and compatibility with recent versions of the Mac OS.

ISA Slots and Cards
On the Macintosh: PCI Slots and Cards

See **PCI Slots and Cards**.

I-N

J

Java
On the Macintosh: Java

Java is a cross-platform programming language developed by Sun Microsystems. It's used primarily on the Internet for small programs, called applets, that can be downloaded and run from web pages. Windows users don't worry about Java applets much, because the Java support within Windows (and from programs like Netscape Navigator) is good.

Unfortunately, Java has never quite measured up on the Macintosh side. Despite recent improvements in Java *virtual machines* on the Mac (software that translates Java instructions), Java programs still don't run as fast on the Mac as they do in Windows.

Worse, although Java is a cross-platform language, different Java virtual machines execute Java code differently, particularly on different platforms. As a result, Java applets have a reputation for being unstable and working poorly on the Macintosh, thanks to Java programmers who fail to test their work on all common Java virtual machines.

Many Java applets today are fairly useless, adding nothing more than sophisticated animation or time-wasting games to web pages. Still, if your travel agency web site or electronic banking web site requires Java, you'd be well advised to visit the Apple web site at *http://www.apple.com/java/* to download and install the latest version of the Apple's MRJ (Macintosh Runtime for Java). Each release is faster and stable or than the previous.

Do note that the current version (4.7) of Netscape Communicator does not use Apple's MRJ, instead relying on its own Java virtual machine that's generally not as good. To use MRJ in a web browser, you're pretty much stuck with Microsoft Internet Explorer 4.5 or later on the Mac.

Joystick Control Panel
On the Macintosh: Individual joystick software

In Windows 95, you can configure and test joysticks using the Joystick control panel; in Windows 98, use the Game Controllers control panel for this purpose. Joysticks are rare in the Macintosh world, so there's no standard Mac OS control panel for configuring them. Instead, each joystick comes with its own custom software.

JPEG
On the Macintosh: JPEG

JPEG, which stands for Joint Photographic Experts Group, is a graphics compression format that's commonly applied to photographic images. Almost every photograph you find on the World Wide Web, for example, is stored in JPEG format (and bears the suffix *.jpg* or *.jpeg* on its name). On the Mac, you can open JPEG files with any web browser, or with the Movie Player application that comes on every Mac hard drive.

JPEG files are 100 percent cross-platform—you can easily transfer JPEG files between Mac and Windows machines with no conversion.

K

Keyboard

On the Macintosh: Keyboard

The PC world has seen a number of keyboard designs over the years, with the most common becoming the 101-key keyboard with the function keys on top, cursor and navigation controls, and a separate numeric keypad. Apple has used a number of different keyboard layouts for Macs as well, but for the most part you won't have any trouble switching from a PC keyboard to a Macintosh keyboard. There are, however, some keys on Macintosh keyboards that you won't recognize. Refer to Table K-1 for an overview, and to individual entries for key usage details.

Keyboard Control Panel

On the Macintosh: Keyboard Control Panel, General Controls Control Panel

The sliders in the Windows Keyboard control panel let you control various aspects of the keyboard; you'll find exactly the same options on the Macintosh, although they aren't all in the same places.

Repeat delay, Repeat rate. The settings let you specify how soon a key begins repeating when you hold it down (to type XXXXX, for example), and how quickly the key repeats once it starts. To find the same controls on the Macintosh, open the Apple menu → Control Panels → Keyboard control panel. (See Figure K-1.)

Cursor blink rate. This control lets you adjust how quickly your insertion point blinks when in a word processor. On the Macintosh, you can make the same adjustment in the Apple menu → Control Panels → General Controls control panel.

Language tab. In Windows, you use this tab to choose from among several different keyboard layouts corresponding to the keys frequently used in various languages. The same feature is available on the Macintosh: choose Apple menu → Control Panels → Keyboard control panel.

Table K-1. Keys Unique to Macintosh Keyboards

Unique Macintosh Keyboard Key	Function / Equivalent
Command key (has an apple and a cloverleaf on it)	Used as a modifier with alphanumeric keys to provide keyboard shortcuts—the exact equivalent of the Ctrl key on Windows.
Clear key (Numeric keypad)	Deletes currently highlighted text or graphics, exactly like the Edit → Clear command.
Help key	Brings up the online help screens in the Mac OS and in applications; works like the F1 function key in Windows.
Option key	Used as a modifier key and to type unusual characters; similar to the Alt key.
Power key	Turns the Macintosh on. If the Macintosh is already running, presents a dialog box for sleeping, restarting, or shutting down; may have nonstandard equivalents on PC keyboards, particularly laptops.

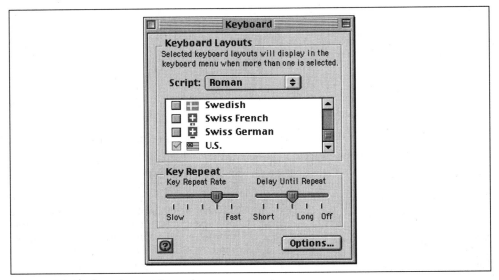

Figure K-1. Keyboard control panel

From now on, you'll see a keyboard menu—represented by a small flag—on the right side of your menu bar. To switch languages, choose a layout from this menu. Or, if you prefer, click the Options button in the Keyboard control panel to specify a keyboard shortcut that, when pressed, switches keyboard layouts.

Keyboard Port
On the Macintosh: ADB (Apple Desktop Bus), USB (Universal Serial Bus)

PCs generally offer several ports for connecting keyboards, mice, and other input devices. On the Macintosh, you connect most input devices—including keyboards, mice, trackballs, and joysticks—to one of two kinds of jacks, depending on the age of the machine All current Macintosh models offer USB ports for connecting such input devices; discontinued models offered proprietary ADB jacks instead.

ADB (Apple Desktop Bus). Because each older Macintosh input device generally offers two ADB jacks, you can chain several ADB devices together and use them simultaneously—a keyboard, mouse, and trackball, for example.

See Figure K-2 for an illustration of the icon that appears next to the ADB port on the back of the Macintosh.

USB (Universal Serial Bus). ADB was a fixture on all Macintosh models from 1987 to 1998. Beginning with the release of the iMac in 1998, however, Apple eliminated ADB in favor of the emerging industry standard called Universal Serial Bus, or USB. The 1999 blue and white Power Macintosh G3 models still offer a single ADB jack, but the rest of the line has moved to USB. Exactly as in Windows, USB devices (and connectors) offer numerous advantages. You can safely connect or disconnect such gadgets from the Macintosh, even while the computer is turned on; with the addition of an inexpensive USB hub, you can add ports for five, ten, or more USB gadgets; and the rectangular USB connectors are idiot-proof when compared with the circular ADB connectors of old.

Figure K-2. ADB icon on the back of Macs

L

List Views

On the Macintosh: List Views

When you're examining your folders and files in a Desktop window, both the Macintosh and Windows offer a list view—a compact textual display of a window's contents. (The alternative Icon view is better suited for windows containing only a few files or folders.)

Looking for List view. The View menu of a Macintosh window doesn't offer an equivalent of the standard Windows List view, in which your icons appear in multiple columns. You can simulate such an arrangement in a Macintosh window, however, like this:

1. Choose View → as Icons.
2. Choose View → View Options.

3. Choose Keep arranged by Name (or specify any sorting order you prefer).
4. Select the small icon size (see Figure L-1). Click OK.

For more information, see **View Menu**.

Looking for Details view. What the Macintosh calls List view (see Figure L-2) is the equivalent of the Windows Details view. As in Windows, you can click the heading above a column (where it says Size, for example) to sort the list by that criterion. To reverse the sorting order (from Z to A instead of A to Z, for example), however, don't click the column header a second time, as on Windows. Instead, click the tiny pyramid above the vertical scroll bar (an option available only in Mac OS 8.1 and later).

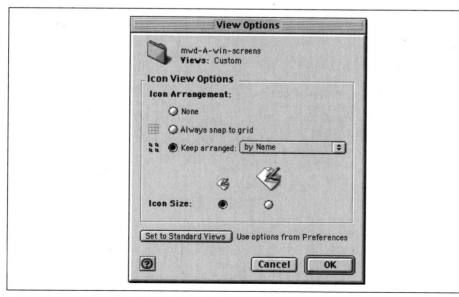

Figure L-1. Simulating the Windows list view

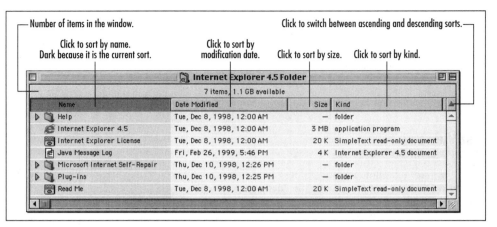

Figure L-2. List view

To specify which columns appear in a particular window, choose View → View Options (or Control-click and then choose View Options); in the resulting dialog box, select a different assortment of columns.

You may also be disoriented by the fact that on the Macintosh, files and folders are sorted alphabetically in the same list, instead of appearing in separate alphabetical clusters as on Windows. To simulate the Windows system of file/folder segregation, click the Kind column header.

Login/Logout

On the Macintosh: Location Manager Control Panel

Windows is nominally a multiple-user system: you can set it to prompt you for a username and password when you turn on the PC. The information you enter at that point changes what you see on the Desktop and in the Start menu, among other things.

In contrast, the Macintosh, through Mac OS 8.6, is essentially a single-user system with no login/logout capabilities. To create a multiple-user scenario on the Macintosh, you have several options:

- Use the Location Manager, which is designed to switch between sets of control panel, networking, Internet, speaker volume, and other settings. For information, see **User Profiles**.

- Buy a program designed for educators, such as At Ease, which maintains a separate set of files and folders for each user a particular machine.

In Mac OS 9, on the other hand, a Windows-style multiple-user feature is seamlessly built in. Visit the Multiple Users control panel to set up accounts and turn the ability to Log Out on or off.

M

Mail Control Panel

On the Macintosh: Internet Control Panel

In Windows, the Mail control panel lets you create and edit different accounts, or profiles, for Windows Messaging (known as Microsoft Exchange in the first version of Windows 95). These accounts make it easy for several people to use Windows Messaging on the same computer. Profiles also simplify the process of switching between modem and network access, and they let you separate different mail services.

On the Macintosh (and in Windows 98), such multiple-user features are generally built right into the email programs themselves. You may prefer, however, the Internet control panel provided with Mac OS 8.5 later. It lets you create and switch between sets of Internet preferences, including email preferences (see Figure M-1).

To create a second set of Internet settings, follow these steps:

1. Open Apple menu → Control Panels → Internet.
2. Choose File → New Set (Command-N).
3. Name the set.
4. Click each tab—especially Personal and E-mail—and fill in the appropriate settings.

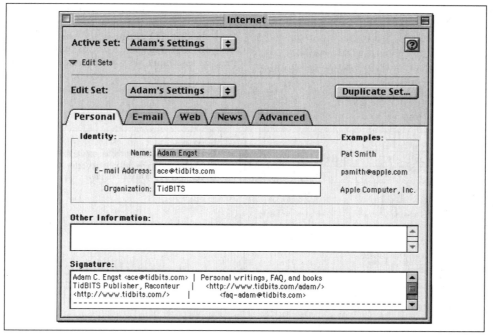

Figure M-1. Internet control panel

Once you've created multiple sets, you can switch between them with these steps:

1. Open Apple menu → Control Panels → Internet.

2. From the Active Set menu, choose the desired set.

3. Close the Internet control panel.

All of this assumes, of course, that you check your email using an email program capable of recognizing the Internet control panel's settings—and that you know how to tell the email program to use those settings.

Macros

On the Macintosh: Macros

Macro programs let you record or script actions—mouse clicks, menu commands, type phrases, and so on—and then play them back with a single keystroke or click. Because a macro program can also be used to reassign keystrokes to other functions, you might find them especially helpful in making your Macintosh behave more like the Windows machine you're used to. For more information on some commercially available macro utilities, visit the following web sites:

- QuicKeys (CE Software—this program is available in both Macintosh and Windows editions):
  http://www.cesoft.com/quickeys/qkhome.html

- KeyQuencer (Binary Software):
  http://www.binarysoft.com/kqmac/kqmac.html

- OneClick (WestCode Software):
  http://www.westcodesoft.com/oneclick/ocinfo.html

Maximizing Windows

On the Macintosh: Zooming Windows

When you click the maximize button in Windows, the window expands to occupy the entire screen, even if there's only, for example, a single icon in the window. On the Macintosh, the zoom box (see Figure M-2) has a similar effect. There's a substantial difference, however: on the Macintosh, clicking the zoom box makes the window only large enough to enclose its contents, thus preserving screen real estate. If you click the zoom box to enlarge a Finder window that contains only three icons, the window may not grow very much at all—just large enough so that all three icons are visible within its boundaries.

Another difference: when you click it, the icon on the Windows maximize button changes. It's now known as a restore button; clicking it restores the window to its original size. The Mac's zoom button works exactly the same way (click once to zoom, click again to restore), but its appearance doesn't change.

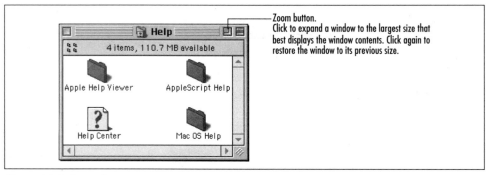

Figure M-2. Zoom button

Memory Usage

On the Macintosh: Memory Usage

Windows' robust virtual memory scheme ensures that it's unlikely that you'll run out of memory when launching multiple programs. The PC might dramatically slow down as it swaps computer code from RAM to your hard disk, but memory management is otherwise handled for you behind the scenes. The Mac OS's memory model is quite different, and often requires some input from you.

Every Macintosh application claims a specific amount of memory when it launches. To see how much memory it will request, select the program's icon. In Mac OS 8.5 or later, choose File → Get Info → Memory (Command-I) or Control-click the file and choose Get Info → Memory. In previous versions of the Mac OS, choose File → Get Info.

Either way, the Get Info window appears, revealing three numbers pertaining to memory requirements (see Figure M-3):

Suggested Size
This non-editable number indicates the amount of memory the software company recommends that you give to the application. (Keep in mind, however,

that marketing departments are sometimes involved in the selection of this number. Increasing the Preferred Size by 10 or 20 percent often makes the program run with more stability.)

Minimum Size
The minimum amount of memory necessary for the application to run at all.

Preferred Size
The amount of memory the application consumes in normal situations.

When you launch an application, the Mac OS allots it the amount of memory in that application's Preferred Size box. The next application you launch is assigned its requested amount of memory, and so on, until you run out of memory.

If the amount of memory indicated in the program's Preferred Size box isn't available, but the amount shown in the Minimum Size box is available, the program still launches. (It may not run as quickly or be as stable, however.) And if even the Minimum Size memory isn't available on the Macintosh, the operating system lets you know—and suggests that you quit applications or close windows. In some cases, it even offers to quit some applications for you.

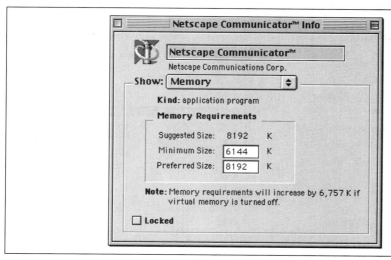

Figure M-3. Memory requirements in the Get Info window

Finding out the machine's total RAM. To find out how much RAM your Macintosh has, and where it's all going, begin at the Desktop (choose Finder from the iconic Application menu in the upper-right corner of your screen). Then choose Apple menu → About This Computer. The resulting dialog box (see Figure M-4) shows how much actual RAM is available ("Built-in memory"), along with how much is being simulated with tricks like virtual memory and programs like RAM Doubler.

Checking and modifying memory usage. You can find out how much memory the Macintosh is using at any time by choosing Apple menu → About This Computer (see Figure M-4).

The About This Computer window lists all the running applications and shows how much memory each has requested. The shaded part of each bar tells you how much of the requested memory is actually in use. If an application is behaving oddly and it's using all of its allotted memory, consider

increasing the Preferred Size setting in the Get Info window.

Memory control panel. The About This Computer window also tells you whether or not your Macintosh is using virtual memory (or RAM Doubler, described later in this entry) and how much additional memory it provides. You configure virtual memory in the Memory control panel, which also lets you change the disk cache size and create a RAM disk (see Figure M-5).

You can always return to the factory settings—in general, a good idea—by clicking Use Defaults.

To use virtual memory, you need at least as much disk space available (for the swap file) as the total amount of physical RAM in the computer. Unlike Windows, the Mac OS does not dynamically change the size of the swap file.

You might want to use a RAM disk for disk-intensive operations that would run much faster in a RAM disk than on your hard disk.

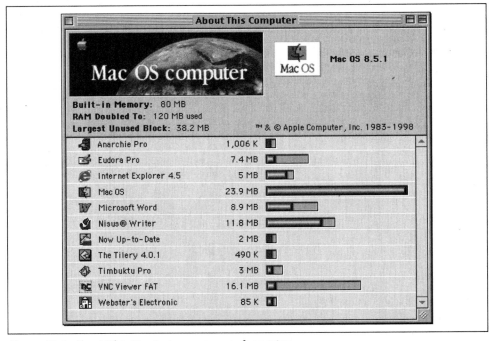

Figure M-4. About This Computer memory information

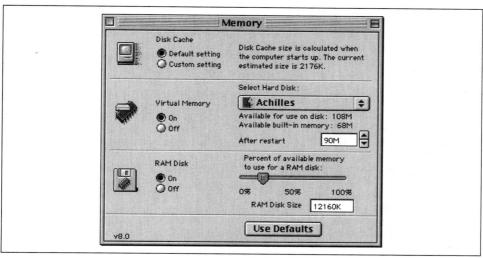

Figure M-5. Memory control panel

After you turn the RAM disk on and configure it in the Memory control panel, you must restart; the same is true if you change the size of the RAM disk later on. RAM disks survive restarts but lose their contents if you shut the Macintosh off. Be careful to copy important files back to your hard disk before shutting down.

Fragmented memory. Here's a problem you won't have seen in Windows. When you quit a Macintosh application, the memory it was using becomes available for use by other programs. But suppose you launched three programs, taking up all but 2 MB of your Mac's free memory—and then quit the second one, which was using 1 MB of RAM. You may be surprised to discover that the Macintosh now won't let you launch a program that requires 3 MB of memory, even though your calculations lead you to believe that 3 MB should now be available.

The culprit is *memory fragmentation*. On a Macintosh, no program can run unless its memory requirement is available in one unbroken chunk.

You can avoid memory fragmentation by quitting applications in the reverse order from which you launched them. That way, memory is freed up from the top down. Of course, quitting all applications also frees up

all your available memory, as does restarting the Macintosh.

Another solution: install the utility called RAM Doubler from Connectix Corporation. RAM Doubler fools the Macintosh into thinking it has up to three times more installed memory than it does; one of these tricks involves using fragmented blocks of memory that are otherwise too small to accommodate a single program. You can find more information about RAM Doubler at *http://www.connectix.com/*. RAM Doubler eliminates the need to use the Mac OS's built-in virtual memory.

Notes. Although this memory model might seem problematic, it generally isn't a problem for Macintosh users for several reasons.

• With RAM as cheap as it is, it's easy to put enough RAM in the Macintosh so you never have to worry about running out. That's less true for people using memory-hungry programs like image editors, but for most users, popping more RAM in makes the problem go away.

• You can use RAM Doubler or turn on the Mac OS's built-in virtual memory to increase the amount of memory available to applications. Another advantage to using either RAM Doubler or virtual memory is that memory requirements for many applications decrease, due to the way they allow code to be loaded and unloaded on the fly. The disadvantages are that both may cause problems with poorly written programs, and virtual memory can be slow when it's forced to swap to disk (just as in Windows).

- An increasing number of applications ask for a relatively small amount of memory and then use system temporary memory when they briefly need more. When the application is done with the memory, it makes it available again so other programs can use it. This technique, which Apple encourages, promotes far more efficient use of memory.

Media Player

On the Macintosh: MoviePlayer, QuickTime Player

The Macintosh is highly touted for its multimedia prowess, but how do you actually see and hear sounds and movies? In Windows, you use ActiveMovie Control or Media Player; but on the Macintosh, turn to MoviePlayer or QuickTime Player, which you'll probably find in Macintosh HD → Applications.

Despite its simple appearance, QuickTime Player is surprisingly full-featured. It can open and play all kinds of QuickTime movies: those that include only sound, sound and video, or even QuickTime VR (still photos whose camera angle you can change by dragging the mouse to look around you). You can also use the Player to extract tracks (such as the sound track from a movie), delete tracks, or even turn tracks on and off before playing them back. In fact, QuickTime Player can even open and display picture files (PICT, GIF, JPEG, TIFF, and so on) and sound files (AIFF, WAV, and more).

Many of QuickTime Player's features aren't available in the free version. Paying $30 for the QuickTime Pro version gives you the ability to edit your movies and sounds and unlocks many useful features.

Once you've opened a movie, you see the standard VCR-like controls for playing the movie, as shown in Figure M-6.

QuickTime VR movies require different controls. Drag anywhere in the image to scroll around; press Shift (or, before QuickTime 3, Option) to zoom forward, and the Control key to zoom out.

Note

In QuickTime 4, Apple replaced MoviePlayer with QuickTime Player, which offers the same basic features, though with fancier window dressing.

Menu Bar

On the Macintosh: Menu Bar

One of the biggest differences between Windows and the Macintosh is that Windows menu bars appear inside each window, whereas on the Macintosh, a single menu bar appears at the top of the screen.

When you switch between applications on the Macintosh, the menus in the menu bar change to reflect the commands offered by the current application. (Only a few menus—the standard Apple, File, Edit, and Help menus—don't change, because almost every program offers them.) The appearance of the current menu bar is one of the Macintosh user's visual clues as to which program is frontmost.

You should also be aware of one final difference between the menu bars on Macintosh and Windows: you can't pull down Macintosh menus from the keyboard. Although you can trigger most individual menu commands using keyboard shortcuts, you must use the mouse to open a menu on the Macintosh (to peruse its contents, for example).

Menus

On the Macintosh: Menus

Menus are one of the primary interface elements of both Windows and the Mac OS. In both Windows and Mac OS 8 and later, you

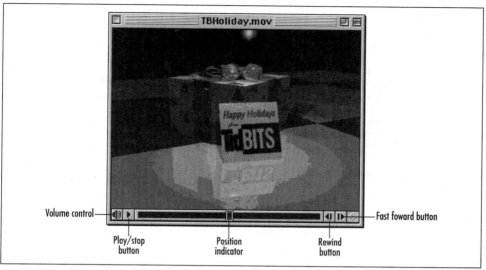

Figure M-6. Movie Player controls

Figure M-6. Movie Player controls

can click once on a menu to open it, after which it stays down, even if you release the mouse button. (In previous versions of the Mac OS, menus stayed open only as long as you held the mouse button down.)

You may notice, by the way, that Macintosh menus don't display telltale keyboard-shortcut underlines, as in Windows. That's because you can't open Macintosh menus from the keyboard at all—you must use the mouse. (Of course, such add-on utilities as Speed Doubler from Connectix can restore this feature if you find it limiting. Visit *http://www.connectix.com/* for details.)

Note

On the Macintosh, if you haven't made a selection, an open menu closes by itself after 15 seconds. It doesn't remain open forever, as on Windows.

After opening a menu, if you decide to close it again without making a selection, you can either wait 15 seconds or use a keystroke: the Mac's Esc key or Command-period.

Microphones
On the Macintosh: Microphones

If you want to plug in a microphone for sound recording or voice recognition, you must install a sound card into your PC (if it didn't come with a preinstalled sound card). Except for the iBook laptop, every Macintosh model since 1989 has included sound-recording circuitry and built-in 1/8-inch microphone jacks. Some models, including the PowerBook and iMac, even have microphones built into the screen. Many Macintosh models, such as the Power Macintosh G3 series, are accompanied by an external microphone that be placed so that it hugs the top of the monitor.

For instructions on using a Macintosh microphone, see **Sound Recorder**.

Microsoft Access
On the Macintosh: FileMaker Pro

There's no Macintosh version of Microsoft Access, the database included in Microsoft Office for Windows.

By far the most popular database program for the Macintosh is FileMaker Pro, from

I-N

FileMaker, Inc. (an Apple subsidiary previously known as Claris). You can learn more about FileMaker Pro at *http://www.filemaker.com/*.

Microsoft Excel

On the Macintosh: Microsoft Excel

The leading spreadsheet program in Windows, Microsoft Excel, is also the leading Macintosh spreadsheet. As with Excel for Windows, it's one of the primary programs in the Macintosh version of Microsoft Office.

The current Macintosh and Windows versions of Excel are nearly identical: Microsoft Excel 97 in Windows corresponds almost perfectly to Excel 98 on the Macintosh. Even the file format is identical. File formats are not guaranteed to be the same between any other versions, so if you're moving files back and forth between two other versions of Excel, make sure to save in the proper format. Generally, newer programs can open files created by older versions, but you must explicitly save them in the older format.

Microsoft Outlook

On the Macintosh: Microsoft Outlook, Microsoft Outlook Express

Microsoft Office 97 for Windows includes Microsoft Outlook, a full-featured email program that includes an integrated calendar and contact database.

Although Office 98 for the Macintosh doesn't include an equivalent version of Outlook, such a program exists. You might consider it a stealth application, however, since it's rarely sold in stores, and is targeted primarily at corporate network users. Contact Microsoft customer service to find out how to get a copy.

Microsoft Outlook Express

On the Macintosh: Microsoft Outlook Express

Microsoft Outlook Express, the free Internet email program that's included with Internet Explorer 4.0 and Windows 98, has a similar Macintosh sibling. The Macintosh version of

Outlook Express is bundled with Mac OS 8.5 and later; you can also download it for free for use with earlier versions from *http://www.microsoft.com/mac/oe/*.

Microsoft PowerPoint

On the Macintosh: Microsoft PowerPoint

PowerPoint, the leading presentation/slide show software on Windows, is also available in a nearly identical version on the Macintosh. It's included with Microsoft Office 98 for the Macintosh, and is also sold separately. As with the other programs in today's Microsoft Office, PowerPoint files are 100 percent cross-platform: you can email (or otherwise transfer) a PowerPoint file back and forth between Windows and Macintosh with no conversion necessary.

Microsoft Word

On the Macintosh: Microsoft Word

You'll have little trouble switching between Word 97 on Windows and Word 98 for the Macintosh. The file formats, menus, and options are identical, so there's no need to worry about conversion when sharing documents or moving from one platform to another.

If you're using an older version of Word for the Macintosh for the first time, however, the transition may not be as seamless. For example:

Word 5.1. Word 5.1 for the Macintosh came out around the same time as Word for Windows 2.0, though it wasn't particularly similar. Word 5.1 lacked macro capabilities, making it immune to the macro viruses that have plagued all subsequent releases of Word on both platforms.

Despite its age, Word 5.1 can open files created in any version of Word, including Word 97 for Windows or Word 98 for Macintosh; you can find the necessary translator at *http://www.microsoft.com/macoffice/prodinfo/office/coexist.htm*. Nor do you need to fear submitting your 5.1 documents to users of more recent Word versions; they can open older documents without any need for converters.

Word 6.0. Word 6.0 for the Macintosh closely resembled Word 95 for Windows. Once again, with the addition of the translator file at *http://www.microsoft.com/macoffice/prodinfo/office/coexist.htm*, Word 6 can open Word documents from any version or platform, older or newer.

Minimizing Windows
On the Macintosh: Hiding Applications, Collapsing Windows

When you want to hide a Windows window, you click the minimize button; the window becomes an icon on the Taskbar. The Macintosh offers two ways to conceal a window.

- Collapsing a Macintosh window is the equivalent of minimizing a single Windows document window. You can also "minimize" an entire Macintosh application, including all of its windows simultaneously. To do so, choose Application menu → Hide *Application* (where *Application* is the name of the frontmost application). Hiding an application makes all of that application's windows, palettes, and toolbars disappear, although the application is still running. You can perform the same feat by Option-clicking the Desktop or any window of another running program.

  To reveal the hidden application's window, choose its name from the Application menu.

- Click the collapse button (see Figure M-7) in the window's title bar. Unlike the first method, which hides all the open windows in an application, clicking the collapse button collapses

only one window so that only its title bar shows. To expand the window, click the collapse button again.

For more information about closing windows for good, see **Closing Windows**.

Note

You can also double-click any Macintosh window's title bar to collapse the window—a broader target than the tiny collapse box.

To enable this feature in Mac OS 8 or later, choose Apple menu → Control Panels → Appearance → Options; turn on the "Double-click title bar to collapse windows" checkbox. In previous versions of the operating system, you'll find the same option offered in the WindowShade control panel.

Modems
On the Macintosh: Modems

In general, modems work exactly alike on Macs and PCs. In fact, you can sometimes move the identical modem between platforms, provided you overcome the incompatibility of connections and driver software. Refer to Table M-1 for information about modem cross-platform compatibility.

When you connect a modem to a PC, Windows detects the modem and tries to install the correct drivers. On the Macintosh, you may have to perform some manual configuration. Start by opening the Apple menu → Control Panels → Modem control panel; from the pop-up menu, choose the specific modem model you're installing. If you don't

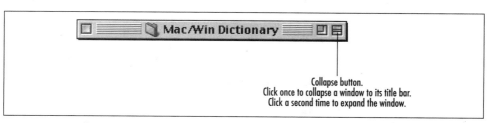

Collapse button.
Click once to collapse a window to its title bar.
Click a second time to expand the window.

Figure M-7. Collapse button

Table M-1. Modem Cross-Platform Compatibility

Modem Type	Compatibility Notes
PC external modems	Almost always compatible with Macs, once you've added a Macintosh serial cable. Make sure the serial cable is labeled "hardware handshaking" for proper operation. When specifying a Macintosh modem script to operate the modem (in the Modem control panel), you can generally get away with choosing Hayes Basic as the modem model; you'll have much better results, however, if you can locate a manufacturer-supplied modem script specific to this modem. Visit the modem manufacturer's web site for assistance.
PC internal modems	Incompatible with Macs, due to both driver and physical connection issues.
PC-oriented PC card modems	Some are compatible with PC Card-capable Macintosh PowerBooks. Contact the modem's manufacturer to verify Macintosh driver compatibility and availability.

see the model listed, visit the modem manufacturer's web site in search of the appropriate modem script. If you find it, install it in your Macintosh HD → System Folder → Extensions → Modem Scripts folder. It now shows up in the Modem control panel pop-up menu.

If you're unable to locate the appropriate script, choosing a basic Hayes modem from the Modem control panel pop-up menu often works. As a last resort, some telecommunications programs, such as America Online, let you manually input the modem's

initialization string, such as AT&F1, which is usually provided in the modem's manual. For more on initialization strings, visit *http://www.tidbits.com/iskm/modems.html*.

For more information about configuring a modem, see **Dial-Up Networking Folder**.

Modems Control Panel
On the Macintosh: Modem Control Panel

Although Windows generally configures modems for you, it provides manual configuration options in the Modems control panel. The Macintosh Modem control panel provides a few of the same functions (see Figure M-8).

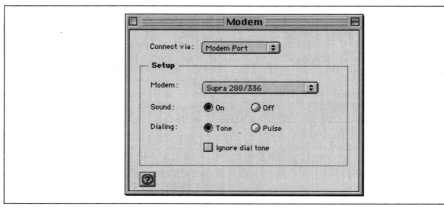

Figure M-8. Modem control panel

The technical details for individual modems are stored in modem scripts, sometimes called CCL scripts, in Macintosh HD → System Folder → Extensions → Modem Scripts. Choose the modem script that matches your modem, or, if there's no exact match, one from the same company. If all else fails, choose one of the Hayes modem scripts. Check the modem manufacturer's web site for new modem scripts.

Writing a modem script from scratch isn't a task for the faint of heart, but if you're an accomplished scripter and familiar with modem commands, consider duplicating one of the existing modem scripts and editing it with a text editor. You may also want to consider using Apple's Modem Script Generator program, available from *http://asu.info.apple.com/swupdates.nsf/artnum/n10664.*

Monitors
On the Macintosh: Monitors

Most monitors sold today are multiple frequency monitors (also called *multisync* monitors), which means, among other things, that they'll work with both PCs and Macs. Better yet, all Macintosh models sold today feature standard PC-style VGA monitor connectors on the back panel. (When installing a PC monitor onto an older Macintosh model, you may need an inexpensive adapter, available from an electronics shop or online mail-order web site, for the video connector.)

If your Macintosh contains slots, such as NuBus or PCI slots, you can add additional video cards to your Macintosh—and thereby connect up to five additional monitors with amazing ease and extraordinary results. The Monitors & Sound control panel lets you designate the additional monitors either as extensions of the same gigantic virtual Desktop or as mirrors of the first. (This same control panel lets you configure resolutions and color settings for each monitor; see **Display Control Panel**.)

You'll find multiple-monitor arrangements far more common on the Macintosh (which has offered this feature for many years) than on Windows PCs, despite the fact that Windows 98 makes multiple-monitor configurations possible for the first time.

Motherboards
On the Macintosh: Motherboards

Thanks to the standardization of components in the PC world, it is relatively common to upgrade a PC motherboard (and the CPU on it) to increase speed. In the Macintosh world, motherboard upgrades are far less common, because Apple is the only manufacturer of Macs and their motherboards. On the other hand, the impossibility of motherboard replacement doesn't mean that you can't speed up your Macintosh. Most of today's Macintosh models feature removable CPUs—that is, the central processing unit is on a removable daughtercard. If you crave more speed, you can remove this miniature card and replace it with one that contains a faster chip. Companies that sell such processor upgrades include:

- MacTell:
  http://www.mactell.com/
- Newer Technology:
  http://www.newertech.com/
- PowerLogix:
  http://www.powerlogix.com/
- Sonnet Technolgies:
  http://www.sonnettech.com/
- XLR8:
  http://www.xlr8.com/

Mouse
On the Macintosh: Mouse

Using a mouse on the Macintosh is almost exactly the same as using it in Windows, with one large exception. Standard PC mice have two buttons, whereas the standard Macintosh mouse has only one. (Apple made this design decision long ago because although sophisticated computer users often prefer multiple-button mice, novices have trouble remembering which button to use for different tasks. With a single button, there's nothing to remember.) The Mac's single mouse button is identical to the left mouse button on a PC mouse.

> **Note**
>
> If you miss having a two-button mouse on your Macintosh, the online mail-order outfits will be delighted to sell you a replacement mouse that features two, three, or even four mouse buttons. The accompanying software lets you specify a function for each of these additional buttons—including Control-clicking, which is the equivalent of the right mouse button in Windows. You can even buy a Macintosh equivalent of the Microsoft IntelliMouse, the one with a scroll wheel nestled between the two buttons.

See **Right-Click** for more information on how the Macintosh provides the features you're used to accessing via the right mouse button. See **Mouse Control Panel** to learn how to change the mouse tracking and double-click speed.

Mouse Control Panel

On the Macintosh: Mouse Control Panel, Trackpad Control Panel

The Mouse control panel in Windows governs tracking speed (how fast the cursor moves when you move the mouse), double-click speed (how quickly you must click twice for the computer to register a double-click instead of two separate clicks), button configuration, and pointer graphics. The Mouse control panel on the Macintosh offers only two options: you can change

tracking speed and double-click speed (see Figure M-9). In Windows, you can also turn on pointer trails; that option appears in the Macintosh Mouse control panel only if you're using a PowerBook.

> **Note**
>
> The Trackpad control panel offers a unique feature: it can turn on the trackpad's mouse-button clicking features. That is, instead of clicking the laptop's trackpad clicker to click the mouse, you may prefer to click directly on the trackpad surface. Three related buttons in the Trackpad control panel let you turn on clicking by tapping; dragging by tapping down and dragging; and drag lock by tapping once, dragging, and tapping again to release.

PowerBook and iBook laptops also come equipped with a Trackpad control panel. It offers the same tracking speed and double-click speed controls as the Mouse control panel, but operates independently, so that you can specify different settings for the Trackpad and an external mouse.

Mouse Port

On the Macintosh: ADB, USB

There's not much involved in connecting a mouse to a Macintosh; there's only one possible place to plug it in, and no software configuration is necessary.

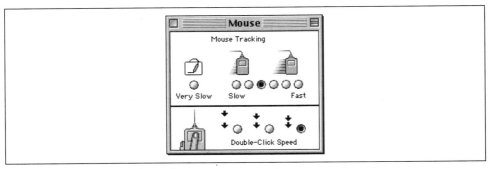

Figure M-9. Mouse control panel.

Figure M-10. ADB icon on the back of Macs

The connector itself has been an ADB (Apple Desktop Bus)-style round connector on every Macintosh model until 1998; beginning with the iMac model, Macintosh mice are instead USB devices. (In the former case, the connector on the back panel of the computer is marked not by mouse icon, but rather by an alien-looking backward capital F, as shown in Figure M-10.)

Note

If your Mac's mouse port is round, it's the ADB-style connection, and caution is warranted. Don't connect or disconnect this kind of mouse when the computer is turned on—you risk damaging the mouse, motherboard, or both. No such caution is necessary when connecting or disconnecting USB mice.

Moving Files

On the Macintosh: Moving Files, Copying Files

To move a Macintosh file icon from one location to another on the same disk, simply drag it from one window to the other. But keep in mind:

- You can drag any icon to the Macintosh Desktop, not just icons from your startup hard disk, as in Windows. The two exceptions: you can't move icons from a locked disk, such as a CD-ROM, and you can't move to the Desktop files from a disk you're accessing over the network. (If you drag an icon from a locked or networked disk to the Desktop, the Macintosh copies it to the Desktop of the startup disk instead of simply moving it.)

In short, the Desktop can contain icons from multiple disks, which isn't true in Windows.

- If you drag an icon from one disk to another, the Finder copies it instead of moving it. There's no Move command on the Macintosh; you must copy a file, and then delete the original.

- When you're dragging an icon to another location on the same disk, pressing Option makes the Macintosh duplicate the file instead of moving it. And if you press Command and Option, you create an alias of the file instead of moving it (see **Shortcuts**).

Note

Suppose you want to move a file icon into a deeply nested folder. Instead of opening window after window to get at your destination, consider using "spring-loaded folders," a feature of Mac OS 8 and later. It works like this:

Drag the icon onto a folder or disk icon and wait—don't let go of the mouse button. After a moment, the folder or disk window opens. Without releasing the mouse button, drag onto the next folder icon until it, too, opens. You can continue this way, opening nested folder after nested folder; when you've finally opened the target window, release the mouse. All the windows you've opened close behind you automatically, and the file has successfully been moved.

In Mac OS 8.5 and later, by the way, you can accelerate the opening of each folder by tapping the Spacebar, even if the prescribed 1.5 seconds of waiting (or whatever you've specified in Edit → Preferences) hasn't yet elapsed.

MS-DOS Prompt

On the Macintosh: None

Whereas Windows is a descendant of DOS, the Macintosh has featured a graphical interface from its first incarnation. It has no command-line features at all.

Multimedia Control Panel
On the Macintosh: Monitors & Sound

The Multimedia control panel in Windows provides a hodge-podge of settings that fall roughly under the heading of multimedia. You can fiddle with advanced settings related to sound input and output, video display, MIDI, CD music, and more.

The closest equivalent on the Macintosh is the Monitors & Sound control panel (which, in Mac OS 9, has been broken into two separate control panels called Monitors and Sound). When you click the Sound icon, here you can specify which Macintosh sound source should be considered the input for sound recording—microphone, CD-ROM, and so on—and what volume should be used for speaker playback, exactly as on the first tab of the Windows Multimedia control panel.

The other tabs of the Multimedia control panel have no equivalents on the Macintosh.

Multitasking
On the Macintosh: Multitasking

Despite the online battles waged by proponents of each platform, you won't notice much difference between the multitasking schemes used by the Macintosh and Windows. On either platform, you can download a file from the Internet while retrieving your email, browsing the Web, and writing in a word processor. For information about switching between different applications on the Macintosh, see **Taskbar**.

My Computer
On the Macintosh: Desktop

The Macintosh has no equivalent to My Computer, the Windows window that contains the disk icons for a Windows system. Instead, the icons for your hard disk, floppy disk, CD-ROM, and so on appear at the right side of the Macintosh Desktop—but only when disks are actually in the corresponding drives (see **Disks**).

The remaining contents of the My Computer window are also available on the Macintosh, but in different locations. For more information, see **Printers Folder**, **Control Panel**, **Dial-Up Networking Folder**, and **Scheduled Tasks**.

N

NetBEUI

On the Macintosh: AppleTalk

The standard protocol for communicating between PCs running Windows is NetBEUI, which stands for NetBIOS Extended User Interface. The comparable proprietary networking protocol in the Macintosh world is AppleTalk. If you're interested in connecting Macs and PCs, stick to a common protocol like TCP/IP.

Netscape Navigator/ Communicator

On the Macintosh: Netscape Navigator/ Communicator

The Macintosh and Windows versions of Netscape Navigator and Communicator are even more alike than the corresponding versions of Microsoft Internet Explorer. You can learn more about the Macintosh version of Netscape Communicator, and download a copy, from *http://www.netscape.com/ computing/download/index.html.*

Net Watcher

On the Macintosh: File Sharing Control Panel, File Sharing Monitor

If you need to see who is connected to your Windows hard disk over the network, use the Net Watcher utility. On the Macintosh, you can see connected users and shared items in Apple menu → Control Panels → File Sharing → Activity Monitor (or, in versions of the Mac OS prior to Mac OS 8.1, in Apple menu → Control Panels → File Sharing Monitor).

Once you're viewing the lists of connected users and shared items (see Figure N-1), you can do two things:

- To disconnect users manually, click a user's name and then click Disconnect.

- To view the sharing privileges for a shared item, select its icon and then click Privileges. Doing so opens the same informational dialog box that appears when you select a folder's icon on the Desktop and then choose File → Get Info → Sharing.

Network Control Panel

On the Macintosh: AppleTalk Control Panel, TCP/IP Control Panel, File Sharing, Printer Sharing

The Network control panel in Windows offers settings for every conceivable aspect of Windows networking. On the Macintosh, the same features are scattered among several different control panels, as follows:

Network components. In the Configuration tab of the Windows Network control panel, you work with four kinds of network components:

Client

Client components help you connect to servers on your network. On the Macintosh, you need the AppleShare extension to access remote file servers. The AppleShare software itself is located in Macintosh HD → System Folder → Extensions, but you access it by choosing Apple menu → Chooser → Apple-Share, as described later.

Adapter

Adapter components let you configure the physical network interfaces, such as Ethernet cards. On the Macintosh, you don't need to configure such devices manually, so there's no equivalent to adapter components. The closest you might get are drivers that let the Mac

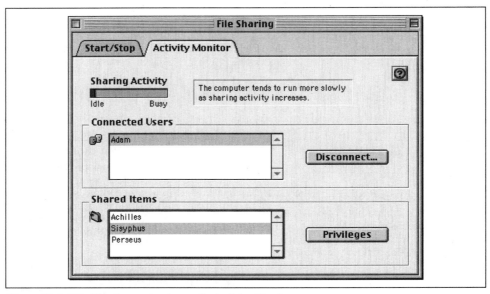

Figure N-1. File Sharing control panel's Activity Monitor

OS recognize the network card, if you aren't using the built-in Ethernet port. Such drivers would go in Macintosh HD → System Folder → Extensions. Check the network card documentation for details.

Protocol

Protocol components let the PC speak specific protocols, or network languages. Computers on the same network can talk to one another only if they support the same protocols. To configure the Macintosh to support TCP/IP, you use the TCP/IP control panel. Similarly, the AppleTalk control panel lets you configure the Macintosh to work on an AppleTalk network.

Although control panels are the front end for working with these protocols, accompanying support files are stored in Macintosh HD → System Folder → Control Panels and Macintosh HD → System Folder → Extensions.

Service

Service components let you share folders and printers with other people on your network. File sharing on the Macintosh is handled by the File Sharing control panel; printer sharing (which is

generally necessary only for inkjet printers; most Macintosh laser printers are designed to work on a network to begin with) requires the Printer Share extension. See **File Sharing** (for details about the Macintosh equivalents to the Identification and Access Control tabs) and **Printer Sharing**.

Configuring Macs to work on AppleTalk networks. Configuring a Macintosh to communicate with other Macs on the same network using AppleTalk is extremely easy. Assuming that you've made the necessary physical connections, open Apple menu → Control Panels → AppleTalk, and then choose the appropriate network type from the Connect via menu: Ethernet, Printer Port (if you're using the slower, but less expensive, PhoneNet cables), Infrared, and so on. When you close the AppleTalk control panel, the Macintosh will be able to communicate with other Macs and printers on the AppleTalk network.

The AppleTalk control panel has three modes: Basic, Advanced, and Administration. You switch between them by choosing Edit → User Mode (Command-U).

- In Basic mode, you can specify a port for connecting to the AppleTalk network: Modem, Printer, or Ethernet, for example. If your network has multiple zones, you can select a zone as well.

- In Advanced mode, you're also given the option to define your AppleTalk address's node and network (see Figure N-2). A hint: Network numbers should be in the upper range of the 0 to 65534 range—if you see a very low number there, it may cause problems for Apple's LaserWriter Bridge software. In general, though, there's no reason to change your AppleTalk address, since it's assigned automatically.

In Advanced mode, two buttons also appear: Info, which provides information about your network address and software versions, and Options, which lets you turn AppleTalk on and off.

- Administrator mode enhances Advanced mode by adding lock buttons that let an administrator lock the settings.

Along with the three user modes, you can also create and switch between different configurations in the AppleTalk control panel. Storing different network configurations in this way is especially useful for PowerBooks that move between different networks. For instance, at work you might connect to an AppleTalk via an Ethernet network, and at home you might use a PhoneNet network to connect to a printer.

The easiest way to create these configurations is to follow these steps:

1. Open Apple menu → Control Panels → AppleTalk.

2. Choose File → Configurations (Command-K) to open the Configurations dialog box.

3. Select the default configuration, and then click Duplicate.

4. Select the newly made copy configuration, click Rename, and then give it a unique name (see Figure N-3).

5. Click Make Active to make your new configuration active.

6. Because your new configuration was a duplicate of the previous default configuration, it has the same settings. Change the settings as desired—by choosing an alternate connection method from the Connect via menu, for instance.

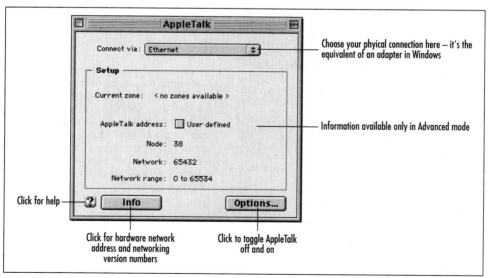

Figure N-2. AppleTalk control panel in Advanced mode

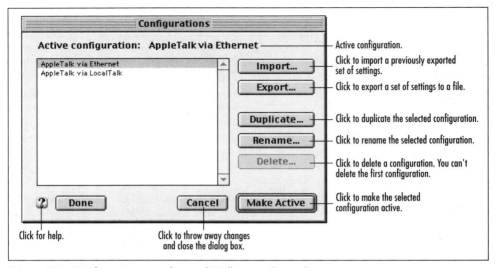

Figure N-3. Configurations in the AppleTalk control panel

7. Close the AppleTalk control panel, saving changes when prompted.

Switching between configurations is as easy as selecting a configuration in the Configurations dialog box and clicking the Make Active button. When you change configurations, you don't have to restart the computer, as you would on Windows.

Configuring Macs to connect to the Internet. As in Windows, there are two basic ways to connect to the Internet: via a modem and via a network that has an Internet connection. (See **Dial-Up Networking Folder**.) The procedures are similar:

1. Open Apple menu → Control Panels → TCP/IP (see Figure N-4).

2. From the Connect via pop-up menu, choose either PPP or Ethernet. Choose PPP if you're connecting via modem, and choose Ethernet if your Ethernet network is connected to the Internet.

3. Next, from the Configure menu, choose the method by which your connection will obtain its settings. The choices are Manually (which requires you to enter all your settings by hand), Using PPP Server (which shows up only if you've chosen PPP as the connection method), Using BootP (which picks up settings from a server on your network), Using

DHCP (which picks up settings from a server on the network), and Using RARP (which picks up your IP address from a server, but none of the other settings).

If you're connecting via PPP via a modem from home, choose Using PPP Server. If you're connecting via Ethernet, the most likely choices are Using DHCP, Using BootP, or Manually. If you don't know which to choose, contact your network administrator or ISP for help.

4. If you've chosen Manually from the Configure menu, enter your IP address, subnet mask, router address, and DNS servers (one per line) in the appropriate fields. You cannot guess at these numbers—if you don't know them, contact your network administrator and ask. Fill in all the blanks except those where you see the words "will be supplied by server."

5. When you're done, close the TCP/IP control panel to change the configuration. There's no need to restart.

Like the AppleTalk control panel, the TCP/IP control has three modes, Basic, Advanced, and Administration. Once again, you switch between them by choosing Edit → User Mode (Command-U). Basic mode is

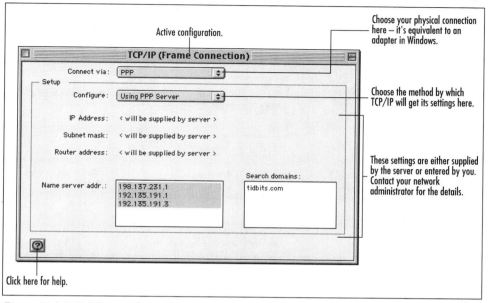

Active configuration.

Choose your physical connection here – it's equivalent to an adapter in Windows.

TCP/IP (Frame Connection)

Connect via: PPP

Setup

Configure: Using PPP Server

IP Address: < will be supplied by server >

Subnet mask: < will be supplied by server >

Router address: < will be supplied by server >

Name server addr.: 198.137.231.1
192.135.191.1
192.135.191.3

Search domains:
tidbits.com

Choose the method by which TCP/IP will get its settings here.

These settings are either supplied by the server or entered by you. Contact your network administrator for the details.

Click here for help.

Figure N-4. TCP/IP control panel set to connect via PPP

all most people ever need to use. Advanced mode lets you specify a few additional options—ignore them unless your network administrator so instructs you. Administration mode provides the same options as Advanced mode, but adds little lock buttons that enable an administrator to lock the settings.

Also like the AppleTalk control panel, you can create and switch between multiple TCP/IP configurations. The process is the same as in the AppleTalk control panel. You might want multiple TCP/IP configurations if you connect to an ISP via a modem some of the time and via a network at other times. Or perhaps you have accounts with multiple ISPs that require different configurations.

Network Neighborhood
On the Macintosh: Chooser, Network Browser

To find and mount a server on your network using Windows, you're used to opening the Network Neighborhood that's on your Desktop. In Mac OS 8.5, the Network

Browser performs exactly the same function. In older versions of the Mac OS, the only way to choose from your available AppleShare servers is through the Chooser (Apple menu → Chooser).

For more information about sharing files and printers, see **File Sharing** and **Printer Sharing**.

Using the Chooser to access file servers. To mount an AppleShare server using the Chooser, follow these steps:

1. Open Apple menu → Chooser.

2. Click the AppleShare icon to display the list of available servers (see Figure N-5).

3. In the "Select a file server" list, select a server name and click OK (or double-click the server name). Alternatively, if the server you want is running Apple-Share IP and you're running Mac OS 8 or later, click Server IP Address, enter the IP address for the server, and then click Connect.

4. Enter your user name and password, and then click Connect (see Figure N-6). If you're connecting to one

N–I

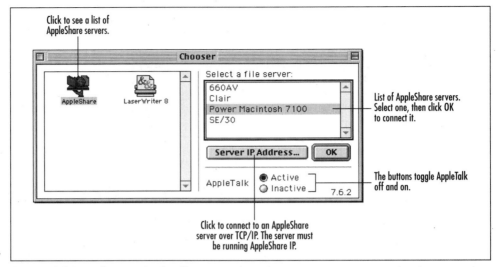

Figure N-5. List of servers in the Chooser

of your Macs as the owner, enter your owner name and owner password as you defined them on that Macintosh in the File Sharing control panel.

5. Choose the shared disks you want to mount on your Desktop, and then click OK.

   If you want the shared disks to appear on the Desktop automatically every time you boot the Macintosh, select the "open on startup" checkbox. Specify whether you want to store your user name only (at which point you'll have to enter your password every time), or both your user name and password (see Figure N-7).

Once the AppleShare volume appears on your Desktop, you can use it just as you would any other disk, although it will respond slowly in comparison to hard disks.

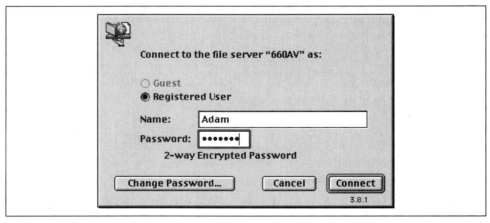

Figure N-6. Connect dialog box

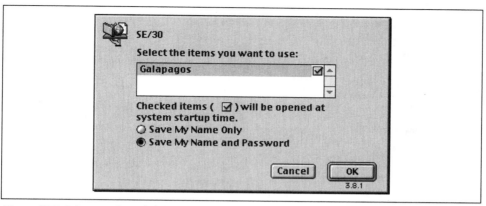

Figure N-7. Selecting shared disks to mount

Using the Chooser to access shared printers.
To access a shared (or network) printer
using the Chooser, follow these steps:

1. Open Apple menu → Chooser.

2. Click the icon corresponding to the
   type of printer you want to access (see
   Figure N-8). If your network includes
   multiple zones, click the appropriate
   zone name in the bottom of the window.

3. In the "Connect to" list, select the name
   of the shared printer and then click OK
   (or double-click the printer name).

4. Enter your password, then click OK.

5. Close the Chooser. The Macintosh creates a Desktop Printer icon for the
   shared printer and designates it the
   default printer. For more information
   on using Desktop Printers, see **Printing
   Files**.

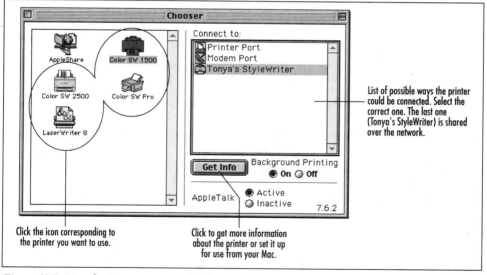

Figure N-8. List of printer access methods in the Chooser

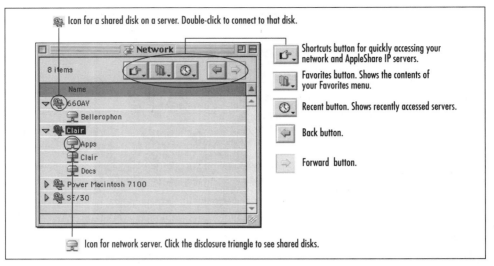

Figure N-9. Network Browser

Using Network Browser to access file servers. If you have Mac OS 8.5 or later, you can use the enhanced Network Browser program to connect to other networked computers.

1. Open Apple menu → Network Browser (see Figure N-9).

2. Either click the disclosure triangle next to a shared computer's name, or double-click the computer's icon to display the login dialog box. Alternatively, if the server you want is running Apple-Share IP, choose Connect to Server from the Shortcut button (a hand icon), enter the IP address for the server, and click Connect.

3. Enter your user name and password. If you're connecting to one of your Macs as the owner, enter your owner name and owner password as you defined them on that Macintosh in the File Sharing control panel. Network Browser displays the available disks on the remote server.

4. Double-click the desired disk in the Network Browser window to mount it as a disk on your Desktop.

Network Browser can't set disks to mount automatically at startup. For that purpose, you'll still have to rely on the Chooser, as described earlier.

Networking Macs and PCs together. Thanks to some ingenious software tools, Macs and PCs can exist on the same network, sharing hard disks and printers as though there were no OS difference whatsoever.

Consider, for example, the Macintosh-side software known as DAVE (*http://www. thursby.com/*). It adds Windows' NetBIOS networking protocol, which permits the Macintosh to connect to Windows machines (versions 3.1, NT, or whatever). DAVE requires no installation on the PC side. Once DAVE is running, PC users see Macs and Macintosh printers through the standard Network Neighborhood program; Macintosh users see PC volumes through the Chooser or Network Browser.

DAVE is great for introducing a Macintosh minority to a larger PC network. If you're in the opposite situation, adding a few Windows machines to a predominantly Macintosh network, buy PC MACLAN instead (*http://www.miramarsys.com/*). It lets a PC access the network's Macintosh printers and hard disks through the standard Network Neighborhood interface. In fact, if you launch the included AppleShare Server software on the Windows machine, the PC can also become available to the Macs on the network—using the same Chooser or Network Browser software the Macintosh users would ordinarily use to access other networked Macs.

Networking

On the Macintosh: Networking

In today's networked world, large portions of both the Mac OS and Windows are linked to networking. The following entries should get you started in networking on the Macintosh.

- For Internet-specific references, see **Internet**.

- For information about basic Macintosh networking, see **Network Control Panel**.

- For information about sharing files on the Macintosh, see **File Sharing**.

- For information about sharing printers on the Macintosh, see **Printer Sharing**.

- For information about connecting a Macintosh to the Internet via a modem, see **Dial-Up Networking Folder** and **Modems**.

- For information about connecting a Macintosh to the Internet via a network, see **Network Control Panel**.

- For information about transferring files from a Windows-based PC to a Macintosh via a network, see **Transferring Files to the Macintosh**.

Notepad

On the Macintosh: SimpleText

Windows ships with both Notepad, a simple, no-formatting text editor, and WordPad, which offers a few more word processing features. The Mac OS equivalent is Simple-Text, which offers a similar level of text-editing features, including the capability to set text fonts, sizes, and styles. SimpleText can also find text in a document, display graphics, record and play back sounds, and speak selected text.

SimpleText can open only documents that contain less than 32K of text, although if a document is larger than 32K because of included graphics or sounds, SimpleText can open it.

Few Macintosh users use SimpleText to create documents; it's mostly used as a reader for ReadMe files. As a result, finding Simple-Text can be tricky. Look first in Macintosh HD → Utilities, and if it's not there, choose File → Find and search for "SimpleText" to see where it has ended up. It's common for applications to install a copy of SimpleText, so you may find multiple copies—feel free to throw out all but the most recent one (check dates by scanning the Date Modified column of the Find window).

Num Lock Key

On the Macintosh: Num Lock Key

Older PC keyboards lacked separate cursor keys; in those days, a press of the Num Lock key turned the number keypad into its alternate function as cursor keys.

That workaround is no longer necessary in this age where every keyboard has a separate bank of cursor keys. Even so, the Num Lock key still appears on most Macintosh keyboards; it's virtually useless except in certain Microsoft programs. For example, in Microsoft Word, pressing this key performs its time-honored function of turning the number keypad into cursor keys.

O

OLE

On the Macintosh: OLE, Publish and Subscribe

Object Linking and Embedding, or OLE, is Microsoft's technology for embedding live, self-updating copies of one kind of data—such as spreadsheet data—in another kind of document, such as a spreadsheet. OLE exists both in Windows and on the Macintosh; the Macintosh-only Publish and Subscribe technology is similar.

OLE. You can insert OLE data from one program, such as a spreadsheet, into another program, such as Word, in one of two ways: as linked data, which updates automatically when you change the source material, and as embedded data, which, like a standard piece of pasted data, maintains no link to any extra document.

Few Macintosh programs offer OLE features; the prominent exceptions are Microsoft applications and Adobe Page-Maker. Consult the application's manual for details on how to link or embed objects appropriately.

Publish and Subscribe. Apple's Publish and Subscribe technology is the same idea as linked objects in OLE: changes in the original "published" material, such as a portion of a spreadsheet, are reflected in any "subscribed" versions (that you have pasted into, say, the word processor). Although many Macintosh programs offer Publish and Subscribe commands, very few Macintosh users use this feature with any regularity.

If your programs offer Publish and Subscribe commands—almost every major Macintosh program does, including Word, Excel, FreeHand, PageMaker, AppleWorks,

WordPerfect, and Photoshop—try the following steps:

1. Highlight some data in the publishing program—a logo in a drawing program, for example, or a range of cells in a spreadsheet.

2. Choose Edit → Create Publisher. (The actual command menu item might be in a submenu, but it's usually in the Edit menu.)

3. Save the "edition" file when prompted. In the original document, a gray nonprinting border generally appears around the material you published. Save this document; if you close the document without saving, your edition file gets cut off from its source material.

4. Switch to the receiving program, position the insertion point in the appropriate location for the inserted data, and choose Edit → Subscribe To. (Again, the menu position may vary by program.)

5. Select the edition file that you just saved.

The data you selected in the first program now appears in the second program, once again enclosed by a nonprinting border. When you open the original publishing document, make changes, and then save the changes, you'll see the subscribed copies update automatically.

Opening Files

On the Macintosh: Opening Files

The basics of opening files are similar in both Macintosh and Windows, but the preferred methods of working differ.

Documents and applications. As in Windows, you can open Macintosh documents and programs in a number of ways:

- Double-click the file's icon (or an alias of it).

- Select the icon, and then choose File → Open (Command-O).

- Drag a document's icon to the icon of a program that can open it. Alternatively, you can open a particular application by double-clicking the icon of a document created by it.

- Drag the document's icon to a window of a program that can read the document. This works primarily when dropping icons into web browser windows.

- Control-click the icon and then choose Open from the contextual menu.

- You can open a document by launching a program that can read it, and then choosing File → Open from within that program.

- Choose a document name from Apple menu → Recent Documents, or choose a program name from Apple menu → Recent Applications. See **Documents Menu** for more information.

- Choose the item from Apple menu → Favorites (if you've designated it as a favorite). See **Favorites Menu**.

- Make an alias of the document or program; place it in Macintosh HD → System Folder → Apple Menu Items, which makes the alias appear in the Apple menu. Then choose its name from the Apple menu. See **Shortcuts** and **Start Menu** for more information.

- Place an alias of the document or program in Macintosh HD → System Folder → Startup Items. The document or program will open automatically every time you boot the Macintosh. For more information, see **Shortcuts** and **StartUp Folder**.

Folders and disks. Use the following methods to open folders and disks:

- Double-click the folder's icon or an alias of the folder.

- In a list view, click the disclosure triangle next to the folder's name.

- Make an alias of the folder and place it in Macintosh HD → System Folder → Apple Menu Items to have it appear in the Apple menu. Then choose the folder from the Apple menu. Note too that you can choose any document or program from the hierarchical menu attached to that folder in the Apple menu. See **Shortcuts** and **Start Menu** for more information.

- Choose the folder from Apple menu → Favorites if you've made that folder a favorite. See **Favorites Menu**.

- Select the folder's icon, then choose File → Open (Command-O).

- Control-click the folder's icon and choose Open from the contextual menu.

- Make an alias of the folder and place it in Macintosh HD → System Folder → Startup Items to have the folder open automatically every time you boot the Macintosh. For more information, see **StartUp Folder**.

S–O

P

Page Setup

On the Macintosh: Page Setup

As in Windows, the Page Setup command is available in almost every program's File menu. It offers a dialog box where you can specify page size, margins, and other program-specific options related to printing (see Figure P-1).

Most people use the Page Setup dialog box to choose a paper size, orientation, and scaling percentage. You can also change a number of PostScript settings in the PostScript Options panel, accessible by choosing PostScript Options from the pop-up menu. Generally the defaults work fine.

PageMaker

On the Macintosh: PageMaker

If you've become accustomed to using PageMaker under Windows, you should have little trouble switching over to PageMaker on the Macintosh. Moving files between platforms may be more complicated, most often because the fonts may not be identical on the two platforms.

Keep in mind that your Macintosh version of PageMaker can open documents created by the same-numbered Windows PageMaker version, but can't open older (or newer) Windows PageMaker documents.

For more information about PageMaker and its successor, InDesign, visit *http://www.adobe.com/*.

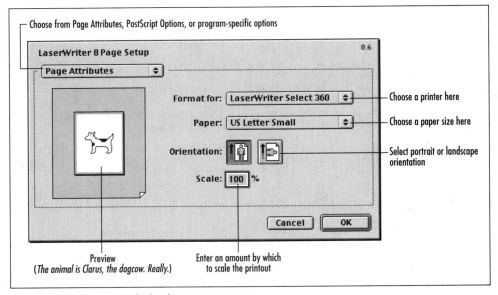

Figure P-1. Page Setup dialog box

Paint
On the Macintosh: None

Long ago, the Macintosh shipped with MacWrite and MacPaint, but Apple soon removed them from the package to encourage third-party developers to create better word processors and painting programs. Today, the equivalent features are found in AppleWorks, a software suite included with every iMac and iBook. On other models, however, no painting software is included with the Mac OS. (The Macintosh shareware download sites are filled with inexpensive Macintosh painting programs—see **Web Sites for Macintosh Software and Information** for some links.)

Parallel Ports
On the Macintosh: Printer Port

Along with serial ports, PCs generally have parallel ports, which are used primarily for connecting to printers. The Macintosh has never had a parallel port; older models featured a pair of serial ports called the modem and printer ports, and current models offer USB ports instead. Most Macintosh inkjet printers connect via a serial cable to the printer or USB port; networked printers connect to the Ethernet jack. For more information about the printer port, see **Serial Ports**.

Passwords Control Panel
On the Macintosh: Password Security Control Panel

Windows offers minimal security through its login dialog box, which is primarily meant to control access to the network and to user profiles. Starting in Mac OS 9, every Macintosh has industrial-strength security through its Multiple Users control panel. Laptop and networked Macs offer security, too. (If you use an earlier verion of the Mac OS on a desktop Macintosh, no security software is built in, but add-on software that provides password protection is available.)

Basic access. Users of Apple laptops can set up the Password Security control panel (Apple menu → Control Panels → Password Security) to require a password at startup. The security offered by the Password Security control panel is quite good, since it works at the hard disk driver level.

Network access. If you're concerned about other people using your Macintosh to access private information on the network, don't save your name and password when setting network volumes to mount automatically in the Chooser. If you choose to have the Mac OS remember only your name, you'll be prompted for your password when the Mac OS first attempts to access the network volume. For details, see **Network Neighborhood**.

Paste
On the Macintosh: Paste

The Windows Paste command (Ctrl-V) pastes whatever is in the clipboard; the Mac's Paste command (Command-V) works exactly the same way.

The only difference: on the Macintosh, the Cut, Copy, and Paste commands work only on material in your documents. They can't operate on files, as in Windows. See **Edit Menu** for details.

PC Cards
On the Macintosh: PC Cards

PC Cards, originally known as PCMCIA cards, are credit card-sized expansion cards commonly used to provide modem or network features to laptops that otherwise lack them. Other uses of PC Cards include hard disk storage, RAM expansion, ISDN adapters, and even GPS systems that use the Global Positioning System satellites to locate your exact position on the planet. The PC Card specification was created by a consortium of over 300 companies, including IBM and Apple, and it enjoys wide acceptance in both the PC and Macintosh worlds, at least for portable computers.

There are three types of PC Cards. Type I cards were designed to be only memory expansion cards; they're 3.3mm thick. Type II cards have many more functions, but are the same size. Type III cards, usually hard disks, are 10.5mm thick. Each type is backward compatible, so you can insert a Type I

S-O

card into a Type II or Type III slot. Better yet, most Macintosh and PC laptops offer a pair of Type II slots on top of one another; the advantage of this arrangement is that you can insert either two Type I or Type II cards, or a single Type III card.

Using PC Cards on the Macintosh is exactly like using them in Windows. You don't have to turn the computer off before inserting or removing PC cards. Unlike Windows, which has a PC Card control panel for managing installed PC Cards, the Mac OS treats PC Cards the way it treats removable disks: when you insert a PC card, it icon appears on the Desktop. You can insert a card at any time, but to eject one, you must choose Special → Eject or drag the icon of the PC Card from your Desktop to the Trash.

PC Cards require driver software to work with the Mac OS. Generic drivers for standard types, such as modem or Ethernet cards, are built into the Mac OS, but for less common PC Cards, you need special software. Unfortunately, many interesting and useful PC Cards come with driver software only for Windows; you can't use every PC Card in a Macintosh. If you wish to use an unusual PC Card in a Macintosh, contact the card's vendor to see if it offers Macintosh driver software.

PCI Slots and Cards
On the Macintosh: PCI Slots and Cards

Over the years, PCs have sported different types of expansion slots and compatible expansion cards, including those based on the ISA bus, the EISA bus, the VESA Local Bus (VL-Bus), and today's modern PCI bus.

On early Macintosh models, the most common slot type was known as the NuBus specification, which was created by Texas Instruments. NuBus never caught on outside of the Macintosh world, where it was used for many years.

A few Macintosh models included high-speed expansion slots called "processor direct slots" (PDS) instead of, or in addition to NuBus. Although fast, PDS slot designs

varied by Macintosh model, making widespread acceptance difficult.

Several years ago, Apple eliminated both NuBus and PDS expansion slots from Macs in favor of the PCI (Peripheral Component Interconnect) bus that's also the standard in the PC world. As a result, many more card manufacturers have created Macintosh versions of their cards (generally by simply writing Macintosh drivers). The economies of scale also means that prices on PCI cards for the Macintosh are often lower than prices for comparable NuBus cards.

Installing a PCI card in a Macintosh is essentially the same as installing one in a PC. Note, however, that the process of opening some older Macintosh models may be difficult. (Apple's most recent Power Macs are extremely easy to open for installing new cards.) Refer to the Mac's manual for instructions on opening the case and installing the PCI card.

Don't assume that you can use a PCI card sold for use in a PC in a Macintosh. You may be able to, but check with the card's manufacturer first to confirm that driver software is available.

PCMCIA
On the Macintosh: PCMCIA

The PCMCIA (Personal Computer Memory Card International Association) specification for credit card-sized expansion cards was considered far too difficult to remember or say (wags claimed it stood for "People Can't Memorize Computer Industry Acronyms"), so PCMCIA cards are now officially known as PC Cards.

Personal Web Server
On the Macintosh: Web Sharing Control Panel

Windows 98 and Windows 95 with Internet Explorer 4.0 include Personal Web Server. This software turns your PC into a small web server, so that you can publish web pages on your hard disk for anyone on the Internet, or—or commonly—on your intranet—to see. On the Macintosh, you get the same feature with the Web Sharing control panel, which first appeared with Mac OS 8. (If the Web Sharing control panel isn't in your Control Panels folder, you can reinstall it from your original Mac OS CD-ROM.)

Using the Web Sharing control panel is easy; the hard part, as on Windows, is ensuring that your Macintosh has a full-time connection to the Internet or office network and making your Mac's private web address known to the appropriate people. To turn on Web Sharing, follow these steps:

1. Open Apple menu → Control Panels → Web Sharing (see Figure P-2).

2. Click the top Select button to select a folder that will contain your web pages. Select the folder from the Open dialog box that appears.

3. Click the bottom Select button to designate a document in your web folder as your home page. This step is optional—if you leave the Home Page set to None, Web Sharing uses Personal NetFinder, a Finder-like view of the files in your web folder.

4. Choose whether you want to give everyone access or restrict access to the settings in the Users & Groups control panel. See **File Sharing** for details on access privileges.

5. Click the Start button.

Once Web Sharing has been turned on, any HTML files in your web pages folder become available to anyone connected to your Macintosh. The Web Sharing control panel reports your address (which may change, if you use a dialup connection to the Internet); choosing Edit → Copy My Address puts the URL to your web site on the clipboard for pasting into email or web browsers.

A few other capabilities are available in the Web Sharing Preferences window, which you open from Edit → Preferences (see Figure P-3).

You can ask Web Sharing to keep a log of all the people who access your web pages, set a maximum size for the log, or control how Web Sharing should handle aliases and write access.

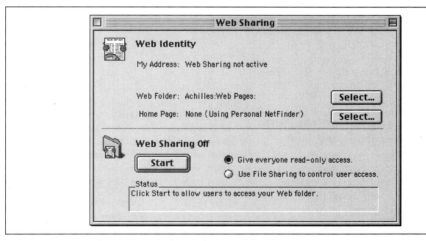

Figure P-2. Web Sharing control panel

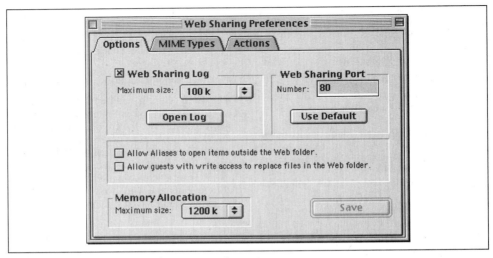

Figure P-3. Web Sharing Preferences window

Photoshop
On the Macintosh: Photoshop

Adobe Photoshop has become the standard program for photo editing and image production for both Macintosh and Windows users. The program is identical on both platforms, and you can exchange Photoshop files—as well as GIF, TIFF, EPS, and other graphics files, of course—without any conversion. For additional information about Photoshop, visit Adobe's web site at *http://www.adobe.com/*.

Power Management Control Panel
On the Macintosh: Energy Saver Control Panel

If your PC supports the Advanced Power Management specification, the Windows 98 Power Management control panel (called the Power control panel in Windows 95) offers control over the energy saving features of the computer. On the Macintosh, look for these features in the Energy Saver control panel, located in Apple menu → Control Panels → Energy Saver.

All current (and most recent) desktop Macs and all Apple laptops support three different energy saving features. A slider bar in the Sleep Setup panel lets you specify what

period of inactivity must elapse before the entire system goes to sleep or shuts down. Click the Show Details button to reveal slider bars that govern when the monitor goes to sleep and the hard disk stops spinning to save power (see Figure P-4).

It's easiest to use just the system sleep settings, but you can set the monitor and the hard disk to sleep on different schedules, as shown in Figure P-4.

Using these power-saving features can save hundreds of dollars worth of electricity over the course of the year, especially if you have more than one computer. Although various hibernation and standby modes on PCs have been known to cause problems, sleep mode on the Macintosh generally works very well.

If you're used to leaving your computer on for backup or other automated maintenance tasks that take place in the middle of the night, you can use the options in the Scheduled Startup & Shutdown panel to, for instance, start up the Macintosh at 2 A.M. and shut it down at 6 A.M., except on weekends.

On PowerBook and iBook laptops, the Energy Saver control panel's Sleep Setup panel is called Idle Sleep; the Scheduled

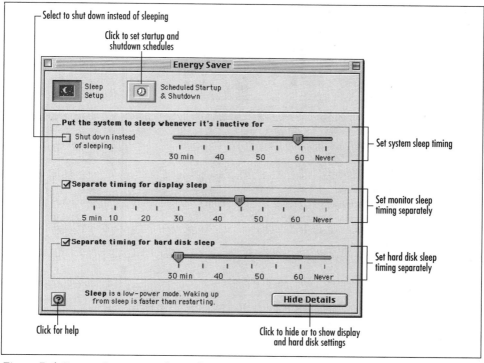

Figure P-4. Energy Saver control panel

Startup & Shutdown controls are relabeled Scheduled Wakeup & Sleep. A third panel, called Advanced Settings, offering several power-saving settings that make sense only for laptops (see Figure P-5).

For each set of laptop settings, you can choose either Battery or Power Adapter from the pop-up menu. In other words, you can define one set of preferences that governs power savings when the computer is running on battery power, and a different set when the laptop is plugged into the wall.

Power Switch
On the Macintosh: Power Key

In general, you turn each brand of PC on or off differently. But every Macintosh made today turns on and off exactly the same way: you simply press the power key on the keyboard. If the computer is off, it turns on; if the computer is running, a dialog box

appears offering Restart and Shut Down buttons, exactly as in Windows.

Some older Macintosh models, such as the LC and 6100 series, don't offer this method of starting up and shutting down. On these models, you turn on the computer by pressing a physical switch; you shut it off by choosing Special → Shut Down, and then pressing the physical switch again.

Print Screen Key
On the Macintosh: Screen Capture

For information about how to take snapshots of screen images, see **Screen Capture**.

Printer Sharing
On the Macintosh: Printer Sharing

Windows lets you share printers attached to your PC in much the same way you share folders on your hard disk. On the Macintosh, network printers, such as most laser

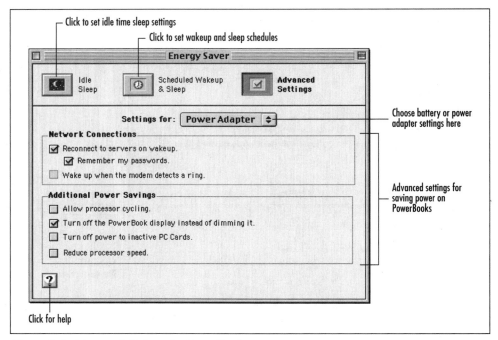

Click to set idle time sleep settings

Click to set wakeup and sleep schedules

Choose battery or power adapter settings here

Advanced settings for saving power on PowerBooks

Click for help

Figure P-5. Advanced Settings for PowerBooks

printers, are automatically available to every Macintosh on the network—no configuration necessary.

Setup on your part is only necessary if you want to make an inkjet printer, such as Apple's discontinued StyleWriter, available to the network. To do so, follow these steps:

1. Make sure you have the Printer Share extension and the appropriate printer driver for your printer in the Extensions folder of all your Macs.

2. On the Macintosh to which the printer is connected, open Apple menu → Chooser, click the icon for the printer you want to share on the left side of the Chooser, and then click the Setup button. The Sharing Setup dialog box appears.

3. Select "Share this Printer," enter a name for the printer, and (if you want to prevent some people on the network from printing on it), enter a password (see Figure P-6).

4. Click OK to close the dialog box and start sharing the printer.

To access the shared printer from another Macintosh, open Apple menu → Chooser, click the icon for that printer, and then select it in the "Connect to" list underneath Printer Port and Modem Port. Click the Get Info button to see which fonts aren't installed on the Macintosh connected to the printer—stick to fonts that are installed on both Macs for high quality printing.

Note that you can't share an inkjet printer attached to a Macintosh with a PC on the same network.

Printers Folder
On the Macintosh: Desktop Printers

In Windows, you configure and access your printers from My Computer → Printers. When you're using Mac OS 8 or later, you use Desktop Printers, which are icons that appear on your Desktop (although you can move them anywhere you like). These

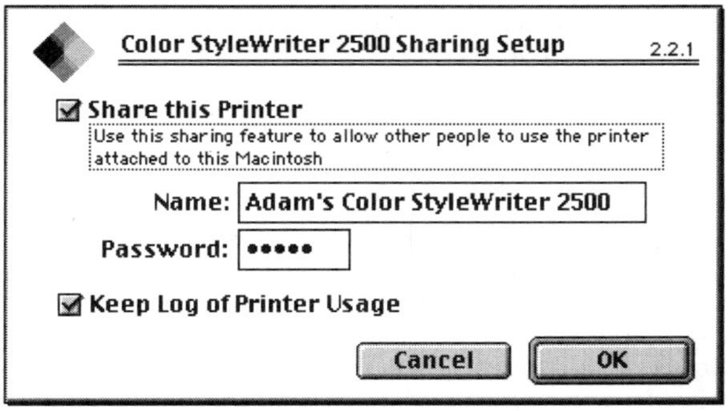

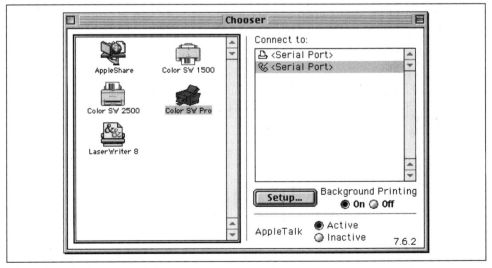

Figure P-6. Sharing a printer

Desktop printer icons offer quick access to printouts in progress, and make it simple to direct a particular printout to a certain printer (if you or your office has more than one printer).

Creating a Desktop Printer. Creating a new printer icon requires use of the Chooser. Follow these steps:

1. Open Apple menu → Chooser.

2. Select the icon representing your printer on the left side of the Chooser (see Figure P-7).

3. Indicate how it's connected to the Macintosh in the Connect to list.

4. Click Setup and set any desired options.

5. Close the Chooser.

The Chooser creates an icon for the printer on your Desktop. You can move it or rename it as you like.

Figure P-7. Setting up a printer

Configuring printers. To change the setup of a printer after you've created its Desktop icon, double-click the icon to open the print queue window. Then choose Printing → Setup. You can change such options as memory configuration and installed paper trays, depending on the individual printer.

Printing to a Desktop Printer. Although you're most likely to print from within programs by choosing File → Print, you can also print documents by dragging them to a printer's icon, or to the open print queue window. The Macintosh then launches the program that created the document—and prints it. For more information about printing, see **Printing Files**.

Modifying the print queue. When you're printing multiple files, you can manipulate them in the print queue window, accessible by double-clicking a Desktop Printer icon (see Figure P-8).

In the print queue window, you can start and stop a printout in progress, select individual printouts and schedule them for specific times, and delete printouts-in-waiting from the queue. You can also drag the printout icons around to print them in a different order.

Finally, in the Printing menu (which appears when the print queue window is open), you can specify whether you want to see alert messages when printing using manual feed;

you can also designate a particular printer to be your default printer.

Printing Files
On the Macintosh: Printing Files

Once properly configured, printing on the Macintosh works almost exactly the same way it does in Windows. For information about setting up Macintosh printers, see **Page Setup**, **Printers Folder**, and **Printer Sharing**. For information about font handling on the Macintosh, see **Fonts**.

As in Windows, there are several different ways of printing on the Macintosh.

- From within an application, choose File → Print (Command-P) to display the Print dialog box, where you can choose which printer to use, which pages to print, how many copies to print, and any other program-specific options (see Figure P-9).

- Drag one or more document icons to either a Desktop Printer icon or an open print queue window (accessed by double-clicking a printer icon). (See **Printers Folder** for details on these printing components.) When you do so, the Mac OS launches the necessary application, displays the Print dialog box, and then prints the document.

The Mac OS can print in the background, just as on Windows.

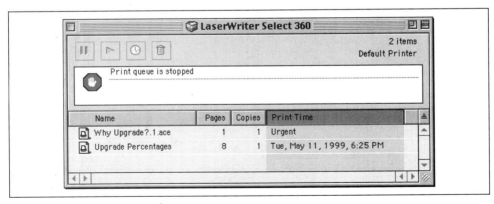

Figure P-8. Print queue window

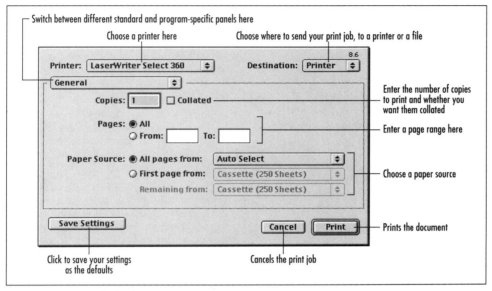

Figure P-9. Print dialog box

Troubleshooting. Although printing is generally a straightforward process, sometimes things can go wrong. Here are a few common problems and solutions:

- The Finder reports, via an alert dialog box, that the printer could not be found on the network. The printer may still be warming up and not yet ready to receive print jobs. If that's not the problem, check the cable connections.

- Fonts seem large and crude. Make sure you're using a TrueType or PostScript font (with ATM installed). Also be sure to use fonts that were designed for printing, rather than for onscreen use. For more information, see **Fonts**.

Program Files Folder
On the Macintosh: Applications Folder

Most Windows installation programs deposit new software in your Program Files folder. The Macintosh is less regimented about storing programs in specific places; although there's an Applications folder on your hard disk, you don't have to store your programs there—and most software installers don't even put new programs there.

In short, feel free to use the Applications folder or not as you wish. You could even create a Program Files folder on the Macintosh and use it as you would in Windows. See **Programs Menu**.

Programs
On the Macintosh: Applications

For a list of programs that work on the Macintosh just as they do in Windows, see **Cross-Platform Programs**.

Programs Menu
On the Macintosh: User-created Programs Menu

Windows users are accustomed to being able to open any program from Start → Programs—a feature not available when you're using a Macintosh. The Mac OS doesn't attempt to group programs in this way—creating such an arrangement is left up to you. As a result, Macintosh users often put aliases (see **Shortcuts**) of their frequently used programs in the Apple menu, in the Favorites menu, or on the Desktop.

To create your own Programs menu on a Macintosh, therefore, follow these steps:

1. Open Macintosh HD → System Folder → Apple Menu Items.

2. Choose File → New to create a new folder in the Apple Menu Items folder. Name it Programs and open it.

3. Choose File → Find to open Sherlock.

4. Search for items whose kind is application (see Figure P-10).

5. In the Sherlock results window, choose Edit → Select All to select all the applications. If you don't want certain applications to appear in your Programs menu, Shift-click their icons to deselect them.

6. Once you have the proper set of icons selected, hold down the Command and Option keys and drag the icons into your Programs window. The Mac OS responds by making aliases of all the dragged icons. Feel free to create additional folders inside the Programs folder, moving aliases into them for even better organization.

Now you can launch all your programs by choosing them from Apple menu → Programs, exactly as in Windows.

Properties Dialog Box
On the Macintosh: Get Info

Whenever you need to change a setting in Windows, you use the Properties dialog box. There's no such universal command on the Macintosh. The properties for an individual Desktop icon—disk, application, document, or whatever—appear when you select the icon and then choose Edit → Get Info; in applications, you generally adjust your settings using a command like Preferences, Options, or Settings.

Beginning with Mac OS 8.5, Apple divided the Get Info windows into multiple panels; you switch among them using the pop-up menu, as shown in Figure P-11.

General Information. The General Information pane, which opens first, gives you basic information about the icon you selected, including its kind, size, location, creation and modification dates, version, label, and comments. The information for an alias also identifies the location of the original file (and provides a button that takes you to it).

Sharing. The Sharing panel appears only for folders, disks, and programs, all of which can be shared over a network. See **File Sharing** for details.

Memory. Only programs have the Memory panel, which lets you modify the memory requirements for the application. See **Memory Usage** for more information.

Status & Configuration. Only Desktop Printers show the Status & Configuration panel, which provides information about the printer hardware. See **Printers Folder** for more information about Desktop Printers.

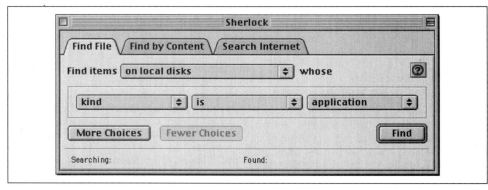

Figure P-10. Finding applications

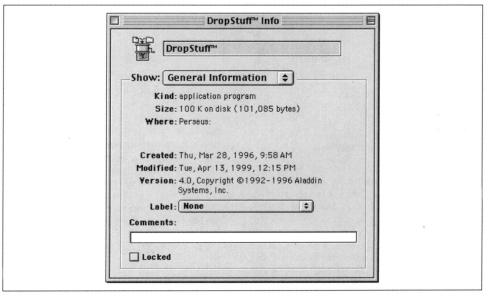

Figure P-11. Get Info window

Fonts. Again, only Desktop Printers have a Fonts panel, which show a list of fonts installed in the printer.

S-O

Q

QuarkXPress
On the Macintosh: QuarkXPress

If you use QuarkXPress on the Macintosh, your skills will translate to the Windows version. Transferring Quark files themselves between Macintosh and PC may not always go smoothly, thanks to both technological differences and font technology differences. For more information, check out Quark's Web site at *http://www.quark.com/* and especially the tech notes at *http://www. quark.com/tech/technotes.html.*

Quicken
On the Macintosh: Quicken

Quicken is available on the Macintosh, but you may be disappointed to discover that it doesn't offer as many features as the Windows version—particularly in the area of Internet connectivity. For more information about the Macintosh version of Quicken, visit *http://www.intuit.com/.*

The Quicken Support web pages also offer information on converting Windows Quicken files for use with the Macintosh version of Quicken—it's not a trivial process, so check the current recommendations.

QuickTime
On the Macintosh: QuickTime

Most people probably think of QuickTime as a way of playing movies on the Macin-

tosh, but the various QuickTime players and plug-ins can also display pictures and play sounds. QuickTime 4 even offers real-time streaming of audio and video over the Internet—great for people who like to listen to the radio via the Internet or watch live "webcasts" of important events. QuickTime can also be a useful file-format conversion utility for use by other applications, including web browsers and email programs.

QuickTime is a cross-platform standard; you may have encountered the occasional Windows program that uses QuickTime as its picture-displaying or sound-playing technology. On the Macintosh, far more programs rely on it. QuickTime is built into the Macintosh OS—use Apple menu → Control Panels → QuickTime Settings to adjust its options—and you can download the latest version for free from *http://www.apple.com.* For about $30, you can upgrade the free copy of QuickTime to QuickTime Pro, which contains tools for creating and editing QuickTime movies.

For more information about QuickTime, visit *http://www.apple.com/quicktime/.*

Quitting Programs
On the Macintosh: Quitting Applications

For information, see **Exiting Programs**.

R

RAM Upgrades

On the Macintosh: RAM Upgrades

If you're familiar with the basics of buying and installing RAM on the PC, you'll have no trouble doing so on a Macintosh. In fact, you'll find it far simpler to buy RAM for your Macintosh; you have far fewer variables to contend with.

What kind to buy. As with PCs, different models of Macs accept different types of SIMMs (30-pin in older Macs, 72-pin in newer models) or DIMMs, different speeds of RAM, different voltages, and so on.

To discover what kind of RAM upgrade boards your particular Macintosh model needs, consider downloading GURU, short for "GUide to RAM Upgrades." Released as freeware by RAM vendor NewerRAM, Inc., GURU is a database of information about every Macintosh model. Using GURU, you can determine everything you need to know about what RAM you should buy for a given Macintosh model, how much RAM that Macintosh can hold, what RAM speeds it supports, and whether the Macintosh supports memory interleaving (a method of increasing speed that requires you install RAM in specific slots). You can download GURU from *http://www.newertech.com/software/guru.html*; revised versions regularly

appear, covering newly released Macintosh models.

If you're researching Macintosh memory upgrades from your PC, you can find much of the same information at *http://www.newerram.com/findmem.html*.

How much RAM to buy. Even with the information from GURU, you may still wonder how much RAM you should install. As on the PC, more is always better, and successive versions of the Mac OS require ever more RAM. Use Table R-1 as a quick reference for how much you'll need.

Installing the RAM. After you've purchased your RAM boards, installing them works precisely as it does on the PC. Open the computer's case, search the motherboard (the large circuit board) for corresponding slots, and snap the new RAM boards in. Today's RAM slots are designed so that you can't install an upgrade board improperly—only when facing the correct direction. Tiny plastic clips at each end of each board snap inward to secure the board's ends.

RAM Usage

On the Macintosh: RAM Usage

See **Memory Usage**.

Table R-1. Suggested Macintosh RAM Configurations

Use	Amount of RAM
Basic productivity applications	32 MB minimum, 64 MB to 96 MB recommended
Games	32 MB and up
Graphics applications	64 MB to 256 MB
Server applications	32 MB to 256 MB, depending on the number of server applications running

Recycle Bin

On the Macintosh: Trash

Like the Recycle Bin in Windows, the Macintosh Trash provides a holding place for files and folders before they're deleted for good. The basics of the Recycle Bin and the Trash are similar, although there are a few differences.

Deleting Items. In Windows, you can move files and folders into the Recycle Bin in numerous ways. On the Macintosh, you move icons into the Trash in any of these ways:

- Drag icons onto the Trash icon.

- Select one or more items in the Finder and then press Command-Delete. This feature, which parallels the use of the Del key to delete files in Windows, arrived with Mac OS 8.

- Select some icons, and then choose File → Move To Trash.

- Control-click an icon in the Finder, and then choose Move to Trash from the contextual menu.

Unlike Windows, the Macintosh doesn't ask to confirm the deletion when you move icons to the Trash—only when you later actually empty the Trash.

Recovering items. Recovering a file or folder from the Trash works just as you'd expect from your experience using the Recycle Bin. Double-click the Trash to open it, and then drag an item out of the Trash window.

In Windows, when you set the Recycle Bin window to the Details view, information columns reveal the original locations and deletion dates of the window's contents. You can't view this kind of data on the Macintosh.

On the other hand, the Macintosh offers a unique feature of its own: if you select icons in the Trash window and then choose File → Put Away (Command-Y), the icons leap back into the folders from which you originally dragged them, even if it was weeks ago. Of course, if you don't know where the original locations are ahead of time, you might have to use File → Find to find where the files end up.

Emptying the Trash. In Windows, you may never even think about emptying the Recycle Bin, which automatically deletes the oldest files when it gets to a certain preset size. The Macintosh, however, never automatically empties the Trash. To remove files from the Trash permanently, choose Special → Empty Trash in the Finder. (You can also Control-click the Trash and choose Empty Trash from the contextual menu.)

Unfortunately, there's no built-in way on the Macintosh to delete just a few files from the Trash or even to delete just the files on a specific disk.

When you empty the Trash, a message tells you how many items are in it and how much space they take up; you're asked if you're sure you want to remove the items permanently. If you tire of clicking the confirmation button each time you empty the Trash, follow these steps:

1. Select the Trash can icon.

2. Choose File → Get Info (Command-I). The Trash Info window appears, as shown in Figure R-1.

3. Uncheck the "Warn before emptying" checkbox.

From now on, no confirmation message will appear when you empty the Trash. The Trash's Get Info window also tells you what's in the Trash, splitting the listing out between files and folders, and counting applications separately.

Trash notes. Although the Macintosh Trash lacks the automatic emptying feature of the Recycle Bin, it does have a few useful features that aren't present in Windows. For instance, in Windows, the Recycle Bin protects files only on hard disks; if you drag a file from a floppy disk, Zip disk, or network drive to the Recycle Bin, Windows deletes it immediately. On the Macintosh, every disk has its own Trash (in the form of a hidden folder)—a fact that explains why an empty Trash can may suddenly bulge when you insert a new disk, for example. Servers have hidden Network Trash folders in addition to the standard hidden Trash folder; this system prevents you from seeing, in your Trash can, all the deleted items

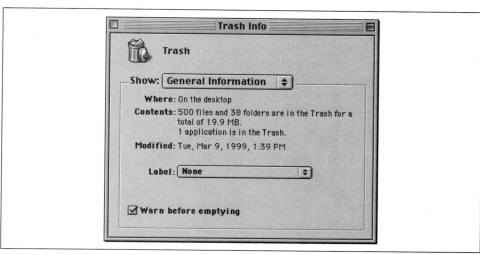

Figure R-1. Trash Info window

in the Trash of every Macintosh on the network, which might be overwhelming.

In Windows, if you drag the icon of a disk to the Recycle Bin, all the files on that disk are deleted. On the Macintosh, doing so simply ejects the disk. (To erase all the files on a Macintosh disk, open the disk's window, select all the files and folders, and then drag the selection to the Trash. Alternatively, just select the disk's icon and then choose Special → Erase Disk.)

Regional Settings
On the Macintosh: Date & Time, Numbers, and Text Control Panels

In Windows, you use the Regional Settings control panel to modify how Windows displays dates, times, numbers, and currencies in countries other than the U.S. On the Macintosh, you make such settings in three different control panels: Date & Time, Text, and Numbers.

Date & Time control panel. In the Date & Time control panel's Date Formats and Time Formats (see Figure R-2) dialog boxes, you can choose a country from a menu or create your own custom settings. Either way,

the Macintosh automatically shows dates and times in the format appropriate for the country you chose. (You'll see the new date formats in, for example, the Date Modified column of Desktop list-view windows.)

Numbers control panel. The Mac's Numbers control panel lets you select decimal and thousands separators and choose a currency symbol (see Figure R-3). Here again, you can specify the settings by choosing from predefined country settings. You can't specify the number of digits in a group, as you can in Windows.

You may have to hunt to see the effect of changes you make in the Numbers control panel. Excel, for example, uses the currency you choose when you apply the Currency format to selected cells.

Text control panel. In addition to the date, time, number, and currency settings, the Mac OS also lets you specify how text behaves according to international customs. Behaviors include sort order, case conversion, and word definitions. You can choose a script system (such as Kanji or Cyrillic) from the Script menu and then a country from the Behavior menu in the Text control panel (see Figure R-4).

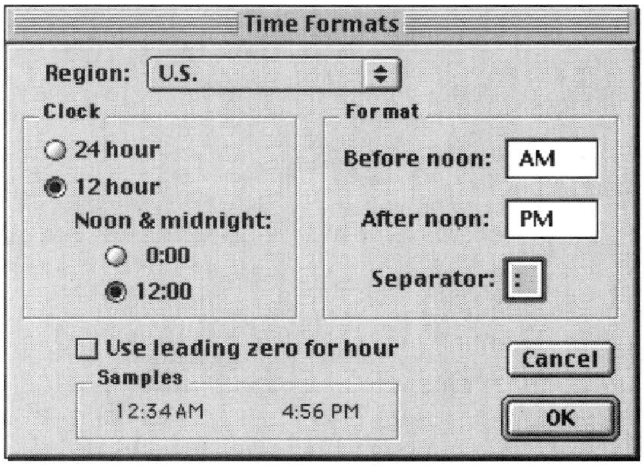

Figure R-2. Time Formats dialog box

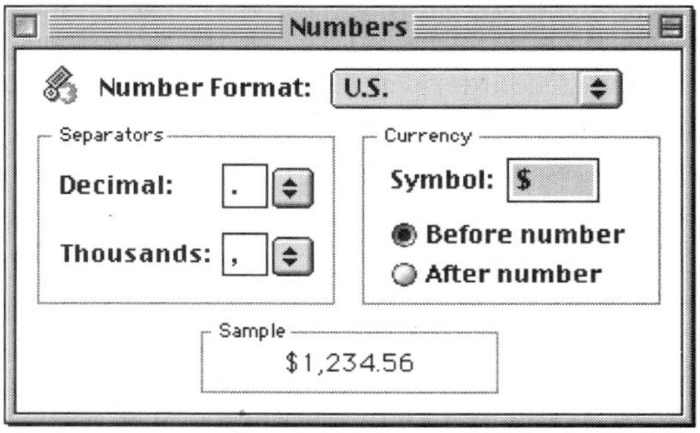

Figure R-3. Numbers control panel

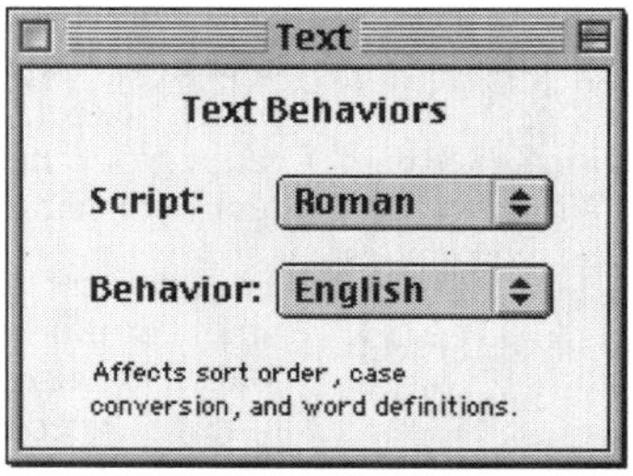

Figure R-4. Text control panel

Registry
On the Macintosh: Preferences Folder

Windows stores configuration settings and preferences for both the operating system and applications in the Registry, a system-level database file. On the Macintosh, the closest equivalent is the Preferences folder (located at Macintosh HD → System Folder → Preferences). Applications generate preference files in this folder; some applications create entire folders of configuration files within the Preferences folder for this purpose.

Here's what you need to know about Macintosh preference files:

- You can't edit them manually, as experienced Windows users can do in the Windows Registry. You can make a change to a preference file only by launching the parent application and changing the preference settings there.

- Files and folders within the Preferences folder must be in the Preferences folder to work. In other words, you can reset most programs to their default settings merely by moving the appropriate preferences file out to the Desktop and then launching the program. Reverting to your old preferences is then as easy as putting that application's preferences file back into the Preferences folder.

- If you want to copy an application from one Macintosh to another, you generally don't need to copy the preferences file. If you do, however, the copy will have exactly the same settings.

- A corrupted preference file—an occasional occurrence on the Macintosh—can explain a wide variety of strange behavior in a particular program. Deleting the preference file is a common, and powerful, troubleshooting technique; the next time you launch the program in question, a fresh and uncorrupted preference file is generated automatically.

Renaming
On the Macintosh: Renaming

Renaming icons on the Macintosh works the same way as in Windows, although it requires one click less. To rename a file on the Macintosh, follow these steps:

1. Click once on the name portion of the file's icon, and then wait for a moment until the "renaming rectangle" opens around the filename. Alternatively, select an icon and then press Return to select the name for editing. (There's no Rename command on the Macintosh.)

2. Make your changes. You're free to use the Cut, Copy, and Paste commands in the Edit menu. You can also use any character except the colon (:); far fewer characters are off-limits on the Macintosh than in Windows.

3. To save your changes to a name, either press Return or click outside the name.

Restrictions. You can't rename the Trash. If file sharing is turned on, you can't change the name of disks that are being shared until you turn file sharing off.

On the other hand, renaming files on the Macintosh—even system files—rarely produces instability and problems, as it might in Windows.

Reset Switch
On the Macintosh: Reset Switch

When you suffer from a truly serious crash in Windows that locks up everything so even Ctrl-Alt-Delete doesn't work, you push the Reset switch. If even that technique doesn't work, you turn the PC off and back on again.

The Macintosh works exactly the same way. If the computer locks up, press Command-Option-Esc to force quit a locked program; if that doesn't work, type the Reset keystroke. On most Macintosh models, this is Control-Command-power key. (The Power key, which you use to turn the Macintosh on, is in the upper-right corner of your keyboard.)

Rarely, a crash prevents the keyboard reset keystroke from working, at which point you'll have to turn the power off and back on again using the power switch on the Macintosh itself. If even that fails, unplug the power cord from the wall.

Resizing Windows
On the Macintosh: Resizing Windows

In Windows, you resize a window by dragging the resize handle in the lower-right corner. The Macintosh has exactly the same resize handle, and it works in exactly the same way.

You can't, however, resize a Macintosh window in only one dimension by dragging any edge, as you can in Windows.

For information about changing the size of windows with a single click, see **Minimizing Windows** and **Maximizing Windows**.

Restart
On the Macintosh: Restart

After installing new software, or when you're experiencing problems and want to start afresh, you restart your PC. The same situation applies to the Macintosh.

To restart a Macintosh manually, choose Special → Restart. Alternatively, press the Power key and click Restart or press the R key. If any documents require saving, you'll be asked if you want to save them; as in Windows, if you click Cancel when asked to save a document, you abort the restarting process.

Right-Click
On the Macintosh: Control-Click

The standard Macintosh mouse has only a single mouse button; as a result, you can't right-click objects to summon contextual menus, as you can in Windows. Instead, Control-click objects. Third-party mice with multiple buttons are available.

Run
On the Macintosh: None

Despite the fact that the move from DOS to Windows encourages PC users to use the graphical interface instead of the DOS command line, many users still prefer to launch programs in Windows by choosing Start → Run and typing the name of the program to run. There's no equivalent in the Mac OS, so you'll have to resort to alternative methods. See **Opening Files** for the possibilities.

S

Safe Mode
On the Macintosh: Extensions Off

In times of troubleshooting, you wouldn't get far without some means of starting a computer from Ground Zero, its native, virginal, factory-fresh state, free from any software you've added to its operating system. In Windows, this condition is known as Safe Mode.

On the Macintosh, restoring the OS to its bare minimum components is called booting with extensions off. To do so, restart the computer while pressing the Shift key. When you see the words "Extensions off" or "Extensions disabled" on the screen, you can release the Shift key; the Macintosh is now running without any system add-ons, such as extensions, control panels, startup items, and so on.

Without these helpers, the Macintosh can't read CD-ROMs, go online, send faxes, connect to networks, and so on. On the other hand, the computer should start up especially quickly and run exceptionally smoothly. The troubleshooting work is halfway done: having determined that whatever problem you're having is a result of corrupted or conflicting extensions, you can now begin the business of determining which ones are causing the problem. For details on this process, see the sidebar "Mastering the Extensions Manager" in **Troubleshooting**.

Saving Files
On the Macintosh: Saving Files

You save documents on the Macintosh exactly the way you do in Windows: by choosing File → Save or by pressing, in the Macintosh case, Command-S.

Only a few differences are worth noting:

- When saving a document for the first time, you may encounter either of two slightly different Save dialog boxes, depending on the version of the Mac OS you're using and the specific program you're using. In Mac OS 8.5, Apple has replaced the old-style Save dialog box (see Figure S-1) with a superior Save dialog box using a technology called Navigation Services (see Figure S-2).

  At this writing, however, few programs take advantage of the new Navigation Services look or features. Most of the time, therefore, you'll encounter the old-style Save dialog box. Fortunately, the process of saving is relatively similar in both and follows these basic steps:

- When you name a file you're saving for the first time, you can use any punctuation except the colon (:). Filenames can be up to 31 characters long, and filename suffixes or extensions aren't necessary. Enter a name for the file. For more information, see **Filenames**.

- The old-style Macintosh Save dialog boxes don't let you switch to any other program while you're using them. In the new Navigation Services dialog boxes, you can switch to another program while saving, just as you can in Windows. See **Dialog Boxes** for details.

- You can't move the old-style Save dialog boxes around on the screen, as you can the new Navigation Services dialog boxes.

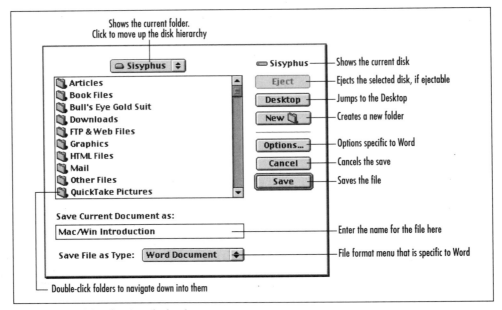

Figure S-1. Old-style Save dialog box

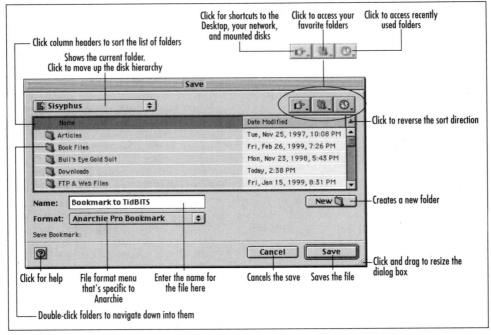

Figure S-2. New Navigation Services dialog box

ScanDisk
On the Macintosh: Disk First Aid

ScanDisk is the built-in Windows program that can repair minor disk corruption. On the Macintosh, you use Disk First Aid for this purpose. (As on Windows, commercial programs like Norton Utilities offer additional features, including file recovery.)

Disk First Aid usually sits in Macintosh HD → Utilities. It's simple to operate:

1. Double-click Disk First Aid's icon to launch the program.
2. Click the icon of the disk you want to check. To select multiple disks, Shift-click their icons (see Figure S-3).
3. Click Verify to verify—generate a report on—the selected disks, or click Repair to verify and repair the disks. Verify makes no change to the disks, whereas Repair fixes any problems it finds.

Scheduled Tasks
On the Macintosh: Macros

In Windows, you can schedule certain tasks, such as a ScanDisk run, to take place auto-

matically on a regular basis. There's no built-in equivalent feature on the Macintosh.

On the other hand, you can schedule some events in the Mac OS, including startup and shut down times (do so in the Apple menu → Control Panels → Energy Saver → Scheduled Startup & Shutdown). You can also set a schedule for Sherlock's Find by Content feature to index your hard disk in, for example, the middle of the night. For more information on Sherlock, see **Find**.

Scraps
On the Macintosh: Clipping Files

In Windows 98, you can drag text and graphics out of certain programs to the Desktop to create a scrap file. Relatively few applications support this feature, so it's not widely used in Windows yet. On the Macintosh, however, the equivalent feature, clipping files, is popular and useful. Not all Macintosh programs support clipping files, but most recent ones do.

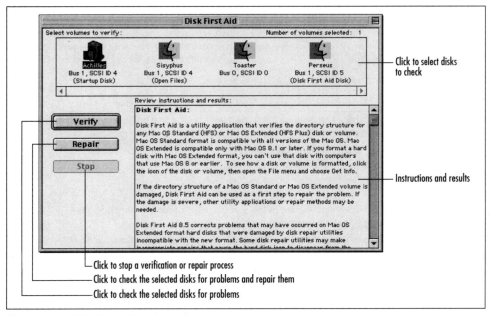

Figure S-3. Disk First Aid

To create a clipping file, select some text or a graphic in a document window; drag it clear out of the window and onto the Desktop. At any time, you can double-click the resulting clipping file on your Desktop to view its contents. To use a clipping file in another document, drag the clipping file's icon from the Desktop to the desired point in an open document.

Screen Capture
On the Macintosh: Screen Capture

For writers of computer books, magazines, and manuals, the screen capture, or screen shot, is a vital tool: it's a graphics file that shows what was on the screen at a precise moment. In Windows, you create screen shots by pressing Print Screen or Alt-Print Screen. On the Macintosh, too, you press specified keyboard keys to create screen shots, as outlined in Table S-1.

Notice the patterns. The key combinations that include the 3 key take a snapshot of the entire screen, whereas those that use the 4 key take a snapshot of a portion of the screen. Adding Control copies the snapshot to the clipboard rather than saving it to a file; finally, if Caps Lock is down, the screen shot is neatly trimmed to include only the window or menu you click after pressing the key combination. Each time, a satisfying camera-shutter sound accompanies the creation of the screenshot.

As on Windows, more powerful screen capture utilities can do things such as saving snapshots in different file formats. Snapz-Pro is one popular example (Ambrosia Software, *http://www.ambrosiasw.com/Products/SnapzPro.html*).

Screen Savers
On the Macintosh: Screen Savers, Energy Saver Control Panel

The Macintosh has no built-in screen saver. Of course, you can buy one, such as the popular After Dark from Berkeley Systems (*http://www.berksys.com/products/afterdark/*). On the other hand, the Mac OS can save your screen far more effectively than any screen saver software by simply darkening your monitor after a specified period of inactivity. For more information, see **Power Management Control Panel**.

SCSI
On the Macintosh: SCSI

SCSI, which stands for Small Computer Serial Interface, is a popular means of attaching high-speed peripherals, such as scanners, Zip and Jaz drives, tape drives, and hard disks, to both Macs and PCs. Because SCSI was built into every Macintosh for many years, products connected by this technology became far more common in the Macintosh world than the PC world.

Table S-1. Screen Capture Options in the Mac OS

Function	Key Combination
Saves the image of the entire screen as a file, called Picture 1, on your startup disk.	Command-Shift-3
Copies the image of the entire screen to the clipboard.	Control-Command-Shift-3
Saves the image of a rectangular section of the screen, which you select by dragging, into a file called Picture 1 on your startup disk.	Command-Shift-4
Copies the image of a rectangular section of the screen, which you select by dragging, to the clipboard.	Control-Command-Shift-4
Captures the image of one particular open menu or window, which you select by clicking, into a file on the startup disk called Picture 1.	Caps Lock-Command-Shift-4, and then click the desired window
Copies the image of one particular open menu or window, which you select by clicking, to the clipboard.	Caps Lock-Control-Command-Shift-4, then click the desired window

For the most part, SCSI devices are storage devices—hard disks, removable cartridge drives, and tape drives.

Two complexities of SCSI technology can cause trouble on any kind of computer—SCSI IDs and termination. Every SCSI device must be set to an ID number between 0 and 6. If you have an older Macintosh whose internal hard disk uses SCSI technology, its ID is 0. (Technically, the Macintosh itself is a SCSI device, too, whose ID is 7.) If you inadvertently attach two SCSI devices with the same ID number to a single Macintosh, dramatic system errors can occur—crashes, bombs, inability to start up, and even multiple copies of the same hard disk icon appearing on the Desktop. The bottom line: use the push button control or wheel on each SCSI gadget to specify a unique ID number before attaching it to a computer.

The other chronic SCSI hazard: If you attach several SCSI devices to a single Macintosh, one gadget connected to the next, you must terminate (attach a special transistor plug designed for this purpose) the far end of the chain. Fortunately, an increasing number of today's SCSI devices include built-in *active termination*, which turns termination on or off automatically as needed.

Usually, it's easy to daisy-chain four or five SCSI devices (including internal devices). But if you try to add more devices, it's a total crapshoot; the devices may not even work unless you try breaking the termination rules. If you must get that ambitious, be sure to perform ritual tofu sacrifices to the SCSI gods beforehand.

The complexity and crankiness of SCSI technology, incidentally, helps to explain why Apple eliminated it from new Macintosh models starting in 1998. SCSI has been replaced in all desktop Macs by the idiot-proof and almost infinitely expandable USB and FireWire technologies.

Serial Ports
On the Macintosh: Modem Port, Printer Port

PCs generally provide one or two RS-232 serial ports for connecting modems and other peripherals. For many years, every Macintosh model also offered two serial ports, although they were RS-422 ports with DIN-8 connectors (see Figure S-4). (Current Macintosh models come with the far faster and more expandable USB ports instead.)

On Macintosh models that included serial ports, a small telephone icon designates the modem port, and a tiny dot-matrix printer icon identifies the printer port. But despite the names, the two ports are generally interchangeable. Most software that requires serial ports, such as PalmPilot or printer software, lets you choose whether you're using the modem port or printer port.

There is one significant exception to the interchangeable nature of the two ports. To connect a Macintosh to a LocalTalk network, the LocalTalk or PhoneNet connector must be connected to the printer port.

Figure S-4. Modem and printer ports

Settings Menu
On the Macintosh: None

In Windows, the Start → Settings menu, for which there's no direct equivalent on the Macintosh, provides access to a number of commands:

Control Panel
> For information about accessing control panels on the Macintosh, see **Control Panel**.

Printers
> For information about configuring printers, see **Printing Files**.

Taskbar
> For information about the Macintosh equivalents to the **Taskbar** and **Start Menu**, see their entries.

Folder Options (Windows 98)
> For information about file types (such as you would find in the Folder Options dialog box), see **File Types**.

Active Desktop & Windows Update (Windows 98)
> The Macintosh has no equivalent for the Active Desktop or Windows Update items in the Settings menu.

Shift Key
On the Macintosh: Shift Key

As on Windows, the Shift key does far more on the Macintosh than simply produce capital letters:

- Hold down the Shift key while the Macintosh boots to prevent all startup items—control panels, extensions, and items in the Startup Items folder—from loading. This trick is extremely useful for troubleshooting; if the Macintosh has been acting up, this technique rules out extension conflicts (a common cause of instability). Keep in mind that many features of the Mac OS won't be available—CD-ROM, Internet connection, and so on—if you boot with the Shift key down.

- Shift-click icons in a Desktop window to select more than one simultaneously, exactly like Ctrl-clicking in Windows.

- Shift-click items in a scrolling list to select a continuous range of items in the list.

- In situations where the Tab key is used for navigation (to move between fields in a dialog box, for example), adding Shift reverses the direction of the navigation, exactly as on Windows.

- When dragging to create a line or rectangle (for example) in a graphics program, hold down Shift to produce a perfectly straight line or perfectly symmetrical rectangle.

Shortcuts
On the Macintosh: Aliases

A Windows shortcut is an icon that represents some other file, folder, or disk and takes up very little disk space, yet opens the original icon when double-clicked. In effect, it lets a file, folder, or disk icon be in more than one place at once. A common usage: put the shortcut for a commonly used item in your Start menu or on your Desktop. On the Macintosh, the equivalent icon duplicates are called aliases.

To create an alias, select the icon of a file, folder, or disk in the Finder. Choose File → Make Alias (Command-M). (Alternatively, Command-Option-drag it to a different window, or Control-click it and choose Make Alias from the contextual pop-up menu.) The Finder creates the alias, appending the word "alias" to the filename (see Figure S-5). In Mac OS 8.5 and later, alias icons are marked by a small arrow, exactly as on Windows shortcuts; in all OS versions, alias names appear in italic type.

You may wish to remove the word "alias" from the name, since the italics make its identity as an alias clear. You can move or copy aliases anywhere you want and use them just as you would the originals.

To find the original of an alias, Control-click it, and choose Show Original from the pop-up contextual menu.

Macintosh aliases are smarter and less likely to stop working than Windows shortcuts, particularly those created in Windows 95. If

Figure S-5. An original file and its alias

you move, rename, or even copy an alias to a different disk, double-clicking still opens the original file. If necessary, the Mac OS will even mount remote AppleShare servers (other shared hard disks on the network), if that's where the original file was located.

Shut Down
On the Macintosh: Shut Down

Exactly as with the PC, you shouldn't shut down a Macintosh simply by cutting its power. If you do so, the Macintosh complains at the next startup, and modern Macs then run the Disk First Aid program to check for any hard disk corruption that your rash action may have caused.

To shut down a Macintosh, choose Special → Shut Down, or press the Power key; click Shut Down in the dialog box that appears (or press Return). The Mac OS then quits all open programs, prompting you to save any changes in open documents. Finally, the Macintosh shuts off. (Some old Macintosh models may prompt you to switch them off

manually, much like PCs without Advanced Power Management.)

Sorting Files
On the Macintosh: Sorting Files

When you're faced with a folder containing a large number of files, sorting the files makes it easier to find the one you want. For more information on sorting files in Desktop windows, see **View Menu**.

You can also choose a sorting criterion from View → Arrange Icons, but clicking column headers is easier.

View as List. The Mac's List View closely resembles Details view in Windows; to sort files in a List View window, click the name of the appropriate column at the top of the window. For example, to sort the files alphabetically by name, click the Name column header, exactly as in Windows. To reverse the direction of the sort, click the pyramid icon to the right of the column headers (see Figure S-6).

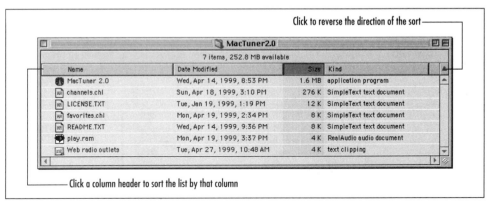

Figure S-6. Sorting files in a list view

Alternative methods exist: you can also choose a sort order from View → Sort List, or Control-click the window and choose a sort order from Sort List.

View as Icons and View as Buttons. As you can read in View menu, the Macintosh offers two other views of the icons in a particular Desktop window: Icon View and Button View. When you're using either of these views, the View → Arrange command sorts the icons in the window. You can arrange icons by name, modification date, creation date, size, kind, or label by choosing the appropriate item from View → Arrange (or by Control-clicking the window and choosing the desired item from the Arrange pop-up menu).

If you rearrange icons in the window, resize the window, or add or remove icons, the icons in a window don't ordinarily arrange themselves to accommodate the new configuration. To force the window to reflect the changes, choose View → Clean Up.

If you'd rather not have to use this Clean Up command repeatedly, use one of the View → View Options → Keep Arranged commands, which make your icons snap to their proper positions whenever you adjust the window or change the number of icons in it. This configuration works much like Windows does when you choose View → Arrange Icons → Auto Arrange.

Sound Recorder
On the Macintosh: SimpleSound

Windows includes a basic sound recording and editing program called Sound Recorder. The Mac's simpler equivalent is called SimpleSound, accessible from Apple menu → SimpleSound.

SimpleSound can record a sound, play a sound, and manage your alert sounds. Of course, you can also do all of this in Apple menu → Control Panels → Monitors & Sound → Alert Sounds → Add. SimpleSound's primary advantage is that only RAM limits the length of the sound you record; the Monitors & Sound method arbitrarily truncates any sound at 10 seconds.

Playing sound files. To play a sound file on your hard disk, open SimpleSound. Choose File → Open, navigate to and open the sound, and then choose Sound → Play.

Recording your own sounds. The most interesting use of SimpleSound is its capability to let you add your own sounds. You might decide, for example, to create your own error beep, to supplement the six basic ones that come with the Macintosh. Follow these steps in SimpleSound (or in the Alerts panel of the Monitors & Sound control panel).

Before attempting to record sounds, make sure the Sound Monitoring Source in Apple menu → Control Panels → Monitors & Sounds → Sound is set to the sound source you want to record, such as External Mic.

1. Choose Apple menu → SimpleSound (or Apple menu → Control Panels → Monitors & Sound → Alerts).

2. Click Add. The recording controls shown in Figure S-7 appear.

3. Click Record; while the virtual tape is rolling, produce some sound. To stop recording, click Stop. Make an effort to prevent recording "dead air" at the end of your sound—alert beeps should be short.

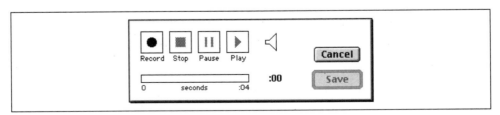

Figure S-7. SimpleSound controls

4. Click Save and name the sound.

5. To review your sound, click it in the Alerts list.

6. If you don't get it perfect on the first try, click Remove (Delete if you're using Monitors & Sound) to remove the sound, and then try again.

Turning your sound into a file. At first, it may occur to you that your sound is only accessible via the list of alert sounds. Fortunately, however, you can easily turn it into a standalone file, suitable for importing into a multimedia program or emailing to a friend.

To do so, open Macintosh HD → System Folder → the System "suitcase" file. Inside, you'll see all your alert sounds represented as icons. Drag one out of the window and onto the Desktop, where it becomes a stand-alone file. The most common Macintosh sound format is known simply as the System 7 format. The shareware world is filled with programs that can convert System 7 sounds into other formats, such as the Windows-compatible AIFF format; see **Web Sites for Macintosh Software and Information** for links.

Sounds Control Panel

On the Macintosh: Appearance Control Panel's Sound Tab, Monitors & Sounds Control Panel's Alerts Panel

Exactly as in Windows, in Mac OS 8.5 and later, you can associate sound effects with various Desktop events—opening and closing windows, opening menus, using scroll bars, and so on.

Appearance control panel. To turn on the sound effects in Mac OS 8.5 or later, open Apple menu → Control Panels → Appearance → Sound. From the Sound Track pop-up menu, choose Platinum Sounds. (Apple originally intended to include various sets of sounds, but included only the Platinum Sound set in the release version of the OS.)

When you do so, you'll see that the control panel offers individual control over the four categories of sound: menus, windows, buttons, and Finder mouse actions (see Figure S-8).

Monitors & Sounds control panel. To choose a different error beep, visit Apple menu → Control Panels → Monitors & Sound → Alerts, where you can switch between alert sounds, change the alert sound volume, add new ones, and remove sounds you don't like (see Figure S-9). (Note that in Mac OS 9, Monitors & Sound has been split into two control panels, named Monitors and Sound.)

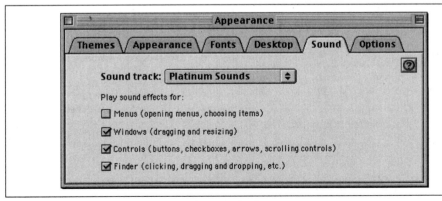

Figure S-8. Appearance control panel's Sound tab

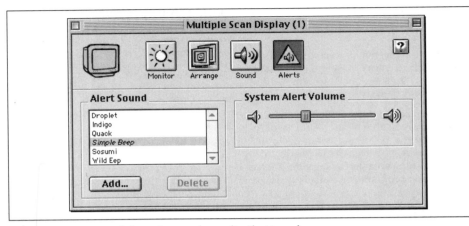

Figure S-9. Monitors & Sound control panel's Alert panel

Speech Recognition
On the Macintosh: Speech Recognition

The Macintosh comes with one built-in form of speech recognition, called PlainTalk. Once you've equipped your Macintosh with a microphone, you can use PlainTalk primarily for launching programs—you can say "Computer, open Microsoft Word" to launch Word. If you're handy with AppleScript, the built-in Mac OS automation software, you can use PlainTalk to open mini programs that open menus, process data, copy and paste, and so on. For more information about PlainTalk, and to download the latest version, visit *http://www.apple.com/macos/speech/*.

However, PlainTalk has no capability for learning your voice, and isn't usable for dictation. If you're interested in speech dictation software on the Macintosh, your prospects once were limited, but now are rapidly improving.

- Dragon NaturallySpeaking, the best-selling continuous-speech recognition program for Windows, is being developed for the Macintosh. Dragon Systems hopes to release the Macintosh version by the end of 1999. For more information about NaturallySpeaking, see *http://www.dragonsys.com/*.

- A Macintosh version of IBM's popular Via Voice speech-recognition software

is also slated for release in winter 1999. IBM (*http://www-4.ibm.com/software/speech*) promises that it will be inexpensive and fast.

- A startup company called MacSpeech, founded by former Dragon employees, is also hard at work developing a continuous-speech recognition program for the Macintosh. The progress of their product, which is based on the Phillips speech-engine technology, is posted at *http://www.macspeech.com/*.

Stand By
On the Macintosh: Sleep

Every recent PC—technically, those that comply with the Advanced Power Management (APM) standard—offers a Stand by, or Suspend, mode. In this state, the computer requires less power, yet springs fully back to life when you press a key. The Macintosh offer a similar feature, called Sleep.

PCs in standby mode may disconnect from the network, and some programs may crash upon waking. The only downside of putting a Macintosh to sleep, on the other hand, is that Apple laptops (but not desktop Macs) lose their network connections.

To put a Macintosh into sleep mode, choose Sleep from the Special menu in the Finder. (If you have an Apple laptop, simply close the lid.) Alternatively, press the Power key on the keyboard; when the dialog box appears, click the Sleep button or press the S key. To wake up a Macintosh that's asleep, press any key on the keyboard (moving the mouse won't do it).

Using the Mac's Energy Saver control panel, which is similar to the Power Management control panel in Windows, you can set the Macintosh to go to sleep automatically after a specified amount of time. The Energy Saver control panel can even wake the Macintosh up, or shut it down, at specific times, too. That trick is handy if, for instance, you want the Macintosh to wake up briefly in the middle of the night to back up, after which it will go to sleep again.

Start Menu
On the Macintosh: Apple Menu (and others)

If anything made Macintosh proponents cry, "Stop, thief!" when Windows 95 debuted, it was the Start menu—a close equivalent to the Mac's Apple menu. Here, at the left side of both computer screens, is a central menu that you can configure to list anything you find important. Here's a rundown of the Start menu's contents, and where to find the Macintosh equivalent of each command.

Shut Down. On the Macintosh, you'll find the Shut Down command in the Special menu. You can also shut down the Macintosh by pressing the power key. For more information, see **Shut Down**, **Stand By**, and **Restart**.

Log Off (Windows 98). In Mac OS 9, the Multiple Users profile duplicates this feature of Windows; in previous Mac OS versions, there's no equivalent to the Log Off command. For additional information, see **User Profiles**.

Suspend. This Windows 95 command is the precise equivalent of the Mac's Special → Sleep command; see **Stand By**.

Run. The Macintosh isn't descended from a command line operating system like DOS; it has no Run command.

Help. To access online help for the Mac OS, choose Help → Mac OS Help in the Finder. For more information, see **Help**.

Find. To search your Macintosh for files, choose Apple menu → Find—or, in Mac OS 8.5 and later, Apple menu → Sherlock. For more information, see **Find**.

Settings. Most Macintosh settings are accessible from Apple menu → Control Panels. See **Control Panel** for additional details.

Documents. Windows keeps track of recently accessed documents in Start → Documents; the Macintosh tracks them in Apple menu → Recent Documents. See **Documents Menu** for more information.

Favorites. In Windows, a "favorite" can either refer to a folder or a web page. On the Macintosh, a favorite can be any icon—folder, disk, document, application, and so on. For more information, see **Favorites Menu**.

Programs. You're probably used to accessing most of your programs from Start → Programs. The fact that the Macintosh doesn't offer a single centralized list of every application on the computer may throw you at first. Instead, the Mac's Apple menu → Recent Applications command lists only the most recently used applications. For details, see **Programs Menu**.

Your own files, folders, and programs. Above the default items in the Start menu is an area where you, and programs you install, can add new commands to the menu. The Mac's Apple menu is equally customizable; Macintosh fans often modify it heavily, loading it up with aliases of frequently used folders, documents, web sites, disks, network servers, and applications.

To edit your Apple menu, follow these steps:

1. Open Macintosh HD → System Folder → Apple Menu Items.

2. To add an icon to the Apple menu, drag it, or an alias of it, into the Apple Menu Items folder. The Apple menu changes immediately to display the new item.

S-O

3. To remove something from the Apple menu, drag its icon out of the Apple Menu Items folder.

To open something listed in your Apple menu, simply choose its name. When you do so, you may be surprised to discover a dramatic difference between the Macintosh Apple menu and the Windows Start menu: on the Macintosh, if you click the name of a disk or folder in the Apple menu, that disk or folder opens. You're not forced to continue onto the hierarchical submenu of the folder's contents to make a selection, as in Windows.

The Apple menu's contents appear alphabetically. If you want to group similar items, consider prefixing them with a special character, such as the bullet character (Option-8). You can also make some files list first by preceding their names with a space.

StartUp Folder
On the Macintosh: Startup Items Folder

In Windows, if you want a certain program or document to open every time you boot the PC, you can place a shortcut to the program or document in the StartUp folder. The Mac's Startup Items folder is exactly the same idea.

To add an item to the Mac's Startup Items folder, first open Macintosh HD → System Folder → Startup Items. Then drag a document, folder, disk, network server, or program—or the alias of any these items—into the Startup Items folder. (See **Shortcuts** if you're not sure how to make an alias.) The next time you boot the Macintosh, that file will open automatically.

You can disable a startup item by dragging its icon out of the Startup Items folder. You can also use the Extensions Manager control panel to manage startup items. Follow these instructions:

1. Open Apple menu → Control Panels → Extensions Manager (see Figure S-10).

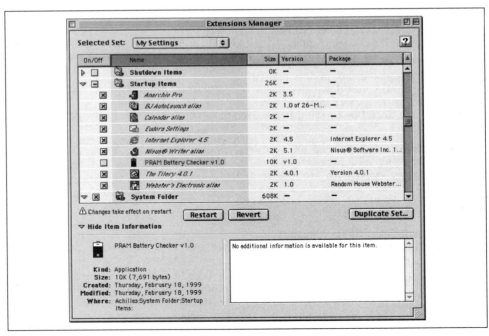

Figure S-10. Extensions Manager

2. Scroll down in the list to Startup Items. (Hint: Click the disclosure triangles next to Control Panels and Extensions to hide those items and make the list much smaller.)

3. To disable a startup item so that it doesn't launch at startup, deselect its checkbox.

4. To enable a disabled startup item so that it will launch automatically at startup, select its checkbox.

5. Close Extensions Manager.

6. Restart the Macintosh to see the results of your changes.

Suspend
On the Macintosh: Sleep

In Windows 98, Microsoft changed the name of the Suspend command. For details, see **Stand By**.

System Information
On the Macintosh: Apple System Profiler

In Windows, you can use the combination of the System Information program and the Windows Report Tool (available from Tools → Windows Report Tool in System Information) to learn more about your system and provide details to tech-support staff.

In Mac OS 8 and later, you can use the Apple menu → Apple System Profiler program to report the same kind of information (see Table S-2), suitable for printing or sending via email.

To use Apple System Profiler, launch the program. Use the Select menu to open various reports. If you want to read all the reports, or if you need to send a report to someone else, choose File → Create Report, and then select the desired options in the dialog box that appears. Apple System Profiler displays the report in a scrolling window; you can save it to disk by choosing File → Save As.

If someone sends you an Apple System Profiler report (usually called ASP Report), you can view it in any word processor. You can also double-click its icon to view it in Apple System Profiler.

Table S-2. Reports Generated by Apple System Profiler

Report	Comments
System Overview	Lists information about your Macintosh, including machine type, CPU type and speed, and various memory configurations.
Networking Information	Provides details about file sharing, your network configuration, the chosen printer, network software versions, and your Internet configuration.
Volume Information	Shows the name, kind, size, free space, SCSI bus, SCSI ID, and other information about your disks.
Device Information	Provides much the same information as the Volume Information report, but focuses on the physical devices, including hard disks, CD-ROM drives, and more.
Control Panel Information	Lists all of your control panels, indicating which are currently turned on. This report can display all control panels, only Apple control panels, or only non-Apple control panels.
Extension Information	Lists all of your extensions, indicating which are currently turned on. This report can display all extensions, only Apple extensions, or only non-Apple extensions.
System Folder Information	Lets you know if more than one System Folder is on your startup disk.
Application Information	Lists the applications on your startup disk.

S-O

System Menu

On the Macintosh: None

Windows provides the system menu in the upper-left corner of every title bar. Commands in the system menu let you minimize, maximize, restore, resize, move, and close the window using either the mouse or the keyboard. The Macintosh has no equivalent to the system menu.

System Monitor

On the Macintosh: About This Computer

The Windows System Monitor utility lets you watch how Windows itself is working. System Monitor provides a vast number of charts, including things like Processor Usage, Disk Cache Size, Unused Physical Memory, and so on.

Although third-party utilities provide some of the same features on the Macintosh (such as the shareware Peek-a-Boo, available from *http://www.clarkwoodsoftware.com/peekaboo*), the Mac OS has nothing comparable—except, perhaps, the About This Computer window, accessible from Apple menu → About This Computer when you're in the Finder. It shows how much memory is allocated to different programs and how much they're actually using, along with the details of the RAM and virtual memory configurations of the Macintosh. For more information, see **Memory Usage**.

T

Tab Key

On the Macintosh: Tab Key

In addition to its traditional function—moving the insertion point to the next Tab stop in a word processor, or advancing to the next cell on a spreadsheet—the Tab key has several special functions on the Macintosh, just as it does in Windows:

- In the Finder, press Tab to select the next icon (alphabetically by name) in the current window. Press Shift-Tab to select the previous icon.

- In dialog boxes (such as Open or Save dialog boxes) or windows with multiple panes, press Tab to move the insertion point from one area to another. For instance, in the Save dialog box, press Tab to switch between the list of files and the text field where you type a name for the file. Similarly, in the Get Info dialog box (select an icon and then choose File → Get Info), press Tab to alternately highlight item's icon and the Comments field.

- In Mac OS 8.5 and later, press Command-Tab to switch between open applications.

Taskbar

On the Macintosh: Application Menu

In Windows, open programs and windows appear as icons in the Taskbar at the bottom of the screen, offering a quick means of switching programs with a single click. On the Macintosh, open programs are listed instead in the application menu in the upper-right corner of the menu bar (see Figure T-1).

In Mac OS 8.5 and later, the application menu's name and icon change to identify the current open program. (In previous OS versions, only the icon, not the name, of the active program appeared.)

Clicking the application menu reveals three commands, along with a list of all the active applications (a checkmark identifies the frontmost application). To switch programs, choose from the application menu. The

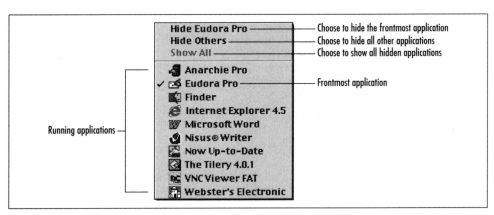

Figure T-1. Application menu

three application menu commands can prove useful:

Hide Application

Hides the front-most application. This Hide command makes all visible aspects of the program's interface disappear—windows, palettes, toolbars, and all. They're not gone, just hidden (or minimized, you might say); to bring them back, choose the program's name from the application menu.

Hide Others

Hides the windows of all programs except the frontmost one. This command can be handy when you find your screen is cluttered and you want to concentrate on a single application, or when you need to view your Desktop in order to drag an icon from it into your email program. If you're used to working in a maximized window in Windows, you may especially appreciate the Hide Others command.

Show All

Displays all windows of all open programs, including any you've hidden. Of course, their windows appear behind those of the frontmost one.

Making the application menu resemble the Taskbar. If you're using Mac OS 8.5 or later, you can turn the application menu into a floating palette of open applications, closely resembling the Windows Taskbar. In fact, you can even move this floating application list to the bottom edge of your screen, where it even more closely simulates the Taskbar. Here's how:

1. Point to the application menu; press the mouse button and drag straight down below the bottom of the now open menu. You'll see a dotted-line rectangle, indicating that you've succeeded in "tearing off" the menu. Release the mouse. The floating palette now on the screen is useful in its own right: a single click on any listed program switches to it.

2. Choose Help → Mac OS Help. In the Search blank, type switcher, and then press Return. Click the help topic called "Switching between open programs."

3. Scroll down in the help window. Click the option called "Open the Application Switcher in a horizontal row in the lower-left corner of the screen and make the window always remain on the screen."

You've created yourself a Macintosh Taskbar. You can adjust the widths of the tiles by dragging the dividing lines horizontally, and you can move this floating taskbar anywhere on the screen by Command-dragging it. For a more Windows-like Taskbar, check out Action GoMac at *http://www. actionutilities.com/site2/html/products/agm. html.*

Text
On the Macintosh: Text

The most common file format on all computer platforms is text, also known as ASCII text after the American Standards Committee for Information Interchange. Text files contain only the characters you can type from the keyboard, without formatting, graphics, sounds, or any other form of binary data. In short, text files are the lowest common denominator between computers, which is why the Web's HTML documents are straight text documents that use specific codes. Any computer can read text files, so basing HTML on text files makes HTML a universally readable format.

Of course, text files are slightly different between platforms. For instance, on the Macintosh, the end-of-line character (such as you get when you press Return) is a carriage return, whereas in Windows, text files use a carriage return/linefeed pair of characters, and Unix text files use a single linefeed character to end each line. The upshot of this is that when you transfer text files from a PC to a Macintosh, you must make sure that the end-of-line characters are translated properly. Most programs that you would use to transfer files between the two systems automatically convert the end-of-line characters appropriately, but if the text file doesn't look right on the other platform, you may have to search and replace to insert the proper end-of-line characters.

Alternatively, use a utility like the Macintosh program Add/Strip, available online at *http://hyperarchive.lcs.mit.edu/ HyperArchive/Archive/text/add-strip-322. hqx*, or the Windows program MacSEE, available at *http://www.reevesoft.com/ macsee_info.htm*.

Text files can differ in one other way between platforms. Only the first 128 characters of the ASCII character set, generally called the lower ASCII characters, are truly standardized, and the Macintosh and Windows may disagree about some of the characters in the upper 128 characters of the ASCII character set. This is seldom a big deal, but occasionally, if someone has relied heavily on characters like the British pound character or the Japanese yen symbol, it might not display correctly on the other platform. The only solution is to perform a search-and-replace in a word processor.

While text files in Windows are identified by the *.txt* extension, text files on the Macintosh seldom have a filename extension.

Title Bar

On the Macintosh: Title Bar

If you've just been plopped in front of a Macintosh, you'll have little trouble using the controls in each window's title bar. They're similar in both operating systems. (See also **Windows**.)

In Windows, a title bar contains the system menu, and the name of the window along with minimize, maximize/restore, and close buttons. You can move the window around the screen by dragging its title bar.

On the Macintosh, title bars contain the name of the window, the close button, the zoom button, and, in Mac OS 8 and later, the collapse button (see Figure T-2). As in Windows, you can drag a window around by dragging the title bar.

Although the names are different, the Windows maximize button and the Macintosh zoom button are roughly equivalent (see **Maximizing Windows**). Similarly, the minimize and collapse buttons are also designed to fulfill the same function; see **Minimizing Windows**. The system menu in Windows lets you resize windows using only the keyboard; there's no such menu in Macintosh windows.

Double-clicking a title bar in Windows is the same as clicking the maximize button; double-clicking a title bar on the Mac OS 8.5 and later is a shortcut for clicking the collapse button (a feature you can turn off in Apple menu → Control Panels → Appearance → Options).

Each Macintosh window also features a close box in the upper-left corner, which closely corresponds to the close box in the upper-right corner of every Windows window. (On the Macintosh, it's possible to close all the windows of particular program without actually quitting the program—a feature that catches some novices, and many former Windows users, by surprise.)

ToolTips

On the Macintosh: Balloon Help, Tool Tips

One of the problems with toolbars and toolbar icons is that you don't always know what an icon does. Microsoft addressed this problem with ToolTips, little yellow rectangles that describe the item underneath the cursor.

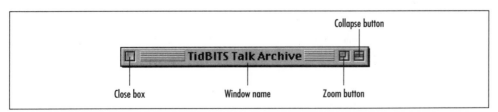

Figure T-2. Macintosh title bar

Although many Macintosh programs offer variations of ToolTips, including programs from Microsoft, Adobe, and others, the Mac OS itself doesn't feature ToolTips to help you identify Macintosh interface components. (Then again, you don't find many unidentified toolbar icons in the Mac OS to begin with.) The Macintosh does, however, offer balloon help, which makes up pop-up descriptive balloon appear to identify a Mac OS icon, menu command, or other element. For a complete discussion, see **Help**.

Trackpad Control Panel
On the Macintosh: Trackpad Control Panel

If you use a PC laptop with a trackpad, you may have a Trackpad control panel that lets you configure the behavior of your trackpad. All Macintosh PowerBooks with trackpads include the Trackpad control panel. Like the Mouse control panel, it lets you set tracking and double-click speed, along with options for using the trackpad for clicking and dragging.

Transferring Files to the Macintosh
On the Macintosh: Transferring Files to Windows

The painful process of transferring files to a Macintosh from a PC running Windows has become significantly easier over the years. You can use various methods, depending on the hardware and software you have available: disks, networks, FTP by Internet, or email. This entry covers only the physical transference of files; for more information about opening or converting the files once you've moved them, see **File Translation**.

Also, no matter how you transfer a file, the Macintosh assigns it a file type based on its filename extension; the File Exchange control panel's file-mapping database controls this assignment so you can change the default mappings if you like, so, for instance, *.txt* files are assigned to a program other than SimpleText. See **File Types** for more information.

Disks. Floppy disks, Zip disks, and similar disks are useful low-tech means of transferring files, especially if the PC and the Macintosh are near one another, or when the computers aren't connected to a network or the Internet.

PCs and Macs use different floppy disk formats; fortunately, the Mac's PC Exchange or File Exchange control panel lets the Macintosh accept disks from Windows PCs. To transfer a file from a PC to a Macintosh, then, just copy it to a PC-formatted floppy disk or Zip disk and insert the disk into the Mac's corresponding drive.

If you prefer to use Macintosh disks in your PC, you'll have to buy an add-on program, such as MacDrive 98 for Windows (*http://www.media4.com/*), Conversions Plus and MacOpener from DataViz (visit *http://www.dataviz.com/*), or MacSEE from Reevesoft (visit *http://www.reevesoft.com/macsee_info.htm*).

Both PC Exchange/File Exchange and its commercial Windows equivalents work with any removable media—floppies, Zip disks, and so on.

Networks. Although both Windows and the Mac OS support networking and can be connected to the same Ethernet network, they don't understand the same network protocols (think of it as a language barrier). Windows uses "File and printer sharing for Microsoft Networks," whereas the Macintosh uses AppleShare. Getting the Macintosh and the PC to speak the same network protocol requires additional software. You have several options.

- Install software like TSStalk from Thursby Software Systems (visit *http://www.thursby.com/*) or PC MACLAN from Miramar Systems (visit *http://www.miramarsys.com/*). These programs let your PC connect to an AppleShare server (such as an everyday Macintosh with file sharing turned on). Then copy files from the PC to the AppleShare server, and if necessary, from the AppleShare server to another Macintosh. (In this arrangement, you bring the Mac's hard disk onto your PC's screen.)

- Use PC MACLAN to run an AppleShare server on a PC. Then connect to the PC MACLAN AppleShare server from the Macintosh, and use the Macintosh to copy files from the PC to the Macintosh. (In this arrangement, you bring the PC's hard disk onto your Mac's screen.)

- Use DAVE from Thursby Software Systems (visit *http://www.thursby.com/*), which provides bidirectional file sharing between Macs and PCs running Windows, although it doesn't use AppleTalk. You install DAVE on both the PC and the Macintosh.

- Install Netopia's Timbuktu Pro (visit *http://www.netopia.com/*) on both the PC and the Macintosh, and then use Timbuktu Pro's built-in file transfer service to move files back and forth. (In this arrangement, you can also view and manipulate one computer's screen in a window on the other computer's screen.)

- If you have a NetWare network, install AppleTalk Filing Protocol on the NetWare server and install MacIPX (which comes with NetWare) on the Macintosh. Doing so lets the Macintosh copy files from the NetWare server, so that you can put a file on the server from a PC, and then copy it down using the Macintosh. For more information, visit *http://www.novell.com/* or talk to a NetWare consultant.

- If you have a Windows NT-based network, install support for Apple File and Print Services. Doing so lets the Macintosh copy files from the NT server, so that you can put a file on the server from a PC, and then copy it down using the Macintosh. For more information, talk to an NT consultant.

- Install Apple's AppleShare IP 6.0 or later (visit *http://www.apple.com/appleshareip/*) on a Macintosh, and then turn on Windows File Sharing, which uses the SMB (Server Message Block) protocol supported by Windows with no additional software. Once you turn on Windows File Sharing in AppleShare IP, the AppleShare IP server appears in the Network Neighborhood like any other Windows server. (In this arrangement, you bring the Mac's hard disk onto your PC's screen.)

Internet: Transferring files by FTP. Transferring files via FTP has two big advantages over the methods previously described. First, the PC and the Macintosh don't have to be near each other or on the same network. Second, doing so doesn't require buying any additional software (although some freeware or inexpensive shareware can simplify the process).

To make this work, you need access to an FTP (File Transfer Protocol) server. You may have one already without even knowing it: most Internet accounts include several megabytes of FTP space. Ask your ISP for details.

If your PC and Macintosh are on the same network, you can run an FTP server on one and connect to it from the other using an FTP client or web browser. Running your own FTP server isn't worth the effort for a single file every now and then, but it might be if you want to transfer files via FTP frequently.

Once you have access to an FTP server, follow these steps:

1. From the PC, run your FTP client and connect to the FTP server.

2. Upload the file from the PC to the FTP server.

3. On the Macintosh, run the Macintosh FTP client or a web browser (web browsers can download from FTP servers but can't generally upload) and connect to the FTP server. If you're using a web browser and need to enter a username and password to access the FTP server, build them into an FTP URL that looks like this:

```
ftp://username:password@ftp.domain.
com/pub/users/tmp/
```

This single address identifies the username, password, machine name for the FTP server, and path to the directory that holds your files. For instance, if I've uploaded a file to my FTP server in the */pub/tidbits/issues/1998* directory,

T-Z

then you have to type the following URL into your web browser to see a list of files in that directory:

```
ftp://ftp.tidbits.com/pub/tidbits/
issues/1998/
```

If you need to enter a username and password to download files from the remote FTP server, you must instead enter something like:

```
ftp://username:password@ftp.tidbits.
com/pub/tidbits/issues/1998/
```

Either way, once you have a directory list, click any filename to download the file—you may need to select where it will appear on your hard disk.

4. Download the file to the Macintosh from the FTP server.

The Mac OS doesn't come with a built-in FTP program. If you don't want to use your web browser, you can download an FTP client from *http://tucows.cyberspacehq.com/mac/ftpmac.html*; try either Anarchie (Stairways Software) or Fetch (Dartmouth College). If you want to set up an FTP server on the Macintosh, check out the shareware NetPresenz from the same company that makes Anarchie—it's at *http://www.stairways.com/*.

Windows includes an FTP client program, but it's a command-line DOS program. Fortunately many better FTP programs are available for Windows, some of which are freeware or shareware. For a list of them (including the shareware FTP server ExpressFS FTP), visit *http://www.winfiles.com/apps/98/ftp.html*.

You can access the Windows FTP client from a DOS shell (Start → Programs → MS-DOS). In the DOS window, type **FTP** followed by the domain name or IP address of the server.

The basic commands you'll need are listed in Table T-1, and you can see a typical session in Figure T-3.

Note

FTP transfers files in either text or binary mode. Windows' FTP client starts in text mode by default. To change to binary mode, type "binary" after you've connected to the FTP server but before you've started file transfer.

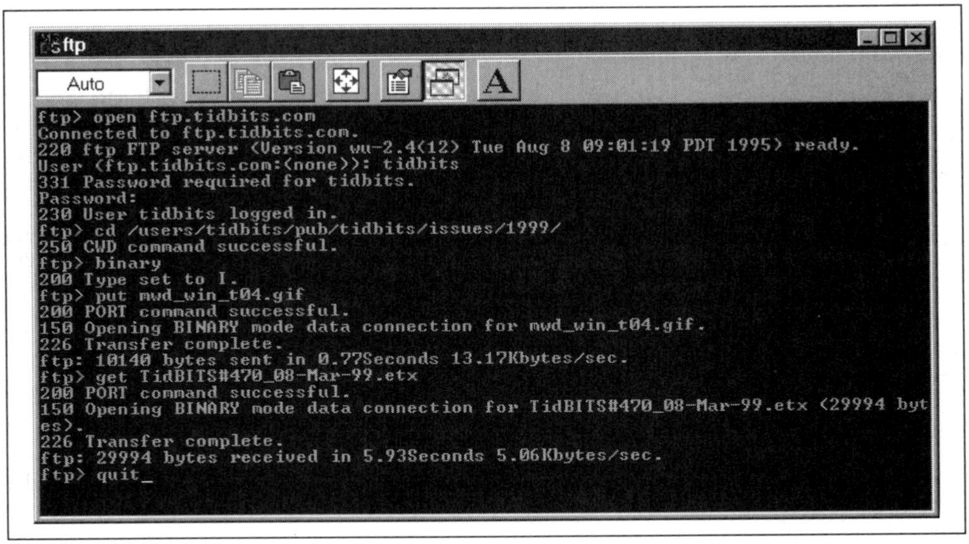

Figure T-3. Typical FTP session

Table T-1. Important FTP Commands

Command	Function
open *ftp.hostname.com*	Opens the connection to the remote FTP server called ftp.hostname.com.
user *username*	Logs you into the FTP server as user *username*. The first time you connect, you're prompted for your username, so you can enter just the username, without the user command.
password *password*	Sends your password to the FTP server. The first time you connect, you're prompted for your password, so you can enter just the password, without the password command.
cd *directory*	Changes the current directory to the specified one.
dir or ls	Lists the files on the remote FTP server.
get *filename*	Retrieves the filename from the remote FTP server.
binary	Sets the file transfer type to binary, which is essential for transferring binary files. The default is ASCII, and if you fail to switch to binary, files that aren't text files may be damaged in transit.
put *filename*	Sends filename to the remote FTP server.
quit	Disconnects from the remote FTP server and exits the FTP program.
help *command*	Displays help information on *command*. For a list of commands, type help by itself.

Email. Email often proves to be the easiest method of sending a file from a PC to a Macintosh. The PC and the Macintosh don't have to be near one another, nor do they have to be connected to an office network. Email often works better than disks, too, because it's much faster.

In practice, however, as any veteran can tell you, not every Macintosh/Windows email file attachment emerges at the other end intact. The reasons are very technical, but they boil down to two problems: encoding differences and incompatibilities with MIME file splitting.

First, any binary components of an email message will be encoded as text. Here's why. Internet email only guarantees 7-bit transfers, so 8-bit files (anything but straight text files) must be encoded to avoid damage. Think of the encoding format as an envelope that protects the file. For this process to succeed, both the sending and receiving program must understand the encoding format used.

The other problem with Macintosh/Windows email attachments is that many email programs split outgoing mail into several chunks, one of which is the attachment. This special formatting system is called MIME, which stands for Multipurpose Internet Mail Extensions. Unfortunately, older email programs may not be MIME-savvy; they may put the encoded attachment in the body of the message instead of recognizing it as an attachment. You, the unlucky recipient, must extract the text and manually decode it with a utility like StuffIt Expander.

In other words, you have two obstacles to successful file transfer by email: attachment encoding formats and MIME. For an attachment to arrive at its destination successfully, the sending and receiving programs must support the same attachment format and recognize MIME for attachments.

In Windows email programs, you may not have the option of turning MIME on or off, depending on the age of the program. But every email program offers a choice of encoding format; Base64 (generally used with MIME) and uuencode (generally used when MIME isn't available) are the most common. A few Windows email programs support BinHex, a Macintosh-specific format.

T-Z

Finding the proper combination of settings is a process of trial and error. Experiment with your email program's settings by sending a small file from your Macintosh to your PC, or vice versa, by email using each of the following settings in turn:

1. BinHex, if available (it's not in Microsoft Outlook Express)
2. Base64
3. uuencode
4. Turn off MIME, and then use uuencode

Once you turn MIME off, there's little point in using anything but uuencode, since programs too old to understand MIME are probably also too old to understand the newer Base64 format. For more information about these file formats (and others you'll see in Macintosh email programs), read "Macintosh Internet File Format Primer" at *http://db.tidbits.com/getbits.acgi?tbart=05066.*

If you receive an email on the Macintosh that's little more than garbled text in the body of the message, the sending program is probably not using MIME. You don't stand much chance of being able to decode the file in that case; if you're determined to try, copy the gobbledygook text, paste it into a new text file, save it, and drop the resulting icon on StuffIt Expander. If that doesn't work, you can try dropping it on Mpack (available at *http://hyperarchive.lcs. mit.edu/HyperArchive/Archive/cmp/mpack-15. hqx*) or YA-Base64 (from *http://www.tss.no/ ~link/NewWatcher/ya/dist/ya-base64-129.hqx*). Don't bet on either of them working, since decoding Base64 manually seldom works.

The best email programs to use for reliable transmission of files to Macs from PCs are those that exist on both platforms, such as Qualcomm's **Eudora** and **Microsoft Outlook Express**.

Tray

On the Macintosh: Menu Bar

A portion of the Windows Taskbar is the Tray, which displays icons for the clock, various system status indicators, and certain utilities. Although the Macintosh has no Tray, some utilities software programs put similar icons on the right side of the menu bar. The Mac's clock appears here, for example.

Troubleshooting

On the Macintosh: Troubleshooting

One of the hardest parts of switching from Windows to the Macintosh is learning how to deal with problems; your Windows experience may not always be helpful.

For complete discussion of troubleshooting the Macintosh, consult a web site like *http:// www.macfixit.com/*, or a book like *Macworld Mac Secrets* (IDG Books) or *Sad Macs, Bombs, and Other Disasters* (Peachpit Press). Here, however, is a basic crash-course in troubleshooting the Macintosh.

- Test to see if the problem is recurrent— quit the program or restart the computer, and then try to recreate the glitch.

- Suspect your extensions (the startup files in System Folder → Extensions folder), which can conflict with each other or with your applications. First, restart the Macintosh while holding down the Shift key to disable extensions. If the problem goes away, an extension is the cause. To figure out which one, use the Apple menu → Control Panels → Extensions Manager program, as described in the sidebar "Mastering the Extensions Manger."

- If the problem is startup related, consider unplugging your SCSI devices, if any.

- If the problem is confined to a single program, consider giving it a larger RAM allotment. To do so, quit the application. Find and highlight its icon on your hard disk; choose File → Get Info. If you see a pop-up menu, choose Memory. Increase the number in the Preferred Size box by 15 percent, and launch the program again.

- Another tip if the problem is confined to a single program: throw away the program's preferences file. You'll find this easily corrupted file in System Folder → Preferences. The next time

Mastering the Extensions Manager

Just as Windows offers features (such as the Taskbar) that simply don't exist on the Macintosh, so the Macintosh offers useful tools with no twin in Windows. One of the most important is Extensions Manager, which is among the Mac's most potent troubleshooting tools. (See Figure S-10.)

You summon this special program by choosing Apple menu → Control Panels → Extensions Manager—or by pressing the Spacebar as the Macintosh starts up. The resulting window lists every extension, control panel, and startup program on your Macintosh. ore importantly, Extensions Manager lets you turn these items on or off by clicking the checkbox next to each. The next time you restart the Macintosh, your new configuration of extensions and control panels takes effect.

Controlling which extensions and control panels load at startup in this way is especially useful when you're troubleshooting a Macintosh. Control panels and extensions occasionally conflict, causing glitches or even crashes. In such a situation, you might use Extensions Manager like this:

First, start up the Macintosh with the Shift key pressed (the equivalent of Windows Safe Mode); you've just turned off all extensions and control panels. If possible, test the application in question again. If the glitch or problem has gone away, open the Extensions Manager.

Turn off half of your extensions and control panels. (Three sources await for figuring out each one's purpose: the Show Item Information button on the Extensions Manager screen; the book Macworld Mac Secrets; or the shareware document InformINIT at *http://www.informinit.com/*.) Then click the Restart button at the bottom of the window.

If the Macintosh doesn't exhibit whatever unpleasant behavior you've been having, one of the extensions you turned off was probably at fault. If the Macintosh does crash or act balky again, repeat the whole process, but this time turn some more extensions off.

Through trial and error, you eventually should be able to figure out which extension is causing the problem. Occasionally the problem is caused by the interaction of two extensions; sometimes, just renaming one so that it alphabetically precedes its enemy is enough to solve the problem.

If all of this sounds like a lot of work, consider buying a program like Conflict Catcher (*http://www.casadyg.com/*). Conflict Catcher does many useful things for managing your extensions, but its main virtue is catching conflicts. It automates the trial-and-error process previously described, ultimately identifying the recalcitrant extension on its own.

you launch the program, the Macintosh will create a fresh and untarnished preferences file for the program in question.

As on Windows, reinstalling the program may solve the problem.

• If all else fails, performing a clean installation of the System Folder is among the most effective and powerful troubleshooting steps you can perform. Fortunately, doing so on a Macintosh is not nearly as complex and

lengthy a procedure as on Windows. See **Clean Install** for instructions.

• When hard disk problems strike—documents can't be saved or copied, for example—run the Disk First Aid program included with every Macintosh.

TrueType
On the Macintosh: TrueType

TrueType is an outline font technology developed by Apple and cross-licensed to Microsoft in exchange for a PostScript clone

T–Z

called TrueImage. Apple got the short end of that deal, since TrueType has become the standard outline font technology in both the Mac OS and in Windows, whereas nothing much ever happened with TrueImage.

You can convert Macintosh TrueType fonts to Windows using the shareware utility TT FontConvert, available at *http://www. netmagic.net/~evan/shareware/*. To convert Windows TrueType fonts for use on the Macintosh, check out TTconverter, available at *ftp://members.aol.com/raymarkcd/ ttconverter.hqx*.

For more information about fonts in general, including where to store the font files, see **Fonts**.

TweakUI
On the Macintosh: ResEdit

If you want to customize Windows interface settings more than is normally possible using the standard control panels, you can use TweakUI. There's no precise equivalent of TweakUI on the Macintosh, although a wide variety of shareware and commercial programs let you tweak different parts of the Mac OS.

However, what the Macintosh does have is ResEdit, which is short for Resource Editor. Many of the interface elements of standard Macintosh programs, such as menus, icons, and pictures, are technically known as resources that are stored in the resource fork of every Macintosh file or program. You can edit almost anything in the resource fork of a file with ResEdit.

ResEdit is primarily for programmers, and it has few protections to prevent you from making mistakes and crippling your applications. You can't, for instance, just add a menu to an application and expect it to work, and doing so may prevent other parts of the application from working.

Most Macintosh users who dare to use ResEdit use it for slight modifications to well-known parts of applications—to give a menu command in a favorite program a new keyboard shortcut, for example. Even then, few people attempt ResEdit modifications without detailed instructions (from a book or magazine, for example). Should you have the necessary instructions, you can download ResEdit from *http://asu.info. apple.com/swupdates.nsf/artnum/n10964*.

U

Undo

On the Macintosh: Undo

The Mac's Undo command, available from Edit → Undo, works much like it does in Windows, although it can't undo Finder actions like moving or deleting a file. Even its keystroke is equivalent: Command-Z.

USB

On the Macintosh: USB

USB, or Universal Serial Bus, is an increasingly popular technology for connecting slow or medium-speed devices to computers. USB connectors and cables can transfer data at up to 12 megabits per second, which makes them useful for gadgets like keyboards, mice, graphics tablets, joysticks, floppy disk drives, Zip drives, scanners, and digital cameras.

Although USB has been available for years in the Windows world, the typical Windows-world chaos of competing drivers and incompatible standards has caused instability in the USB racket, which in turn dissuades users and vendors from adopting USB with more enthusiasm.

In the Macintosh world, however, USB is a stable and increasingly popular standard. All current Macintosh desktop models, including the popular iMac, feature USB jacks. By attaching an inexpensive USB hub to one of the Mac's available USB ports, or even stringing one USB hub to another, Macintosh users can theoretically connect up to 127 printers, scanners, hard disks, and other devices to a single computer—in addition to the keyboard and mouse, which are standard USB devices on all current Macintosh models.

For more information about USB itself and availability of USB-based peripherals, visit *http://www.usb.org/*. For information about USB on the Macintosh, see Apple's page on the topic at *http://www.apple.com/usb/*.

User Profiles

*On the Macintosh: Location Manager
Control Panel, Multiple Users Control Panel*

Windows is nominally a multiple-user system: Using the Users control panel, you can set up Windows to prompt you for a username and password when you turn on the machine. The information you enter at that point changes what you see on the Desktop and in the Start menu, along with settings for email and web favorites.

In contrast, the Macintosh before MacOS 9 is essentially a single-user system and never prompts users for passwords at startup. (The Multiple Users control panel of Mac OS 9, on the other hand, behaves exactly like an easier-to-use version of the Windows-like user profiles.)

On the other hand, you can simulate some multiple-user features using the Location Manager, which was designed to switch between sets of settings for PowerBook users and other people who used Macs in different places. To create different working environments, just create two "locations," one for each user. To create a location, follow these steps:

1. Open Apple menu → Control Panels → Location Manager.

2. Choose File → New Location and name your new location.

3. Once you've created two locations, associate specific settings with each location by selecting a setting in the list and clicking Edit (see Figure U-1). Note that many of the settings require you to create sets in another control panel

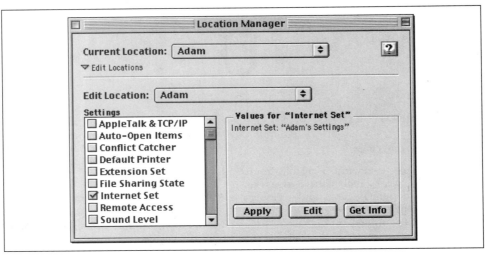

Figure U-1. Location Manager control panel.

before you can manage them in the Location Manager control panel.

See Table U-1 for an explanation of the different settings, and for more information about any of them, select it in the Location Manager control panel and click Get Info. The most important settings for simulating user profiles are Extension Set, Internet Set, and Remote Access.

Table U-1. Settings Available to the Location Manager

Setting	Function
AppleTalk & TCP/IP	Network settings primarily of use for PowerBooks that move on and off different networks.
Auto-Open Items	Use this setting to open files, folders, or network servers automatically when you switch to the associated location. You could automatically open a different user's email settings, documents folder, and the like.
Default Printer	Switch to a different default printer. Primarily useful for traveling Power-Books.
Extension Set	Use this setting to choose which extensions should load for each set. Along with the fact that some extensions may not be appropriate in different locations, this setting also enables different users to load completely different sets of system-modifying extensions.
File Sharing State	Turns File Sharing on or off depending on the chosen location. Useful primarily with PowerBooks that are often disconnected from a network.
Internet Set	Use this setting to switch between sets of Internet settings, which can be specific to each user. Very important for multiple users.
Remote Access	Use this setting to choose between different ways of connecting to the Internet or to other Macs. Although this may seem primarily useful for traveling PowerBooks, since many people have separate Internet accounts (one at a business, the other at a university, say), this setting is also useful for multiple user situations.

Table U-1. Settings Available to the Location Manager (continued)

Setting	Function
Sound Level	Switches sound levels for different locations (turn it off on planes) or user preferences.
Time Zone	Use this setting if you regularly move between different time zones and can associate them with specific locations. Useless for multiple users.

Uuencode

On the Macintosh: uuencode

Uuencode is a method of converting 8-bit binary files into 7-bit text files. It's used mostly for Internet email attachments, since Internet email guarantees only 7-bit trans- fers. Uuencode is relatively common in the PC world, but much less so in the Macintosh world. For more information on when to use uuencode for email attachments, see the "Email" section of **Transferring Files to the Macintosh**.

U-Z

V

Video Connector
On the Macintosh: Monitor Port

PCs generally have only a standard 15-pin video connector these days, but in the more controlled world of the Macintosh, there are in fact four different video connectors (usually referred to as monitor ports) in use.

"Standard" Apple monitor port. The most common, though recently discontinued, monitor port, found on pre-1999 Power Macintosh models, among others, is a 15-pin port with two rows of pins (see Figure V-1), as opposed to the three rows in the standard VGA connector. To connect a multisync monitor to this port, you need an adapter. These adapters are usually available from the company that makes the monitor, often for free, and you can buy more full-featured adapters that provide switches for different resolutions and other settings. Be careful with the free adapters—sometimes they restrict you to specific resolutions.

Standard VGA 15-pin monitor port. In a welcome move toward standardizing with the PC world, current Power Macs and the PowerBook G3 Series use the same 3-row 15-pin VGA-style video connector to which you're accustomed on the PC (see Figure V-2). Ironically, these PowerBooks come with an adapter as well, in case you want to connect a Macintosh-specific monitor with the 2-row 15-pin connector.

VID-14 PowerBook monitor port. The PowerBook 500 and 5300 series laptops feature unusual VID-14 monitor connectors. These PowerBooks come with adapter cables that convert the VID-14 (a thin connector, required because of the PowerBook's slim design) into the fatter Apple 15-pin connector.

HDI-45 monitor port. The Power Macintosh 6100, 7100, and 8100 have an unusual HDI-45 monitor port. The 7100 and 8100 also sport the standard Apple 15-pin monitor port, which makes it easy to hook up multiple monitors to those computers (no additional video adapter is necessary). Like the VID-14 monitor port, you need an adapter to convert the HDI-45 pin layout to the standard Apple 15-pin layout. That adapter comes with the 6100 but must be purchased separately for the other machines.

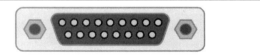

Figure V-1. Standard Apple monitor port

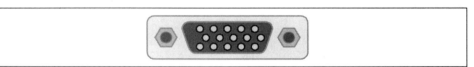

Figure V-2. Standard VGA 15-pin monitor port

View Menu
On the Macintosh: View Menu

As in Windows, you can view the icons in a Macintosh window in several different ways. Most of the commands you're used to seeing in the View menu (or the contextual menu for any window) have close relatives on the Macintosh, as follows:

Toolbar, Status Bar. These commands have no equivalent on the Macintosh.

Explorer Bar, as Web Page, Customize This Folder (Windows 98). As part of its Browser Über Alles strategy, Microsoft has created web browser-like toolbars that you can graft onto normal Desktop windows. The Mac OS offers no equivalent features.

Icon and List views. Windows offers two ways of viewing icons in a window: Large Icons and Small Icons. The Macintosh offers similar views; as in Windows, you can specify every window's view independently.

When you're in Icon view on the Macintosh (choose View → as Icons when the desired window is open), you can choose View → View Options to set the icon size to large or small, thus mimicking the Large Icons and Small Icons views in Windows. The same View Options dialog box offers options to align the Windows icons to an invisible grid, or keep them sorted (by name, modification date, creation date, size, kind, or label) even if the number of icons changes or you resize the window (see Figure V-3).

List view. The Macintosh has no built-in equivalent to the Windows List view, in which icons are aligned in multiple columns, which may require horizontally scrolling to see them all. But creating the same effect is easy enough: open a Macintosh window, choose View → as Icons, choose View → View Options, click the smallest icon size, click the Keep arranged button, specify a sorting criterion, and click OK.

Details view. On the Macintosh, the single-column view known as Details view in Windows is called List view (choose View → as List). In successive columns to the right of the filenames, you can see each file's size, kind, and modification date. You can add other columns, such as Creation Date, Label, Comments, and Version, by choosing View → View Options and then clicking the corresponding checkboxes.

Other unique options available in the Mac's View Options dialog (see Figure V-4) are:

Use relative date
When this option is turned on, your list view identifies appropriate modification and creation dates as "Today," "Yesterday," and even (if you've been fiddling with your Mac's clock) "Tomorrow," instead of showing the actual corresponding dates.

Calculate folder sizes
Macintosh list views, like the corresponding Windows views, show blanks for the sizes of folders; actual sizes are displayed only for files. On the Macintosh, however, you can turn this option on; after a moment of computation, you'll see the size of every folder in your list view displayed. (As with all of these features, this one applies only to the current open window.)

Table V-1 summarizes how the different views compare.

Arrange Icons. In Windows, you can arrange icons in any of the views by name, type, size, or date. In Macintosh icon views, those same options and more are available from View → Arrange. To force Macintosh icons to remain sorted even if the window size changes or the number of icons changes, choose View → View Options → Keep Arranged.

When you're in List view on the Macintosh, the Keep Arranged command changes to View → Sort List; it can sort the files in the window by any criterion for which a column is visible.

Line Up Icons. When you're in an icon view, you may want to get your icons to line up in neat rows. In Windows, that's done with View → Line Up Icons; on the Macintosh, you use View → Clean Up.

Refresh. There's no equivalent to View → Refresh on the Macintosh because it's unnecessary. The Finder watches for new or

T-Z

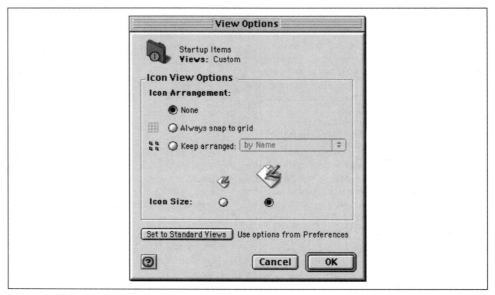

Figure V-3. View Options for Icon view

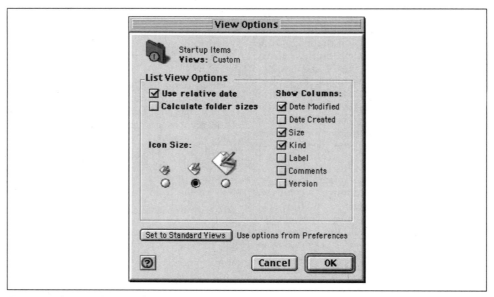

Figure V-4. View Options for List view

deleted files and updates the window display automatically.

Folder Options (Windows 98) / Options (Windows 95). The Windows View → Folder Options command lets you configure how Desktop windows look and act to an incredible degree. The Mac OS doesn't offer as much control; on the other hand, many of the options in the General tab are related

Table V-1. View Comparisons

Windows View	Macintosh View
Large Icons	Icon view, with the large icon size selected in View → View Options
Small Icons	Icon view, with the small icon size selected in View → View Options
List	Icon view, with the small icon size and Keep Arranged by Name option selected in View → View Options
Details	List
Equivalent view requires custom settings	Button

to the Windows 98 pseudo-web browser feature not found on the Macintosh.

View tab

Most of the options in View → Folder Options → View tab pertain to filenames, offering control over capitalization and filename extensions; because these filename restrictions don't exist on the Macintosh, you won't find an equivalent comands.

One View → Folder Options → View option does have a Macintosh equivalent, however: Like Current Folder. You can indeed establish one set of Windows settings that all subsequently created Windows adopt. To do so (in Mac OS 8.5 and later), choose Edit → Preferences → Views to set the default options. You can specify these options independently for list and icon views. The changes you make here will apply to any window whose look you haven't changed. (If you have changed the view options for a particular window, you can make it "snap back" to the standard options you establish here by clicking View → View Options → Set to Standard Views.)

File Types tab

The Macintosh has no equivalent for the View → Folder Options → File Types tab; behind the scenes, every Macintosh files has creator and type codes that link documents to the applications that created them (see **File Types**). You don't have to manually associate filename extensions with particular applications on the Macintosh.

Tricks and tips. As in Windows, the Macintosh list view is filled with clickable inter-

face elements that let you manipulate such a window to your heart's content:

- In Mac OS 8.5 and later, you can drag the names of columns in list view (except the Name column) to rearrange them, as you can in Windows 98. (Choose View → Reset Column Positions to reset those column positions to their factory defaults.)

- You can also adjust the relative widths of the columns by dragging the dividing line between their names, exactly as in Windows.

- In both the Windows Details view and the Macintosh List view, you can sort the list by clicking the column titles at the top of the window. To sort the list in the opposite direction (Z to A, for example), click the tiny pyramid above the right scrollbar (an option in Mac OS 8.1 and later).

Virtual Memory
On the Macintosh: Virtual Memory

See **Memory Usage**.

Viruses
On the Macintosh: Viruses

The virus problem is far more serious in the PC world than on the Macintosh—according to some sources, there are over 40,000 viruses and virus variants, fewer than 100 of which run on the Macintosh. Furthermore, few Macintosh viruses are as unpleasant as PC viruses, which often try to erase files or damage your hard disk. The most destructive Macintosh viruses simply display a

T-Z

taunting message, make the Macintosh feel slower, and so on.

If your Macintosh becomes infected, consider an antivirus program such as Norton AntiVirus for Macintosh (*http://www. symantec.com/avcenter/vinfodb.html*) or Dr. Solomon's Virex for Macintosh (*http://www. drsolomon.com/products/virex/index.cfm*).

Today, only two viruses pose any threat at all to the Macintosh, and both are extremely easy to defeat. First is the AutoStart virus—to make your Macintosh invulnerable to it, choose Apple menu → Control Panels → QuickTime Settings → AutoPlay, and turn off the Enable CD-ROM AutoPlay option. Now your computer can't be infected by the AutoStart virus.

The other concern is Word macro viruses, which are just as dangerous on the Macintosh as on Windows. Both Norton AntiVirus and Dr. Solomon's Virex can help find and eliminate Word macro viruses on the Macintosh. Furthermore, whenever you open a document containing Word macro files, Word 98 on the Macintosh offers to disable macros in documents when you're opening them—a convenient solution that rules out any possibility that the document you're about to open will infect your system.

VL-Bus Slots and Cards
On the Macintosh: PCI Slots and Cards

See **PCI Slots and Cards**.

Volume Control
On the Macintosh: Monitors & Sound Control Panel

In Windows, you can adjust your speaker volume using the corresponding icon on your Taskbar Tray. On the Macintosh, you'll find precisely the same control on your Control Strip (see **Tray**).

For more control over a Windows PC's sound, you can also use the Volume Control application in Start → Programs → Accessories → Entertainment. On the Macintosh, the equivalent program is Apple menu → Control Panels → Monitors & Sound → Sound (see Figure V-5). Here, you can adjust the Computer System Volume and Balance, as well as specify sound input and output options. By clicking the Alerts icon at the top of the window, you can also adjust the volume of your error beeps.

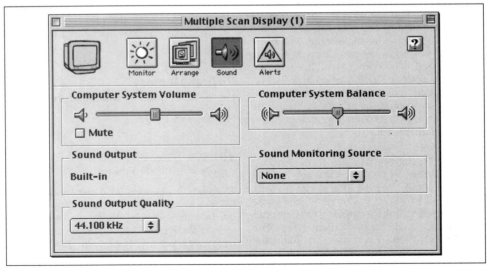

Figure V-5. Monitors & Sound volume settings

W

Wallpaper
On the Macintosh: Background

In Windows, you can apply a pattern "wallpaper" to your Desktop (talk about a mixed metaphor!). To do the same on the Macintosh, see **Background**.

Web Sites for Macintosh Software and Information
On the Macintosh: Web Sites for Windows Software and Information

The Web is full of useful Macintosh software and information; here are some of the best sites.

Apple Computer Support. When you're having trouble with a Macintosh, go to the source. Apple's Support Web pages offer a huge amount of information. Especially useful is the Tech Info Library, which contains thousands of tech notes covering every problem Apple has documented. See *http://www.apple.com/support/*.

Apple Mailing List Directory. Often the best way to find the answer to a question is to ask on a mailing list, but how do you find the appropriate list? Simple: search Apple's mailing list directory. It may not be complete, but it's a good start. See *http://www.lists.apple.com/*.

Info-Mac HyperArchive. Info-Mac is both a digest-based mailing list for issues related to the Macintosh and the most complete archive of Macintosh freeware and shareware programs on the planet. Although numerous mirrors of the Info-Mac Archive exist, the easiest way to find files in it is via the Info-Mac HyperArchive at MIT. See *http://hyperarchive.lcs.mit.edu/HyperArchive.html*.

MacFixIt. Ted Landau is the author of a comprehensive Macintosh troubleshooting book, *Sad Macs, Bombs, and Other Disasters*, and his associated MacFixIt site is an invaluable repository of bug reports, conflicts, and troubleshooting information. See *http://www.macfixit.com/*.

MacInTouch. Ric Ford's MacInTouch web site offers some of the best Macintosh-related news on the Web. It's definitely worth a visit if you're trying to track down a conflict or compatibility issue. See *http://www.macintouch.com/*.

MacWindows. The MacWindows web site is the most appropriate for readers of this book, because it focuses on information of interest to people using both Macs and Windows-based PCs—or switching from one platform to another. See *http://www.macwindows.com/*.

Macworld Magazine. *Macworld* magazine remains the best source for high-quality hardware and software reviews. Since *Macworld* has the only testing lab in the Macintosh industry, its hardware comparison articles are the most comprehensive. (This book's authors both write for *Macworld*.) See *http://www.macworld.com/*.

TidBITS. Adam Engst, one of this book's authors, has been publishing *TidBITS* since 1990, making it one of the oldest Internet publications. Every week *TidBITS* offers news, reviews, technical information, and industry analysis. Perhaps the highest compliment *TidBITS* has received comes in the form of the large number of Windows users who read it, though much of the information is Macintosh-specific. See *http://www.tidbits.com/*.

T-Z

WIN Key

On the Macintosh: None

Most modern PC keyboards feature a left and right WIN (Windows-logo) key. (It's generally located next to the Alt key.) Pressing and releasing it opens the Start menu; it also triggers a few special commands (WIN-F summons the Windows Find command; WIN-M hides all Windows and returns to the Desktop).

The Macintosh has no equivalent.

Windows

On the Macintosh: Windows

Windows can attach a wide variety of toolbars and other window dressing to its standard Desktop windows, which isn't true of the standard Mac OS windows (see Figure W-1).

Macintosh windows can be free-floating, as you'd expect from Windows, or they can dock to the bottom of the screen. Docked windows have only a title bar that looks like a file folder tab (see Figure W-2).

You can find extensive information on manipulating and understanding Macintosh windows in **List Views**, **Minimizing Windows**, **Title Bar**, **Resizing Windows**, and **View Menu**. In the meantime, here's a crash course on Macintosh windows:

- Move a window by dragging its title bar, exactly as on Windows, or by dragging its puffy gray edges.

- Close a window by clicking the tiny square in the upper-left corner.

- Resize a window by dragging the square handle in the lower-right corner.

- Scroll a Desktop window in any direction by Command-dragging inside it (or, of course, by using the scroll bars).

- You can "zoom" a window, making it expand until it's exactly large enough to fit everything inside it (subject to the limits of your screen) by clicking the

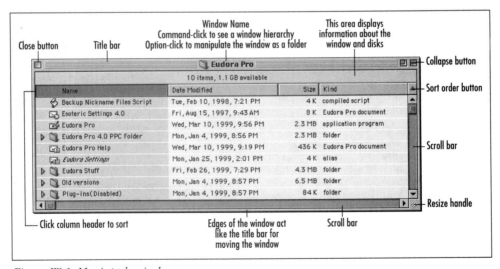

Figure W-1. Macintosh window

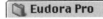

Figure W-2. Docked Macintosh window

first of the two upper-right title bar squares. Click that button again to restore the window to its original size.

- You can collapse, or "window shade" a window, by clicking the tiny square at the far right of its title bar (Mac OS 8 and later). Doing so makes the area of the window itself disappear, so that only the title bar remains floating on the screen. Click that button again to restore the window.

- If you drag the title bar of the Desktop window all the way to the bottom edge of the screen, it "docks," turning into a tab hugging the bottom of the screen. You just created a pop-up window. Click the tab to make the window pop into view; click outside the window (or double-click something inside the window) to make the window collapse back into a tab. (Turn it back into a regular window by dragging the tab upward all the way.)

- Use the View menu to do the same kinds of things you would do in Windows—change to list view, icon view, and so on.

Windows Folder
On the Macintosh: System Folder, Folders

The Windows folder in Windows, located in your main hard disk window, is the equivalent of the Mac OS's System Folder: it contains the operating system itself. You may be pleased to notice that the Macintosh System Folder is better organized than the Windows folder; instead of hundreds of loose files, the Macintosh System Folder contents are neatly organized into folders.

The most important files in the System Folder are the System, Finder, and (on iMacs and other recent models) the Mac OS ROM files. Without these files in their factory-installed locations, the Macintosh cannot boot. For information on the most important folders within the System Folder, see **Folders**.

Moving or renaming files in the Windows folder could cause Windows to stop working. The Mac OS is far more forgiving, but

caution is still advised. Actually, adding new files to the System Folder generally isn't a problem; in fact, if you drop certain kinds of files onto the System Folder icon (such as fonts, control panels, sounds, extensions, and so on) the Mac OS automatically deposits them into the appropriate folder within the System Folder. Removing files is riskier; if you're careful, however, you're unlikely to cause any damage.

For detailed information about every file you're likely to find in your System Folder, consult a book like David Pogue's *Macworld Mac Secrets*, or download a copy of Dan Frakes's shareware InformINIT document from *http:// www.informinit.com/*.

Windows Messaging
On the Macintosh: Microsoft Outlook Express

Microsoft's name for its email and communications features has changed several times. (In Windows 98, these features have found a home in the standalone Microsoft Outlook Express program.) The Mac OS has no built-in email program, but Outlook Express is included with every Macintosh. For more information, see **Microsoft Outlook Express**.

Windows Scripting Host
On the Macintosh: AppleScript

Windows Scripting Host (Windows 98 and later) lets you automate Windows using a variety of scripting languages. On the Macintosh, the best known scripting language is AppleScript, but you can also control the operating system using scripting languages like Frontier, or even parts of common Unix scripting languages, including Perl. For more information on AppleScript, see **Batch Language**.

Wizard
On the Macintosh: Assistant

It's common in Windows for a wizard, a small program, to walk you through such tasks as installing a new printer, screen by screen, prompting you for one piece of

W-Z

information after another until the task is complete.

On the Macintosh, wizards are sometimes known as assistants. You don't encounter them as often on the Macintosh as in Windows, but AppleWorks (included with every iMac and iBook) offers dozens of them, and you run into Internet and Macintosh Setup assistants the first time you turn on a new Macintosh.

Windows Help
On the Macintosh: Help

To read about the Mac's online help systems, see **Help**.

WordPad
On the Macintosh: SimpleText

Windows comes with both NotePad, a simple, no-formatting text editor, and Word-Pad, which lets you specify fonts, sizes, and styles for your text. The Mac OS equivalent of WordPad is SimpleText, which offers a similar level of formatting and editing features. SimpleText can also find text in a document, display graphics, record and play back sounds, and speak selected text.

Unlike WordPad, SimpleText can open only documents that contain less than 32K of text, although if a document is larger than 32K because of included graphics or sounds, SimpleText can open it. SimpleText cannot open Word files, as WordPad can, nor does it offers such advanced word processing features as bullet lists and rulers.

Few Macintosh users use SimpleText to create documents; it's mostly used as a reader for ReadMe files. As a result, finding SimpleText can be tricky. Look first in Macintosh HD → Utilities; if it's not there, choose File → Find and search for SimpleText. It's common for each program you install to donate an additional copy of SimpleText, so you may find multiple copies—feel free to throw out all but the most recent one (check dates by scanning the Date Modified column of the Find window).

Z

Zip

On the Macintosh: StuffIt

The standard compression and archiving format in Windows is Zip. Although Macs can create and open Zip archives (using, for example, Aladdin's StuffIt program), the primary compression and archiving format on the Macintosh is the StuffIt format. You can identify a "stuffed" file by the letters *.sit* at the end of its name, just as the letters *.zip* identify a Zip file.

Because StuffIt is a proprietary format, most of the software available for working with StuffIt archives comes from Aladdin (or is based on software modules from Aladdin). To survive in the Macintosh world, you'll probably need, sooner or later, some of the following programs (all of which can be found at *http://www.aladdinsys.com*):

Expansion. StuffIt Expander is a simple utility that can expand any StuffIt archive, along with many other formats, including Zip. (StuffIt Expander is included with every new Macintosh; use your Apple menu → Sherlock command to locate it.) When you download a file from the Internet, most email or web browser programs automati-cally launch StuffIt Expander to expand the newly arrived software.

If you receive a file attachment by email that doesn't automatically expand in this way, you may have to drag the file's *.sit* icon onto the StuffIt Expander icon. (Many Macintosh users leave the StuffIt Expander icon, or an alias of it, on the Desktop for just this purpose.)

Compression. You can create StuffIt archives using, for example, the shareware Drop-Stuff or the commercial StuffIt Deluxe. DropStuff works like StuffIt Expander—just drag one or more file icons on its icon to create a compressed StuffIt archive containing those files. StuffIt Deluxe is more like WinZip: it lets you add files to, and remove files from, the archive by dragging them into and out of what looks like a standard Desktop window.

Working with Zip archives. Despite the dominance of the StuffIt format on the Macintosh, Zip archives aren't uncommon. StuffIt Expander can expand them, as previously noted, but to create or manipulate Zip archives, use the shareware utility ZipIt, available from author Tom Brown at *http://www.awa.com/softlock/zipit/zipit.html*.

About the Authors

Adam Engst is the publisher of *TidBITS*, a free email and web publication that reports on topics of interest to the Macintosh Internet community (visit *http://www.tidbits.com/*). He has also written numerous computer books, including the best-selling *Internet Starter Kit for Macintosh* and *Internet Starter Kit for Windows* series.

David Pogue (*http://www.davidpogue.com/*) writes the award-winning Desktop Critic column for *Macworld* magazine. His 15 bestselling books include *PalmPilot: The Ultimate Guide, The iMac for Dummies*, and *Macworld Mac Secrets*.

Colophon

Our look is the result of reader comments, our own experimentation, and feedback from distribution channels. Distinctive covers complement our distinctive approach to technical topics, breathing personality and life into potentially dry subjects.

The animals featured on the cover of *Crossing Platforms: A Macintosh/Windows Phrasebook* are a European edible frog (*Rana esculenta*) and an Eastern cottontail rabbit (*Sylvilagus floridanus*).

The European edible frog has been found all over Europe, with the exception of Spain, for many centuries, possibly as far back as the days of the cave man. This type of frog is mostly aquatic, leaving its pond only to travel to another source of water or sometimes to eat. Its diet consists of worms, beetles, various insects, and even butterflies. The male's unique mating call is a vociferous, rattle-like croak, amplified by two inflated sacs, one on either side of his face. One female can lay 5000–10,000 eggs per breeding season. Metamorphosis of the larvae into the frog takes a few months, and sexual maturity occurs at around two years. An adult frog is three inches in length. Because their legs are considered a delicacy, European edible frogs have been hunted by humans for centuries.

The Eastern cottontail rabbit is one of the most widely known small wild mammals in the United States, as well as one of the most prolific. Commonly found in the woods and undergrowth of the eastern half of the U.S., this rabbit grows to 14–17 inches, weighs about three pounds, and features its trademark two-inch snow-white cottony tail. Its diet includes virtually all grasses, vegetables, bark, and berries. Conversely, it is a source of food for almost every carnivorous animal as well as snakes and various larger birds. Although this type of rabbit can live up to eight years, every year two-thirds of the population dies, mostly from predators, leaving the remaining third to replenish the species in the following Spring. In one breeding season, a single rabbit can have up to five litters, with each litter producing up to seven babies.

Clairemarie Fisher O'Leary was the production editor and copyeditor for *Crossing Platforms: A Macintosh/Windows Phrasebook*. Nancy Wolfe Kotary was the production manager. Jane Ellin and Maureen Dempsey provided quality control. Mike Sierra provided FrameMaker technical support.

Edie Freedman designed the cover of this book, using a 19th-century engraving from the Dover Pictorial Archive. The cover layout was produced with Quark-XPress 3.32 using the ITC Garamond font. Whenever possible, our books use RepKover™, a durable and flexible lay-flat binding. If the page count exceeds RepKover's limit, perfect binding is used.

The inside layout was designed by Alicia Cech and implemented in FrameMaker 5.5 by Mike Sierra. The text fonts are ITC Garamond Light and Garamond Book and the heading fonts are Franklin Gothic Light and Franklin Gothic Book. The illustrations that appear in the book were produced by Robert Romano and Rhon Porter using Macromedia FreeHand 8 and Adobe Photoshop 5. This colophon was written by Nicole Arigo.

 # More Titles from O'Reilly

In a Nutshell Quick References

Windows 98 in a Nutshell

By Tim O'Reilly, Troy Mott & Walter Glenn
1st Edition August 1999
642 pages, ISBN 1-56592-486-X

From the authors of the bestselling *Windows 95 in a Nutshell* comes this easy-to-use quick reference for all serious users of Windows 98. It summarizes differences between Windows 95 and Windows 98, covers almost every Windows 98 command and utility available, gives advice for using the Registry, includes short-hand instructions on many important Win98 tasks, and much more.

Mac OS in a Nutshell

By Rita Lewis
1st Edition June 2000 (est.)
376 pages (est.), ISBN 1-56592-533-5

Mac OS in a Nutshell is a comprehensive, compact reference for serious users of Mac OS that systematically unveils little-known details of the operating system in a consistent reference format. It covers almost every command and utility, Internet configuration and access, and clever ways to do familiar and not-so-familiar tasks.

PC Hardware in a Nutshell

By Robert Bruce Thompson & Barbara Frichtman Thompson
1st Edition March 2000 (est.)
450 pages (est.), ISBN 1-56592-599-8

PC Hardware in a Nutshell is a comprehensive guide to buying, building, upgrading, and repairing Intel-based PCs for novices and seasoned professionals alike. It features buying guidelines, how-to advice on installing, configuring, and troubleshooting specific components, plus ample reference material and a complete case study on building a PC from components.

Windows 95 in a Nutshell

By Tim O'Reilly & Troy Mott
1st Edition June 1998
528 pages, ISBN 1-56592-316-2

A comprehensive, compact reference that systematically unveils what serious users of Windows 95 will find interesting and useful, capturing little known details of the operating system in a consistent reference format.

Windows Programming

Learning DCOM

By Thuan L. Thai
1st Edition April 1999
502 pages, ISBN 1-56592-581-5

This book introduces C++ programmers to DCOM and gives them the basic tools they need to write secure, maintainable programs. It clearly describes the C++ code needed to create distributed components and the communications exchanged between systems and objects, providing background, a guide to Visual C++ development tools and wizards, and insight for performance tuning, debugging, and understanding what the system is doing with your code.

Learning Perl on Win32 Systems

By Randal L. Schwartz,
Erik Olson & Tom Christiansen
1st Edition August 1997
306 pages, ISBN 1-56592-324-3

In this carefully paced course, leading Perl trainers and a Windows NT practitioner teach you to program in the language that promises to emerge as the scripting language of choice on NT. Based on the "llama" book, this book features tips for PC users and new NT-specific examples, along with a foreword by Larry Wall, the creator of Perl, and Dick Hardt, the creator of Perl for Win32.

O'REILLY®

TO ORDER: **800-998-9938** • **order@oreilly.com** • **http://www.oreilly.com/**
OUR PRODUCTS ARE AVAILABLE AT A BOOKSTORE OR SOFTWARE STORE NEAR YOU.
FOR INFORMATION: **800-998-9938** • **707-829-0515** • **info@oreilly.com**

Windows Programming

Inside the Windows 95 File System

By Stan Mitchell
1st Edition May 1997
378 pages, Includes diskette
ISBN 1-56592-200-X

In this book, Stan Mitchell describes the Windows 95 File System, as well as the opportunities and challenges it brings for developers. Its "hands-on" approach will help developers become better equipped to make design decisions using the new Win95 File System features. Includes a diskette containing MULTIMON, a general-purpose monitor for examining Windows internals.

Inside the Windows 95 Registry

By Ron Petrusha
1st Edition August 1996
594 pages, Includes diskette
ISBN 1-56592-170-4

An in-depth examination of remote registry access, differences between the Win95 and NT registries, registry backup, undocumented registry services, and the role the registry plays in OLE. This book shows programmers how to access the Win95 registry from Win32, Win16, and DOS programs in C and Visual Basic. It includes VxD sample code and comes with a diskette that contains registry tools.

Developing Windows Error Messages

By Ben Ezzell
1st Edition March 1998
254 pages, Includes CD-ROM
ISBN 1-56592-356-1

This book teaches C, C++, and Visual Basic programmers how to write effective error messages that notify the user of an error, clearly explain the error, and most important, offer a solution. The book also discusses methods for preventing and trapping errors before they occur and tells how to create flexible input and response routines to keep unnecessary errors from happening.

Win32 Multithreaded Programming

By Aaron Cohen & Mike Woodring
1st Edition December 1997
724 pages, Includes CD-ROM
ISBN 1-56592-296-4

This book clearly explains the concepts of multithreaded programs and shows developers how to construct efficient and complex applications. An important book for any developer, it illustrates all aspects of Win32 multithreaded programming, including what has previously been undocumented or poorly explained.

Windows NT File System Internals

By Rajeev Nagar
1st Edition September 1997
794 pages, Includes diskette
ISBN 1-56592-249-2

Windows NT File System Internals presents the details of the NT I/O Manager, the Cache Manager, and the Memory Manager from the perspective of a software developer writing a file system driver or implementing a kernel-mode filter driver. The book provides numerous code examples included on diskette, as well as the source for a complete, usable filter driver.

Windows NT SNMP

By James D. Murray
1st Edition January 1998
464 pages, Includes CD-ROM
ISBN 1-56592-338-3

This book describes the implementation of SNMP (the Simple Network Management Protocol) on Windows NT 3.51 and 4.0 (with a look ahead to NT 5.0) and Windows 95 systems. It covers SNMP and network basics and provides detailed information on developing SNMP management applications and extension agents. The book comes with a CD-ROM containing a wealth of additional information: standards documents, sample code from the book, and many third-party, SNMP-related software tools, libraries, and demos.

O'REILLY®

TO ORDER: **800-998-9938** • **order@oreilly.com** • **http://www.oreilly.com/**
OUR PRODUCTS ARE AVAILABLE AT A BOOKSTORE OR SOFTWARE STORE NEAR YOU.
FOR INFORMATION: **800-998-9938** • **707-829-0515** • **info@oreilly.com**

Windows Programming

Transact-SQL Programming

By Kevin Kline, Lee Gould & Andrew Zanevsky
1st Edition March 1999
836 pages, Includes CD-ROM
ISBN 1-56592-401-0

Full of examples, best practices, and real-world advice, this book thoroughly explores Transact-SQL, a full-featured procedural language that extends the power of SQL on both Microsoft SQL Server 6.5/7.0 and Sybase version 11.5. Comes with a CD-ROM containing extensive examples.

Python Programming on Win32

By Mark Hammond & Andy Robinson
1st Edition December 1999 (est.)
450 pages (est.), ISBN 1-56592-621-8

Despite Python's increasing popularity on Windows, *Python Programming on Win32* is the first book to demonstrate how to use it as a serious Windows development and administration tool. This book addresses all the basic technologies for common integration tasks on Windows, explaining both the Windows issues and the Python code you need to glue things together.

How to stay in touch with O'Reilly

1. Visit Our Award-Winning Web Site

http://www.oreilly.com/

★ "Top 100 Sites on the Web" —*PC Magazine*
★ "Top 5% Web sites" —*Point Communications*
★ "3-Star site" —*The McKinley Group*

Our web site contains a library of comprehensive product information (including book excerpts and tables of contents), downloadable software, background articles, interviews with technology leaders, links to relevant sites, book cover art, and more. File us in your Bookmarks or Hotlist!

2. Join Our Email Mailing Lists

New Product Releases

To receive automatic email with brief descriptions of all new O'Reilly products as they are released, send email to:
listproc@online.oreilly.com
Put the following information in the first line of your message (*not* in the Subject field):
subscribe oreilly-news

O'Reilly Events

If you'd also like us to send information about trade show events, special promotions, and other O'Reilly events, send email to:
listproc@online.oreilly.com
Put the following information in the first line of your message (*not* in the Subject field):
subscribe oreilly-events

3. Get Examples from Our Books via FTP

There are two ways to access an archive of example files from our books:

Regular FTP

- ftp to:
  ftp.oreilly.com
  (login: anonymous
  password: your email address)
- Point your web browser to:
  ftp://ftp.oreilly.com/

FTPMAIL

- Send an email message to:
  ftpmail@online.oreilly.com
  (Write "help" in the message body)

4. Contact Us via Email

order@oreilly.com
To place a book or software order online. Good for North American and international customers.

subscriptions@oreilly.com
To place an order for any of our newsletters or periodicals.

books@oreilly.com
General questions about any of our books.

software@oreilly.com
For general questions and product information about our software. Check out O'Reilly Software Online at **http://software.oreilly.com/** for software and technical support information. Registered O'Reilly software users send your questions to: **website-support@oreilly.com**

cs@oreilly.com
For answers to problems regarding your order or our products.

booktech@oreilly.com
For book content technical questions or corrections.

proposals@oreilly.com
To submit new book or software proposals to our editors and product managers.

international@oreilly.com
For information about our international distributors or translation queries. For a list of our distributors outside of North America check out:
http://www.oreilly.com/www/order/country.html

O'Reilly & Associates, Inc.
101 Morris Street, Sebastopol, CA 95472 USA
TEL   707-829-0515 or 800-998-9938
        (6am to 5pm PST)
FAX   707-829-0104

International Distributors

UK, EUROPE, MIDDLE EAST AND AFRICA (EXCEPT FRANCE, GERMANY, AUSTRIA, SWITZERLAND, LUXEMBOURG, LIECHTENSTEIN, AND EASTERN EUROPE)

INQUIRIES
O'Reilly UK Limited
4 Castle Street
Farnham
Surrey, GU9 7HS
United Kingdom
Telephone: 44-1252-711776
Fax: 44-1252-734211
Email: josette@oreilly.com

ORDERS
Wiley Distribution Services Ltd.
1 Oldlands Way
Bognor Regis
West Sussex PO22 9SA
United Kingdom
Telephone: 44-1243-779777
Fax: 44-1243-820250
Email: cs-books@wiley.co.uk

FRANCE

ORDERS
GEODIF
61, Bd Saint-Germain
75240 Paris Cedex 05, France
Tel: 33-1-44-41-46-16 (French books)
Tel: 33-1-44-41-11-87 (English books)
Fax: 33-1-44-41-11-44
Email: distribution@eyrolles.com

INQUIRIES
Éditions O'Reilly
18 rue Séguier
75006 Paris, France
Tel: 33-1-40-51-52-30
Fax: 33-1-40-51-52-31
Email: france@editions-oreilly.fr

GERMANY, SWITZERLAND, AUSTRIA, EASTERN EUROPE, LUXEMBOURG, AND LIECHTENSTEIN

INQUIRIES & ORDERS
O'Reilly Verlag
Balthasarstr. 81
D-50670 Köln
Germany
Telephone: 49-221-973160-91
Fax: 49-221-973160-8
Email: anfragen@oreilly.de (inquiries)
Email: order@oreilly.de (orders)

CANADA (FRENCH LANGUAGE BOOKS)
Les Éditions Flammarion ltée
375, Avenue Laurier Ouest
Montréal (Québec) H2V 2K3
Tel: 00-1-514-277-8807
Fax: 00-1-514-278-2085
Email: info@flammarion.qc.ca

HONG KONG
City Discount Subscription Service, Ltd.
Unit D, 3rd Floor, Yan's Tower
27 Wong Chuk Hang Road
Aberdeen, Hong Kong
Tel: 852-2580-3539
Fax: 852-2580-6463
Email: citydis@ppn.com.hk

KOREA
Hanbit Media, Inc.
Sonyoung Bldg. 202
Yeksam-dong 736-36
Kangnam-ku
Seoul, Korea
Tel: 822-554-9610
Fax: 822-556-0363
Email: hant93@chollian.dacom.co.kr

PHILIPPINES
Mutual Books, Inc.
429-D Shaw Boulevard
Mandaluyong City, Metro
Manila, Philippines
Tel: 632-725-7538
Fax: 632-721-3056
Email: mbikikog@mnl.sequel.net

TAIWAN
O'Reilly Taiwan
No. 3, Lane 131
Hang-Chow South Road
Section 1, Taipei, Taiwan
Tel: 886-2-23968990
Fax: 886-2-23968916
Email: taiwan@oreilly.com

CHINA
O'Reilly Beijing
Room 2410
160, FuXingMenNeiDaJie
XiCheng District
Beijing, China PR 100031
Tel: 86-10-66412305
Fax: 86-10-86631007
Email: beijing@oreilly.com

INDIA
Computer Bookshop (India) Pvt. Ltd.
190 Dr. D.N. Road, Fort
Bombay 400 001 India
Tel: 91-22-207-0989
Fax: 91-22-262-3551
Email: cbsbom@giasbm01.vsnl.net.in

JAPAN
O'Reilly Japan, Inc.
Kiyoshige Building 2F
12-Bancho, Sanei-cho
Shinjuku-ku
Tokyo 160-0008 Japan
Tel: 81-3-3356-5227
Fax: 81-3-3356-5261
Email: japan@oreilly.com

ALL OTHER ASIAN COUNTRIES
O'Reilly & Associates, Inc.
101 Morris Street
Sebastopol, CA 95472 USA
Tel: 707-829-0515
Fax: 707-829-0104
Email: order@oreilly.com

AUSTRALIA
WoodsLane Pty., Ltd.
7/5 Vuko Place
Warriewood NSW 2102
Australia
Tel: 61-2-9970-5111
Fax: 61-2-9970-5002
Email: info@woodslane.com.au

NEW ZEALAND
Woodslane New Zealand, Ltd.
21 Cooks Street (P.O. Box 575)
Waganui, New Zealand
Tel: 64-6-347-6543
Fax: 64-6-345-4840
Email: info@woodslane.com.au

LATIN AMERICA
McGraw-Hill Interamericana
Editores, S.A. de C.V.
Cedro No. 512
Col. Atlampa
06450, Mexico, D.F.
Tel: 52-5-547-6777
Fax: 52-5-547-3336
Email: mcgraw-hill@infosel.net.mx